THE RENT ACTS 1920-1957

THE
RENT ACTS
1920-1957

*The texts of the principal Acts prefaced by a complete guide
to the state of the law on the passing of the new Act
with a complete index to the whole*

by

NORMAN C. ABBEY

Legal Associate Member of the Town Planning Institute;
Associate of the Institute of Housing; Lecturer on the Law
of Real Property, Housing and Town Planning, Dilapida-
tions, and Valuations at South-West Essex Technical
College and School of Art. Formerly of the Ministry of
Housing and Local Government.

Author of *A Companion to the Town and Country Planning Acts
and Orders* and *A Companion to the New Law of Landlord and
Tenant.*

London 1957
EYRE & SPOTTISWOODE

*Made and printed in Great Britain
for Eyre & Spottiswoode (Review
Publications) Ltd., 15 Bedford Street,
London, W.C.2, by Staples Printers Ltd.
at their Rochester, Kent, establishment*

Contents

Preface

THIS work is designed to show as concisely as possible not only the effect of the Rent Act, 1957, but also the operation of the whole of the law which comprises what is commonly known as "the Rent Acts" and the law which controls the letting of furnished premises.

The Act of 1957 is probably the most extensive measure which has been passed to amend this code of legislation. It provides for the decontrol of a large portion of the unfurnished houses which were first controlled or re-controlled in 1939; for further reduction in the scope of the Acts by Ministerial order; for new lettings to be free from control; and for a completely new system for fixing maximum rents of houses which remain controlled in England and Wales.

Although the number of houses which remain controlled is being reduced there is no easement of the difficulties which have long been apparent in understanding the law relating to rent restrictions. In fact the Act of 1957 is equal to its older associates in maintaining the reputation of this branch of law; any brief moments of clarity are quickly made "subject to the provisions" of a Schedule the aggregate of which take up more than half the text of the Act.

I have planned this book on the lines of my earlier works and allowed a chapter for each of the important aspects of the law. The form of presentation is designed to provide a continuity of the material relating to the two matters which are of general interest (i) controlled tenancies (Chapters II to VII); and (ii) decontrol (Chapters VIII and IX). For Scotland, Chapters X and XI are substitutes of Chapters III and IV in regard to rents and repairs. The remaining chapters, except Chapters XVI and XVIII, deal with special subjects.

The history of the Rent Acts shown in Chapter I is intended as a background from which may be gathered the principles on which the law has operated for the last forty years. Up to the Act of 1957 the pattern has been much the same—control of rents and security of tenure. The new Act, however, seems to take a stage further the attempt made by the Acts of 1954—which were not very successful—to preserve property as well as to protect tenants. Chapter II shows the basis for claiming protection under the Acts, the rights of succession and the new provision for the assignment of statutory tenancies.

In Chapter III there is a full explanation of the new rent structure for England and Wales. The time which the Act allows for the full

extent of the scheme to become operative precludes any immediate
assessment of the way in which it will work; the chapter explains in
detail how it is designed to work. The machinery of the scheme,
however, is very closely linked with the provisions for repair which
are dealt with in the succeeding chapter.

The question of dilapidations is always a problem, even with
tenancy agreements which lay down the responsibility of the parties.
The experiment in the Act of trying to get repairs done through the
medium of prescribed forms will be watched with interest by people
in the professions who for years have battled with the interpretation
of repairing covenants and, in particular, the extent to which a want
of repair should be shown the notice of repair. Chapter IV shows
the liability of in the parties for doing repairs and the procedure to be
followed under the Act for getting repairs done. These provisions of
the Act are of vital importance to the tenant who, although not
denied any right he may have at common law to claim damages, has
become accustomed to the remedy provided by the Acts of withholding part of the rent if repairs are not done. The extent to which
this sanction may be imposed is explained in the chapter.

Chapter V shows the risks which are run in any attempt to defeat
the objects of rent limits by claiming a premium or other sum in a
manner which the law declares to be illegal. As the Acts use the
same machinery for both controlled and newly decontrolled premises
in making such payments an offence I have in this chapter departed
from the general lay-out of the work and dealt with all provisions
as to premiums and other like payments in respect of unfurnished
lettings.

In general a sub-tenant is entitled to the same protection as a
tenant but in 1947 the courts decided that Crown sub-tenants had
no protection; and in 1949 and 1950 that sub-tenants of large houses
and houses let at low rents were not necessarily protected after their
landlord's interest came to an end. Special legislation has now been
passed to give greater protection to these sub-tenants and it is
explained in Chapter VI.

The rule that a tenant is protected against ejectment by his
landlord has always been subject to certain qualifications. A landlord can get possession if he finds suitable alternative accommodation for his tenant; the courts have power to grant possession in such
cases and on certain grounds without proof of other accommodation
being available. Chapter VII examines the question of "suitable
alternative accommodation" and shows the various provisions which
enable a landlord to get possession against his tenant.

One of the declared intentions of the Act of 1957 is to provide for "release from control under Rent Acts". This is the first time in eighteen years that there has been any measurable shedding of control and in order to assist in the transition from statutory protection the Act postpones for a period after the time of decontrol the operation of the ordinary law of contract. During that time a short-term or statutory tenant can continue to enjoy security of tenure without any increase in his rent. The way in which this scheme is to work is described in Chapter VIII. Other tenancies which are excepted from control are listed in Chapter IX.

In Scotland, the established pattern of the Rent Acts as to rent limits and the right to claim increases for doing repairs has been retained owing to the reform of the system of valuation for rating. Chapters X and XI explain in detail what a landlord may claim in the way of rent and how the Act of 1957 has extended his right to claim further increases for repairs.

The new provisions for decontrol apply also to the control of mortgages. This is dealt with in Chapter XII. The effect of the Act of 1957 on the special Act passed in 1951 to protect the interests of personnel of the reserve forces during their period of service is described in Chapter XIII. In Chapter XIV I have explained the operation of the Act of 1955 for the de-requisitioning of houses and the rights of a statutory tenant under that Act whose dwelling is within the range of decontrol. The rights of tenants of furnished lettings which become decontrolled are set out in Chapter XV which deals with the whole of the law on this subject. I have included in Chapter XVI a note on the new provision which requires a minimum period of four weeks for a notice to quit. Chapter XVII is in the nature of an addendum to my *Companion to the New Law of Landlord and Tenant* and explains the effect of the Act of 1957 on long tenancies and tenancies of business and professional premises.

The final chapter contains the texts of the principal enactments within the Rent Acts. In order to keep the work to a reasonable size I have not included in this chapter the Housing Repairs and Rents Act, 1954, as I have been able to deal fully with the sections which remain operative on rent restrictions in the earlier chapters. The Housing (Repairs and Rents) (Scotland) Act, 1954, has also been omitted as the sections which refer to the repairs increase need re-writing almost in full to show the effect of the 1957 Act increase. This kind of treatment would have made the chapter somewhat unwieldy and as an alternative to such duplication, or a cumbersome notation, I have dealt separately with the two types of repairs increase in Chapter XI which seemed to be a more practical method of showing the difference between the two schemes.

It will be seen from Chapter XVIII that in consequence of amendments and repeals which have been made from time to time some of the statutes have become rather fragmentary in character. To assist in uniting these pieces I have noted in the earlier chapters references to sections of Acts which apply to a particular subject. In this notation, unless it is otherwise clear from the immediate text:

"the Act of 1920" and "/1920 Act" mean the Increase of Rent and Mortgage Interest (Restrictions) Act, 1920;

"the Act of 1923" and "/1923 Act" mean the Rent and Mortgage Interest Restrictions Act, 1923;

"the Act of 1933" and "/1933 Act" mean the Rent and Mortgage Interest Restrictions (Amendment) Act, 1933;

"the Act of 1938" and "/1938 Act" mean Increase of Rent and Mortgage Interest (Restrictions) Act, 1938;

"the Act of 1939" and "/1939 Act" mean the Rent and Mortgage Interest Restrictions Act, 1939;

"the Act of 1943" and "/1943 Act" mean the Rent of Furnished Houses Control (Scotland) Act, 1943;

"the Act of 1946" and "/1946 Act" mean the Furnished Houses (Rent Control) Act, 1946;

"the Act of 1949" and "/1949 Act" mean the Landlord and Tenant (Rent Control) Act, 1949;

"the Act of 1952" and "/1952 Act" mean the Crown Lessees (Protection of Sub-Tenants) Act, 1952;

"the Acts of 1954" and "/1954 English Act" or "/1954 Scottish Act" mean the Housing Repairs and Rents Act, 1954, and the Housing (Repairs and Rents) (Scotland) Act, 1954;

"the Act of 1957" and "/1957 Act" mean the Rent Act, 1957.

N. C. A.

June 1957.

Table of Statutes

Page numbers in heavy type indicate where the particular statute or section is set out in full.

TABLE OF STATUTES xiii

Page

Housing Act, 1925 . . . . . 293, 294
Housing (Scotland) Act, 1925 293
Rent and Mortgage Interest (Restrictions Continuation)
Act, 1925 . . . . . 4, 277 n., **285**
Rating and Valuation Act, 1925, s. 68 . . . 41, 234
Housing (Rural Workers) Act, 1926, s. 3 . 38, 128, 202, 210, 239
Expiring Laws Continuance Act, 1927 . . . 4
Landlord and Tenant Act, 1927 . . . . 103, 305
 s. 1 . . . . 105, 227
 s. 13 . . . . 106, 228
 s. 16 . . . . 24, 214, 237
Rating and Valuation (Apportionment) Act, 1928 . . 310
Expiring Laws Continuance Act, 1928 4
Expiring Laws Continuance Act, 1929 4
Land Drainage Act, 1930, s. 24 . . . . 28, 214
Expiring Laws Continuance Act, 1930 4
Expiring Laws Continuance Act, 1931 4
Expiring Laws Continuance Act, 1932 4
Rent and Mortgage Interest Restrictions (Amendment) Act,
1933 . . . . 4, **286**, 310

s. 1 .	*Page* 113, **286**, 314	s. 11	*Page* 185, 240, **291**
s. 2 .	108, 276 n., 307	s. 13	16, 262 n., **291**, 299
s. 3 .	78, 79, 80, 258,	s. 14	180, 240, 270 n., **292**
	286, 302, 325	s. 15	185, 270 n., **292**
s. 4 .	84, 237, 258,	s. 16	185, **294**
	288, 314, 343	s. 17	263 n., **295**
s. 5 .	314	s. 18	**295**
s. 6 .	116, **289**, 314, 344	First Schedule .	75, 80,
s. 7 .	121, 122, 255 n., **289**		158, 217, 240, 258,
s. 8 .	181, 237, **290**		279, 282, **296**, 315
s. 9 .	**290**, 314	Second Schedule	279 n., **298**
s. 10 .	185, 240, **291**	Third Schedule.	**298**

County Courts Act, 1934, s. 134 179
Increase of Rent and Mortgage Interest (Restrictions) Act,
1935 . . . . 5, **299**
Housing (Scotland) Act, 1935 . . . 304, 329
Public Health Act, 1936 81
 s. 94 . . . . 51, 195
 s. 95 . . . . 57, 219
 s. 289 15

s. 41   .   .   *Page* 76   s. 49   .   .   *Page* 213
s. 42   .   .   .   16   s. 50   .   .   .   186
s. 43   .   .   .   83   Third Schedule .   .   163
s. 45   .   .   .   114   Fourth Schedule   148, 150

Landlord and Tenant Act, 1954   . 8, 14, 15, 24, 58, 61, 92, 95,
                                112, 188, 189, 203, 211, 226, 238

s. 2 .   *Page* 189, 213, 239   s. 43   .   *Page* 229, 242
s. 3   239   s. 55   .   .   .   85
s. 6 .   . 85, 148, 150, 238   First Schedule .   24, 81,
s. 7   238   215, 238
s. 10   .   .   .   81, 82   Second Schedule 81, 215, 239
s. 12   .   .   .   240   Third Schedule .   .   242
s. 15   . 74, 75, 112, 113   Ninth Schedule .   .   75
s. 19   .   .   .   239

County Courts Act, 1955, s. 12   78
Requisitioned Houses and Housing (Amendment) Act, 1955   8,
                                        92, 159, 211, 212

s. 1 .   .   .   *Page* 159   s. 7 .   .   .   *Page* 165
s. 2   160   s. 8   161
s. 3 .   .   .   160, 161   s. 14   159
s. 4 .   . 162, 163, 203, 212   s. 18   160
s. 5   165   s. 20   160
s. 6   165

Local Government (Street Works) (Scotland) Act, 1956   121, 208
Administration of Justice Act, 1956   278
Clean Air Act, 1956, s. 12   .   35, 121, 136, 197, 242, 243
Slum Clearance (Compensation) Act, 1956   .   .   .   50
Valuation for Rating (Scotland) Act, 1956   115, 116, 122, 147, 213
Sexual Offences Act, 1956   88
Expiring Laws Continuance Act, 1956   166
Rent Act, 1957   .   .   .   .   8, 90, **193**

s. 1 .   *Page* 20, 21, 23, 24,   s. 8 .   *Page* 130, 132, 140,
              27, 31, **193**   144, 145, **199**
s. 2 .   .   21, 26, 27, 28,   s. 9 .   .   123, 133, 134,
              37, 49, 63, **194**   142, 146, **200**
s. 3 .   .   .   29, **196**   s. 10   .   .   128, **201**
s. 4 .   .   .   32, **196**   s. 11   10, 85, 86, 90, 91, 92,
s. 5 .   33, 34, 35, 36, **197**   164, 169, 189, **202**
s. 6 .   .   25, 26, 33, **198**   s. 12   .   156, 168, 169,
s. 7 .   131, 143, 145, **198**   170, 171, 177, **203**

Table of Cases

CHAPTER I

The Rent Acts from 1915 to 1957

THE history of the Rent Acts dates back to 1915 when Parliament imposed restrictions on the increases in rent of unfurnished residential property then being made by landlords and in the rate of interest on a mortgage of such property, particularly in towns where munitions were being made for World War I. The statutes in the present series of legislation known collectively as "the Rent and Mortgage Interest Restrictions Acts, 1920 to 1939", which were amended in 1949, 1951, 1952, 1954 and 1955, have now been subjected to a major revision by the Rent Act, 1957. Throughout this work they are referred to as "the Rent Acts". The principal objects of the Acts are:

(*a*) to protect the tenant against his landlord by

   (i) limiting the rent he can be called upon to pay, and

   (ii) providing him with security of tenure so long as he pays his rent; and

(*b*) to protect the landlord against his mortgagee by

   (i) limiting the rate of mortgage interest he can be called upon to pay, and

   (ii) providing against the calling in of the mortgage so long as the interest is paid.

In 1943 (for Scotland) and 1946 (for England and Wales) a separate code of legislation was established to control the letting of furnished premises which, for all practical purposes, replaced the limited control of such lettings provided by the Rent Acts.

1. The Acts in operation between 1915 and 1920

The houses controlled by the Increase of Rent and Mortgage Interest (War Restrictions) Act, 1915, were those of a standard rent or rateable value of not more than £35 in London, £30 in Scotland and £26 elsewhere in England and Wales. The broad effect of the Act was to restrict the amount of rent or mortgage interest recoverable in respect of any such house to the rent at which the premises were let or the rate of interest charged on the 3rd August 1914. The

Act did not apply to a house let with land, or to a dwelling-house let at a rent which included board, attendance, or use of furniture, or a dwelling-house let at a rent of less than two-thirds of the rateable value; or to a mortgage repayable by instalments extending over a term of not less than ten years, or to a mortgage of land where the controlled dwellings were less than one-tenth of the rateable value of the whole of the mortgaged property. If the landlord carried out any improvements he was permitted to increase the rent by an extra 6 per cent. per annum of the amount expended on the improvements; he could also recover for increases in rates where the tenant paid an "inclusive rent". The payment of premiums in addition to rent was not allowed. A landlord could not recover possession of a dwelling so long as his tenant paid his rent and performed his covenants, except on the ground that the tenant had committed waste, or was a nuisance or annoyance to neighbours, or that the landlord required the premises for his own occupation or for an employee. A mortgagee was not permitted to call in a mortgage so long as the mortgagor paid the interest and instalments of principal, performed his covenants and kept the mortgaged property in a proper state of repair. The Act of 1915 was amended by the Courts (Emergency Powers) Act, 1917, which allowed premiums to be accepted on leases for twenty-one years and upwards and permitted a tenant or mortgagor to recover within six months any overpayments of rent or mortgage interest. The Increase of Rent, &c. (Amendment) Act, 1918, prevented a landlord, who had bought his house since the 30th September 1917, from recovering possession for his own occupation. The Increase of Rent and Mortgage Interest (Restrictions) Act, 1919—which doubled the rental limits of the Act of 1915 and was passed as a result of the Report of the Hunter Committee (Cmd. 9235)—prolonged the duration of the Acts until Lady Day 1921. It allowed a landlord to increase the rent of a controlled dwelling-house by not more than 10 per cent., except where the sanitary authority had issued a certificate of disrepair; and allowed mortgage interest to be raised by not more than one-half per cent. subject to a maximum of 5 per cent. per annum; and placed a limitation on the rent of houses let furnished. The Act also excepted from control any house erected after or in the course of erection on the 2nd April 1919. The Increase of Rent, &c. (Amendment) Act, 1919, which repealed the Act of 1918, revised the grounds on which a landlord could claim possession of a dwelling-house against his tenant.

2. The Acts in operation between 1920 and 1957

In 1920 the Salisbury Committee, appointed to inquire into the working of the Acts, presented their Report (Cmd. 658) and the Increase of Rent and Mortgage Interest (Restrictions) Act, 1920, was passed to give effect to the Committee's recommendations. That Act repealed the previous legislation and is the statute around which has been built the subsequent legislation dealing with limitations of rent and security of tenure for tenants of unfurnished residential premises. One of the principal changes made by the Act of 1920 was to treble the rental limits of the Act of 1915, thereby extending control to dwellings with a standard rent or rateable value of not more than £105 in London, £90 in Scotland and £78 elsewhere in England and Wales. It retained the provisions in the Rent and Mortgage Interest (Restrictions) Act, 1919, of excepting from protection dwelling-houses erected after or in the course of erection at the 2nd April 1919, and extended that exception to houses being converted or which were converted after that date. The Act retained the principle that the standard rent or the standard rate of interest on a mortgage of a controlled dwelling should be the rent at which it was let or the rate of interest charged on the 3rd August 1914, but expanded the range of permitted increases in rent which could be claimed by the landlord or mortgagee. This rent structure is still retained in Scotland—see Chapter X. The Act revised the grounds on which a landlord could obtain possession, which were subsequently replaced by the Act of 1923 and later amended by the Act of 1933. Restrictions on the calling in of mortgages and on the payment of premiums were retained as well as limitations on the rent of houses let furnished. The Act, which applied to business and professional premises until the 24th June 1921 (28th May 1921 in Scotland), was intended to remain in force for the protection of residential tenants until the 24th June 1923 (28th May 1923 in Scotland). By the Increase of Rent and Mortgage Interest Restrictions (Continuance) Act, 1923, it was continued until the 31st July 1923. The rule established in *Kerr* v. *Bryde* [1923] A.C. 16, that an increase in rent, as permitted by the Act of 1920, could not be made unless the contractual tenancy was terminated by a valid notice to quit, was side-stepped by the Rent Restrictions (Notices of Increase) Act, 1923, which provided that a notice of increase of rent could operate also as a notice to quit. This Act has been replaced in England and Wales by provisions in the Act of 1957 but it still applies in Scotland. The Report of the Onslow Committee (Cmd. 1803), published in 1923, recommended the continuance of the Acts and this proposal was accepted by the passing of the Rent and Mortgage Interest Restrictions Act, 1923, which prolonged the legislation until the 24th June 1925 (28th May 1925 in Scotland). That Act introduced the first stage of decontrol after World War I by releasing from control any premises which came into the possession of the landlord (otherwise than by order or judgment for possession on the ground of non-payment of rent), or which were let on lease for a term ending after the 24th June 1926, being a term of not less than two years. In either case a lawful sub-tenant remained protected. The Act also made it clear that the provisions in the Act of 1920 which excludes from control a dwelling-house bona fide let at a rent which includes payments in respect of board, attendance, or use of furniture applies only if the rent which is fairly attributable to the attendance or the use of furniture, regard being had to the value of the same to the tenant, forms a substantial portion of the whole rent. In the following year the Prevention of Eviction Act, 1924, was passed to prevent the unreasonable eviction of a tenant by a landlord who wanted to occupy the house himself. By the Rent and Mortgage Interest (Restrictions Continuation) Act, 1925, the Acts were kept in force until the 25th December 1927 (28th May 1928 in Scotland), and subsequently, by the Expiring Laws Continuance Acts, 1927, 1928, 1929, 1930, 1931 and 1932, to the 25th December 1933 in England and Wales and to the 28th May 1934 in Scotland.

In 1931 the Marley Committee reported that houses in the higher ranges of rateable value could be decontrolled and that those in the lower ranges were being decontrolled too quickly. As a result of that Report (Cmd. 3911) the Rent and Mortgage Interest Restrictions (Amendment) Act, 1933—which prolonged the operation of the Acts to the 24th June 1938 (28th May 1938 in Scotland)—divided controlled houses into three categories, usually referred to as Class A, Class B and Class C. The division was made by reference to rateable values in England and Wales and yearly values in Scotland. Class A houses consisted of those with a rateable value or yearly value over £45 in London and Scotland, and over £35 elsewhere. The rateable or yearly values for Class B were over £20 but not over £45 in London, over £26 5s. but not over £45 in Scotland, and over £13 but not over £35 elsewhere; and for Class C houses, £20 or under in London, £26 5s. or under in Scotland and £13 or under elsewhere. The Act decontrolled Class A houses in England and Wales as from the 29th September 1933, and in Scotland from the 28th November 1933. Class B houses continued to become decontrolled on the landlord obtaining possession or on the grant of a lease for a term of not less than two years; Class C houses no longer became decontrolled when the landlord obtained possession or granted a lease for a specified period. If, however, a Class C house had been let as a separate dwelling before the 18th July 1933, and the landlord claimed that it had become decontrolled during the period 1923–1933 he could preserve the release from control by registering the house with the local authority. Such registrations had to be made within three months of the passing of the Act. Local authorities were not required to investigate any claim made by a landlord and a certificate of registration was evidence of registration only and not evidence of decontrol. The burden of proving that a house was controlled rested on the tenant, both in the case of a Class B house and a Class C house registered as decontrolled. The Increase of Rent and Mortgage Interest (Restrictions) Act, 1935, cleared up an anomaly under the Acts which previously had not allowed the widow or other member of a tenant's family to claim the statutory tenancy if the tenant died leaving a will.

The process of decontrol begun in 1933 was taken a stage further by the Increase of Rent and Mortgage Interest (Restrictions) Act, 1938, which was based on the Report of the Ridley Committee (Cmd. 5621) published in 1937. The Act—which provided for continuance of control until the 24th June 1942 (28th May 1942 in Scotland)—divided Class B into two parts and houses with a rateable value exceeding £35 in London and Scotland and exceeding £20 elsewhere were decontrolled as from the 29th September 1938 in England and Wales, and as from the 28th November 1938 in Scotland. The remaining houses within the Class, except separately let parts of houses, no longer became subject to decontrol on the landlord obtaining possession. The Act provided, however, that any house in Class B which remained within the limits of control but in respect of which the landlord claimed decontrol under the Act of 1923 by his having obtained possession, or by the grant of a lease for a specified period, should not be re-controlled provided they were registered with the local authority before the 26th August 1938.

The local authorities in England and Wales responsible for registering landlords' claims to decontrol under the Acts of 1933 and 1938 were county borough councils, non-county borough councils and urban and rural district councils; in Scotland, the councils of burghs and counties.

In the case of dwellings which were decontrolled under the Acts of 1933 and 1938 any tenants holding under statutory tenancies were given just over two months' security of tenure in England and Wales and four months in Scotland in 1933, and four and six months respectively in 1938, and were entitled to one month's notice to give up possession. The restrictions on mortgages on these dwellings were continued for six months after the passing of the Acts.

The threat of war was responsible for the passing on the 1st September 1939 of the Rent and Mortgage Interest Restrictions Act, 1939, which brought under control practically all privately owned houses let unfurnished at a rack rent—whether built before or after the passing of the Act—with a rateable value not exceeding £100 in London, £90 in Scotland and £75 elsewhere in England and Wales. The Act, however, fixed the standard rent and the standard rate of interest on a mortgage by reference to the rent at which a newly controlled or re-controlled house was let, or the rate of interest charged, on the 1st September 1939. Houses which had remained subject to control under the Rents Acts, 1920 to 1938, were not affected by this new measure of control of rents and mortgage interest. The Act of 1939 restricted the "permitted increases" which could be claimed by a landlord in respect of the new standard rents and did not allow any increase in the new standard rate of mortgage interest. There were thus established two forms of control and those houses which remained subject to the Acts of 1920 to 1938 have become known as "old control" houses, and the houses which became subject to control under the Act of 1939 have become known as "new control" houses. The Act stopped all forms of decontrol and provided for the continuance of the Rent Acts until six months after the date declared by Order in Council to be the end of the "emergency".

In consequence of the provisions in the Act of 1957 for fixing rents of houses in England and Wales the distinction between "old control" and "new control" is of less importance south of the border than in Scotland, where the two types of control remain effective for determining the limits of recoverable rent.

In 1943 the Rent of Furnished Houses Control (Scotland) Act was passed to provide for the more effective control of rents of furnished lettings and authorised the Secretary of State to set up rent tribunals for that purpose. This idea was adopted for England and Wales by the Furnished Houses (Rent Control) Act, 1946, following a recommendation by the Ridley Committee in their Report (Cmd. 6621) published in 1945. The Acts are on a temporary basis and are renewed annually by the Expiring Laws Continuance

Act. The main difference between the two Acts as originally written was that the Scottish Act gave no security of tenure to the tenant whereas under the English Act a tenant could get up to three months' security of tenure after his case had been referred to the rent tribunal.

The Ridley Committee included in their recommendations proposals for extending security of tenure for tenants of furnished lettings and for the setting up of rent tribunals for fixing fair rents of unfurnished houses controlled by the Rent Acts. The Committee suggested a complete ban on the payment of premiums for leases of controlled dwellings; and that the position should be clarified as to shared accommodation. These matters (including security of tenure for tenants of furnished lettings in Scotland) were dealt with in the Landlord and Tenant (Rent Control) Act, 1949, but not to the extent recommended by the Committee. In view of the new system of fixing rent limits in England and Wales as laid down by the Act of 1957, rent tribunals no longer have jurisdiction to vary the rents of unfurnished lettings except in Scotland.

Wider aspects of control of leaseholds followed the Reports of the Leasehold Committee set up in 1948, under the Chairmanship of the late Lord Uthwatt (who was succeeded by Lord Justice Jenkins). The Committee issued in March 1949 an Interim Report on the Tenure and Rents of Business Premises (Cmd. 7706) and a Final Report (Cmd. 7982) in June 1950. Two important recommendations of the Committee—(i) that the protection of the Rent Acts be extended to occupying ground lessees of houses, and (ii) that greater security of tenure be given to tenants of business premises—were accepted in temporary and modified form by the passing of the Leasehold Property (Temporary Provisions) Act, 1951. At the same time the Long Leases (Temporary Provisions) (Scotland) Act, 1951, provided protection for tenants of long leases in Scotland. The operation of these Acts was extended by the Leasehold Property Act and Long Leases (Scotland) Act Extension Act, 1953. The Tenancy of Shops (Scotland) Act, 1949, which was based on the Interim Report (Cmd. 7603) of the Guthrie Committee, already provided shop tenants in Scotland with the right to apply to the sheriff for the renewal of shop tenancies. This Act is renewed annually by the Expiring Laws Continuance Act. The provisions in the two Acts of 1951 have since been put on a permanent basis. The Long Leases (Scotland) Act, 1954, enables lessees and sub-lessees occupying residential property in Scotland under certain long leases to obtain a feu right of such property on certain conditions. The Landlord and

Tenant Act, 1954,[1] provides security of tenure for tenants in England and Wales holding under tenancies granted in respect of residential premises for more than twenty-one years at low rents and for tenants of business and professional premises. By the Rent Act, 1957, the protection in the Act of 1954 for residential tenants in England and Wales applies to all holders of long tenancies, whether or not they hold at a low rent. The Reserve and Auxiliary Forces (Protection of Civil Interests) Act, 1951, includes provisions for protecting the interests of tenants called up or volunteering for certain naval, military or air force service or for doing work or training under the National Service Act, 1948. Sub-tenants of the Crown have been given the protection of the Rent Acts against their immediate land-lords by the Crown Lessees (Protection of Sub-Tenants) Act, 1952.

The Housing Repairs and Rents Act, 1954, and the Housing (Repairs and Rents) (Scotland) Act, 1954 (both of which came into force on the 30th August 1954), made more extensive amendments of a general character to the Rent Acts. They entitled the landlord of a controlled dwelling, which had been let before the 1st September 1939, to claim an increase in rent for keeping the property in good repair and for the increased cost of services; lettings by local authorities, development corporations, housing associations and trusts, and National Health Service Executive Councils in Scotland, as well as houses erected or produced by conversion after the 29th August 1954, were excluded from the Rent Acts.

The Requisitioned Houses and Housing (Amendment) Act, 1955, repealed the power under the Defence Regulations to requisition property for housing purposes and provided for winding up the use of requisitioned houses by the 31st March 1960. The Act includes a provision which enables a local authority to invite the owner of any such property to accept the licensee under requisitioning as a statutory tenant under the Rent Acts.

3. The Rent Act, 1957

This Act introduces what is probably the most extensive system of decontrol in the history of the Rent Acts. In addition to houses in the London area and Scotland with a rateable value exceeding £40, and elsewhere in England and Wales exceeding £30, being taken out of control altogether and provision being made for further decontrol by stages, the Act entitles landlords to claim decontrol of

---

[1] The effect of this Act and other statutory provisions relating to tenancies in England and Wales are dealt with in the author's "Companion to the New Law of Landlord and Tenant."

dwellings when they come into possession. But the short-term and statutory tenant whose dwelling has been decontrolled is entitled to protection for a minimum period of fifteen months during which time he has security of tenure and his rent remains the same. Furthermore, whilst there is no restriction on the freedom of the landlord to sell on his own terms when a dwelling comes into possession, he is not entirely free if he decides to re-let. For three years from the 6th July 1957 there is an absolute prohibition to charge a premium in addition to the rent of premises decontrolled, unless a lease is granted for more than twenty-one years; and during that time the payment of rent in respect of such lettings more than one rental period or at most six months in advance is illegal.

Certain loans made in connection with a tenancy are now treated as premiums.

In regard to houses in England and Wales which remain controlled the Act provides a new rent structure based on the gross value for rating of the property; in Scotland the existing formula is retained for calculating the recoverable rent of a dwelling-house with provision for increasing the repairs increase allowed by the Act of 1954 and for a new form of repairs increase at half rate where the landlord cannot prove the expenditure test to claim the full increase.

The Act was passed on the 6th June 1957 and came into operation on the 6th July 1957 (s. 27).

CHAPTER II
Controlled and Statutory Tenancies

As a general principle the protection of the Rent Acts can be claimed only through a contractual tenancy; the Acts do not give any rights to "squatters". There is, however, the exception in the Act of 1955 where a licensee of a requisitioned house is taken over as a statutory tenant (see Chapter XIV); and the provision for the assignment of a statutory tenancy to facilitate the exchange of controlled dwellings (para. 3 below).

The Act of 1957 does not disturb this principle but as a general rule it restricts the protection to existing tenants. At the same time the right of a widow or other relative to claim a statutory tenancy on the death of the tenant is preserved; and the protection of the Acts continues to apply to the first tenant taking a controlled tenancy of a house after possession has been obtained on grounds of over-crowding (p. 92).

The effect of the Act is to shift control from a dwelling-house as such to an existing tenancy held in respect of the dwelling-house. Under the Act of 1920 (s. 12 (6)) the emphasis on control was on the dwelling-house itself and not on the rights of a particular tenant. Thus, when property changed hands the new owner acquired subject to the Act and a new tenant got the same protection as did his predecessor. The provision for decontrol on possession in the Act of 1923, however, reversed this rule and limited the protection to existing tenancies; but it was partly revived by the Acts of 1933 and 1938 which preserved control of the smaller dwelling-houses. The Act of 1939 stopped any form of decontrol and thus perpetuated the control of a dwelling; it went further than the Act of 1920 (which did not apply to houses converted or erected on or after the 2nd April 1919) and applied to new as well as existing dwellings, even if they were erected after the Act. This form of control remained absolute until the Acts of 1954 allowed houses erected or produced by conversion after the 29th August 1954 to be free from control.

1. Controlled tenancies

The effect of the decontrol provisions in the Act of 1957 (s. 11 (1) (2)) is that as from the 6th July 1957 the Rent Acts will apply only to existing tenancies of unfurnished lettings in respect of dwelling-houses the rateable value of which on the 7th November 1956 (p. 97), did not exceed:

   (i) £40 in the Metropolitan Police District (p. 185) or the City of London;
  (ii) £30 elsewhere in England and Wales;
 (iii) £40 in Scotland.

The transitional provisions for the protection of short-term and statutory tenants of houses which became decontrolled on that date have the effect of preserving control in such cases for at least fifteen months (see Chapter VIII).

(1) *Dwellings within the Acts*

By Section 12 (2) of the Act of 1920 the Rent Acts apply only to "a house or part of a house let as a separate dwelling".

Any rooms in a dwelling-house subject to a separate letting wholly or partly as a dwelling are treated as a part of a dwelling-house let as a separate dwelling (s. 12 (8) *ibid.*).

The burden of proving that the Rent Acts do not apply to any dwelling-house rests on the landlord (s. 7 (1) / 1938 Act).

(2) *Premises let as a separate dwelling*

The tenant must have a true tenancy giving him the right to the exclusive possession of the premises or part which has been let to him. A licensee, such as a service occupier (e.g., a caretaker, chauffeur or gamekeeper), a lodger or the occupier of requisitioned premises (p. 162), is not protected by the Acts. In the case of a "tied" cottage, the occupier is protected if it is let to him as tenant; but not if it is occupied by him under a contract of service.

(3) *Shared accommodation*

The acute shortage of living accommodation in the years immediately after World War II produced a series of problems on the application of the Rent Acts to shared accommodation. In *Neale* v. *Del Soto* [1945] K.B. 144, it was decided that where the tenant shared some living accommodation with the landlord it was not a letting as a separate dwelling. In subsequent decisions it was held that a kitchen constituted living accommodation (*Cole* v. *Harris* [1945] K.B. 474) even if it was used only for cooking (*Kenyon* v. *Walker* [1946] 2 All E.R. 595) and it made no difference whether the sharing was with the landlord or with another tenant (*Banks* v. *Cope Brown* [1948] 2 K.B. 287; *Llewellyn* v. *Christmas* [1948] 2

K.B. 385). On the other hand, a shared lavatory or bathroom is not sufficient to take a tenancy out of the Acts (*Cole* v. *Harris, supra*); and in *Goodrich* v. *Paisner* [1956] 2 W.L.R. 1053, it was held that where a tenant used a back bedroom in common with the landlord it was not sufficient to deprive the tenant of the protection of the Acts. As the House of Lords pointed out in that case the earlier decisions did no more than produce a general guide as to the kind of sharing which might take a letting outside the scope of the Rent Acts.

The Landlord and Tenant (Rent Control) Act, 1949, amended the effect of the earlier decisions and dealt with the problem in two ways.

(i) *Sharing with the landlord or the landlord and others:* Section 7 of that Act provides that where the tenant has exclusive occupation of some accommodation (which if let on its own would be a controlled tenancy) together with the use of other accommodation in common with the landlord or with the landlord and other persons the Rent of Furnished Houses (Scotland) Act, 1943, or the Furnished Houses (Rent Control) Act, 1946, as the case may be, shall apply to the letting even if the contract does not include payment for the use of furniture or for services. In any such case the rent tribunal can settle the rent and give security of tenure to the tenant as if it were a furnished letting (see p. 173).

(ii) *Sharing with others but not the landlord:* If the tenant holds separate accommodation (which if let on its own would be a controlled tenancy) and also shares accommodation with persons other than the landlord the Act of 1949 (s. 8) provides that the Rent Acts shall apply to the separate accommodation.

So long as the tenant is in possession of separate accommodation either under a contract of tenancy or as a statutory tenant any attempt to terminate or modify his right to the use of any of the shared accommodation which is living accommodation is void. On the other hand, the landlord can exercise any right under the tenancy to make the shared accommodation available to any other persons in common with the tenant.

While the tenant is in possession of the separate accommodation no order or judgment for the recovery of any of the shared accommodation or for the ejectment of the tenant therefrom may be made or given unless a like order or judgment has been made or given in respect of the separate accommodation. The landlord, however, can apply to the county court or, in Scotland, to the sheriff for an order for the termination or modification of the right of the tenant to use the whole or any part of the shared accommodation which is not living accommodation (e.g. a bathroom).

(4) *Sub-tenants using shared accommodation*

A tenant of controlled premises does not lose the protection of the Rent Acts by sub-letting part of the premises if the only reason is that the sub-tenant is sharing accommodation with other persons (s. 9 / 1949 Act).

(5) *Furnished sub-lettings*

The tenant of controlled premises does not lose the protection of the Rent Acts by reason only that he has sub-let part of the premises as a furnished letting (s. 9 *ibid.*).

(6) *Decontrol and rent limits of lettings which include shared accommodation*

The provisions in the Act of 1957 as to decontrol and as to new rent limits apply to lettings which include shared accommodation in the same way as they apply to other furnished and unfurnished lettings.

(i) *Sharing with the landlord or the landlord and others:* In this type of case the provisions for decontrol and as to the amount of rent payable apply as if the letting were a contract for a furnished tenancy (see Chapter XV).

(ii) *Sharing with others but not the landlord:* If it is necessary to apportion the rateable value (p. 98) of the separate accommodation in this type of case in order to establish whether the letting has become decontrolled the circumstances of the shared accommodation must be taken into account (s. 8 (2) / 1949 Act). For the purpose of fixing new rent limits an apportionment of the gross value may be made as in any other case (p. 40); in Scotland, the provisions of the Act of 1949 continue to apply if there is any dispute as to the amount of recoverable rent (p. 119).

(7) *Premises let for mixed purposes*

An essential requirement of the Rent Acts is that the premises must be let as a dwelling. But a house or part of a house is not excluded from the protection of the Acts by reason only that part of the premises is used as a shop or office or for business, trade or professional purposes (s. 12 (2) / 1920 Act: s. 3 (3) / 1939 Act). The tenancy is protected even if the greater part of the premises is used for such purposes (*Vickery* v. *Martin* [1944] K.B. 679), provided it was let as a dwelling-house (*Whiteley* v. *Wilson* [1953] 1 Q.B. 77); or if let for business purposes and lived in provided the tenant is not precluded by the terms of the lease from living there (*Levermore and Another* v. *Jobey* [1956] 1 W.L.R. 662). But if the residential part and the part used for business purposes are sub-let separately, only the sub-tenancy of the residential part will be protected by the Acts (*Phillips* v. *Hallahan* [1925] 1 K.B. 756). The sub-tenant of the business premises may be able to claim protection under Part II of the Landlord and Tenant Act, 1954.

(8) *Premises excepted from the Acts*

The various classes of premises and lettings which are not protected by the Rent Acts are shown in Chapters VIII and IX.

2. Statutory tenancies

(1) *Status of the tenant*

The Rent Acts do not create a tenancy in the accepted form of giving the tenant a legal estate in the land. They merely allow him to retain possession of the dwelling after his contractual tenancy has been terminated or has expired. In other words the tenant has only a personal right of occupation and the so-called "statutory tenancy" is "a mere status of irremovability" which can come into existence even if the tenant was in breach of covenant at the end of his contractual tenancy (*Tideway Investment and Property Holding Ltd.* v. *Wellwood* [1952] Ch. 791). He loses the right if he ceases to occupy the premises (*Ebner* v. *Lascelles* [1928] 2 K.B. 486) but not if it is only a temporary measure, e.g. on account of illness (*Wigley* v. *Leigh* [1950] 2 K.B. 305). On the other hand, the controlled dwelling need not be the only place of residence and the owner of a house in the country can claim protection in respect of the flat he rents in town, provided he uses it regularly, e.g. two nights a week (*Langford Property Co. Ltd.* v. *Tureman* [1949] 1 K.B. 29) but not if he only stays there occasionally (*Beck* v. *Scholz* [1953] 1 Q.B. 570). The tenant has no right to assign (*Keeves* v. *Dean* [1924] 1 K.B. 685) except with the consent of the landlord and, in some cases, a superior landlord (see para. 3 below). If the tenant sub-lets the whole of the property he ceases to be protected (*Roe* v. *Russell* [1928] 2 K.B. 117). He cannot bequeath the right by will (*Lovibond & Sons Ltd.* v. *Vincent* [1929] 1 K.B. 687) but in certain cases on the tenant's death the widow or a near relative can claim the statutory tenancy (see below). The tenancy does not vest in his personal representatives if he dies without leaving a will (*Drury* v. *Johnston* [1928] N.I. 25), nor can it be claimed by the trustee in bankruptcy if the tenant goes bankrupt (p. 179).

(2) *Conditions of a statutory tenancy*

A tenant who retains possession of any dwelling-house as a statutory tenant under the Rent Acts must observe and is entitled to the benefit of all the terms and conditions of his original contract of tenancy so far as they are consistent with the provisions of the Acts (s. 15 (1) / 1920 Act). No qualifying period of occupation is required before a person can claim a statutory tenancy, unless he claims it as a member of the family of a deceased tenant (see below).

By virtue of Section 16 of the Act of 1957 no notice by a landlord or a tenant to quit any controlled premises in England and Wales is valid unless it is given not less than four weeks before the date on which it is to take effect (p. 187). Paragraphs 28 to 30 of the Sixth Schedule to the Act apply the same rule to controlled tenancies in Scotland.

It is a condition of every statutory tenancy that the tenant will give the landlord facilities for executing any repairs which he is entitled to do (s. 16 (2) / 1920 Act).

A landlord may also obtain an order of a court of summary jurisdiction permitting him to execute any work which he is required to do under a sanitary notice served by the local authority (s. 289, Public Health Act, 1936). There is a similar provision in Section 159 of the Housing Act, 1936, and in Section 161 of the Housing (Scotland) Act, 1950, for enabling a landlord to execute repairs.

The Landlord and Tenant Act, 1954, enables a tenant holding under a long lease, where the landlord takes steps to terminate the lease either at the end of its term or after it has been continued by the Act, to apply for what the Act calls a "statutory tenancy", the terms of which may be agreed between the landlord and tenant or may be determined by the court. A statutory tenancy of that type may have completely new terms (see Chapter XVII).

(3) *Preservation of tenancy on the death of the tenant*

Although a statutory tenant has only a personal right of occupation the Acts provide on his death for some security of tenure for his widow or near relative who has been living with him. This protection applies also in the case where a statutory tenant has exchanged his tenancy (see below). Section 12 (1) (*g*) of the Act of 1920, as amended, provides that the expression "tenant" includes:

(*a*) the widow of a tenant who was residing with him at the time of his death, or

(*b*) where the tenant leaves no such widow or is a woman, such member of the tenant's family residing with him at the time of his death as may be decided in default of agreement by the county court or, in Scotland, by the sheriff.

It is clear that the widow of the deceased tenant has the first claim to the tenancy provided she was living with him at the time of his death; and her right is not affected if she re-marries (*Apsley* v. *Barr* [1928] N.I. 183). But if the widow was not residing with the tenant at the time of his death a member of his family can claim the tenancy, provided he or she was residing with the tenant at the time of the tenant's death (s. 42 (1) / English Act 1954: s. 33 (1) / Scottish Act 1954).

In the case of a tenant dying after the 18th July 1933 a member of the family (but not the widow) must have resided with the tenant for not less than six months immediately before his death in order to be able to claim the statutory tenancy (s. 13 / 1933 Act).

The widow or other relative is entitled to succeed even in the case of a suspended order for possession if the landlord had not attempted to enforce the order during the tenant's lifetime (*Sherrin* v. *Brand* [1956] 1 All E.R. 194).

There is no definition in the Acts as to what is meant by a "member of the tenant's family". It has been held to include a husband (*Salter* v. *Lask* (No. 2) [1925] 1 K.B. 584); a daughter (*Tickner* v. *Clifton* [1929] 1 K.B. 207); an adopted child (whether or not there has been a legal adoption) (*Brock* v. *Wollams* [1949] 2 K.B. 388); brothers and sisters (*Price* v. *Gould* (1930) 46 T.L.R. 411); and in one case an unmarried wife who had two children by the tenant (*Hawes* v. *Evenden* [1953] 1 W.L.R. 1169).

These provisions as to transmission on death only operate once so that when the claimant dies the tenancy does not pass to any other member of the family (*Pain* v. *Cobb* (1931) 47 T.L.R. 596), e.g. on the death of the widow the tenancy will not pass to a son or daughter.

There is, however, an exception to this rule in the case of an assignment of a tenancy. The agreement for the exchange—which needs the consent of all landlords—can provide that even if a tenant who is a party to the agreement is a statutory tenant by succession the rule as to transmission on death shall apply for the benefit of his widow or near relative who may have been living with the tenant for the six months immediately before his death (see below).

(4) *Preservation of tenancy for a deserted wife*

If a statutory tenant deserts his wife it seems that she is assumed to have a licence from her husband to remain in occupation of the matrimonial home so long as she pays the rent and performs the obligations under the tenancy, even if he has no intention of returning to her (*Old Gate Estates Ltd.* v. *Alexander* [1950] 1 K.B. 311: *Middleton* v. *Baldock* [1950] 1 K.B. 657). But the wife is a licensee of a special character, she is not her husband's agent and cannot assign her interest (*R.* v. *Twickenham Rent Tribunal: ex parte Dunn* [1953] 2 Q.B. 425).

3. Exchange of statutory tenancies

In an effort to provide some freedom of movement without losing the protection of the Acts Section 17 of the Act of 1957 provides facilities for the exchange of statutory tenancies.

(1) *Exchanges to be voluntary*

A statutory tenant may agree in writing to transfer his tenancy to another person. As from the date specified in the agreement the incoming tenant is deemed to be the statutory tenant of the dwelling.

Whilst the provision is designed chiefly to allow statutory tenants to exchange their dwellings it is possible for the outgoing tenant to take a tenancy which is not controlled, such as a council house, or to buy the controlled tenancy and let the vendor into occupation as a statutory tenant. In other words there is no obligation on the outgoing tenant to take a tenancy at all.

(2) *Landlords' consents to agreement*

An exchange agreement is of no effect unless the landlord of the controlled dwelling is a party to it (s. 17 (2) *ibid.*). If both the dwellings are subject to statutory tenancies the landlords of the two dwellings must be parties to the agreement. If the outgoing tenant is taking a contractual tenancy he should ensure that the landlord has no objection to the transfer, except where the incoming tenant can assign without consent.

If either or both the statutory tenancies are held under a superior lease a superior landlord must be a party to the exchange agreement or agreements if his consent would have been necessary to an assign-

c

ment of the contractual sub-tenancy out of which the statutory sub-tenancy arose.

If a landlord is not prepared to enter into an agreement he cannot be challenged on the grounds that his action is unreasonable.

(3) *Transmission of exchanged tenancy on death of incoming tenant*

The widow or other near relative of the incoming tenant can claim the tenancy on his death (see para. 2 (3) above), except in the case where the outgoing tenant is a statutory tenant who succeeded to the tenancy on the death of the former statutory tenant. In that case the exchange agreement can provide for the tenancy to pass to the widow or other relative on the death of the incoming tenant (s. 17 (3) *ibid.*) but otherwise—as in any other case—there is no second transmission on death.

(4) *Prohibition on premiums in respect of exchange agreements*

It is unlawful to require the payment of any pecuniary consideration, such as a premium, for entering into an agreement for the exchange of a statutory tenancy. The amount of any such payment is recoverable by the person by whom it was made either in proceedings for its recovery or, if it was paid to the landlord, by deduction from the rent.

(5) *Penalty for demanding a premium*

Any person who demands a pecuniary consideration in respect of an exchange agreement is liable on summary conviction to a fine not exceeding £100, and the court may order him to repay the consideration.

(6) *Payments between outgoing and incoming tenants*

The above-mentioned provisions relating to illegal payments do not prevent the outgoing tenant claiming payment from the incoming tenant

(a) of so much of any outgoings discharged by the outgoing tenant as is referable to any period after the date of exchange;

(b) of any sum not exceeding the amount of any expenditure reasonably incurred by the outgoing tenant in carrying out any structural alteration of the dwelling-house or in providing or improving fixtures which are not tenant's fixtures;

(c) where the outgoing tenant was himself an assignee, of a sum not exceeding any reasonable amount paid by him to his assignor for expenditure incurred by that assignor, or by any previous assignor, in carrying out any structural alteration or in providing or improving fixtures which are not tenant's fixtures; or

(d) where part of the dwelling-house is used as a shop or office, or for business, trade or professional purposes, of a reasonable amount in respect of any goodwill of the business, trade or profession, being goodwill transferred to the incoming tenant in connection with the agreement of exchange or accruing to him in consequence thereof (s. 17 (4) *ibid.*).

CHAPTER III

The Rent Limits in England and Wales

ONE of the fundamental principles of the Rent Acts is the limitation of the amount of rent which a landlord may recover from the tenant of controlled property.

The Act of 1957 introduces a new scheme for fixing the rent limits of controlled dwelling-houses in England and Wales. The scheme of the Acts of 1920 to 1939, which limited the standard rent to the amount which was charged on the 3rd August 1914 in the case of "old control" houses, and on the 1st September 1939 in the case of "new control" houses, has been superseded by a common formula which can be applied to all controlled houses. This scheme has abolished the system which allowed the landlord of "old control" houses to claim "permitted increases" for being responsible for repairs and also the "repairs increase" under the Act of 1954 in respect of lettings made on or before the 1st September 1939. On the other hand, the rent limit of all controlled houses can be adjusted to take account of the responsibility of the landlord or the tenant for repairs.

The original scheme of the Rent Acts continues to apply to houses which became decontrolled on the 6th July 1957, where the tenant is entitled to remain in possession (Chapter VIII) and to Scotland (Chapters X and XI).

1. The rent limit

The general effect of the Act is that the annual rent of a controlled dwelling-house (excluding rates, charges for services or furniture) can be raised to the level of twice the gross value of the dwelling, although in some cases this can only be achieved in stages. In other cases the factor of two is subject to adjustment to take account of repairing obligations, and is liable to be reduced if the property is not kept in good repair.

Section 1 (1) of the Act provides that, subject to adjustments for responsibility for repairs, the rent recoverable for any rental period from the tenant under a controlled tenancy is not to exceed the following limit:

    (1) a rent of which the annual rate is equal to the 1956 gross value of the dwelling multiplied by two, together with

(2) (*a*) the annual amount of any rates for the basic rental period borne by the landlord or a superior landlord; and

(*b*) such annual amount as may be agreed in writing between the landlord and the tenant or determined by the county court to be a reasonable charge for

(i) any services for the tenant provided by the landlord or a superior landlord during the basic rental period, or

(ii) any furniture which under the terms of the tenancy the tenant is entitled to use.

An agreement or determination by a rent tribunal made under Section 24 (3) (*b*) of the Act of 1954 as respects furniture or services remains valid until a new agreement or determination is made under the Act of 1957 (para. 1, Seventh Schedule / 1957 Act).

The above limit, which is called "the rent limit" (s. 1 (2) *ibid.*), is of general application and can be claimed notwithstanding any statutory restriction previously imposed (s. 2 (1) *ibid.*), e.g., in the case of a subsidised private house (p. 37), but it is subject to adjustment if there is any change in the rates (p. 29), or as respects services or furniture (p. 32), or if any improvements completed on or after the 6th July 1957 are carried out at the landlord's expense (p. 33), or if the tenant is entitled to a reduction on grounds of disrepair (p. 58). A landlord need not claim the full amount of the rent limit but adjustments to the rent are arbitrary amounts and, in those cases, neither more nor less can be claimed.

The "basic rental period" means the rental period comprising the 6th July 1957, or in the case of a controlled tenancy beginning after that date, the first rental period of the tenancy (s. 25 (1) *ibid.*). For the meaning of "1956 gross value" see page 40, and for "rates" page 28. The meanings of services, furniture and improvements are discussed in paragraphs 9 and 10 *post*.

2. Adjustments of factor for responsibility for repairs

In fixing the rent limit the Act takes account of the fact that there is no general rule (apart from Section 2 of the Housing Act, 1936, see page 46) as to responsibility for repairs of unfurnished lettings and it provides for adjustment of the factor of two in the following cases (Part I, First Schedule, *ibid.*).

(1) *Repairs other then internal decorations*

(*a*) *Where the tenant is responsible for all repairs:* If under the terms of the tenancy the tenant is responsible for all repairs, the appropriate factor is four-thirds instead of two in fixing the rental limit by reference to the 1956 gross value.

(*b*) *Where the tenant is responsible for some repairs:* If under the terms of the tenancy the tenant is responsible for some, but not all, repairs, the appropriate factor is such number less than two but greater than four-thirds as may be agreed in writing between the landlord and the tenant or determined by the county court.

(2) *Internal decorations*

In both of the above cases the expression "repairs" does not include internal decorative repairs; so the tenant cannot claim an adjustment of the factor of two because he is responsible for doing internal decorations.

On the other hand, the landlord can claim an adjustment of the rent limit—

(*a*) if he is responsible for internal decorative repairs under the terms of the tenancy, or

(*b*) if neither he nor the tenant is so responsible under the tenancy but the landlord elects to be treated as being responsible for such work.

In either of these cases—

(i) where the tenant is not responsible for any repairs, the appropriate factor is seven-thirds instead of two;

(ii) where the tenant is responsible for all other repairs, the appropriate factor is five-thirds instead of four-thirds;

(iii) where the tenant is responsible for some but not all other repairs, the appropriate factor is such number less than seven-thirds but greater than five-thirds as may be agreed in writing between the landlord and the tenant or determined by the county court.

As a general rule, therefore, the landlord can put up the rent by one-third of the 1956 gross value for doing internal decorations.

(3) *Landlord's election to do internal decorations*

In the case where neither the landlord nor the tenant is responsible for internal decorations but the landlord elects to be responsible for the work he must give notice in the prescribed form to the tenant. The notice will continue to have effect if there is a change in the person of the landlord.

If a landlord has been in receipt of a rent which is higher than the rent limit by reason of the fact that he was getting a higher rent under the old law (see para. 3 *post*) he is not deprived of the right to adjust the rent on electing to do internal decorations. As respects any rental period beginning after the election the question of fixing the rent limit under the Act is to be determined as if the election had always had effect. The result of this provision is that if the rent limit plus one-third of the 1956 gross value for internal decorations is higher than the rent which the landlord has been getting he can claim that higher amount. But the increased amount the tenant has to pay will probably be less than one-third of the 1956 gross value.

(4) *Tenant's objection to landlord doing internal decorations*

A tenant can object to the election by the landlord to do internal decorations. If within one month of the service of notice by the landlord of his election to do the decorations the tenant dissents from it the election has no effect.

The tenant, however, must be prepared himself to do the decorations because after he has dissented and he fails to do the decorating it becomes a ground on which the landlord can claim possession. The Act provides that if the tenant duly dissents it shall be a ground for possession that the tenant has failed to keep the dwelling in a reasonable state of internal decorative repair, having regard to its age, character and locality (p. 80).

3. No reduction where existing rent above limit

Where on the 6th July 1957 the recoverable rent payable in respect of a controlled tenancy is higher than the rent limit under the Act the rent can remain at that higher level (s. 1 (3) *ibid.*). It will, however, be subject to adjustment if there is a change in the rates (p. 29), or as respects services or furniture (p. 32), or if any improvements are carried out (p. 33), or to an abatement on grounds of disrepair (p. 58).

This rule applies also in the case where a tenancy remains controlled on a subsidised private house (p. 38) or to a house which is subject to a statutory tenancy following a long lease (s. 20 (1), para. 8, Sixth Schedule *ibid.*).

This higher rent limit can be increased if the landlord elects to do internal decorations (see para. 2 (3) *ante*).

4. Calculation of rent

In calculating the recoverable rent of a controlled dwelling the landlord is entitled—

(*a*) to exclude any sums recoverable as rent under Section 16 of the Landlord and Tenant Act, 1927, by reason of increases in taxes, rates or fire premiums ascribable to improvements, made by tenants, other than

    (i) sums so recoverable in respect of increases in rates, or

    (ii) sums referable to improvements executed by the tenant before the 1st April 1956, or

    (iii) sums referable to improvements executed by him after that date but affecting the 1956 gross value by reason of a proposal made before the 1st April 1957;

(*b*) to exclude any sums recoverable as rent which are payments for accrued tenant's repairs, in respect of a long lease, under the First Schedule to the Landlord and Tenant Act, 1954;

(*c*) to leave out of account—

    (i) any deduction from rent as recovery of premiums, under the First Schedule to the Landlord and Tenant (Rent Control) Act, 1949, or

    (ii) any reduction of rent by order of a court on the failure of a landlord to carry out initial repairs under the Landlord and Tenant Act, 1954, where the tenant retains possession as a statutory tenant after the termination of a long lease (s. 25 (3) / 1957 Act).

5. Increase of rent limit not automatic

The provisions in the Act of 1957 which enable a landlord to increase the rent of a controlled tenancy do not apply automatically. The rent which could be claimed under the repealed law remains the recoverable rent under the tenancy until the procedure under the Act is put into effect for increasing or decreasing the rent (s. 1 (4) *ibid*.). In any case a landlord is not entitled to vary the rent of a contractual tenancy except under the terms of the contract.

6. Variation of rent under a contractual tenancy

The Act follows the principle of previous Rent Acts and does not allow any variation of rent during the currency of a contractual tenancy. Thus, if the landlord wishes to increase the rent of a periodic tenancy and there is no provision in the agreement enabling him to do so, he must first terminate the contract. If the tenancy is for a fixed term the landlord has no power under the Rent Acts, or the Act of 1957, to increase the rent during the currency of the term, unless the agreement provides for making an increase.

(1) *Prohibition on rent increases during contractual period*

A notice of increase cannot operate to increase the rent under a controlled tenancy for any contractual period except in so far as may be consistent with the terms of the tenancy; nor can the rent be increased for any contractual period in order to allow for adjustments as respects services and furniture (s. 6 / 1957 Act). The "contractual period" means a rental period beginning while a tenancy is current.

(2) *Termination of contractual tenancy for purposes of rent increases*

In order to claim an increase in rent a landlord does not have to serve a notice to quit as well as a notice of increase. The latter can operate also as a notice to quit. This provision is a re-statement of the law in the Rent Restrictions (Notices of Increase) Act, 1923, which has been repealed so far as it applied to England and Wales.

Where a notice of increase is served during the currency of a tenancy which could, by a notice to quit served at the same time, be brought to an end before the date or earliest date specified in the notice of increase, the latter operates to convert the tenancy into a statutory tenancy as from that date. The effect of this provision is that no notice of increase can operate during the currency of a tenancy granted for a fixed term; in the case of some periodic tenancies, e.g., a yearly tenancy terminable by six months' notice, the date of increase must be postponed to the end of the period required to terminate the contractual tenancy.

(3) *Adjustment for services not within terms of tenancy*

Section 40 (now repealed) of the Housing Repairs and Rents Act, 1954, enabled a landlord under a controlled tenancy made on or before the 1st September 1939 to claim—notwithstanding anything in the terms of the tenancy or statutory tenancy—an increase in rent in respect of any rise over the period between the 3rd September 1939 and the 30th August 1954, in the cost of services for the tenant

  (i) provided by the landlord under the terms and conditions of the letting; or

  (ii) provided by the landlord but not under the terms of the tenancy.

Where the parties agreed or the landlord obtained a determination from the rent tribunal for an increase in respect of services provided by the landlord but not under the tenancy, i.e. within category (ii)—which might be termed "non-contractual services"—any subsequent change in the provision of the services, either withholding or restoring, were regarded as transfers of burdens and liabilities as between landlord and tenant.

This arrangement is preserved by the Act of 1957 in Section 6 (4) and where the landlord was receiving an addition in rent for such services under a contractual tenancy current on the 6th July 1957 and the services are withheld in whole or in part during the contractual period, the rent recoverable for that period is to be decreased by an appropriate amount. The amount of the decrease must be settled by agreement in writing between the landlord and the tenant or by the county court. The decrease may be back-dated and will continue to be effective until revoked or varied by agreement in writing between the landlord and the tenant or by the county court.

(4) *Rent decreases during contractual period*

Subject to the above provisions for decreasing rent where non-contractual services are withheld, the Act of 1957 does not affect the operation of any lease or agreement in so far as it provides for a reduction in rent during any contractual period.

7. Procedure for increasing rents

Section 2 of the Act lays down the procedure which must be followed before a landlord can claim an increase in rent.

(1) *Notice of increase*

The landlord must serve on the tenant a notice of increase in the prescribed form specifying the amount of the increase. If the landlord wishes to claim the total increase up to the rent limit in stages he can serve separate notices for each increase either on the same day or on different days, or a notice may specify more than one date and amount. The landlord must fix more than one date where the limit of seven shillings and six pence per week (see sub-para. (3) below) falls short of the full increase claimable under the Act. No notice of increase could be served before the 6th July 1957.

The county court may rectify any error or omission in a notice if satisfied that it is due to a bona fide mistake on the part of the landlord (s. 6 / 1923 Act).

(2) *Date of increase*

The notice must specify the date when the increase is to take effect, which in any case cannot be earlier than three months after service of the notice; so that a tenant is always entitled to three months' notice of a rent increase (s. 2 (2) (a) / 1957 Act).

"Three months" for the purpose of fixing the date of an increase means three calendar months (s. 3, Interpretation Act, 1889).

(3) *Limitation of amount of initial increase*

The total of the increases which may be specified in any notice or notices taking effect less than nine months after service of the first notice must not exceed seven shillings and six pence per week. But a notice may specify more than one date and amount (s. 2 (2) (b) / 1957 Act).

The general effect of this provision is that for at least three months from the 6th July 1957 a landlord will not be able to claim any increase in rent, except for authorised adjustments (see below), and for the next six months the amount of increase which he may claim (excluding such adjustments) will be limited to seven shillings and six pence per week.

This restriction applies only to the first notice and to any subsequent notice in so far as it takes effect within the nine months after service of the first notice. Thus, if a second notice is served three months after the first notice the tenant will get three months' notice of the second increase but will only be able to claim the limitation of seven shillings and six pence during the next three months.

The limitation, however, does not mean that the landlord must forfeit any increase over and above the seven shillings and six pence per week. The rent recoverable for any rental period is reckoned on an annual basis (s. 1) and not in relation to a particular rental period, such as a week.

(4) *Increases not subject to restrictions*

The minimum period of three months for the operation of a notice of increase and the limitation to seven shillings and six pence per week for the first six months does not apply in the case of authorised adjustments in respect of rates, services, furniture or improvements (pp. 29–33). The tenant may, therefore, have to pay more than an increase of seven shillings and six pence per week. On the other hand, no increase can be claimed during the period of a contractual tenancy (para. 6 (1) *ante*).

(5) *Restrictions on rent increases where property is unfit*

The restrictions on the right of a landlord to claim an increase in rent where the property has been declared by a local authority to be unfit or where the tenant has served a notice of disrepair are set out in Chapter IV (p. 45).

(6) *Restrictions on right of overseas companies to increase rent*

If the landlord is a corporate body incorporated outside the United Kingdom a notice of increase can be given only after a certificate of repair has been issued by a local authority; and the notice will be cancelled from the date when it took effect if subsequently the local authority issue a notice of disrepair—see Chapter IV, p. 45.

8. Inclusion of rates in rent

Where the rent of a controlled dwelling includes an amount in respect of rates borne by the landlord or a superior landlord the Act makes special provision for the calculation of the amount of rates to be included in the rent and for adjustments to be made on any subsequent change in the rates. This provision replaces that in Section 2 (1) (b) of the Act of 1920 which allowed a landlord to claim a "permitted increase" for any increase in rates payable by him.

(1) *Meaning of "rates"*

"Rates" include water rents and charges but not an owner's drainage rate within the meaning of Section 24 (2) (a) of the Land Drainage Act, 1930. Under that provision an owner's drainage rate is a rate raised for the purposes of defraying expenses incurred by a drainage board in connection with new works or the improvement of existing works and charges in respect of contributions to be made by the board to a Rivers Board.

Any reference to rates in respect of a dwelling includes a reference to such proportion of the rates of a hereditament of which the dwelling forms part (e.g. the rooms on one floor of a house) as may be agreed in writing between the landlord and the tenant or determined by the county court (s. 25 (1) / 1957 Act).

(2) *Calculation of amount of rates*

The amount for rates which may be included in the rent for any rental period must be calculated in the same proportion as the length of the rental period bears to the length of the rating period. Thus, in the case of a weekly tenancy where the local authority levy a rate each half year the amount for rates included in the weekly rent will be one twenty-sixth part of the whole rate (Second Schedule *ibid.*).

In regard to a new rating period the amount for rates included in the rent continues to be calculated on the same basis as for the previous rating period until the amount of the new rate is known.

Any discount, and any allowance for compounding with the rating authority for payment of rates by the owner instead of by the occupier, is left out of account in fixing the amount of rates included in the rent. The effect of this provision is that a landlord can charge his tenant more than is actually paid out as rates.

(3) *Adjustments as respects rates borne by the landlord*

If there is any change in the amount of rates demanded for the new rating period the amount of rates included in the rent must be recalculated to take account of the new rate demand. Any such recalculation is not to affect the amount of rates ascertained for any rental period beginning more than six weeks before the date of service of the demand for the new rate.

If the settlement of a rating proposal results in a decrease in the amount of rates payable by a landlord, the amount of rates included in the rent must be recalculated to give effect to the decrease. The recalculation must not affect the amount of rates ascertained for any rental period beginning more than six weeks before the date of the settlement of the proposal.

The two limitations as to back-dating an adjustment mean that a landlord or tenant is only entitled to a proportion of the adjustment if it relates to a retrospective period of more than six weeks. Any adjustments which relate to earlier periods are not recoverable.

Where any rates are borne by the landlord or a superior landlord and they differ from the amount of rates for the basic rental period the rent limit is to be increased or decreased by the amount of the difference (s. 3 / 1957 Act). This is an arbitrary adjustment and differs from the provision in Section 2 (1) (*b*) of the Act of 1920 by virtue of which the landlord could claim a "permitted increase" not exceeding the increase in rates.

The increase cannot be inconsistent with the terms of a contractual tenancy (p. 25) but where the notice can be back-dated any rent underpaid becomes due on the day after service of the notice.

An increase of rent due to an increase in rates is disregarded in fixing the limit of seven shillings and six pence per week in respect of any notices taking effect less than nine months after service of the first notice of increase (p. 27).

An increase is not limited to the case where a higher rate is levied; it may be claimed where the rates are increased through a revision in the rateable value of the premises (*Steel* v. *Mahoney* [1918] W.N. 253).

The Act makes no provision for the service of a notice, either by the landlord or the tenant, where there is a decrease in the amount of rates.

(4) *Sub-tenancies*

The above provisions relating to the payment of rates included in rent apply equally to sub-tenancies. A tenant who charges his sub-tenant a rent which includes rates must make increases or decreases in consequence of any changes in the rates. Where the landlord pays the rates the tenant must pass on to the sub-tenant the whole or part of any increase or decrease in rates demanded or allowed by his landlord (i.e. the superior landlord of the sub-tenant), if the rent of the sub-tenancy includes rates, unless it is a contractual sub-tenancy which does not allow such adjustments to be made.

9. Provision of services or furniture by the landlord

The provision in the Act of 1957 which enables a landlord to include in the rent of a controlled tenancy a reasonable charge for any services for the tenant provided by the landlord or a superior landlord or for the use of furniture does not introduce any new law for the control of lettings with services or furniture. It merely provides as to the charge which may be made in any case under the Rent Acts where the tenancy remains controlled even if there is provision for services or for use of furniture.

By virtue of Sections 12 (2) of the Act of 1920 and 3 (2) of the Act of 1939 the Rent Acts do not apply to a dwelling-house bona fide let at a rent which includes payments in respect of board, attendance or use of furniture (p. 166). A house is not regarded as being let furnished or with attendance unless the amount of rent representing the value of the attendance or the use of the furniture to the tenant forms a substantial portion of the whole rent (s. 10 (1) / 1923 Act). It is only in the case where the value of services or of use of furniture falls short of this rule that the tenancy is controlled by the Rent Acts. The bulk of what are commonly called "furnished lettings" are subject to control under the Rent of Furnished Houses Control

(Scotland) Act, 1943, and the Furnished Houses (Rent Control) Act, 1946 (see Chapter XV).

(1) *Meaning of "services" and "furniture"*

There is no definition in the Act of 1957 as to the meaning of "services" or "furniture". It seems clear, however, that the provision of services, unlike the use of furniture, is not limited to services provided under the terms of the tenancy. Section 1 (1) (*b*) provides that services but not furniture may be provided by a superior landlord.

In *R.* v. *Paddington North Rent Tribunal, ex parte Perry* [1956] 1 Q.B. 229, it was held that services included the provision of central heating, constant hot water, passenger and service lifts, the lighting and heating of a lounge, passages and staircase, the provision of a porter, the cleaning of parts used in common with other tenants, the removal of refuse, the control of pests and the provision of floor covering to parts used in common with other tenants. That case dealt with the meaning of "services" under (the now repealed) Section 40 of the Housing Repairs and Rents Act, 1954, which enabled a landlord under a controlled tenancy made on or before the 1st September 1939 to claim an increase in rent in respect of any rise, over the period between the 3rd September 1939 and the 30th August 1954, in the cost of provision of services.

With regard to furnished lettings the term "services" is defined in the Acts of 1943 and 1946 (p. 168).

The term "furniture" applies only to articles commonly and currently regarded as such (*Palser* v. *Grinling* and *Property Holding Company Ltd.* v. *Mischeff* (reported together) [1948] A.C. 291), and the terms of the tenancy agreement are not conclusive as to what may be regarded as furniture. In that case it was said that as against the tenant the landlord must have a proprietory right in articles regarded as furniture. The term did not include articles provided in halls and passages for the common use of tenants. Loose articles generally come within the term, while "fixtures" may or may not be furniture according to the nature and degree of attachment. In such a case, even if the articles would otherwise rank as "furniture", the test should be that if they cannot be detached without appreciable damage to or alteration of the fabric or themselves they ought not to be regarded as furniture.

Articles which have been regarded as furniture are a moveable electric refrigerator where its only attachment to the fabric was the connection through a plug in the wall; linoleum and rubber floor covering (*Property Holding Co. Ltd.* v. *Mischeff, supra.*); crockery and kitchen utensils (*Maddox Properties Ltd.* v. *Kless* [1946] 1 All E.R. 487). On the other hand, such articles as electric panel fires and an electric immersion heater have not been regarded as furniture (*R.* v. *Rent Tribunal for Hampstead and St. Pancras, ex parte Ascot Lodge Ltd.* [1947] K.B. 973); nor have built-in wardrobes although they performed the functions of conventional furniture (*Palser* v. *Grinling, supra*). But there is no precise dividing line and in the *Mischeff* case a fitted medical chest in a bathroom was treated as furniture.

(2) *Adjustments as respects services and furniture*

Provision is made in Section 4 of the Act for adjusting the payments made in respect of services provided for the tenant by the landlord or a superior landlord or use of furniture by the tenant, under the terms of the tenancy, where there is any change subsequent to the basic rental period.

If there is any difference, in comparison with the basic rental period, as respects the provision of services or the use of furniture by the tenant or any circumstances relating thereto the rent limit is to be increased or decreased by an appropriate amount. The adjustment may be made only where the charge is such as to affect the amount of the rent which it is reasonable to charge. On the other hand, in so far as the difference can be measured in value to the tenant the change is arbitrary and an adjustment must be made.

An increase or decrease as respects services or furniture must be settled by agreement in writing between the landlord and the tenant or by the county court. The right to apply to the county court is not limited to cases where there is disagreement between the parties. A determination whether made by agreement or by the county court may be back-dated in the case of a statutory tenancy and will continue to be effective until revoked or varied by agreement in writing between the landlord and the tenant or by the county court (s. 4 (2) *ibid.*). Thus, the adjustments will continue to apply if there is a new landlord, or if there is a new tenant after the landlord has obtained possession on grounds of over-crowding (p. 92), or if the widow or other relative claims the tenancy on the death of the tenant (p. 15).

A rent increase as respects services or use of furniture is payable without the service of any notice; it may be claimed in addition to the limitation of seven shillings and six pence per week during the initial period of increase (p. 27); and notwithstanding any restriction on increases on grounds of unfitness (p. 49).

(3) *Variation under a contractual tenancy*

If the rent includes a charge for services or furniture it cannot be increased or decreased on account of such items during any contractual period, except in so far as it is consistent with the terms of the tenancy (s. 6 (2) (5) *ibid.*); or it is permissible to make a reduction due to any change in the value of non-contractual services (p. 97).

(4) *Sub-tenancies*

If any services provided by a landlord are made available to a sub-tenant under the terms of the sub-tenancy the same rights as to the amount to be charged or adjustments to be made will apply as between tenant and sub-tenant as exist between landlord and tenant.

10. Increases for improvements

The Act of 1957 follows the earlier Rent Acts and allows a landlord to claim an increase in the rent limit in respect of improvements completed on or after the 6th July 1957 (s. 5 / 1957 Act).

(1) *Meaning of improvements*

An improvement is defined as including structural alteration, extension or addition and the provision of additional fixtures or fittings, but does not include anything done by way of decoration or repair (s. 25 (1) *ibid.*).

In the case of some works it is not easy to distinguish between an improvement and a repair. Under the similar provision in Section 2 (1) of the Act of 1920 the cost of substituting a water closet for an earth closet has been held to qualify for an increase (*Free* v. *Callenders' Trustees* [1927] S.L.T. (Sh. Ct. Rep.) 17); and a water closet for a privy at the end of the garden (*Strood Estates Co.* v. *Gregory* [1936] 2 K.B. 605). In *Wates* v. *Rowlands* [1952] 2 Q.B. 12, the raising of foundations was treated as an improvement but a new tiled floor to replace a wooden floor, which rested on the foundations and which had become rotten through a rise in the water level, was regarded as a repair.

It was held in *Morcom* (*Grey Coat Hospital Governors*) v. *Campbell-Johnson and Others* [1956] 1 Q.B. 106, that the question to be decided was whether there was the provision of something new for the benefit of the tenant, or whether something already existing had been replaced in which case the work was that of repair and not improvement even if more modern equipment was used. In that

D

case the replacement of drainage and cold-water systems by new and modern systems in a block of flats built sixty years ago and the lowering of an adjoining area below the damp course were held to be repairs. It seems to follow from the dictum in that case that the works listed in the Ministry of Housing and Local Government publication *New Homes for Old*, which qualify for an improvement grant under the Housing Act, 1949, will not necessarily be regarded as improvements under the Rent Acts in respect of which the landlord may claim the addition in the rent limit.

(2) *Private street works qualify as improvements*

Where private street works are carried out at the expense of the landlord or a superior landlord under Section 150 of the Public Health Act, 1875, or the Private Street Works Act, 1892, or the corresponding provisions of any local Act, the works qualify as an improvement (s. 18 / 1957 Act).

The increase may be claimed only in respect of expenditure incurred by the landlord or a superior landlord on or after the 6th July 1957 where they do the work or in respect of private street works charges for which they become liable after that date where the work is done by the highway authority. Where the charges are payable by instalments the landlord is not entitled to claim a rent increase on interest payable on the charges. On the other hand, a landlord appears to be able to include in his expenditure any out-of-pockets incurred by him, such as solicitor's or surveyor's fees, where the work is done by the highway authority.

If other premises belonging to the landlord or superior landlord benefit from the works the expenditure is to be apportioned between the controlled dwelling and the other premises by agreement in writing between the landlord and the tenant or determined by the county court. The right to apply to the county court is not limited to cases where there is disagreement between the parties.

(3) *Amount of increase*

The rent limit under any controlled tenancy of the dwelling for rental periods beginning after the completion of the improvement may be increased by 8 per cent. per annum of the amount expended on the improvement by the landlord or any superior landlord or any person from whom the landlord or any superior landlord derives title (e.g. a previous owner) (s. 5 (1) *ibid.*). This increase is arbitrary and differs from the former provision in Section 2 (1) (a) of the Act of 1920 which allowed the landlord to claim an increase not exceeding the permitted increase of 8 per cent. per annum of the expenditure incurred (or 6 per cent. per annum if the expenditure was incurred before the 2nd July 1920).

(4) *Deductions from expenditure qualifying for increase*

In calculating the amount expended on improvements, the following must be deducted:

   (i) the amount of an improvement grant made under Section 20 of the Housing Act, 1949;

   (ii) the amount of repayment made by a local authority under Section 12 of the Clean Air Act, 1956, for the adaptation of fireplaces in private dwellings in smokeless zones (s. 5 (4) *ibid.*);

   (iii) any statutory contribution which diminishes the liability for private street works charges (s. 18 (3) *ibid.*).

(5) *Improvements reflected in gross value not subject to the increase*

The increase cannot be claimed in respect of an improvement the value of which is reflected in the 1956 gross value under the provisions which apply for the establishment of that value (p. 40). In that case the landlord is only entitled to claim the increase in respect of improvements completed after the date of variation of the gross value (para. 8, Fifth Schedule, *ibid.*).

(6) *Date and operation of increase*

The date specified by a notice of increase, as the date from which the increase for improvements is to take effect, may be any date after service of the notice (s. 5 (2) *ibid.*), provided it is not inconsistent with the terms of a contractual tenancy (p. 24).

The increase is disregarded in fixing a limit of seven shillings and six pence per week in respect of any notices taking effect less than nine months after service of the first notice of increase (p. 27).

(7) *Tenant's right of appeal against increase*

Not later than one month after service of a notice of increase relating to improvements, or such longer time as the court may allow, the tenant may apply to the county court for an order cancelling or reducing the increase on the ground—

   (a) that the improvement was unnecessary; or

   (b) that a greater amount was expended on it than was reasonable.

The court may make an order accordingly which can be made to have retrospective effect (s. 5 (3) *ibid.*).

No application can be made on the ground that an improvement was unnecessary—

(*a*) if an improvement grant has been made in respect of the improvement under Section 20 of the Housing Act, 1949, or

(*b*) if a tenant under a controlled tenancy consented in writing to the improvement and the consent contained an acknowledgement (however expressed) that the rent could be increased on account of the improvement. This limitation will include the case where the consent has been given by a former tenant (e.g. on a widow succeeding to a tenancy on the death of her husband), and precludes a sub-tenant from objecting where the tenant has given his consent.

A tenant has no right of appeal against a notice of increase which relates to expenditure on private street works (s. 18 (4) *ibid.*); and, as he is not an "owner" for the purposes of the Acts of 1875 or 1892, he does not appear to have any right to challenge the amount of charges demanded by the highway authority where they act in default under the former Act or to object to the proposed works under the latter Act.

(8) *Sub-tenancies*

A tenant may pass on to a sub-tenant the whole or part of a claim made by the landlord for improvements—depending on the extent to which the sub-tenant's premises benefit by the work—unless it is a contractual sub-tenancy which does not allow the increase to be made. Where the increase is claimed from a sub-tenant he has a right to object thereto, except on the ground that the work was unnecessary in cases where an improvement grant has been made or where the tenant has given his consent.

(9) *Rent adjustments for improvements completed before 6th July 1957*

Where a notice of increase in respect of an improvement was served under the Act of 1920 less than four weeks before the 6th July 1957, it can take effect after the expiration of four weeks from the time of service until the rent is increased under the new procedure (para. 2 (2), Seventh Schedule, *ibid.*).

Where an improvement was completed after the 1st April 1956

and has not affected the 1956 gross value of the dwelling, the rent limit under the Act of 1957 can be increased by 8 per cent. per annum of the amount expended (para. 2 (3) *ibid.*). A certificate by the valuation officer that the improvement has not affected the 1956 gross value is conclusive evidence on the matter (para. 2 (6) *ibid.*).

In either of the foregoing cases the tenant can challenge the increase as if it were an improvement completed on or after the 6th July 1957 (see sub-para. (7) above), with the modification that if no notice of increase was served the appeal to the court must be made within one month from that date, or such longer period as the court may allow, and without restriction as to any consent having been given (para. 2 (4) *ibid.*). If the tenant had appealed to the court before the 6th July 1957 against the increase, no further application can be made; but if the appeal is pending it may be proceeded with (para. 2 (5) *ibid.*).

11. Penalty for false information in a notice of increase

If a notice of increase contains any statement or representation which is false or misleading in any material respect the landlord will be liable on summary conviction to a fine not exceeding £50 unless he proves that the statement was made innocently and without intent to deceive (s. 2 (4) *ibid.*).

12. Prohibition on premiums

Section 2 of the Landlord and Tenant (Rent Control) Act, 1949, makes it illegal to charge a premium in addition to rent on the grant, renewal, continuance or assignment of a controlled tenancy. See Chapter V.

13. Rents of subsidised private houses

Provisions are made in certain statutes for the payment of a grant by the State or by local authorities towards the provision or improvement of private houses. These Acts lay down the conditions on which the subsidies are payable, including the amount of rent which may be charged for a house. The Housing Act, 1952, makes the same kind of provision in respect of council houses which are sold by local authorities. Section 20 of the Act of 1957 allows the rent in respect of such subsidised and former council houses to be increased to not less than the rent limit of the Act during the time the conditions continue to apply.

The conditions attached to grant-aided private houses to which this rule applies are contained in:

(a) Section 2 of the Housing (Financial Provisions) Act, 1924, where State subsidy was provided towards the cost of houses built by a non-profit-making society, body of trustees or company established for the promotion of dwelling-houses for the working classes;

(b) Section 3 of the Housing (Rural Workers) Act, 1926, where grants were made by local authorities (with Government aid) for the reconditioning of private houses for agricultural workers and others engaged in rural industries;

(c) Section 3 of the Housing (Financial Provisions) Act, 1938, where grants are made by local authorities (with Government aid) towards the provision of private housing accommodation for members of the agricultural population;

(d) Section 23 of the Housing Act, 1949, where grants are made by local authorities (with Government aid) towards the modernisation of older type houses by improvement and conversion schemes; and

(e) Section 3 of the Housing Act, 1952, which lays down the conditions which may be imposed by local authorities on the disposal of council houses.

(1) *Controlled houses which are subsidised*

In the case of a tenancy of a subsidised or former council house in private ownership which is controlled the condition as to the amount of rent which may be charged, if imposed before the 6th July 1957, is modified to permit the rent to be raised to the rent limit under the Act of 1957 (s. 20 (1)). In regard to conditions imposed on or after that date the rent which may be charged is the rent limit under the Act. In either case the increase is subject to the proper notice of increase being given (p. 27). If a condition imposed before the 6th July 1957 has been registered in the register of local land charges the entry must be amended accordingly (s. 20 (2) *ibid.*).

(2) *Controlled subsidised houses with rent above limit*

If the condition as to the amount of rent which may be charged for any such controlled house was imposed before the 6th July 1957 and allows a rent in excess of the rent limit, the higher rent may continue to be charged. The higher rent is subject to adjustment for rates (p. 29), services or furniture (p. 32), or for improvements (p. 33), and to abatement on grounds of disrepair (p. 58).

(3) *Decontrolled houses which are subsidised*

Where the tenancy of a subsidised or former council house is decontrolled, and the house does not belong to a housing association or a housing trust, the condition attached to the house which fixes the rent limit, if imposed before the 6th July 1957, is modified to permit a rent limit of twice the 1956 gross value of the house. The factor of two may be adjusted to take into account the responsibility for repairs.

If the condition allows a rent which exceeds that rent limit the higher rent may continue to be charged.

In the case of conditions imposed on or after the 6th July 1957, the maximum rent is the rent limit which would be obtained by multiplying the 1956 gross value by two or the appropriate factor which applies for taking account of the responsibility for repairs.

If the dwelling has been produced by conversion which has resulted in a change in the valuation list after the 7th November 1956, any entry in the list before the change is disregarded (s. 20 (3) *ibid.*).

The provisions in the Act which enable the rents of controlled tenancies to be increased apply in the above cases; a notice of increase cannot take effect under three months; the increase is limited to seven shillings and six pence per week for the first six months of the initial increase. The increase cannot be claimed if the local authority have taken action on grounds of unfitness by reason of disrepair (p. 49). But the tenant cannot claim an abatement of rent on the grounds that he has served a notice requiring the land-lord to do repairs (para. 16, First Schedule, *ibid.*). The jurisdiction of the county court applies as in the case of a controlled tenancy.

(4) *Decontrolled houses belonging to a housing association or housing trust*

Special provision is made for the modification of conditions attached to subsidised houses which belong to a housing association or a housing trust and which were decontrolled on the 30th August 1954 (p. 108).

If the condition was imposed before the 6th July 1957, it may be amended to limit the rent to such amount as may be agreed between the association or trust and the local authority or, in default of agreement, by the Minister of Housing and Local Government. Until that amendment is made no increase in rent may be charged. The London County Council are regarded as a local authority for this purpose in respect of housing schemes promoted by them or improvement grants made by them under the Housing Act, 1949.

In the case of conditions imposed on or after the 6th July 1957, the same principle applies and the rent limit is the amount agreed between the association or trust and the local authority or the London County Council, or determined by the Minister (s. 20 (4) *ibid.*).

14. Meaning of 1956 gross value

(1) *General*

The 1956 gross value of a dwelling is the gross value thereof as shown in the valuation list on the 7th November 1956, or where the dwelling is part only of a hereditament shown in that list such proportion of that gross value as may be agreed in writing between the landlord and the tenant or determined by the county court. The right to apply to the county court is not limited to cases where there is disagreement between the parties (s. 25 (1) *ibid.*).

The Act, however, provides for the modification of the 1956 gross value in the following cases.

(2) *Notional 1956 gross value*

If a rating proposal is made—

    (i) before the 1st April 1957, or

    (ii) on the ground of a change in the occupier or in the circum-stances of occupation

and, in consequence thereof, the gross value of the hereditament as shown in the valuation list on the 7th November 1956 is varied, then, as regards any rental period (whether beginning before or after the variation) the 1956 gross value of a dwelling being or forming part of the hereditament is to be ascertained by reference to the gross value as so varied (para. 6, Fifth Schedule, *ibid.*).

(3) *Dwellings without assessments on the 7th November 1956*

If a dwelling is or forms part of a hereditament for which there was no gross value on the 7th November 1956, the first subsequent date on which a gross value for the hereditament is shown in the valuation list is to be treated as the date of the 1956 gross value (para. 7 *ibid.*).

(4) *Improvements reflected in gross value*

Special provision is made to avoid the tenant paying twice for an improvement (p. 35) in respect of which the value is reflected in the 1956 gross value.

Where in pursuance of a rating proposal made on the ground of a change in the occupier or circumstances of occupation the gross value shown in the valuation list is varied so as to take account of the state of the dwelling at a date on or after the 6th July 1957, the landlord is only entitled to claim an increase of 8 per cent. per annum of the amount expended on improvements completed after the date of variation of the gross value (para. 8 *ibid.*).

(5) *Mixed hereditaments with single assessments*

In cases where the dwelling is or forms part of a mixed hereditament, such as a flat over a shop, the gross value will, by virtue of Section 4 (3) of the Valuation for Rating Act, 1953, reflect a 1939 value for the private dwelling and a current value for the remainder of the hereditament, thus giving the premises as a whole a higher gross value than if the whole hereditament were used as a private dwelling. In this type of case the gross value of the part of the premises not used as a private dwelling or dwellings is reduced by four-sevenths in order to obtain a uniform gross value at the 1939 level for the whole of the hereditament. The 1956 gross value for such premises is, therefore, the aggregate of the full 1956 gross value for the residential part and three-sevenths of that value for the non-residential part. A certificate of the valuation officer is conclusive evidence as to the amount of gross value attributable to the part of the premises not used as a private dwelling (para. 9 *ibid.*).

(6) *Mixed hereditaments with more than one assessment*

The principle of the previous sub-paragraph is applied also where the dwelling extends over more than one rating assessment, e.g. a flat over a shop which are let together and have separate assessments. Where a dwelling consists of or forms part of more than one hereditament, the 1956 gross value of the dwelling is to be ascertained by determining that value in respect of each hereditament or part as if it were a separate dwelling and aggregating the gross values so determined. In determining the 1956 gross value of any hereditament—such as a shop—which is assessed at current value (i.e. under Section 68 of the Rating and Valuation Act, 1925) the gross value as shown in the valuation list is to be reduced by four-sevenths (para. 10 *ibid.*).

15. Reduction of 1956 gross value for tenant's improvements

In certain cases a tenant can obtain a reduction in the gross value of his dwelling-house for improvements not done by the landlord and so avoid the payment of rent for an improvement which has been carried out at a tenant's expense, e.g. the provision of a garage (Fifth Schedule *ibid.*).

Where the tenant, or any previous tenant, under a controlled tenancy which was current on the 6th July 1957 has made or contributed to the cost of an improvement on the premises he may claim a reduction in the 1956 gross value of the premises.

A reduction in the 1956 gross value on these grounds does not alter the actual gross value for rating purposes.

(1) *Improvements which qualify*

A claim can be made for any improvement made before the 7th November 1956 by the execution of works amounting to structural alteration, extension or addition (para. 11 *ibid.*).

(2) *Time for making the claim*

The claim must be made within six weeks from the 6th July 1957, by serving on the landlord a notice in the prescribed form requiring him to agree to a reduction.

(3) *Appeal to county court on validity of claim*

The tenant can appeal to the county court on any of the following matters which have not been agreed in writing between the parties:

(a) whether the improvement specified in the notice qualifies for the reduction;

(b) what works were involved in the improvement;

(c) whether the tenant or a previous tenant had made the improvement or contributed towards its cost;

(d) what proportion his contribution, if any, bears to the whole cost.

The determination of the court is final and conclusive (para. 12 *ibid.*).

(4) *Time for lodging appeal*

The appeal must be made to the court within three weeks after the expiration of six weeks from service of the notice of claim on the landlord; the court has power to extend the period for making the appeal.

(5) *Amount of reduction*

(a) *By agreement between the parties:* The amount of the reduction may at any time be agreed in writing between the landlord and the tenant.

(b) *By the valuation officer in default of agreement:* Where it is agreed between the parties or determined by the county court that there is a valid claim and the landlord and tenant cannot agree as to the reduction in the gross value the tenant may apply to the valuation officer for a determination (para. 13 *ibid.*).

The tenant must wait two weeks from the time of the agreement or determination of the court that he has a valid claim before making the application; but it must be made within the next two weeks.

The application must be in the prescribed form and must state the name and address of the landlord.

The certificate of the valuation officer must state—

(*a*) whether or not the improvement has affected the 1956 gross value of the premises, and

(*b*) if it has, the amount by which that gross value would have been less if the improvement had not been made.

The valuation officer must send a copy of the certificate to the landlord. Except where the landlord and tenant otherwise agree in writing, the amount of the reduction in the 1956 gross value,

(*a*) if the tenant or a previous tenant met the whole cost of the improvement, is the amount shown in the certificate, or

(*b*) that amount proportionately reduced where part only of the cost was contributed by the tenant or a previous tenant.

(*c*) *Deferment of certificate where rating proposal pending:* If a proposal to amend the valuation list relating to the hereditament is pending at the time of the tenant's application and the alteration would have effect from a date earlier than the 8th November 1956, the valuation officer must not issue the certificate until the proposal is settled (para. 13 (5) *ibid.*).

16. Conclusion of rating proposals

A rating proposal is regarded as settled when an alteration is made in the valuation list to give effect to it, or to an agreement made in consequence of it, or when final proceedings on appeal or arbitration relating to an objection to the proposal are determined, or when the proposal is withdrawn, whichever first occurs (para. 17 *ibid.*).

17. Effect of variation or reduction in gross value on previous increases of rent

Any notice of increase served before the variation or reduction of the 1956 gross value is settled will remain valid but take effect so

far as it can without causing the rent to exceed the rent limit
(para. 16 *ibid.*).

18. Concurrence of superior landlords to agreements

If the landlord is himself a tenant, then unless he is holding under
a tenancy for a term with more than seven years to run, any agreement
with his tenant as to the amount or reduction of the 1956 gross value
will not have effect except with the concurrence in writing of his
immediate landlord (s. 23 *ibid.*).

CHAPTER IV

Repairs and Rent Reductions for Disrepair in England and Wales

ALTHOUGH the Act of 1957 follows the principle of previous Rent Acts and does not impose a duty upon a landlord to do repairs to controlled property in England and Wales he may forfeit the right to claim the increases in rent allowed by the new rent structure if his property is not in a reasonable state of repair. Furthermore, a landlord who allows his property to fall into disrepair after he has claimed the increases runs the risk of the increased rent being seriously diminished unless he takes steps to remedy the defects within a reasonable time.

1. Responsibility for repairs

For the purposes of the Rent Acts a landlord can assume to be responsible for any defects for which the tenant is not expressly responsible, provided that in the case of internal decorations the landlord must first elect to be responsible unless he is already liable to do the work under the terms of the tenancy. On the other hand, the fact that a landlord has assumed the responsibility for repairs does not appear to impose a liability as between himself and the tenant to do the repairs. If the landlord does the work the tenant cannot challenge his right to claim the full rent limit on the ground that he was not obliged to do the repairs; if the landlord fails to repair that rent limit may be reduced so long as the dilapidations remain unremedied. The extent of implied liability is governed by Section 2 of the Housing Act, 1936 (see below), and it has been said that the standard of repair required by that provision is "a humble standard. It is only required that the place must be decently fit for human beings to live in" (*Jones* v. *Geen* [1925] 1 K.B. 659).

(1) *Landlord's liability at common law*

At common law as a general rule a landlord is under no implied obligation to repair a dwelling which is let unfurnished (*Gott* v. *Gandy* (1853) 2 E. & B. 845). In the case of a furnished letting for immediate occupation there is an implied condition that the premises are at the commencement of the tenancy in a fit state for human habitation (*Smith* v. *Marrable* (1843) 11 M. & W. 5).

45

In the case of an unfurnished letting the extent of the landlord's liability to repair must be gathered from the express terms of the tenancy; if the tenancy is silent as to repairs the tenant must take the premises as he finds them.

(2) *Landlord's liability under statute*

(a) *Tenancies entered into before 6th July 1957:* In considering the extent to which a landlord is liable for repairs regard should be had to the provisions of Section 2 of the Housing Act, 1936. That section provides that in respect of the tenancy of a house let for human habitation, which in the county of London is let at a rent not exceeding £40 or £26 elsewhere in England and Wales, there is implied a condition that the house is at the commencement of the tenancy—and an undertaking that it will throughout the tenancy be kept by the landlord—fit for human habitation. Contracting out of the provision is illegal. The implied condition applies to cottages let to agricultural workers under a contract of employment (s. 3 *ibid.*); but not to leases granted for a fixed term of three years or more where the tenant undertakes to put the property in a condition reasonably fit for human habitation; nor to houses let under contracts made before the 31st July 1923 at a rent of more than £16, and situate outside the county of London or a borough or urban district with a population of 50,000 or more.

For the purpose of the above provisions "rent" means the actual contractual rent irrespective of any liability of the landlord or tenant to pay rates (*Rousou* v. *Photi* [1940] 2 K.B. 379).

The implied condition referred to above does not apply in the case of a house situated in a clearance area and purchased or retained by a local authority, or purchased by them in lieu of making a demolition order, or when the demolition of a house under a clearance order has been postponed on its being let to the authority for temporary use for housing purposes (s. 20 (2) / 1954 Act).

(b) *Tenancies entered into on or after 6th July 1957:* In the case of a contract of tenancy entered into on or after the 6th July 1957 the rental limits in Section 2 of the Act of 1936 have been doubled, so that in respect of such contracts the implied condition applies to any house let for human habitation in the county of London at a rent not exceeding £80 and £52 elsewhere in England and Wales (para. 22, Sixth Schedule / 1957 Act).

(c) *Parts of premises used in common:* In the case of a controlled tenancy of a dwelling which forms part of other premises owned by or under the control of the landlord or a superior landlord—

(a) any disrepair of the roof or of any other part of those premises which results, or may result, in disrepair of the dwelling, and

(b) any disrepair of any staircase or other approach to the dwelling contained in those premises

is treated for purposes of disrepair under the Act of 1957 as if it were disrepair to the dwelling (para. 13, First Schedule, *ibid.*).

(3) *Tenant's liability*

If the contract of tenancy is silent as to repairs the common law implies that the tenant will use the premises in a tenantlike manner and not commit waste, doing such repairs as will enable him to deliver up the premises in substantially the same condition as when he entered them (*Marsden* v. *Edward Heyes, Ltd.* [1927] 2 K.B. 1).

For the purpose of the Act of 1957 a tenant is assumed to be responsible for:

(a) defects for the remedying of which, as between the landlord and the tenant, the tenant is responsible, or

(b) defects which are due to any act, neglect or default of the tenant or any person claiming under him or any breach by the tenant or such a person of any express agreement (paras. 15 and 21, First Schedule / 1957 Act).

2. Meaning of repair

The Act of 1957 not only abandons any attempt to define what is meant by "repair" it seems to enable a tenant to specify defects which may not come within the ordinary definition of "repairs". If the dwelling or any part thereof is in disrepair the tenant may specify in his notice to the landlord "defects" which ought reasonably to be remedied having due regard to the age, character and locality of the dwelling. The practical effect of this provision appears to be

(a) that, in so far as the defects are repairs, there will be cases where the tenant is not entitled to a very high standard of repair, e.g. where the useful life of the dwelling is nearly exhausted, and

(b) that the tenant can require the landlord to do work which, as an inherent defect, may rank as an improvement rather than a repair, e.g. in order to cure dampness in walls it may be necessary to insert a damp-proof course.

In so far as the provision is applied to repairs it seems that the obligation of the landlord will be fulfilled by the replacement of the worn-out part by another (new or second-hand) part; but this does not necessarily mean that the requirement of a particular tenant—which may be very low—will be sufficient for the purpose.

The case of *Anstruther-Gough-Calthorpe* v. *McOscar and Another* [1924] 1 K.B. 716, is a useful guide as to the extent to which a covenantor is obliged to repair. The property in question was situated at Calthorpe Street, Gray's Inn Road, and was held for a term of ninety-five years from the 24th June 1824. The tenant covenanted that "the lessee, his executors, administrators, and assigns, should well and sufficiently repair, support, uphold, maintain, paint, pave ... and keep the said houses", and yield up the same so repaired and kept at the end of the term. Gray's Inn Road was semi-rural and a fashionable residential district in 1824 but at the termination of the lease in 1919 the character of the neighbourhood had changed, the houses would then let either singly or in tenements to short-term tenants. The landlord contended that the tenant was responsible to repair the premises without limitation to such repairs as would satisfy the requirements of reasonably minded persons of the class who would be likely to become occupiers of the premises. The tenant contended that the effect of the covenant was limited to the extent of imposing an obligation to carry out such repairs as, having regard to the age, character, and locality of the premises, would make them reasonably fit to satisfy the requirements of reasonably minded tenants of the class who would be likely to occupy them. The Queen's Bench Division decided in favour of the tenant but the Court of Appeal reversed that decision and followed that of *Morgan* v. *Hardy* (1887) 35 W.R. 588, where it was decided, in the case of a fifty years' lease, that it was a wholly untenable proposition that the depreciation of the neighbourhood ought to lower the amount of damages for breach of covenant to repair. In the view of the Court of Appeal (Scrutton, L.J.) that could only mean that the fact that the class of persons who would use the house at the end of the term had deteriorated, so that their requirements in the way of repairs were less, was immaterial in ascertaining the repairs that the tenant was bound to execute. *Proudfoot* v. *Hart* (1890) L. R. 25 Q.B.D. 42, was distinguished as it was concerned with a lease for three years only and there was no suggestion of any change in the character of the house or of its probable tenants between the beginning and the end of the term. In the *Calthorpe* case the tenants were held liable for the cost of putting the premises into the state of repair in which they would be found if they had been managed by a reasonably minded owner, having regard to their age, to their character and ordinary uses, or to the requirements of tenants of the class likely to take them at the commencement of the term.

The Act does not go so far as the decision in the *Calthorpe* case but imposes on the landlord an obligation to do repairs which "ought reasonably to be remedied". On the other hand, where the remedying of defects necessitates making an improvement the obligation to do the work seems to be governed by the same principle. If the defect specified by the tenant in his notice of disrepair amounts to an improvement it will enable the landlord to claim an increase in rent for doing the work (p. 33).

3. Local authority or tenant's action restricting landlord's claims for rent

The scheme of the Act of 1957 for restricting the right of a landlord to recover an increase in rent of a controlled dwelling-house, on the ground that it is unfit, operates in two ways: (i) where action has been taken by the local authority; (ii) where notice of disrepair has been served by the tenant.

4. Rent restrictions on property declared unfit by local authority

Where action has been taken by a local authority on the ground that the dwelling falls short of the standard of fitness for human occupation laid down by a particular statute the right of the landlord to claim a full rent is restricted (s. 2 (2) (c), *ibid.*).

(1) *Cases to which the restriction applies*

The classes of houses to which the restrictions apply are:

    (i) *Slum property* where the dwelling

        (*a*) is within a clearance area under the Housing Act, 1936; or

        (*b*) is or forms part of premises with respect to which a demolition order or closing order under the Act, or a closing order under Sections 10 or 11 of the Local Government (Miscellaneous Provisions) Act, 1953, has been made and has not ceased to be in force.

Under Section 25 of the Housing Act, 1936, a local authority must declare as a clearance area any area in their district on which they are satisfied

E

(*a*) that the houses in the area are unfit for human habitation, or are by reason of their bad arrangement, or the narrowness or bad arrangement of the streets, dangerous or injurious to the health of the inhabitants of the area, and that the other buildings, if any, in the area are for a like reason dangerous or injurious to the health of the said inhabitants; and

(*b*) that the most satisfactory method of dealing with the conditions in the area is the demolition of all the buildings.

Thus, it is possible for a local authority to include in a clearance area houses which are not unfit for human habitation but are "obstructive buildings" because their bad arrangement, or the narrowness or bad arrangement of the streets, make them dangerous or injurious to the health of the inhabitants of the area.

The Housing Act, 1936, moreover, makes an important distinction as to the compensation payable to the owner of an unfit house and one which is an obstructive building. The owner of an unfit house is required to demolish the property at his own expense or if the local authority buy the property they merely pay site value, i.e. the value of the land as a site cleared of buildings and available for development in accordance with the building byelaws (s. 40 *ibid.*). The exception to this rule is the owner-occupier who bought his house between the 1st September 1939 and the 12th September 1955, and who, under the Slum Clearance (Compensation) Act, 1956, is entitled to payment which ensures that any such owner-occupier of a condemned house which is pulled down or which is bought by the local authority receives compensation at the same rate as would be payable if the house had not been declared unfit.

On the other hand, the owner of an obstructive building is entitled to full market value if the local authority acquires his property; or if he demolishes the property in accordance with the requirements of a demolition order he may claim compensation from the local authority for the loss sustained (s. 55 *ibid.*). The effect of the Act of 1957 in this type of case is that, as the compensation is related to the letting value of the house, the owner who has served a notice of increase of rent which has not become effective before the declaration of the clearance area may get compensation at a lower rate although his property is not in need of repair.

(ii) *Property with outstanding repairs notices*, i.e. where works of repair remain unexecuted as respects the dwelling in regard to which

(a) a notice has been given under Section 9 of the Housing Act, 1936; or

(b) an order has been made under

    (i) Section 94 of the Public Health Act, 1936; or

    (ii) paragraph 7 of the Fifth Schedule to the Public Health (London) Act, 1936.

The provisions in the statutes referred to above are of wider application than works of repair.

Section 9 of the Act of 1936 provides that where a local authority are satisfied that a house is unfit for human habitation, but is capable of being made fit at reasonable expense, they must call upon the person having control of the house to execute within a reasonable time the necessary works to make it fit. In considering whether a house is so unfit Section 9 of the Housing Repairs and Rents Act, 1954, provides that regard shall be had to its condition in respect of the following matters—repair; stability; freedom from damp; natural lighting; ventilation; water supply; drainage and sanitary conveniences; and facilities for storage, preparation and cooking of food and for the disposal of waste water. It frequently happens that a notice under the Act of 1936 requires the carrying out of works which are improvements and not repairs. Some local authorities prefer the Public Health Act, 1936, to the Housing Act for the purpose of getting repairs done but it has been held in *Salisbury* v. *Roles* [1948] W.N. 412, that it is improper to use the Public Health Act for this purpose if the repairs cannot be dealt with under the Housing Act on the grounds of cost.

The provisions in the Public Health Acts (referred to in (b) above) refer to "nuisances which may be dealt with summarily". They refer not only to premises which are in such a state as to be prejudicial to health or a nuisance but also to such matters as nuisances arising from the keeping of animals or from any accumulation or deposit. The abatement proceedings operate in two stages. In the first place a local authority must serve what is termed an "abatement notice" or, in the London Act, a "nuisance notice". If the notice is disregarded, or the nuisance is likely to recur, the sanitary authority are required to apply to a court of summary jurisdiction (in London, a petty sessional court) for a "nuisance order" for the abatement or prohibition of the nuisance. It is only at this second stage after a nuisance order has been made that there is a restriction on the operation of rent increases.

In either event, whether the notice has been served under the

Housing Act or a nuisance order has been made under one of the Public Health Acts, a landlord is only deprived of the right to an increase in rent where repairs—and not other works—have not been executed.

(iii) *Unfit property in redevelopment areas*, i.e. where an order has been made under paragraph 9 of the Fifth Schedule to the Town and Country Planning Act, 1944, declaring a dwelling or a house of which it forms part unfit for human habitation and not capable at reasonable expense of being rendered so fit, and either

(a) the Minister of Housing and Local Government has not yet decided whether to confirm the order, or

(b) he has confirmed it and less than two years have elapsed since its confirmation.

The said paragraph 9 deals with unfit houses in areas being acquired for planning purposes. Under the provision an order can be made in respect of an unfit house so that it can be acquired as if it were condemned property under the Housing Act, 1936, and purchased at site value (p. 50). The provision has been extended to apply to unfit houses in areas designated as new towns (s. 23, New Towns Act, 1946), to land designated by a development plan as subject to compulsory acquisition for planning purposes (s. 44 (4), Town and Country Planning Act, 1947), and to land required for purposes in connection with town development (s. 6 (6), Town Development Act, 1952).

5. Effect of local authority notices and orders on rent increases

In any of the cases referred to in the previous paragraph

(i) a notice of increase served whilst the dwelling is so unfit is void;

(ii) if a notice of increase has been served before and becomes effective during the time when the dwelling has become so unfit any increase specified in the notice remains in abeyance so long as the dwelling remains unfit.

These restrictions do not affect notices of increase given for the purposes of adjustments for rates (p. 29) or for increases for improvements (p. 33).

The immediate effect of these provisions is that a landlord is not able to claim an increase under the Act of 1957 in respect of slum property which had been condemned before the 6th July, 1957, and in the case of other property which was within the classes named on that date the landlord must carry out the repairs before he can serve a notice of increase of rent.

(iii) if a notice has been given and has become effective before the property becomes so unfit it continues to operate but the tenant may be able to claim an abatement of rent for disrepair (see below).

6. Rent restrictions on tenant's notice of disrepair

The procedure to be followed by a tenant in order to secure a reduction in rent on grounds of disrepair is more complicated than the system hitherto operated under the Rent Acts. In the first place the tenant under a controlled tenancy must serve on the landlord a notice in the prescribed form stating:

(i) that the dwelling or any part thereof is in disrepair by reason of defects specified in the notice, and

(ii) that those defects ought reasonably to be remedied, having due regard to the age, character and locality of the dwelling

and requesting the landlord to remedy them (para. 3, First Schedule / 1957 Act). Until this notice has been served the landlord is not under any obligation under the Act to do the repairs and then only to the extent of the works specified in the notice.

The notice can be served even if there has been no increase in rent under the Act.

The tenant should keep very carefully a copy of his notice of disrepair in case he is called upon to prove it in the court.

Certificates of disrepair issued by local authorities before the 6th July 1957 remain effective unless in proceedings pending the county court orders any such certificate to be revoked (para. 3, Seventh Schedule *ibid.*).

7. Certificates of disrepair

(1) *Tenant's application for certificate on landlord's default to repair*

If any of the defects specified in the notice of disrepair remain unremedied after six weeks from service of the notice the tenant may apply on the prescribed form to the local authority for a certificate of disrepair. The tenant must forword with his application a copy of the notice of disrepair (para. 4 (1) First Schedule *ibid.*).

The local authorities for this purpose are:

   (i) if the premises are situated in the City of London, the Common Council of the City;

  (ii) elsewhere in the county of London, the metropolitan borough councils;

 (iii) elsewhere in England and Wales, the county borough councils, non-county borough councils, urban and rural district councils.

(2) *Landlord's undertaking to remedy defects*

A tenant cannot apply to the local authority for a certificate of disrepair if the landlord has given an undertaking in the prescribed form to remedy the defects specified in the tenant's notice which remain unremedied or such of them as the tenant may agree in writing to accept as sufficient.

(3) *Issue of certificate of disrepair*

Where the local authority are satisfied

(*a*) that the dwelling or any part thereof is in disrepair by reason of defects specified in the notice of disrepair, and

(*b*) that all or any of those defects ought reasonably to be remedied, having due regard to the age, character and locality of the dwelling,

they must issue to the tenant a certificate of disrepair accordingly (para. 4 (2) *ibid.*). The certificate must be in the prescribed form and must specify the defects as to which the local authority are satisfied under (*a*) and (*b*) above.

In considering the issue of a certificate the local authority do not seem to be in a position to take into account a condition of disrepair due to a defect not specified in the tenant's notice without running the risk of acting outside their powers under the Act. In order to get such repairs done the tenant must serve another notice on the landlord or it may be a defect in respect of which the local authority can use their statutory powers (e.g. under Section 9 of the Housing Act, 1936). No time limit is imposed within which a local authority must issue a certificate of disrepair.

A local authority cannot include in a certificate any defect in the state of internal decorative repair unless the landlord is responsible for internal decorations under the tenancy or he has elected to be responsible for the work (p. 22). The local authority is to treat the landlord as being responsible for internal decorations if the application for the certificate alleges that he is or has elected to be respon-

sible. In any other case the landlord is not regarded as being responsible for such work (para. 11 *ibid.*).

The local authority must serve on the landlord a copy of every
certificate of disrepair (para. 14 *ibid.*).

(4) *Assumptions as to responsibility for defects*

A local authority is not required to inquire into any obligation as
between a landlord and tenant or into the origin of any defect (para.
4 (4) *ibid.*).

The position seems to be that notwithstanding provisions as to
repairs in the tenancy agreement the certificate of disrepair can include any repair work listed in the notice of disrepair, including
internal decorations for which the tenant alleges the landlord is or
has elected to be responsible. If he is responsible for some but not all
repairs, the work needed to put right a defect originating from a
source outside the scope of that liability (other than internal
decorations for which the landlord is not or has not elected to be
responsible) can be included in the certificate, e.g. dilapidations
arising from "fair wear and tear", which are frequently excluded
from repairing covenants.

(5) *Rights of appeal against a certificate of disrepair*

(*a*) *By the tenant:* A tenant may challenge a local authority who
have failed to issue a certificate of disrepair, or have left out of a
certificate an item of disrepair which the tenant included in his
notice, by appeal to the county court (para. 4 (3) *ibid.*). If the court
is satisfied that the local authority ought to have issued a certificate
as respects any defects it must direct the local authority to proceed
on the footing that, in relation to those defects, the dwelling is in
disrepair and that the defects ought reasonably to be remedied.
This direction has the effect of requiring a local authority to issue a
certificate of disrepair. If the authority have not included in their
certificate all the items listed in the tenant's notice, the court, on the
application of the tenant, can order that any item so omitted shall be
deemed to have been specified in the certificate.

These rights of appeal to the court are not short-cuts for getting
repairs done. They merely provide machinery of appeal where the
local authority

> (i) are not satisfied that the items of disrepair in the tenant's
> notice are of the kind which ought reasonably to form the
> subject matter of a certificate, or

(ii) have not proceeded with reasonable speed in the issue of the certificate, or

(iii) have left out of a certificate an item included in the tenant's notice of disrepair.

(*b*) *By the landlord:* A landlord can appeal to the county court on the ground that any defect specified in a certificate of disrepair—

(i) is the responsibility of the tenant, or

(ii) if it is an internal decorative repair, is not a defect for which the landlord is responsible under the tenancy or that he has not elected to be responsible for the work, or

(iii) ought not to have been specified.

If the court upholds the contention of the landlord it must cancel the certificate in respect of the defect in dispute (paras. 4 (3) (4), 11 (3) *ibid.*). The landlord may be able to prevent the rent being reduced while the court proceedings are pending (p. 59). Where a certificate is cancelled, either wholly or in part, it is deemed never to have had effect to the extent of the cancellation (para. 4 (5) (6) *ibid.*).

(6) *Suspension of issue of certificate of disrepair*

Before issuing a certificate of disrepair the local authority must give three weeks' notice in the prescribed form to the landlord stating that they propose to issue the certificate and specifying the defects to which it is to relate. If within the period of three weeks the landlord gives an undertaking in the prescribed form to remedy the defects and serves a copy thereof on the local authority, the authority cannot issue the certificate (para. 5 *ibid.*).

(7) *Local authority's refusal to accept landlord's undertaking*

A local authority may refuse to accept the undertaking of a landlord and may issue a certificate of disrepair in any of the following cases:

(*a*) where a previous certificate has been issued against the landlord in respect of the dwelling or any part thereof;

(*b*) where the landlord has previously become liable under Section 10 (3) of the Housing Act, 1936, as the person having control of the dwelling or of any premises comprising the dwelling, to repay to the local authority any expenses incurred by them for doing work in default to make a house fit for human habitation;

(c) where the landlord has previously given an undertaking to remedy defects in respect of the dwelling, or any other dwelling in the area of the local authority, and any of the defects to which that undertaking related remained unremedied for six months;

(d) where the landlord has previously been convicted of—

    (i) an offence under Section 95 of the Public Health Act, 1936, of failing to comply with, or contravening, a nuisance order; or

    (ii) an offence under paragraph 12 of the Fifth Schedule to the Public Health (London) Act, 1936, of failing to comply with an abatement order or contravening a prohibition order or a closing order.

If the local authority refuse to accept an undertaking and issue a certificate of disrepair the undertaking is deemed never to have been given (para. 5 *ibid.*).

(8) *Cancellation of certificate of disrepair*

A landlord can apply to the local authority for the cancellation of the certificate of disrepair on the ground that the defects specified in the certificate have been remedied. This is an important provision for so long as a certificate remains in force—even if the repairs have been done—the tenant is entitled to claim an abatement of rent.

Upon receipt of any such application the local authority must serve on the tenant a notice to the effect that unless an objection from him is received by them within three weeks from the service of the notice on the ground that the defects or any of them have not been remedied, the local authority propose to cancel the certificate. If the tenant does not object, or if in the opinion of the local authority the objection is not justified, they must cancel the certificate as from the date of the landlord's application or such later date as appears to them to be the date on which the defects were remedied (para. 6 *ibid.*).

(9) *Appeal to county court in regard to cancellation of a certificate of disrepair*

(a) *By the landlord:* A landlord may appeal to the county court where a local authority have not cancelled a certificate of disrepair after an application has been made to them in that behalf. The Act does not fix any time within which a local authority must deal with an application for cancellation of a certificate. If the court is satisfied that the certificate ought to have been cancelled it may order that the certificate shall cease to have effect as from the date of the order or such earlier date as may be specified in the order (para. 6 (3) *ibid.*).

(*b*) *By the tenant:* A tenant can appeal to the county court where a local authority have cancelled a certificate of disrepair. If the court is satisfied that the certificate ought not to have been cancelled it may order that the certificate shall be deemed always to have remained effective (para. 6 (4) *ibid.*).

8. Abatement of rent on grounds of disrepair

The Act deals separately with the case where notice of increase of rent is served during a period when a certificate of disrepair is operative and where the notice is operative when the certificate is issued (para. 7 *ibid.*); and applies the same rules where a landlord fails to fulfil an undertaking given by him (para. 8 *ibid.*).

(1) *Suspension of new notices of increase*

Any notice of increase served during the period beginning six months before the date of application by the tenant for a certificate of disrepair and ending when the certificate ceases to be in force has no effect as respects any rental period beginning while the certificate is in force. This suspension does not apply to any increase in respect of rates (p. 29) or of improvements (p. 33). Thus, the notice will remain effective if the certificate relates solely to defects which amount to improvements.

(2) *Reduction in rent on account of certificate of disrepair*

For any rental period beginning while a certificate of disrepair is in force the appropriate factor (p. 21) is four-thirds (para. 7 (2) *ibid.*).

This rule applies also where the rent recoverable is higher than the rent limit because:

(*a*) a higher rent was payable on the 6th July 1957 (p. 23), or

(*b*) it is a subsidised private house (p. 37), or

(*c*) it is a statutory tenancy under the Landlord and Tenant Act, 1954, following a long tenancy (p. 188).

(3) *Where notice of increase void*

A notice of increase served while a certificate of disrepair is in force is void unless it contains a statement that it will not take effect while the certificate remains in force (para. 7 (3) *ibid.*). But a notice so served is not void in so far as the increase specified in it is in respect of rates (p. 29) or of improvements (p. 33).

(4) *Additional right to back-date abatement of rent*

In addition to the right to claim an abatement of rent whilst a certificate of disrepair is in force (under the preceding sub-paras.), a tenant is entitled to a reduction of rent during the period between the date of his application and the date of granting the certificate. This further reduction cannot be claimed until the certificate has been issued. Then the tenant is entitled to assume that the certificate has been back-dated to the first rental period beginning on or after the date of his application for the certificate and that the appropriate factor has been four-thirds for the retrospective period (para. 7 (4) *ibid.*).

The effect of this provision is that for a time the tenant will be entitled to double the amount of the reduction. For example, the application of the factor of four-thirds may have the effect of reducing rent by five shillings a week. This reduction operates from the issue of the certificate of disrepair. Then assume that a period of six weeks had elapsed between the time of the application for the certificate and the time of its issue. The provision for back-dating the decrease entitles the tenant in that case to claim a further reduction of five shillings a week for six weeks—making a total reduction of ten shillings a week for six weeks. After that period, if the repairs have not been done, the decrease will be five shillings a week. On the other hand, there is no guarantee that the tenant will recover all back-payments. He is entitled to deduct such payments only so long as the certificate remains in force.

(5) *Limitation on rent reduction while proceedings pending*

A landlord can prevent the rent being reduced whilst his appeal is before the county court for the cancellation of a certificate of disrepair on the ground that the defects specified

   (i) are the responsibility of the tenant, or

   (ii) if, in the case of internal decorative repairs, the landlord is not responsible under the terms of the tenancy, or he has not elected to be responsible for the work, or

   (iii) ought not to have been specified.

If he makes his application to the county court within three weeks after the issue of the certificate the rent is not to be reduced on account of the certificate while proceedings on the appeal are pending and until they are concluded (para. 7 (5) *ibid.*). This provision applies only in the case where the appeal is made to cancel the certificate in respect of all the defects specified therein.

(6) *Rent reduction where landlord's undertaking not fulfilled*

The fact that a landlord has given an undertaking to remedy defects does not enable him to escape the provisions of the Act for reducing rent on grounds of disrepair if he does not fulfil his undertaking. A landlord is allowed six months to do the work from the time he gives an undertaking after the tenant has served a notice of disrepair (p. 54) or after the local authority have stated that they propose to issue a certificate of disrepair (p. 56).

Where an undertaking has been given the landlord or the tenant can apply to the local authority for a certificate as to whether any, and if so which, of the defects to which the undertaking related remain unremedied. That certificate is evidence in any proceedings until the contrary is proved of the matters certified.

If any defects to which an undertaking relates remain unremedied at the end of the period of six months the same consequences will follow as if a certificate of disrepair had then been issued and had continued in force until the defects had been remedied (para. 8 *ibid.*). For this purpose it is to be assumed that if the undertaking was given after the tenant had given notice of disrepair and before he had applied for a certificate of disrepair (p. 53) an application for a certificate had been made when the undertaking was given.

The effect of the provision is to apply the rules relating to abatement of rent (sub-paras. (1) to (4) above) to the case where a landlord does not carry out his undertaking to do repairs, thus:

(a) *Suspension of new notices of increase:* Any notice of increase served during the period beginning six months before—

- (i) the landlord gave the undertaking after the tenant had given notice of disrepair without any application being made for a certificate of disrepair, or

- (ii) if the landlord did not give an undertaking until after the tenant had applied for a certificate of disrepair, the date of that application, and

- (iii) ending when the certificate deemed to have been given ceases to be in force;

has no effect as respects any rental period beginning while the certificate is deemed to be in force. This suspension does not apply to any increase in respect of rates (p. 29) or of improvements (p. 33).

(b) *Reduction in rent on account of deemed certificate of disrepair:* For any rental period beginning while a certificate of disrepair is deemed to be in force the appropriate factor is four-thirds (p. 58). This rule applies also where the recoverable rent is higher than the rent limit because:

(i) a higher rent was payable on the 6th July 1957 (p. 23), or

(ii) it is a subsidised private house (p. 37), or

(iii) it is a statutory tenancy under the Landlord and Tenant Act, 1954, following a long tenancy (p. 188).

(c) *Where notice of increase void:* A notice of increase served while a certificate of disrepair is deemed to be in force is void unless it contains a statement that it will not take effect while the certificate is so deemed to be in force. But a notice so served is not void in so far as the increase specified in it is in respect of rates (p. 29) or of improvements (p. 33).

(d) *Additional right to back-date abatement of rent:* In addition to the right to claim an abatement of rent whilst a certificate of disrepair is deemed to be in force (sub-paras. (a), (b) and (c) above) a tenant is entitled to a reduction of rent in respect of the period between—

(i) the date when the landlord gave an undertaking after the tenant had given notice of disrepair without any application being made for a certificate of disrepair, or

(ii) if the landlord did not give an undertaking until after the tenant had applied for a certificate of disrepair, the date of that application,

and the date when the certificate of disrepair is deemed to have been granted.

The tenant can claim that the certificate of disrepair deemed to have been granted be made retrospective to the first rental period beginning on or after the date of the landlord's undertaking or, as the case may be, the date of the tenant's application for a certificate of disrepair; then the appropriate factor is four-thirds in settling the rent limit for the back-dated period.

This provision will enable a tenant to double the amount of the reduction until he has recovered the over-payment for the back-dated period, provided the repairs are not done in the meantime (see the example on p. 59). There is no guarantee that the tenant will recover the whole of the over-payment.

(7) Reduction of a sub-tenant's rent

Where a certificate of disrepair is issued to a tenant and he has
sub-let the whole or part of the dwelling to which it relates it is
assumed that a certificate to the like effect has been issued to the
sub-tenant at the same time, unless he has obtained one for the same
defects in his own right. The effect of this provision is that the sub-
tenant can claim an abatement of rent on the certificate against the
tenant and he can appeal to the court against the cancellation of the
certificate. At the same time, the sub-tenant has power to obtain a
certificate of disrepair against the tenant and to claim a reduction in
rent on the failure of the tenant to carry out an undertaking to do
repairs (para. 9 *ibid.*).

9. Payment of fees for certificates

On any application for—

(i) a certificate of disrepair, or

(ii) a certificate as to whether any defects to which a landlord's
undertaking relates remain unremedied (p. 60)

a fee of two shillings and six pence is payable to the local authority.

The tenant is entitled to deduct the fee payable for a certificate of
disrepair from any subsequent payment of rent and also for a
certificate relating to a landlord's undertaking if the local authority
reveal that any of the defects remain unremedied (para. 12 *ibid.*).

If the county court cancel a certificate of disrepair on the grounds
that the repairs are the responsibility of the tenant, or being internal
decorative repairs are not the responsibility of the landlord, or ought
not to have been specified (p. 56) the landlord can recover any fee
deducted from rent by the tenant.

A fee of two shillings and six pence is payable on application to a
local authority for the cancellation of a certificate of disrepair.

10. Repair provisions run with the property

The above-mentioned provisions relating to abatement of rent
for disrepair continue to apply, so long as the premises are controlled,
notwithstanding any change in the person of the landlord or the
tenant (para. 10 *ibid.*). A new landlord, therefore, is bound by any
undertaking given by his predecessor in title; a widow or other
relative claiming the tenancy on the death of the tenant is entitled
to the rights which flow from a notice to remedy defects given by the
deceased tenant.

11. Property belonging to overseas companies

Special provision is made for the protection of a tenant whose landlord is a body corporate incorporated outside the United Kingdom (s. 2 (3), paras. 17 to 21, First Schedule, *ibid.*).

(1) *Certificates of repair*

In any such case a notice of increase of rent will not have effect unless either—

(*a*) a certificate of repair has been issued to the landlord with respect to the dwelling not earlier than twelve months before the service of notice of increase, or

(*b*) a previous notice of increase served by that landlord in respect of the dwelling has had effect.

This restriction does not apply where the tenant is responsible for all repairs.

(2) *Application for certificate of repair*

An overseas company can obtain a certificate of repair from the local authority for the district in which the dwelling is situated by application made in the prescribed form. The name of the tenant must be stated. The application must be accompanied by a fee of two shillings and six pence.

If the local authority are satisfied that the state of repair of the dwelling is such that no certificate of disrepair could be issued they must issue a certificate of repair. In so far as the dwelling may be in need of internal decorative repair the local authority are not required to have regard to the fact that the landlord may not be responsible for such repairs. The local authority must serve a copy of the certificate of repair on the tenant.

If the local authority are not satisfied that the state of repair of the dwelling is such that no certificate of disrepair could be issued they must send to the landlord a statement of the defects in consequence of which they are unable to issue a certificate of repair.

(3) *Appeal to county court for certificate of repair*

The landlord can appeal to the county court against a refusal of the local authority to issue a certificate of repair on the grounds that all the defects specified in the statement are either—

(*a*) defects for which the tenant is responsible, or

(*b*) defects amounting only to internal decorative disrepair and for which the landlord is not responsible.

If the court is satisfied that the landlord's case has been proved on either of those grounds it must order the local authority to issue a certificate of repair.

(4) *Effect of the subsequent issue of a certificate of disrepair*

If after the issue of a certificate of repair a certificate of disrepair is issued in respect of the same dwelling, the certificate of repair is deemed never to have been issued. The effect of this provision is that upon the issue of the certificate of disrepair the tenant can recover from the landlord the amount of increased rent paid in consequent of any notice of increase, subject to the limitation for the recovery of excess rent (p. 178).

CHAPTER V

Restrictions on Premiums, Loans and Advance Payments of Rent

In an endeavour to enforce rent limits the Rent Acts make it illegal to charge a premium in addition to rent as a condition of the grant, renewal, continuance or assignment of a controlled tenancy. The Act of 1957 extends this principle to loans made in regard to a controlled house. Furthermore, for a period of three years after a dwelling-house has become decontrolled, the Act makes it an offence to charge a premium, or to require a loan to be made or rent to be demanded in advance, except for a strictly limited period, on a new letting.

1. Meaning of "premium"

Some difficulty may be experienced in determining what is meant by a premium. It is defined by Section 18 (2) of the Act of 1949 as including any fine or other like sum and any other pecuniary consideration in addition to rent.

In the case of a dwelling which is not controlled there is no limit as to the amount of rent which may be charged other than the maximum sum which a tenant is willing to pay; and a payment which looks like a premium is not necessarily required by a landlord as a condition of the grant or assignment of a tenancy (*Woods* v. *Wise* [1955] 2 Q.B. 29).

2. General prohibition in respect of controlled dwellings

The payment of any premium in addition to rent—

(a) as a condition of the grant, renewal or continuance of a tenancy, or

(b) as a condition of the assignment of a tenancy,

of a controlled dwelling is prohibited by Section 2 of the Landlord and Tenant (Rent Control) Act, 1949.

The prohibition does not affect the taking of a premium by the Crown (s. 1 (3), Crown Lessees (Protection of Sub-Tenants) Act, 1952); nor does it apply to any interest held under the Crown if the premium was required by an agreement made before the 8th February 1952.

3. Exemption for long leases

The general prohibition on the taking of a premium as a condition of the assignment of a tenancy does not apply to a lease granted for a fixed term of more than twenty-one years where the assignment was made on or after the 30th August 1954 (s. 38 (now repealed) / 1954 English Act); nor to the grant, renewal, continuance or assignment of such a lease made on or after the 6th July 1957 (s. 21 / 1957 Act).

4. Premiums payable before the 2nd June 1949

If before the 2nd June 1949 a premium had been paid in respect of the grant, continuance or renewal of a controlled tenancy, and since the creation of that tenancy no superior tenancy has been granted (or, in Scotland, a premium was paid on assignment before that date), a premium may be charged on the assignment of the tenancy. Section 8 (3) of the Act of 1920—which was repealed by the Act of 1949—allowed premiums to be charged on the grant of tenancies for fixed terms of fourteen years and upwards.

The amount of the premium which may be taken in any such case is a proportion of the original premium and must be in ratio with the term of the tenancy and the unexpired balance of the term at the date of assignment (s. 2 (2) / 1949 Act: s. 29 / 1954 Scottish Act).

In regard to any such premiums a payment is not to be treated as a premium if it consisted only of such outgoings, sum or amount as mentioned in the next paragraph. If the premium included any such payments they are to be disregarded in calculating the amount of the premium (s. 39 (1) / 1954 English Act: s. 30 (1) / 1954 Scottish Act).

5. Payments between assignor and assignee

An assignor may, if apart from the prohibition he would be entitled to do so, require the payment by the assignee—

(a) of so much of any outgoings discharged by the assignor as is referable to any period after the assignment takes effect;

(b) of any sum not exceeding the amount of any expenditure reasonably incurred by the assignor in carrying out any structural alteration of the dwelling-house or in providing or improving fixtures which are not tenant's fixtures;

(c) where the assignor was himself an assignee, of a sum not exceeding any reasonable amount paid by him to his assignor for expenditure incurred by that assignor, or by any previous assignor, in carrying out any structural alterations or in providing or improving fixtures which are not tenant's fixtures; or

(d) where part of the dwelling-house is used as a shop or office, or for business, trade or professional purposes, of a reasonable amount in respect of any goodwill of the business, trade or profession, being goodwill transferred to the assignee in connection with the assignment or accruing to him in consequence thereof (s. 2 (4) / 1949 Act).

6. Recovery of premiums paid

Any premium paid under an agreement made after the 25th March 1949 is recoverable by the person by whom it was paid. An agreement made between that date and the 2nd June 1949 for the payment of a premium which was lawful under previous law was made voidable at the option of either party (s. 2 (5) *ibid.*).

7. Adjustments in rent where premiums paid

In placing a prohibition on premiums the Act of 1949 made provision for adjustments in rent in cases where the premium had been paid before the commencement of the Act. Where an application was made to the rent tribunal before the 2nd June 1950 for the determination of a reasonable rent of a dwelling-house in respect of which a premium had been paid before the 2nd June 1949 and had not been fully repaid or recovered, the tenant could apply for the tribunal's certificate under the Act. If a certificate was issued certain limitations were made on the rent payable and, in some cases, the tenant was entitled to recover at least part of the premium. For a limited period after the issue of the certificate the reasonable rent was reducible by the rental equivalent of the premium. Where the tribunal were satisfied and certified accordingly that between the date of payment of the premium and the 25th March 1949 the reversion had been sold for valuable consideration, the tenant was entitled to recover from the person to whom the premium had been paid an amount equal to the rental equivalent of the premium (First Schedule *ibid.*).

8. Penalty for demanding a premium

Any person demanding a premium is liable to a fine not exceeding £100. The court may also order the premium to be refunded (s. 2 (6) *ibid.*).

A person is not guilty of an offence by reason only of the payments for outgoings, improvements or goodwill as between assignor and assignee as referred to in paragraph 5 above; nor by reason only that—

(a) any payment of outgoings required by him on an assignment was a payment of outgoings referable to a period before the assignment took effect; or

(b) any expenditure incurred by him in carrying out structural alterations of a dwelling-house, or in providing or improving fixtures therein, being expenditure in respect of which he required the payment of any sum on the assignment of a tenancy of the dwelling-house, was not reasonably incurred; or

(c) any amount paid by him to his assignor for expenditure incurred by that assignor, or by any previous assignor, in carrying out any structural alterations or in providing or improving fixtures which are not tenant's fixtures, was not a reasonable amount; or

(d) any amount required by him to be paid on an assignment in respect of goodwill was not a reasonable amount (s. 39 (2) / 1954 English Act: s. 30 (2) / 1954 Scottish Act).

9. Excessive prices for furniture, etc., to be treated as premiums

Where the purchase of any furniture, fittings or other articles has been required as a condition of the grant, renewal, continuance or assignment of a tenancy of controlled premises and the price exceeds the reasonable price of the articles, the excess may be treated as if it were a premium. Any person who is required to purchase any such articles can request the seller to state in writing the price he is demanding for the articles. If, without reasonable excuse, the seller fails within fourteen days to produce the written statement, or knowingly makes a false statement, he is liable to a fine not exceeding £10 (s. 3 / 1949 Act).

10. Illegal demands of tenant for "key money"

It is an offence for a statutory tenant, as a condition of giving up possession of controlled premises, to ask or receive the payment of any sum, or the giving of any other consideration, by any person other than the landlord. A tenant who requires furniture or other articles to be bought at an excessive price is regarded as demanding an illegal payment under this provision (s. 9 (2) / 1923 Act). The penalty on conviction for such an offence is a fine not exceeding

£100 and the court may order the refund of the payment (s. 15 (2) / 1920 Act).

11. Prohibition of premiums in respect of exchange agreements for controlled dwellings

The prohibition on premiums in respect of agreements for the exchange of statutory tenancies is dealt with in Chapter II (p. 10).

12. Prohibition of premiums in respect of furnished lettings

The prohibition on premiums in respect of furnished lettings is dealt with in Chapter XV (p. 166).

13. Premiums not to be charged for decontrolled premises

It is illegal at any time during the period of three years beginning with the 6th July 1957 to charge a premium in addition to rent as a condition of the grant, renewal, continuance or assignment of a tenancy of a dwelling-house which was decontrolled on that date (p. 90), or which became decontrolled on possession being obtained by the landlord (p. 91) (s. 13 (1) / 1957 Act). This restriction will apply to the assignment of a new tenancy entered into by a sitting tenant of decontrolled premises (p. 102).

If a premium is demanded in any such case the same consequences follow as in the case of a controlled dwelling (paras. 2 to 9 above). The prohibition does not affect leases granted for more than twenty-one years. Payments on assignment of portions of premiums taken before the 2nd June 1949 are permissible and also payments between an assignor and assignee for outgoings, cost of improvements or goodwill. Any person demanding within the period of three years a premium in respect of a decontrolled house is liable to a fine not exceeding £100 and he may be ordered to refund the premium.

(1) *Application to tenancies at low rents*

This prohibition applies also to a dwelling-house which is within the above categories of decontrol but outside the operation of the Rent Acts by reason of the fact that it was let at a rent of less than two-thirds of the rateable value of the premises, unless it was let for more than twenty-one years. On the other hand, this prohibition does not affect the assignment of a tenancy at a low rent granted before the 6th July 1957 and not renewed or continued thereafter.

(2) *Application to orders for future decontrol*

A Ministerial order which decontrols further categories of houses in the future (p. 90) may provide for the application of the above prohibition to houses within the scope of the order and may substitute a period shorter than three years during which the taking of a premium will be illegal (s. 13 (2) *ibid.*).

14. Loans treated as premiums

The provisions in the Act of 1949 relating to the prohibition on premiums apply to the making of a loan (whether secured or not) as a condition of the grant, renewal, continuance or assignment of a tenancy of a controlled dwelling and, for three years from the 6th July 1957, of dwellings decontrolled on that date or which become decontrolled on the landlord obtaining possession.

An agreement for a loan or any security issued in pursuance of such an agreement is not invalid but the loan is repayable to the lender on demand notwithstanding any term in the agreement (s. 14 *ibid.*).

15. Restrictions on advance payments of rent of decontrolled tenancies

A requirement in a tenancy granted, continued or renewed during the period of three years from the 6th July 1957 in respect of a dwelling-house which became decontrolled on that date, or subsequently on the landlord obtaining possession, is void if it requires rent to be paid—

    (*a*) before the rental period to which it relates begins to run (e.g. in the case of a weekly tenancy before the beginning of the week in respect of which it is due), or

    (*b*) if the rental period is longer than six months, earlier than six months before the end of the period in respect of which it is due (e.g. where rent is payable annually in arrear it cannot be claimed until six months of the period have elapsed) (s. 15 *ibid.*).

(1) *Extent of restriction*

The restriction applies whether the requirement is imposed as a condition of the grant, renewal or continuance of the tenancy or under the terms thereof.

Any rent which is void under the restriction is irrecoverable from the tenant.

(2) *Penalty for wrongful demand of rent in advance*

A person who purports to impose any requirement in order to avoid the restriction is liable on summary conviction to a fine not exceeding £100. The court may also order that the rent which was wrongfully paid be refunded to the person by whom it was paid.

CHAPTER VI

Sub-letting

IF the contractual tenancy allows the tenant to sub-let he may continue to do so during the period of his statutory tenancy, subject to the terms and conditions of the original contract of tenancy being observed, e.g. to the granting of the landlord's consent to sub-let. If the tenant sub-lets the whole of the dwelling-house he loses the protection of the Rent Acts. In any such case a sub-tenant to whom the whole or any part of the premises had been lawfully sub-let becomes the tenant of the landlord upon the same terms as he held from the tenant (s. 15 (3) / 1920 Act). In *Esdaile and Others* v. *Lewis* [1956] 2 All E.R. 357, a condition that "no sub-letting allowed without the consent of the landlord" was not broken because the tenant sub-let part of the premises. The decision was based on the principle that a covenant not to sub-let did not forbid the sub-letting of part of the dwelling-house and the landlords were not entitled to possession against the sub-tenant.

Any order or judgment against the tenant for recovery of possession of the dwelling-house does not affect the right of any sub-tenant to whom the premises or any part thereof had been lawfully sub-let before the proceedings against the tenant had been commenced (s. 5 (5) / 1920 Act). If the sub-letting was in breach of covenant of the head lease the sub-tenant is not protected (*Dick* v. *Jacques* (1920) 36 T.L.R. 773); but the sub-tenant will not lose possession unless he was aware of the unlawful sub-letting (*Ward* v. *Larkins* (1923) 130 L.T. 184). On the other hand, the sub-tenant must be holding under a controlled or statutory tenancy (*Solomon* v. *Orwell* [1954] 1 W.L.R. 629).

It is the duty of a tenant to supply his landlord with particulars of any sub-letting; and a landlord may obtain possession against a tenant in order to prevent overcharging for sub-letting (p. 84).

1. Decontrol of sub-tenancies

The provisions of the Act of 1957 with regard to decontrol (Chapter VIII) apply to sub-tenancies in the same way as they apply to tenancies. A sub-tenancy of a dwelling-house which on the 7th November 1956 had a rateable value exceeding—

(i) £40 in the Metropolitan Police District or the City of
    London;
(ii) £30 elsewhere in England and Wales;
(iii) £40 in Scotland

became decontrolled on the 6th July 1957. Statutory sub-tenants
and short-term contractual sub-tenants in occupation on that date
have the same protection for fifteen months as tenants (p. 93); but
sub-tenancies created by contract on or after that date will not be
controlled, and further categories of sub-tenancies may be decontrolled in the future by Ministerial order (p. 90).

One important effect of these provisions is that a controlled tenant
who, either expressly or impliedly, is allowed to sub-let will after the
time of decontrol be free to charge any rent which is not excessive
in respect of any new sub-tenancy of an unfurnished letting. If the
tenant charges an excessive rent he will be liable to lose possession
(p. 84).

2. Decisions restricting a sub-tenant's rights of protection

In three classes of case the courts have given decisions on the
limitations of a sub-tenant's rights of protection. In *Rudler* v. *Franks*
[1947] K.B. 530, it was held that a sub-tenant of the Crown had no
protection against his immediate landlord; in *Knightsbridge Estates
Trust Ltd.* v. *Deeley* [1950] 2 K.B. 228, it was held that the sub-tenant
of a leaseholder at a low rent had no protection when the head lease
came to an end; and in *Cow* v. *Casey* [1949] 1 K.B. 474, it was
decided that where a house outside the limits of the Rent Acts was
sub-let in parts the sub-tenants were not entitled to protection when
the head lease came to an end.

The Leasehold Property (Temporary Provisions) Act, 1951, provided interim protection for some sub-tenants of the *"Knightsbridge"*
and *"Cow* v. *Casey"* classes and subsequent legislation has provided
further protection for sub-tenants in all three classes.

3. Crown sub-tenants

In *Rudler* v. *Franks*, *supra*, following *Clarke* v. *Downes* (1931)
145 L.T. 20, it was decided that a sub-tenant of the Crown had no
protection under the Rent Acts against his immediate landlord. This
exemption, which denied to the sub-tenant any security of tenure
or rights as to limitation of rent, was abolished by the Crown
Lessees (Protection of Sub-Tenants) Act, 1952, without in any way

affecting rights of the Crown as landlord, lessor or mortgagee. The effect of the Act is that, from the 1st September 1952, mesne tenants and assignees from the Crown are bound by the Rent Acts so far as their own tenants and sub-tenants are concerned. But a tenant or sub-tenant is not protected as against the Crown, e.g. if a tenant's lease is terminated a sub-tenant cannot claim to become the direct tenant of the Crown. The right of the Crown to take a premium is not affected.

The effect of making such sub-lettings subject to the provisions of the Rent Acts is to give protection also to mortgagors of such interests.

Where any order or judgment had been made or given by a court before the 1st September 1952 against a Crown sub-tenant, but had not been executed the court were empowered, on the application of the sub-tenant, to review the decision.

4. The decision in Knightsbridge Estates Trust Ltd. v. Deeley [1950] partly overruled

Until 1950 it was generally assumed that a sub-tenant with a rack rent tenancy who was holding under a lease at a rent which did not amount to two-thirds of the rateable value of the premises was protected against the superior landlord upon the expiration or determination of the head lease. In *Knightsbridge Estates Trust Ltd.* v. *Deeley, supra,* however, it was decided that when the head lease came to an end the sub-tenant was unprotected. In that case the landlord had let a house, which was within the limits of the Rent Acts, at a rent of less than two-thirds of the rateable value, i.e. a letting outside the scope of the Acts (s. 12 (7) / 1920 Act). The tenant sub-let the property at a rack rent. It was held that the sub-tenant was protected against the tenant but not against the landlord when the head lease came to an end.

With some limitations Section 15 of the Landlord and Tenant Act, 1954, reversed that decision. It provided that for the purposes of Section 15 (3) of the Act of 1920 (i.e. where the interest of a tenant comes to an end for any reason, a lawful sub-tenant of the whole or part of the premises is deemed to become the tenant of the superior landlord) the interest of a tenant under a long tenancy (p. 188) is not to be disregarded by reason only that the rent payable in respect of that tenancy is one falling within Section 12 (7) of the Act of 1920 (i.e. a rent of less than two-thirds of the rateable value). The Act of 1954 applied, therefore, only in the case where the head lease was a long tenancy or a tenancy at a low rent granted in continuation of the long tenancy in respect of property within the limits of the Rent Acts. The Act of 1957 provides for the application of the Act of 1954 to long tenancies not at low rents as it applies to long tenancies at low rents and the curtailment of the limits of the Rent Acts does not affect the protection of long tenancies under the Act of 1954 (p. 188). The *"Knightsbridge"* decision still applies where the head lease was granted for a term of twenty-one years or less at a low rent (which is comparatively rare), and to property outside the limits of the Rent Acts on or before the 5th July 1957. But where a sub-tenant of property let on a long lease at a low rent and outside the limits of the Rent Acts was protected by Section 7 of the Leasehold Property (Temporary Provisions) Act, 1951, immediately before the Act of 1954 came into operation on the 1st October 1954, he continues to be protected by the Rent Acts (para. 3, Ninth Schedule / 1954 Act).

Section 15 of the Act of 1954 also excluded from protection any sub-tenancy created after the 30th September 1954 out of a long tenancy if at the time of the creation of the sub-tenancy—

(a) a notice had been given to terminate the long tenancy; or

(b) the long tenancy was being continued after the term date by virtue of the Act,

unless the sub-tenancy was created with the written consent of the person who at the time was the competent landlord. Any sub-tenancy for a period of twenty-one years or less created by contract on or after the 6th July 1957 is decontrolled.

The protection afforded to a sub-tenant by Section 15 is without prejudice to the right of a landlord to apply for an order for possession (under paragraph (d) of the First Schedule to the Act of 1933 (p. 82)) where the tenant has sub-let the whole of the premises (s. 15 (2) / 1954 Act).

5. Sub-tenancies of tenancies at low rents in Scotland

Section 32 of the Housing (Repairs and Rents) (Scotland) Act, 1954, applies the same principle as that contained in Section 15 of the Landlord and Tenant Act, 1954, and provides that a sub-tenant does not lose the protection of Section 15 (3) of the Act of 1920 because the tenant's rent is less than two-thirds of the rateable value of his dwelling-house. This protection, however, is without prejudice to the landlord's right to claim possession where the tenant has sub-let the whole of the premises (see previous paragraph).

6. The decision in Cow v. Casey [1949] overruled

In *Cow* v. *Casey, supra,* it was held that where a large house, which was outside the protection of the Rent Acts, was sub-let in parts, a sub-tenant, who was protected by the Acts against his own landlord, could not retain that protection when his landlord's tenancy came to an end if the interest of the next superior landlord was not one to which the Acts applied.

Section 41 of the Housing Repairs and Rents Act, 1954, overruled that decision and applies the protection of the Rent Acts to sub-tenants of parts of such premises as and when the superior tenancy (not itself protected by the Acts) comes to an end.

A sub-sub-tenant is protected if the property comprised in the sub-tenancy as well as the tenancy is outside the limits of the Rent Acts, provided he holds a tenancy controlled by the Acts (*Cadogan (Earl) and Another* v. *Hinthorne* [1956] 3 All E.R. 8 ı).

CHAPTER VII

Restrictions on the Right to Possession of Controlled Premises and Decontrolled Premises during the "Standstill" Period

A CONTROLLED tenancy may be terminated (i) by the tenant giving notice to quit (unless it is for a fixed term); (ii) by an order of the court for possession; (iii) to stop overcrowding; (iv) by the destruction of the house; (v) by the tenant ceasing to occupy the premises; (vi) by the tenant changing his status; or (vii) by the exercise of statutory powers.

The rules as to termination of a controlled tenancy apply also to the tenant of a dwelling decontrolled by the Act of 1957 who retains possession after the time of decontrol (p. 93).

1. Notice to quit by the tenant

The tenant of a controlled dwelling holding under the terms of the original contract of tenancy who wishes to terminate his tenancy must give proper notice under the contract; if the tenancy is for a fixed term then, in the absence of a special provision in the lease (such as a "break clause" to terminate at the end of seven or fourteen years in a twenty-one years lease), he is not entitled to terminate the contract until the expiration of the term.

A tenant who retains possession as a statutory tenant is entitled to give up possession only—

(a) by giving such notice as would be required under the original contract of tenancy, or

(b) if no notice would have been so required, on giving not less than three months' notice (s. 15 (1) / 1920 Act); unless the landlord agrees to accept a surrender (*Boyer* v. *Warbey* [1953] 1 Q.B. 234).

By Section 16 of the Act of 1957 not less than four weeks' notice to quit is required (p. 187).

It is an offence for a statutory tenant as a condition of giving up possession of controlled premises to ask or receive the payment of any sum, or the giving of any other consideration, by any person other than the landlord. If the tenant asks an excessive price for furniture or other articles as a condition of giving up possession the excess is treated as if it were an illegal payment under this provision (s. 9 (2) / 1923 Act). Any person convicted of such an offence is liable to a fine not exceeding £100 and the court may order the refund of the payment (s. 15 (2) / 1920 Act).

2. Restrictions on the right of the court to make an order for possession

No order or judgment for the recovery of possession of a controlled dwelling-house or for the ejectment of a tenant therefrom may be made unless the court considers it reasonable to make such an order or give such a judgment, and either—

   (i) the court is satisfied that suitable alternative accommodation is available for the tenant or will be available for him when the order or judgment takes effect; or

   (ii) the court has power to do so on any of the grounds set out in the First Schedule to the Act of 1933 without proof of alternative accommodation being available (s. 3 (1) / 1933 Act).

See paragraph 1 (3) of Chapter II (p. 11) as to the recovery of possession of shared accommodation.

There is no right of appeal from the county court if the court can grant possession only on being satisfied that it is reasonable to do so (s. 12 (4), County Courts Act, 1955).

(1) *Suitable alternative accommodation*

A certificate by the local authority for the area that they will provide suitable alternative accommodation for the tenant by a date specified in the certificate, is conclusive evidence that suitable alternative accommodation will be available for him by that date (s. 3 (2) / 1933 Act). But the production of such a certificate does not bind the court and before making an order for possession it must consider whether or not it is reasonable to do so.

A certificate by a local authority for a neighbouring area that they are willing to accept the tenant as their tenant does not satisfy the requirement as to suitable alternative accommodation (*Sills* v. *Watkins* [1956] 1 Q.B. 250).

Where no certificate is produced to the court, accommodation may be deemed to be suitable if it consists either—

   (*a*) of a controlled house; or

(*b*) of premises to be let as a separate dwelling on terms which will, in the opinion of the court, afford the tenant security of tenure reasonably equivalent to that obtained by the tenancy of a controlled house.

In view of the fact that contractual tenancies entered into on or after the 6th July 1957 will not be controlled, the landlord may have to offer a substantial tenancy to meet the requirements of this provision. In *Scrace* v. *Windust* [1955] 1 W.L.R. 475, the controlled house was to be converted into two flats and the statutory tenant was offered one on a weekly tenancy as alternative accommodation. As the proposed conversion would have taken place after the 29th August 1954 the flat would not be controlled (p. 107) and the court decided that it was not suitable alternative accommodation. The court did suggest, however, that if the landlord was prepared to offer the flat for a term of years he might be able to satisfy the requirement of the Act of 1933.

The Act of 1957, however, seems to suggest that as time goes on the whole position with regard to security of tenure will be due for review as, apart from a few cases which are negligible, all new tenancies created under contract will have no greater protection than the common law. In bargaining for premises the majority of tenants are not likely to seek security of tenure by taking a term of years and will accept as a maximum the four weeks' notice to quit laid down by the Act.

In settling suitable alternative accommodation the court must also be satisfied that it is reasonably suitable to the needs of the tenant and his family as regards proximity to place of work, and either—

(i) the rent and size of the house is similar to local council houses provided for persons whose needs are similar to those of the tenant and his family; or

(ii) is otherwise reasonably suitable to the means of the tenant and to the needs of himself and his family as regards extent and character (s. 3 (3) / 1933 Act).

A certificate given by a local housing authority stating—

(*a*) the extent of the accommodation afforded by houses provided by them to meet the needs of tenants with families of such number as may be specified in the certificate; and

(*b*) the rent charged for such houses,

is conclusive evidence of the facts so stated. Any such certificate

signed by the clerk to the authority will be received in evidence
without further proof unless the contrary is shown (s. 3 (4) (5) / 1933
Act).

Alternative accommodation will not be deemed to be suitable to
the needs of a tenant and his family if their occupation would make
it an overcrowded house for the purposes of the Housing Act, 1936,
or the Housing (Scotland) Acts, 1950 and 1952 (s. 7 (3) / 1938
Act).

If the controlled dwelling consists of mixed premises, e.g. a house
and shop, there appears to be no obligation to provide a shop with
the alternative accommodation; all that is required is to provide
suitable alternative living accommodation (*Middlesex County Council*
v. *Hall* [1929] 2 K.B. 110; *Miller* v. *Corrigall* [1950] S.L.T. (Sh. Ct.)
70).

(2) *Without proof of Alternative accommodation*

The court has power to make an order for possession of a controlled
dwelling-house without proof of alternative accommodation (where
the court considers it reasonable so to do) (First Schedule. 1933
Act) if—

(a) the tenant has not paid his rent or carried out his other
    obligations as tenant, whether under his tenancy or under
    the Rent Acts:

    Under this provision a tenant is liable to lose possession—

    (i) if he is in breach of covenant under the terms of his
        original tenancy agreement, e.g. taking in paying
        guests in breach of covenant not to use the premises
        for business (*Tendler* v. *Sproule* [1947] 1 All E.R. 193);

    (ii) if he does not comply with any condition deemed to
         have been included in his statutory tenancy, e.g.
         by not giving the landlord the necessary facilities to
         execute repairs (see s. 16 (2) / 1920 Act);

    (iii) if he objects to the landlord's election to do internal
          decorations and then fails himself to keep the
          dwelling in a reasonable state of internal decorative
          repair, having due regard to its age, character and
          locality (para. 2 (3), First Schedule / 1957 Act).

    A judgment or order for the recovery of possession of a
dwelling-house is subject to restriction on execution if the
judgment or order is made on the sole ground that the rent

had not been paid and the tenant is a service man who can claim protection under the Reserve and Auxiliary Forces (Protection of Civil Interests) Act, 1951 (s. 4 (2)). When a service man is prevented by service commitments from performing civil employment as an obligation of a tenancy the landlord is not entitled to treat such non-performance as a ground for claiming recovery of possession under this heading (s. 20 (1) *ibid.*).

A landlord is not entitled to obtain possession under this heading against a statutory tenant under the Landlord and Tenant Act, 1954, by reason only that the act or default occurred before the date of termination of the long tenancy (s. 10 (2) / 1954 Act). If a tenant, holding under a statutory tenancy granted under that Act, fails within a reasonable time to carry out initial repairs which he is under an obligation to do, or defaults in making payment for accrued tenant's repairs, or any part or instalment of such a payment, the failure or default may be treated as a breach of the obligation of the statutory tenancy and a ground for applying for an order for possession under this heading (para. 17, First Schedule; para. 4, Second Schedule / 1954 Act).

(*b*) the tenant or any person residing or lodging with him or a sub-tenant—

   (i) has been guilty of conduct which is a nuisance or annoyance to adjoining occupiers (a "nuisance" for this purpose is not necessarily a statutory nuisance under the Public Health Act, 1936 (*Timmis* v. *Pearson* [1934] 1 L.J.N.C.C.R. 115)); or

   (ii) has been convicted of using the premises or allowing them to be used for immoral or illegal purposes (e.g. a conviction for receiving stolen property on the premises—*S. Schneiders, Ltd.*, v. *Abrahams* [1925] 1 K.B. 301); or

   (iii) by neglect or default has allowed the condition of the dwelling-house to deteriorate,

and, where the person at fault is a lodger or sub-tenant, the court is satisfied that the tenant has not taken reasonable steps to remove him:

A landlord cannot obtain possession on the above grounds against a statutory tenant under the Landlord and Tenant

G

Act, 1954, by reason only that the act or default occurred before the date of termination of the long tenancy (s. 10 (2) / 1954 Act).

(c) the tenant has given notice to quit and in consequence of which the landlord has contracted to sell or let the house or has taken other steps and would be seriously prejudiced if he could not obtain possession:

A mere intention to sell is not enough; the landlord must have contracted to do so (*Barton* v. *Fincham* [1921] 2 K.B. 291).

(d) the tenant without the consent of the landlord has, after the 31st July 1923, in the case of "old control" property, or after the 1st September 1939, in the case of "new control" property, or after the termination of a long lease, assigned or sub-let the whole of the dwelling-house, or sub-let part the remainder being already sub-let:

This provision applies where there is no restriction as to assignment or sub-letting (*Regional Properties Ltd.* v. *Frankenschwirth* [1951] 1 K.B. 631). The wider issue of assigning or sub-letting in breach of covenant is covered by paragraph (a) above. As a statutory tenancy under the Rent Acts cannot be assigned (except with the consent of the landlord under Section 17 of the Act of 1957 (p. 17)) the reference to assignments seems to apply only to assignments of contractual tenancies, or to assignment of statutory tenancies created under the Landlord and Tenant Act, 1954.

(e) the dwelling-house is the subject of an off-licence and the tenant—

(i) has committed an offence as licensee; or

(ii) has not conducted the business to the satisfaction of the licensing justices or the police; or

(iii) has carried on the business in a manner detrimental to the public interest; or

(iv) the renewal of the licence has for any reason been refused:

(f) if the dwelling-house is badly overcrowded and it could have been abated by the removal of a lodger or sub-tenant:

This provision was repealed as to England and Wales by the Act of 1938.

Under the Housing Act, 1936, and the Housing (Scotland) Act, 1950, a landlord is entitled to obtain possession of a dwelling-house which is overcrowded (see para. 3, *post* p. 85).

(*g*) the house is reasonably required by the landlord for a full-time employee, or for a tenant's full-time employee, as a condition of employment and the tenant was formerly employed by the landlord or a previous landlord and was let to him in consequence of his employment: •

A farm employee of a hospital who went to work in their laundry when they gave up the farm but remained in the farm cottage did not cease to be in the employment of the former landlord to enable the present farmer to get possession (*Duncan* v. *Hay* [1956] 1 W.L.R. 1329).

The provision under this heading which enabled the court to give the landlord possession of a dwelling-house, on production of an agricultural certificate, when the landlord required the house for an agricultural worker, was repealed as to England and Wales by Section 43 of the Housing Repairs and Rents Act, 1954.

The grounds of this paragraph do not apply in the case of an application for possession during a reserve forces man's period of service (s. 20 (2), Reserve and Auxiliary Forces (Protection of Civil Interests) Act, 1951).

(*h*) the dwelling is reasonably required by the landlord for residential occupation for—

(i)   himself; or

(ii)   any son or daughter of his over eighteen years of age; or

(iii)   his father or mother.

A landlord is not entitled to possession under this heading if he became landlord by purchase after the 7th November 1956. This provision was revised by the Act of 1957 (paras. 21 and 33, Sixth Schedule) by the application of a single date for all classes of controlled houses. Hitherto there were various dates from the 6th December 1937 in the case of "old control" houses to dates in 1954 for sub-tenancies of properties belonging to local and public authorities.

In any case where an application for an order for possession is made on the grounds of this heading the court may not make an order if satisfied that having regard to all the

circumstances, including the question of alternative accommodation for the landlord or tenant, greater hardship
would be caused by granting the order than by refusing to
grant it. The onus of proving "greater hardship" is, therefore, on the tenant.

(3) *Possession through overcharging a sub-tenant*

An order for possession may be obtained against a tenant to
prevent excessive charges for sub-letting. The court may make an
order for possession or for the ejectment of a tenant of a controlled
house, if it is considered reasonable to do so, when the tenant is
charging an excessive rent for any sub-let part of the dwelling-house.
The rent is regarded as being excessive if it is greater than the
recoverable rent for the sub-let part. Whether or not an order for
possession is made in respect of a house in Scotland, the sheriff must
in any such proceedings apportion the standard rent as between the
dwelling-house and the sub-let part, or make a determination of the
recoverable rent of the sub-let part, unless any such apportionment
or determination has already been made. In England and Wales
the county court must make a determination of the recoverable rent
of the sub-let part if it has not already done so. If after the apportionment or determination the tenant overcharges he is liable to a
fine not exceeding £100, unless he can prove that he did not know
and could not ascertain that the rent was excessive or that the excess
was due to an accidental miscalculation (s. 4 / 1933 Act: para. 4,
Sixth Schedule / 1957 Act).

A tenant is under a general obligation to send particulars of any
new sub-letting to his landlord. Failure to supply the information
may make the tenant liable to a fine not exceeding £10 (s. 4 (4)
ibid.). A landlord of a house in Scotland may request a tenant to
supply to him in writing, within fourteen days, particulars of any
sub-letting and of the rent charged. If without reasonable excuse the
tenant fails to supply the information or makes a false statement in
any material particulars he is liable to a fine not exceeding £2
(s. 7 (2) / 1923 Act).

(4) *Suspension of orders for possession*

The court has power to suspend the operation of any order or
judgment for the recovery of possession of a controlled house (s. 5
(2) / 1920 Act). An order for possession on account of arrears of
rent is often suspended so long as the tenant fulfils an undertaking
to pay off the arrears by instalments specified by the court.

(5) *Possession on false evidence*

If the landlord obtains an order for possession on the ground that he requires the house for his own occupation or for a member of his family or for an employee and subsequently it transpires that the order was obtained by misrepresentation or the concealment of material facts, the court may order the landlord to compensate the former tenant for any loss or damage sustained (s. 5 (6) (7) / 1920 Act: s. 3 (1) / 1939 Act: s. 6 / Landlord and Tenant Act, 1954).

There is a similar provision in general terms in Section 55 of the Landlord and Tenant Act, 1954, where the landlord obtains possession on false evidence of a dwelling-house comprised in a long tenancy or of business premises.

(6) *No notice to quit required when order for possession obtained*

A landlord who obtains an order or judgment for the recovery of possession of a dwelling-house or for the ejectment of a tenant is not required to give any notice to quit to the tenant (s. 15 (1) / 1920 Act).

(7) *Acceptance of rent after notice to quit*

When a landlord has served notice to quit on a tenant the acceptance of rent by the landlord for a period not exceeding three months from the expiration of the notice does not prejudice any right to possession of the premises and, if an order for possession is made, any payment of rent so accepted is treated as mesne profits (s. 16 (3) / 1920 Act).

3. Possession on account of overcrowding

Sections 65 (1) of the Housing Act, 1936, and 55 (1) of the Housing (Scotland) Act, 1950, provide that when a dwelling-house is overcrowded in such circumstances as to render the occupier thereof guilty of an offence, nothing in the Rent Acts shall prevent the landlord from obtaining possession of the house. Where possession is obtained under these provisions the landlord cannot claim decontrol in respect of the first tenancy created thereafter (s. 11 (6) / 1957 Act).

4. Possession of houses sub-divided or let in lodgings and overcrowded

The Rent Acts do not prevent possession being obtained of any house or part of a house which is sub-divided or let in lodgings in order to limit the number of persons accommodated on the premises

(s. 11 (2) / 1954 English Act). Where possession is so obtained the landlord cannot claim decontrol in respect of the first tenancy created thereafter (s. 11 (6) / 1957 Act).

5. Destruction or damage of a dwelling-house

When a house is destroyed (e.g. by a bomb) a contractual tenant may claim the right to possession of any new house erected on the site (*Simper* v. *Coombs* [1948] 1 All E.R. 306); but the tenancy may be determined by notice—unless it is granted for a fixed term—before the new house is ready for occupation. In any such case the tenant cannot claim a statutory tenancy before the new house is habitable (*Ellis & Sons Amalgamated Properties, Ltd.* v. *Sisman* [1948] 1 K.B. 653).

If the house is only damaged and does not lose its original identity a statutory tenant is entitled to claim the right to occupy after repairs have been done to the house if he has shown an intention to do so (*Morleys (Birmingham) Ltd.* v. *Slater* [1950] 1 K.B. 506).

6. Loss of possession by tenant ceasing to occupy

A tenant may forfeit the status of statutory tenant by ceasing to occupy the premises. Absence may be sufficiently prolonged, e.g. by a period of imprisonment, to compel the inference of a cesser of possession. Each case is a question of degree and of fact (*Brown* v. *Brash and Ambrose* [1948] 2 K.B. 247).

7. Change of tenant's status

A tenant may lose the protection of the Rent Acts by a change in the status of his occupation. For example, if he has agreed to buy the freehold, and remains in occupation until completion, he ceases to be a statutory tenant (*Turner* v. *Watts* (1928) 44 T.L.R. 105).

On the other hand, a tenant is not treated as having abandoned his rights as a statutory tenant and become a mortgagee in possession where he becomes mortgagee of the landlord's mortgage on the premises (*Silsby* v. *Holliman and Another* [1955] 2 W.L.R. 1090).

8. Exercise of statutory powers

Possession of controlled property may be obtained by the exercise of statutory powers in the following cases:

(1) *The Housing Acts*

Nothing in the Rent Acts are deemed to affect the provisions of the Housing Acts in relation to the obtaining of possession (s. 156, Housing Act, 1936)—

(i) of a house in respect of which a demolition order has been made (i.e. demolition of an insanitary house or the demolition of an obstructive building); or

(ii) of a house in respect of which a clearance order has been made; or

(iii) of any house which a local authority require for the purpose of exercising their powers under any enactment relating to housing; or

(iv) of any house required for the purpose of enabling re-development in accordance with a re-development plan (prepared under the Housing Acts) to be proceeded with; or

(v) of any premises where an undertaking has been given by the owner that the premises will not be used for human habitation; or

(vi) of any part of a building or underground room in respect of which a closing order is in force; or

(vii) of a house in respect of which a closing order has been made where the local authority consider it inexpedient to make a demolition order (s. 10, Local Government (Miscellaneous Provisions) Act, 1953).

There are similar provisions in Section 158 of the Housing (Scotland) Act, 1950.

In many of the above cases the local authority must provide alternative accommodation, or be satisfied that such accommodation will be available, in advance of any displacement.

Under Section 50 (2) of the Housing Act, 1936, if a local authority are satisfied that, for the purpose of enabling re-development to be carried out in accordance with an owner's proposals which have been approved by the authority, it is necessary that any controlled dwelling should be vacated and that suitable alternative accommodation is or will be available for the tenant, the authority may issue a certificate to that effect for the purpose of enabling the landlord to obtain possession.

(2) *The Town and Country Planning Acts*

Section 30 of the Town and Country Planning Act, 1944, provides that if development or re-development involves the displacement of persons living in the area, the local planning authority or the highway authority, as the case may be, must make reasonable provision for alternative accommodation before the displacement is due to take place.

When an authority requires immediate possession of a house the Minister of Housing and Local Government may certify accordingly and the effect of his certificate is to place the property outside the protection of the Rent Acts. The operation of the Act of 1944 has been largely superseded by later Acts but Section 30 has been incorporated into—

(i) *The New Towns Act, 1946* (s. 6 (1) (*d*)), under which it is the duty of a development corporation, or the local highway authority, to provide reasonable alternative accommodation for residents who are displaced by re-development work in new towns. If either the development corporation or the highway authority require immediate possession of a house the Minister may issue his certificate;

(ii) *The Town and Country Planning Act, 1947* (s. 44 (1)), under which the duty of providing reasonable alternative accommodation is placed on a local authority acquiring houses for the purpose of carrying out development under the provisions of the Act; the Minister having power to issue a certificate if immediate possession of a house is required; and

(iii) *The Town Development Act, 1952* (s. 6 (2) (5)), under which the local authority must provide reasonable alternative accommodation for persons displaced from residential property in connection with the extension of existing towns; the Minister having the same power to issue a certificate if immediate possession of a house is required.

There is a similar provision in Section 29 of the Town and Country Planning (Scotland) Act, 1945, which has been incorporated into the New Towns Act, 1946, in its application to Scotland, and into the Town and Country Planning (Scotland) Act, 1947.

9. Premises used for immoral purposes

Section 35 of the Sexual Offences Act, 1956, provides that when the tenant of any premises has been convicted of knowingly permitting the premises to be used as a brothel the landlord can require him to assign his lease or other contract (e.g. in the case of a furnished letting) to some other person approved by the landlord, who must not unreasonably withhold his approval. If the tenant does not assign the lease or contract within three months the landlord is entitled to determine it and the court which convicted the tenant may make a summary order for possession. If the landlord, after having had notice of the conviction, fails to exercise his rights and the offence is repeated he is deemed to be a party to that offence, unless he can show that he has taken all reasonable steps to prevent the recurrence of the offence. If, after the first conviction, the land-lord determines the lease or contract and then grants a fresh tenancy either to or for the benefit of the convicted tenant, without inserting in the new tenancy all reasonable provision to prevent a recurrence of the offence, he is deemed to be a party to any subsequent offence unless he shows that he took all reasonable steps to prevent the recurrence of the offence.

CHAPTER VIII

Decontrol under the Rent Act, 1957

ONE of the main objects of the Rent Act, 1957, is to release certain classes of dwelling-houses from control under the Rent Acts. This is done—

(a) by providing for the immediate decontrol of certain categories of dwelling-houses;

(b) by enabling further categories of dwelling-houses to be decontrolled from time to time by order made by the Minister of Housing and Local Government or the Secretary of State for Scotland; and

(c) by exempting new tenancies from control.

1. Immediate decontrol

Section 11 (1) of the Act provides that the Rent Acts shall not apply to any dwelling-house the rateable value of which on the 7th November 1956 exceeded—

(i) £40 in the Metropolitan Police District or the City of London;

(ii) £30 elsewhere in England and Wales;

(iii) £40 in Scotland.

Subject to the scheme for the protection of short-term sitting tenants (para. 10 below), the effect of this provision is that dwelling-houses with rateable values in excess of the above figures are decontrolled as from the 6th July 1957, the date when the Act came into operation.

As to the meaning of "rateable value" for this purpose see page 97, and the area of the Metropolitan Police District is shown on page 85.

2. Future decontrol

Further categories of dwelling-houses may be released from control by order of the Minister or Secretary of State for Scotland, as the case may be, under Section 11 (3) of the Act. As from such date as may be specified in the order the Rent Acts will cease to apply to dwelling-houses the rateable value of which exceeds such amount as may be specified. The order will fix the date on which the rateable value is to be ascertained for this purpose. An order may be made so as to relate to—

(i) the whole of England and Wales;

(ii) the whole of Scotland; or

(iii) such area or areas in England and Wales or in Scotland as may be specified in the order,

and so as to apply generally or only to, or except to, such classes or descriptions of dwelling-houses as may be so specified.

An order must be made by statutory instrument and will not have effect until it has been approved by a resolution of each House of Parliament.

3. Decontrol of new tenancies

Section 11 (2) of the Act provides that the Rent Acts shall not apply to a tenancy created by a lease or agreement coming into operation at or after the 6th July 1957, and when the tenancy comes to an end the tenant will not be entitled to retain possession as a statutory tenant.

On the other hand, a tenant under a controlled tenancy on that date does not lose the protection of the Rent Acts by taking a new tenancy of premises which are the same, or consist of or include part of, the premises held by him under a controlled tenancy.

The general effect of this provision is that when a dwelling is given up by a tenant who was in possession up to the 6th July 1957, a new tenant who takes over on or after that date is not protected by the Rent Acts; furthermore, dwellings which are let for the first time on or after that date will not be controlled.

The rule that, in certain cases, a widow or other relative may claim the right to continue in occupation on the death of the tenant (p. 15) applies where the deceased tenant held a controlled tenancy immediately before the 6th July 1957, even if he entered into a new tenancy on or after that date. In other words, when the widow or other relative succeeds after the death of the tenant it does not count as a new tenancy. On the other hand, where a new tenant takes a tenancy on or after that date his widow or other relative will not be able to claim the tenancy on his death, except in so far as the ordinary law of succession applies.

4. Sub-tenancies

A sub-tenancy is subject to the provisions for decontrol in the same manner as a tenancy (see Chapter VI).

5. Tenant-landlords

Where a tenant holds a tenancy of a dwelling which is above the limits of rateable value and lives in part only of the dwelling, having sub-let a part or parts, the tenancy of the tenant becomes decontrolled and he has no greater protection under the Act than any other tenant. The tenancy of a sub-tenant of the dwelling, however, if it does not exceed the limits of control, will remain controlled and if the head tenant is given notice to quit the sub-tenant is entitled to remain in his part of the dwelling on the same terms either as the direct tenant of the landlord or as sub-tenant of a new tenant.

6. Protection of long tenancies not affected

The above-mentioned provisions relating to immediate or future release from control or to the decontrol of new tenancies do not apply to a lease granted for a term of more than twenty-one years in respect of residential premises which is protected by Part I of the Landlord and Tenant Act, 1954 (s. 11 (4) / 1957 Act) (p. 188).

7. Dwellings formerly requisitioned

Under the Requisitioned Houses and Housing (Amendment) Act, 1955, local authorities have power to invite owners of requisitioned houses to accept as statutory tenants the occupiers holding as licensees during the time of requisitioning (see Chapter XIV). Where a licensee has been accepted as statutory tenant—whether before, on or after the 6th July 1957—he or his statutory successor is not entitled to retain possession after the 31st March 1965 if the dwelling is within the range of decontrol (s. 11 (5) / 1957 Act).

8. Possession on account of overcrowding

A landlord cannot claim decontrol where a dwelling comes into his possession by virtue of action taken under Section 65 of the Housing Act, 1936, Section 55 of the Housing (Scotland) Act, 1950, or Section 11 of the Housing Repairs and Rents Act, 1954, for the abatement of overcrowding. In any such case the provisions relating to decontrol of new tenancies (para. 3 *ante*) do not apply to the first tenancy of the whole or any part of the dwelling which is created after possession is so obtained. It would seem that the new tenancy must be one which apart from decontrol would be subject to the Rent Acts and that the landlord cannot circumvent the provision by letting in a manner which is not within the scope of the Acts, e.g. by a tenancy at a nominal rent. The effect of such a letting would be merely to suspend the rule. If the landlord sells the property the purchaser will buy subject to the rule.

9. Special protection for Forces Reservists

The Act makes special provision for the protection of serving members of the Reserve and Auxiliary Forces—see Chapter XIII, page 153.

10. Protection for short-term and statutory tenants occupying decontrolled premises

Where a tenant is occupying a dwelling at the time of decontrol on the 6th July 1957, and he could under the terms of his tenancy or by reason of being a statutory tenant be dispossessed within fifteen months from that date, he is given security of tenure for at least that period and during that time the rent cannot be increased against his will, except to take account of changes in rates. In the case of future releases from control the period of security can be reduced to six months. If a tenant quits either before or at the end of the period of security of tenure he may be able to claim compensation for improvements which he has carried out on the premises.

The "time of decontrol" means, in the case of dwellings subject to immediate release from control, the 6th July 1957, and, in the case of future releases from control, the date specified in the order providing for decontrol (para. 1, Fourth Schedule / 1957 Act).

(1) *Tenancies which are protected*

Where immediately before the time of decontrol the dwelling-house is the subject—

(i) of a statutory tenancy, or
(ii) of a controlled tenancy which would or might come to an end during the period of security of tenure after decontrol either by effluxion of time or notice to quit,

the tenant is entitled to retain possession until given notice by the landlord (para. 2 (1) *ibid.*).

The effect of this provision is that a tenant holding under a tenancy which extends beyond the period of security of tenure after decontrol becomes subject to the terms of his tenancy from the time of decontrol, except in the cases referred to in paragraph 14 (p. 96).

A power in a lease to terminate at stated intervals is not regarded as a power to terminate by notice to quit for the purpose of ending a tenancy which otherwise would extend beyond the period of security or for claiming compensation for improvements (p. 103).

(a) *Rent Acts conditions continue to apply:* A tenant who is protected and retains possession after the time of decontrol does so in the like circumstances, to the like extent and subject to the like provisions (including in particular provisions as to recovery of possession by the landlord) as if the Rent Acts had not ceased to apply to the dwelling-house. Thus, if the tenant ceases to occupy any part of the dwelling and he was a statutory tenant or he does not pay his rent the landlord can apply to the court for an order for possession on the grounds set out in Chapter VII.

(b) *Period of security for immediate decontrol:* The landlord of a dwelling which became decontrolled on the 6th July 1957 cannot give notice to the tenant who is protected so as to require him to give up possession earlier than fifteen months after the time of decontrol; therefore the tenant is entitled to retain possession until, at the earliest, the 5th October 1958 (para. 2 (2) *ibid.*).

(c) *Not less than six months' security on future decontrols:* An order of the Minister or the Secretary of State providing for the release from control of further categories of dwelling-houses may provide that the period of security of tenure may be shorter than fifteen months but in no case can it be less than six months (para. 13 *ibid.*).

(d) *Six months' notice to quit:* As an additional measure of security, a tenant of decontrolled premises who is protected is always entitled to not less than six months' notice to quit. A landlord's notice is void if it requires the tenant to give up possession earlier than six months after service of the notice (para. 2 (2) *ibid.*). Where the tenancy is terminable by notice to quit but has not been terminated by the date specified in the notice, the notice operates to terminate the tenancy on that date (para. 2 (5) *ibid.*).

(e) *Protection for statutory successors:* The protection for occupying tenants after the time of decontrol extends to the widow or other relative who would have been entitled on the death of the tenant to retain possession if the Rent Acts had not ceased to apply to the dwelling (p. 15) (para. 14 *ibid.*). Thus, if the tenant of a dwelling which became decontrolled on the 6th July 1957 dies in March 1958, his widow, if she is living with him at the time, is entitled to retain possession of the dwelling until the 5th October 1958, and to six months' notice to quit.

(f) *Orders for possession before decontrol:* The above-mentioned provisions for the protection of occupying tenants of decontrolled premises do not prevent the execution of an order for possession obtained by the landlord before the time of decontrol (para. 2 (2) *ibid.*).

(g) *Possession of part of a dwelling:* In the case of a part of a dwelling which has no separate rateable value no notice can be served which requires the tenant to give up possession until the rateable value of the dwelling has been apportioned (para. 2 (3) *ibid.*). See page 98 as to the apportionment of rateable values.

(2) *Tenancies of business and professional premises*

Where as the result of decontrol a tenancy of business or professional premises qualifies for protection under Part II of the Landlord and Tenant Act, 1954, the above-mentioned provisions for the protection of occupying tenants to not apply (see Chapter XVII).

11. Rent payable by short-term and statutory tenants remaining in possession after decontrol

Where a tenant is entitled to retain possession (para. 10 (1) above) after the time of decontrol the rent payable by him is the same as was recoverable from him for the last rental period beginning before that time.

The dwellings which became decontrolled on the 6th July 1957 all fall within the former classification of "new control" houses and the rents payable during the period of security will be either—

(a) the rent at which the dwelling was let on the 1st September 1939, or

(b) if the dwelling was first let after that date, the rent of the first letting, subject to any subsequent adjustment made by a rent tribunal,

together with any "permitted increases" payable before the 6th July 1957 for improvements or rates and, in the case of the former group, any repairs increase and any increase on account of a rise in the cost of services (p. 25).

During the period of security after the time of decontrol the only alterations permitted in any such rent are adjustments for changes in rates (para. 3 *ibid.*).

Where at the time of decontrol any proceedings were pending for the variation of rent no further steps are to be taken in the proceedings except in relation to costs (para. 6 *ibid.*).

12. Rents of decontrolled subsidised private houses

The rents which may be charged in respect of decontrolled subsidised private houses are shown in Chapters III and X.

13. Tenant's notice to quit after decontrol

If a tenant who is entitled to retain possession after the time of decontrol wishes to give up possession and he is—

(a) a contractual tenant

    (i) under a periodic tenancy, he must give notice to quit as required under the terms of the tenancy which cannot in any case take effect less than four weeks after service of the notice (s. 16 *ibid.*); or

    (ii) under a fixed term, he is entitled under common law to leave at the end of the term and without notice unless the agreement requires notice to be given; or

(b) a statutory tenant claiming possession by virtue of

    (i) a periodic or other tenancy, he must give such notice as would have been required under the contract of tenancy which cannot in any case take effect less than four weeks after service of the notice (s. 16 *ibid.*); or

    (ii) a tenancy which required no notice to quit, e.g. a tenancy for a fixed term, he must give not less than three months' notice to quit (s. 15 (1) / 1920 Act.

See paragraph 10 (1) *ante* as to a landlord's right to obtain possession during the period of security.

14. Occupying tenants of decontrolled premises who are not protected

Where a decontrolled tenancy extends beyond the period of security after decontrol, e.g. a tenancy for a fixed term with three years to run, the provisions for security of tenure, notice to quit or as to rent payable after decontrol (paras. 10 and 11 *ante*) do not apply (para. 2 (1), Fourth Schedule, *ibid.*).

In any such case the tenancy continues under the terms of the agreement (subject to the modifications referred to in (1) and (2) below); the tenant is not entitled to six months' or any notice to quit unless it is provided for in the agreement and, if a notice is required, it must be for a period of not less than four weeks (s. 16 *ibid.*).

(1) *Rent payable on decontrol*

Where the rent payable under the tenancy has been added to by statute, e.g. to cover increased cost of services, the rent does not revert to the amount fixed by the tenancy agreement. The landlord is still entitled to claim the addition, notwithstanding that the statutory authority to do so has been repealed. Where the addition was agreed or determined under Section 40 of the Housing Repairs and Rents Act, 1954, or Section 31 of the Housing (Repairs and Rents) (Scotland) Act, 1954, in respect of services which under the terms of the tenancy the landlord is not liable to provide (see page 25) and those services are withheld in whole or in part after the time of decontrol the rent is to be decreased by an appropriate amount. The amount of the decrease must be settled in writing between the landlord and the tenant or by the county court (or, in Scotland, by the sheriff). The decrease may be back-dated and will continue to be effective until revoked or varied by agreement in writing between the parties or by the county court or sheriff (para. 7 *ibid.*).

(2) *Tenant's right to elect to terminate tenancy*

If the tenancy allows the landlord to increase the rent by an unspecified amount (otherwise than in respect of rates, the provision of services or the use of furniture), the rent cannot be increased for at least three months from the time of decontrol.

During that period the tenant can elect to surrender the tenancy and secure the protection of the Act during the period of security after decontrol as if it were a letting which would or might come to an end during that time.

The tenant may make the election by giving notice in writing to the landlord.

Where the tenant elects to surrender his tenancy any sub-tenancy is terminated on service of the notice; the sub-tenant then obtains the same protection as a tenant who is entitled to retain possession after the time of decontrol (p. 93).

A sub-tenant holding under the kind of tenancy referred to above may exercise the right of election notwithstanding that the tenant has not made an election (para. 9 *ibid.*).

15. Meaning of "rateable value"

The following rules apply as to the ascertainment of the rateable value of a dwelling-house on a particular date for the purposes of decontrol (para. 1, Fifth Schedule, *ibid.*).

(1) *England and Wales*

(a) *Separately rated dwellings:* If the dwelling-house is a hereditament which is separately rated the rateable value is that shown in the valuation list on the particular date; or if that rateable value

H

differs from the net annual value, it is the net annual value on that date. The "particular date"—which is called "the date of ascertainment"—is the 7th November 1956, in the case of dwellings which became decontrolled on the 6th July 1957, and the date in a Ministerial order on which rateable value is to be ascertained, in the case of future decontrols.

(*b*) *Apportionment of rateable value:* If the dwelling-house is not separately rated and is part only of a hereditament, the rateable value is such proportion of that value or net annual value as may be agreed in writing between the landlord and the tenant or determined by the county court.

In the case of an apportionment of a letting which includes accommodation shared with others but not the landlord the circumstances of the sharing must be taken into account in fixing the rateable value of the separate accommodation (s. 8 (2) / 1949 Act).

(*c*) *Aggregation of rateable values:* If the dwelling-house consists of or forms part of more than one separately rated hereditament, the rateable value is—

   (i) the aggregate of the rateable values or net annual values of the hereditaments as shown in the valuation list on the particular date; or

  (ii) where the hereditaments (or the whole of them) are not separately rated on that date such value as may be agreed in writing between the landlord and the tenant or determined by the county court.

An application may be made to the county court by either party without first attempting to reach agreement. The court can make such apportionment as seems just and its decision is final and conclusive (s. 12 (3) / 1920 Act: s. 19 (4) / 1957 Act).

(2) *Scotland*

In applying the above rules (and those in the next sub-paragraph) to premises in Scotland, references to the valuation list and to a hereditament mean the valuation roll and to lands and heritages. The reference to annual value does not apply (para. 5, Fifth Schedule, 1957 Act).

Any reference to rateable value on the date of ascertainment is construed as a reference to the rateable value of the premises as shown in the valuation roll on that date or, where the premises form part only of lands and heritages shown in the roll, to such proportion of that rateable value as may be agreed in writing between the landlord and the tenant or determined by the sheriff.

The provision for the aggregation of rateable values does not apply to Scotland.

(3) *Ascertainment where rating proposals pending*

The Act makes provision for the adjustment of rateable values in cases where rating proposals are pending at the date of ascertainment (e.g. on the 7th November 1956).

In England and Wales this provision applies only in cases where—

(*a*) a proposal was made before the 1st April 1957 in respect of a dwelling which became decontrolled on the 6th July 1957; or

(*b*) a proposal was made before such date as may be specified in a Ministerial order in regard to dwellings which become decontrolled in the future.

Where the valuation list is altered in such a case, so as to vary the rateable value of a hereditament shown in the list on the 7th November 1956, or on the date specified in a Ministerial order, and the alteration takes effect not later than such respective date (e.g. the 7th November 1956), the rateable value or net annual value for the purposes of decontrol is the amount of that value shown in the list as altered (para. 2 *ibid.*). This provision applies also for the purpose of making an apportionment or aggregation of rateable value.

In applying the above rule to Scotland the reference to a proposal means an appeal or complaint made in accordance with the provisions of the Lands Valuation (Scotland) Act, 1854, as amended, against an entry in the valuation roll. An appeal or complaint is regarded as being settled when an alteration is made in the roll to give effect to it, or when the appeal or complaint (including any further appeal to the Lands Valuation Appeal Court) is finally determined, or when the appeal or complaint is withdrawn, whichever first occurs.

(4) *Security of tenure while rating proposal pending*

In cases where the proposals mentioned above are pending at the time of decontrol the question whether the dwelling is to be decontrolled is postponed until the rating proposal has been settled. This provision applies only in the case of a dwelling-house which was due for release on the 6th July 1957 where the rating proposal was for the reduction of rateable value and that value on the 31st March 1956 (in Scotland, the 15th May 1956) was within the new limits of control (para. 3 *ibid.*).

(5) *Furnished lettings*

As to the ascertainment of rateable values for furnished lettings, see Chapter XV.

16. Reduction of rateable value in England and Wales for tenant's improvements

Special provision is made to prevent a dwelling-house in England and Wales being decontrolled on the 6th July 1957 where the rateable value is above the limits of control on account of improvements done at the expense of a tenant, such as adding a garage.

In the case of a controlled dwelling-house which became due for release from control on that date the tenant may claim a reduction in rateable value to save the dwelling from decontrol if he, or any previous tenant, has made or contributed to the cost of an improvement on the premises (Fifth Schedule *ibid.*).

Where a reduction in rateable value is secured it is only a notional value for the purpose of decontrol and does not affect the actual rateable value for rating purposes which remains unaltered.

(1) *Improvements which qualify*

A claim can be made for any improvement made before the 7th November 1956 by the execution of works amounting to structural alteration, extension or addition (para. 11 *ibid.*).

(2) *Time for making claim*

The claim must be made within six weeks from the 6th July 1957 by serving on the landlord a notice in the prescribed form requiring him to agree to a reduction in the rateable value.

(3) *Appeal to county court on validity of claim*

The tenant can appeal to the county court on any of the following matters which have not been agreed in writing between the parties:

- (*a*) whether the improvement specified in the notice qualifies for the reduction;
- (*b*) what works were involved in the improvement;
- (*c*) whether the tenant or a previous tenant had made the improvement or contributed towards its cost;

(*d*) what proportion his contribution, if any, bears to the whole cost.

The determination of the court is final and conclusive (para. 12 *ibid.*).

(4) *Time for lodging appeal*

The appeal must be made to the court within three weeks after the expiration of six weeks from service of the notice of claim on the landlord; the court has power to extend the period for making the appeal.

(5) *Amount of reduction*

(*a*) *Agreement between the parties:* The amount of the reduction may at any time be agreed in writing between the landlord and the tenant.

(*b*) *Determination in default of agreement:* Where it is agreed between the parties or determined by the court that there is a valid claim and the landlord and tenant cannot arrive at a written agreement as to the reduction in the rateable value the tenant may apply to the valuation officer for a determination (para. 13 *ibid.*).

The tenant must wait two weeks from the time of the agreement or determination of the court that he has a valid claim before making the application; but it must be made within the next two weeks.

The application must be in the prescribed form and must state the name and address of the landlord.

The certificate of the valuation officer must state:

(*a*) whether or not the improvement has affected the rateable value on the 7th November 1956, and

(*b*) if it has, the amount by which that rateable value would have been less if the improvement had not been made.

The valuation officer must sent a copy of the certificate to the landlord.

Except where the landlord and tenant otherwise agree in writing, the amount of the reduction in the rateable value—

(*a*) if the tenant or a previous tenant met the whole cost of the improvement, is to be the amount shown in the certificate, or

(*b*) that amount proportionately reduced where part only of the cost was contributed by the tenant or a previous tenant.

(*c*) *Deferment of certificate where rating proposal pending:* If a proposal

to amend the valuation list relating to the hereditament is pending
at the time of the tenant's application and the alteration would have
effect from a date earlier than the 8th November 1956, the valuation
officer must not issue the certificate until the proposal is settled
(para. 13 (5) *ibid.*). A proposal is regarded as settled when an
alteration is made in the valuation list to give effect to it, or to an
agreement made in consequence of it, or when final proceedings on
appeal or arbitration relating to an objection to the proposal are
determined, or when the proposal is withdrawn, whichever first
occurs (para. 17 *ibid.*).

(6) *Retention of control pending settlement of claim*

Where the rateable value is reduced and, in consequence, the
dwelling remains controlled it is to be assumed that the dwelling
remained controlled from the 6th July 1957 to the time when the
reduction was agreed or determined (para. 14 *ibid.*).

17. Reduction of rateable value for tenant's improvements on future decontrols

A Ministerial order providing for the decontrol of further
categories of dwelling-houses (para. 2 *ante*) may contain provisions
for the reduction of rateable values on account of improvements
done at the expense of a tenant (para. 15, Fifth Schedule, *ibid.*).

18. Further security of tenure by lease

The fact that a tenant is entitled to retain possession after the time
of decontrol does not prevent the landlord and tenant entering into
a new tenancy agreement to come into operation either before or
when the period of possession has expired. But a new tenancy
agreement cannot be arranged as a means of defeating the object
of the Act, which is to give the tenant the right to stay in possession
for a minimum period after the time of decontrol.

On the other hand, if the landlord is prepared to give the tenant
at least three years' security of tenure the period of possession after
decontrol (on the old terms) can be shortened. If, before the date
on which the right to retain possession ends, the landlord and tenant
enter into a new tenancy agreement which will not expire, or be
terminable by notice to quit given by the landlord, earlier than
three years from the commencement thereof, the before-mentioned
provisions for retaining possession after the time of decontrol will
cease to apply as from the commencement of the new tenancy
(para. 4, Fourth Schedule, *ibid.*). The use of this provision not only

enables the tenant to obtain a longer period of security of tenure, provided he observes the terms of the agreement; it also enables the landlord to negotiate a new rent earlier than he can otherwise do under the Act.

There is no right of appeal against a landlord's refusal to negotiate a new tenancy.

19. Compensation for improvements made by tenants

The Act of 1957 introduces a new principle in law by enabling certain tenants of decontrolled premises to claim compensation for improvements carried out at a tenant's expense (para. 5, Fourth Schedule, *ibid.*). The scheme is based on that in the Landlord and Tenant Act, 1927, which entitles a tenant of trade, business or professional premises to claim compensation for improvements.

(1) *Tenants entitled to claim*

A tenant is entitled to claim compensation if immediately before the time of decontrol he held the dwelling-house under—

(*a*) a statutory tenancy, or

(*b*) a controlled tenancy which would or might come to an end during the period of security of tenure after decontrol either by effluxion of time or notice to quit, and

he gives up possession at the end of the tenancy or at the end of the period of security of tenure after decontrol (para. 5 (1) *ibid.*). A tenant is not deprived of the right to claim compensation merely on the ground that he gives up possession before the expiration of the period of security of tenure. On the other hand, the rule is not of general application and does not apply to a tenancy for a fixed term which is of longer duration than the period of security of tenure; nor does it apply where a tenant takes a new tenancy for a period of not less than three years certain (para. 18 *ante*); in that case, a tenant who desires to be reimbursed for any improvements made during the period of the old tenancy must negotiate an adjustment in settling the terms of his new tenancy.

(2) *Time for making claim*

The claim may be made by the tenant at any time before he gives up possession (para. 5 (1) *ibid.*).

(3) *Improvements for which claim may be made*

A claim may be made in respect of any improvement on the

dwelling-house, not being a fixture which the tenant is by law entitled to remove, which on his giving up possession adds to the value of the dwelling-house.

The improvement must have been made—

(a) by the tenant, or

(b) by any other person who retained possession of the dwelling-house after the time of decontrol, or

(c) by any other person being a tenant under the statutory or controlled tenancy.

Cases which come within classes (b) and (c) include a relative who has retained possession after the death of the tenant, an assignee who paid for an improvement carried out by the assignor or a previous assignor (p. 66), and a sub-tenant.

Claims may be made only in respect of improvements completed after the 15th August 1945. There is no backward limit as to when the improvement was begun.

As to the meaning of improvement, see page 33.

(4) Assessment of compensation

The sum to be paid as compensation for any improvement must not exceed the net addition to the value of the dwelling-house as a whole which may be determined to be the direct result of the improvement.

In making the assessment an allowance must be made for any benefits which may have been received from the landlord or his predecessors in title in consideration expressly or impliedly of the improvement. A typical example of such a benefit is where the landlord had contributed towards the cost of the improvement.

In determining the amount of the net addition, regard must be had—

(a) to the intended use of the dwelling-house after the tenant has given up possession; and

(b) if it is shown that it is intended to demolish or to make structural alterations in the house or any part thereof or to use it for a different purpose the effect of such demolition, alteration or change of use on the additional value attributable to the improvement must be taken into account; and

(c) the length of time likely to elapse between the giving up of possession and the demolition, alteration or change of use (para. 5 (2) ibid.).

There must also be taken into account in determining the amount of compensation, any diminution in the value of any other property belonging to the landlord, or to any superior landlord from whom the immediate landlord directly or indirectly holds, which is the direct result of the improvement (para. 5 (3) *ibid.*).

(5) *Improvements for which compensation may not be claimed*

No compensation is payable—

(i) if the improvement is one of a kind for which a claim for compensation may be made under Section 1 of the Landlord and Tenant Act, 1927, i.e. an improvement which adds to the letting value of property used wholly or partly for carrying on any trade or business (including premises regularly used for carrying on a profession) (this provision does not apply to Scotland); or

(ii) if the person by whom the improvement was made was under an obligation to make it in pursuance of a contract entered into for valuable consideration; or

(iii) if the improvement was made in breach of covenant; or

(iv) if before the improvement was completed the landlord objected in writing to it (para. 5 (4) *ibid.*).

(6) *Determination of claims*

. The amount of compensation payable (if any) must be determined by the county court or, in Scotland, by the sheriff (para. 5 (5) *ibid.*).

If the court determines that, on account of the intention to demolish or alter, or change the use of the dwelling-house, no compensation or a reduced amount shall be paid, the claimant may be authorised to make a further application if the demolition, alteration or change of use is not carried out within the time fixed by the court.

(7) *Refund of compensation paid by mesne landlords*

Where the landlord is himself a tenant he may be entitled to recover from his landlord the whole or part of the compensation paid. The amount of refund may be agreed between the parties or determined by the county court (or, in Scotland, by the sheriff) having regard to the terms of the superior tenancy, and in particular the length of the unexpired term thereof, and to all other relevant circumstances. A superior landlord may be able to recover from his

landlord the whole or part of the refund made to the mesne landlord
(para. 5 (6) *ibid.*).

(8) *Power to use capital money for compensation*

The power in Section 13 of the Landlord and Tenant Act, 1927, is
applied to the above provisions to enable a trust or certain uni-
versities and colleges to apply and raise capital money for the
purpose of meeting claims for compensation or other sums (including
costs, charges and expenses) (para. 5 (7) *ibid.*). This provision does
not apply to Scotland.

20. Concurrence of superior landlords to agreements on rateable value

If the landlord is himself a tenant, then unless he is holding under
a tenancy for a term with more than seven years to run, an agreement with his tenant as to the apportionment or aggregation of
rateable value (para. 15 (1) (*b*) (*c*) *ante*), or as to the validity of a
claim for or amount of reduction of rateable value on account of
tenant's improvements (para. 16 (3) (5) *ante*), will not have effect
except with the concurrence in writing of his immediate landlord
(s. 23 / 1957 Act).

21. Outstanding liabilities and repayments

Where at the time of decontrol any rent has been underpaid or
there has been an overpayment by the tenant the Act of 1957 does
not affect the right under the Rent Acts to recover such repayments.
In the case of an overpayment the tenant is entitled to deduct the
amount from future rent (para. 8, Fourth Schedule. *ibid.*).

CHAPTER IX

Tenancies Excepted from Various Controls

IN addition to the categories of tenancies which are or may be released under the Act of 1957 (Chapter VIII), certain tenancies or dwelling-houses are excluded from the protection of the Rent Acts, either by the Acts themselves, or by other legislation, or by decisions of the courts. Some tenancies which are so excluded are protected by other Acts, e.g. furnished lettings.

The following paragraphs indicate the cases where lettings are excluded from statutory control and the tenancies and other lettings which are controlled by special legislation.

1. Houses converted or erected after 2nd April 1919

The provisions of the Rent Acts relating to "old control" (p. 3) do not apply to a dwelling-house erected after or in the course of erection on the 2nd April 1919 or to any dwelling-house which has since that date or was at that date being bona fide reconstructed by way of conversion into two or more separate and self-contained flats or tenements (s. 12 (9) / 1920 Act). Such dwellings, however, may be subject to "new control" (p. 6).

2. Houses converted or erected after 29th August 1954

Section 35 of the Housing Repairs and Rents Act, 1954, and Section 27 of the Housing (Repairs and Rents) (Scotland) Act, 1954, expressly exclude from the provisions of the Rent Acts any dwelling-house which consists of:

(*a*) separate and self-contained premises produced by conversion, after the 29th August 1954, of other premises, with or without the addition of premises erected after that date;

(*b*) premises erected after the 29th August 1954.

Premises qualify for this exemption if the conversion or erection was commenced before and completed on or after the 30th August 1954.

In order to claim decontrol by conversion the work must be something more than improvement and alteration. The mere fact that premises are part of a house which has not previously been separately let and self contained is not sufficient, otherwise a landlord might be able to escape from control by doing a trifling amount of work such as putting in a new bathroom (*Higgins* v. *Silverston* [1956] 2 All E.R. 893).

The exemption does not apply to premises converted into dwellings with the aid of grants payable under the Housing Act, 1949.

3. Houses decontrolled by possession before the 1st September 1939

The provisions relating to "old control" do not apply to premises which were decontrolled by possession before the 1st September 1939 (s. 2 / 1923 Act: s. 2 / 1933 Act: s. 3 / 1938 Act).

The majority of such houses were re-controlled on the 2nd September 1939 and became subject to the provisions relating to "new control".

4. Property of the Crown

The Rent Acts do not apply to the Crown (*Clarke* v. *Downes* (1931) 145 L.T. 20).

This exemption applies also to a Territorial Forces Association (*Territorial Forces Association* v. *Philpot* [1947] 2 All E.R. 376); but not to the British Transport Commission (*Tamlin* v. *Hannaford* [1950] 1 K.B. 18).

In *Rudler* v. *Franks* [1947] K.B. 530, it was decided that a sub-tenant of the Crown had no protection under the Rent Acts against his immediate landlord. That rule was abolished by the Crown Lessees (Protection of Sub-Tenants) Act, 1952 (p. 73).

5. Lettings by local authorities, development corporations, and housing associations and trusts

(i) *Tenancies created as from the 30th August 1954*

As from the 30th August 1954 the following tenancies were expressly excluded from the Rent Acts (s. 33 / 1954 English Act: s. 25 / 1954 Scottish Act):

Any tenancy where the landlord—

(a) is a local authority;

This provision for decontrol brought all dwellings owned by local authorities into line with council houses. The majority of such houses were not subject to control as they were built since the 2nd April 1919 and therefore exempt from "old control"; and they were expressly excluded from "new control" by Section 3 (2) (c)—now repealed—of the Act of 1939. Property held by a parish council or by the representative body of a rural parish not having a separate parish council, e.g. parish property transferred to a parish council under Section 6 of the Local Government Act, 1894, appears to have been excluded from this provision for decontrol.

(b) is a development corporation established under the New Towns Act, 1946;

(c) is a housing association;

A "housing association" means a society, body of trustees or company established for the purpose of, or amongst whose objects or powers are included those of, constructing, improving or managing or facilitating or encouraging the construction or improvement of houses, being a society, body of trustees or company who do not trade for profit or whose constitution or rules prohibit the issue of any capital with interest or dividend exceeding the rate for the time being prescribed by the Treasury, whether with or without differentiation as between share and loan capital (s. 188 (1), Housing Act, 1936: s. 184 (1), Housing (Scotland) Act, 1950). But for the purpose of claiming decontrol it must be shown

(i) that the premises comprised in the tenancy were provided by the association in pursuance of an arrangement with a housing authority, under Section 94 of the Housing Act, 1936, or Sections 80 or 121 of the Housing (Scotland) Act, 1950, or under corresponding provisions in earlier Acts, to provide housing accommodation; or

(ii) that the association is registered under the Industrial and Provident Societies Act, 1893, and the provision of such premises forms part of the purposes for which its business is mainly conducted, and, in Scotland, those premises were provided by the association before the 30th August 1954; or

(iii) that the premises comprised in the tenancy were provided by the association with the assistance of a local authority or county council under Section 93 (3) of the Housing Act, 1936, or of a local authority under Section 79 (2) of the Housing (Scotland) Act, 1950, or were provided or improved by the association in accordance with arrangements made under Section 31 of the Housing Act, 1949, or Section 121 of the Housing (Scotland) Act, 1950 (paras. 26 and 32, Sixth Schedule / 1957 Act). Where the Minister of Housing and Local Government, or the Secretary of State for Scotland, is satisfied that any arrangement should be varied because of these provisions he may approve any variation between the local authority and the association.

(d) is a housing trust

  (i) in England and Wales which is subject to the jurisdiction of the Charity Commissioners; or

  (ii) in Scotland which was in existence on the 13th November, 1953;

A "housing trust" for this purpose means a corporation or body of persons which, by the terms of its constituent instrument, is required to devote the whole of its funds, including any surplus which may arise from its operations, to the provision of houses, and to other purposes incidental thereto and, in England and Wales, a similar corporation or body which must devote the whole or substantially the whole of its funds to housing and other charitable purposes (e.g. The Peabody Donation Fund, London).

(e) in Scotland is

  (i) the Scottish Special Housing Association;

  (ii) any authorised society within the meaning of the Housing Act, 1914;

  (iii) a National Health Service Executive Council.

(ii) *Tenancies existing at 30th August 1954*

Any existing tenancy, within the above classes, which was controlled immediately before the 30th August 1954 did not become decontrolled before the expiration of six months from that date.

After the expiration of such period of six months a tenant was not entitled, as against a local authority, corporation, association, trust or council to retain possession of a dwelling as a statutory tenant.

(iii) *Sub-tenancies*

A sub-tenant is protected against his own landlord but not against the local authority, corporation, association, trust or council when the interest of the mesne landlord comes to an end (ss. 33 (1): 25 (1) / 1954 Acts).

(iv) *Fixing the rents of sub-tenancies*

The Acts of 1954 provided for the fixing of recoverable rents of sub-tenancies as and when the head tenancies became decontrolled. In England and Wales the rents of the sub-tenancies are now governed by the new rent structure of the Act of 1957 (Chapter III). In Scotland the provisions in the Act of 1954 for fixing such rents still apply. In ascertaining what rent is recoverable from a sub-tenant in Scotland the Rent Acts and the Act of 1949 are applied as if the superior tenancy was a controlled tenancy and neither the premises nor any part thereof had ever been let before the beginning of that tenancy. The rent payable under the sub-tenancy then becomes a rent payable under a first letting and either party is entitled to refer the matter to the rent tribunal for review (p. 118).

(v) *Sub-tenants of council houses*

The sub-tenant of a council house was placed in a better position under the Acts of 1954 than under the previous law where the dwelling itself was excluded from the protection of the Rent Acts. He became protected against his immediate landlord, unless that landlord happened to be an exempted authority, e.g. a council house let by a district council to the county council and sub-let by them to a policeman.

(vi) *Sub-tenancies existing before the 30th August 1954*

In the application of the Rent Acts to a sub-tenancy in existence before the 30th August 1954, and created out of an interest of an exempted authority, the following modifications (so far as still relevant) were applied:

> (a) the standard rent under the sub-tenancy was the rent charged on the 11th November 1953 or, if there was no such sub-letting on that date, the rent charged on the first sub-letting before the 30th August 1954. The same limitations were applied in regard to mortgage interest (p. 150);

> (b) the mesne landlord could claim the permitted increase of 8 per cent. only for improvements carried out since the 11th November 1953 if the premises were then sub-let or, in any other case, from the date of the first sub-letting before the 30th August 1954;

(c) any permitted increase in respect of an increase in rates being calculated by reference to the rates payable on the 11th November 1953 if the premises were then sub-let or, in any other case, on the date of the first sub-letting before the 30th August 1954;

(d) if the mesne landlord wanted to obtain possession against the sub-tenant on the ground that he required the premises for himself; or for a son or daughter over eighteen years of age; or for his father or mother, he had to prove that he had acquired his interest not later than the 11th November 1953 or, if the premises were not then sub-let, not later than the first sub-letting before the 30th August 1954. Under the Act of 1957 he will now have to prove that he acquired his interest not later than the 7th November 1956 (p. 83).

6. Long tenancies

The Rent Acts do not apply to any tenancy of residential premises granted for a term of more than twenty-one years, which is protected by Part I of the Landlord and Tenant Act, 1954. But a sub-tenant holding a controlled tenancy under such long tenancy is protected by the Acts. If the tenant under the long tenancy is ejected or dispossessed of the premises the sub-tenant becomes the direct tenant of the landlord (s. 21 / 1957 Act)—see Chapter XVII.

7. Short tenancies at low rents

The letting of a house or part of a house for a term not exceeding twenty-one years at a rent of less than two-thirds of the rateable value of the dwelling-house is not protected by the Rent Acts (s. 12 (7) / 1920 Act: Part I of the Landlord and Tenant Act, 1954).

8. Sub-tenancies created out of short tenancies at low rents

A sub-tenancy created out of a lease of residential premises granted for twenty-one years or less at a rent of less than two-thirds of the rateable value of the dwelling-house, after the head lease has come to an end is not protected by the Rent Acts (*Knightsbridge Estates Trust Ltd.* v. *Deeley* [1950] 2 K.B. 228: s. 12 (7) / 1920 Act: s. 15 (1) Landlord and Tenant Act, 1954).

9. Sub-tenancies created after the 30th September 1954 out of long tenancies

A sub-tenancy created after the 30th September 1954, out of a long tenancy of residential premises let at a rent of less than two-thirds of the rateable value of the dwelling-house or after the 5th July 1957 at any rent, is not protected by the Rent Acts if at the time of its creation

(*a*) a notice had been given to terminate the long tenancy; or

(*b*) the long tenancy was being continued after the term date by virtue of the Landlord and Tenant Act, 1954,

unless the sub-tenancy was created with the written consent of the person who at the time was the competent landlord (s. 15 (1) / 1954 Act: s. 21 (2) / 1957 Act).

10. Furnished lettings

The Rent Acts do not apply to furnished lettings—see Chapter XV.

11. Licensed premises

On-licensed premises are exempted from the provisions of the Rent Acts (s. 1 (3) / 1933 Act: s. 3 (2) / 1939 Act).

Off-licensed premises, as such, are not excepted from the Rent Acts.

12. Agricultural holdings

The Rent Acts do not apply to any dwelling-house which is comprised in an agricultural holding and is occupied by the person responsible for the control (whether as tenant or as servant or agent of the tenant) of the farming of the holding (s. 95: Seventh Schedule, Agricultural Holdings Act, 1948).

13. Houses let with land

The provisions of the Rent Acts relating to "old control" premises do not apply to a house let together with land (other than the site of the house), except where the house is let with land or premises and the rateable value of the land or premises, if let separately, would be less than one-quarter of the rateable value of the house (s. 12 (2) / 1920 Act).

For the purposes of the provisions relating to "new control" any land or premises let together with a dwelling-house are treated as part of the house, unless the land or premises so let consists of agricultural land exceeding two acres in extent (s. 3 (3) / 1939 Act).

14. Lettings of accommodation registered under Defence Regulations

The Rent Acts and the Furnished Houses (Rent Control) Act, 1946, do not apply to accommodation which was registered under

I

Defence Regulation 68CB where the letting has continued after the repeal of the regulation on the 7th December 1954 (s. 45 / 1954 Act).

Section 12 (10) of the Act of 1920 provides that where possession was taken of any dwelling-houses by a Government department during the 1914–18 war, under the Defence of the Realm regulations, for the purpose of housing workmen, the Act applies to such houses as if the workmen were in occupation as tenants of the landlords.

15. Premises let to a company

It has been held that a company is not entitled to claim the protection of the Rent Acts against dispossession (*Hiller* v. *United Dairies (London) Ltd.* [1934] 1 K.B. 57); but a company is entitled to the benefits of the Acts as to restrictions on the increase of rent (*Carter* v. *S.U. Carburetter Co. Ltd.* [1942] 2 K.B. 288).

16. Parsonage houses

Parsonage houses are not protected by the provisions of the Rent Acts which restrict the right to possession (*Bishop of Gloucester* v. *Cunningham* [1943] K.B. 101). This exemption has been held to apply to a cottage in the parsonage grounds if it is necessary for the convenient occupation of the parsonage (*Neale* v. *Jennings* [1946] K.B. 238).

17. Recovery under other Acts of Parliament

The various Acts of Parliament which allow the recovery of possession of controlled houses for specific purposes are shown in Chapter VII.

CHAPTER X

The Rent Limits in Scotland

THE Act of 1957, in its application to Scotland, retains the structure of the earlier Rent Acts as to the recoverable rent of a controlled dwelling. This is due to the fact that the law relating to valuation and rating in Scotland is in process of amendment by virtue of the Valuation and Rating (Scotland) Act, 1956. The recoverable rent, therefore, continues to be based on the principle of "old control" and "new control" tenancies (p. 6) made up of the standard rent with "permitted increases" as laid down by the Acts prior to the Act of 1957, together with the increase for cost of services and repairs increase under the Housing (Repairs and Rents) (Scotland) Act, 1954. The new Act, however, makes three important changes in the fixing of the rent limit: (i) the tenant is no longer permitted to withhold the 15 per cent. and 25 per cent. increases in rent on "old control" houses in case of disrepair; (ii) the amount of the "repairs increase" has been increased; and (iii) there is a new kind of repairs increase known as the "1957 Act increase" where the tenancy does not qualify for a repairs increase under the Act of 1954.

1. Standard rent

The standard rent means in the case of—

(*a*) an "old control" house, the rent at which it was let on the 3rd August 1914 (s. 12 (1) (*a*) / 1920 Act);

(*b*) a "new control" house, the rent at which it was let on the 1st September 1939 (s. 3 (1), First Schedule / 1939 Act);

(*c*) a Crown sub-tenancy, the rent at which the dwelling was let on the 8th February 1952, or if it was not let on that date the rent at which it was first let thereafter, or the date on which the sub-tenancy became protected, before the 6th July, 1957 (s. 2, Crown Lessees (Protection of Sub-Tenants) Act, 1952);

(*d*) a sub-tenancy of property belonging to an exempted authority (p. 110), the rent of the sub-letting on the 13th November 1953; or if the first sub-letting took place between that date and the 30th August 1954, the rent charged on such sub-letting; or if the first sub-letting was after the 30th August

1954 and before the 6th July 1957, the rent charged on such sub-letting which, in any such case, is subject to review by the rent tribunal (s. 25 / 1954 Act),

and "net rent" means, where the "standard rent" includes occupiers' rates, the standard rent less such rates and in any other case the standard rent (s. 12 (1) (c) / 1920 Act).

(1) *Ascertainment of standard rent in certain cases*

If, in the case of (a) or (b) above, the house was not let on the relevant date the standard rent is the rent at which it was last let before that date. If a house was first let after the relevant date and before the time of decontrol—not being a house erected or produced by conversion after the 29th August 1954 (p. 107)—the standard rent is the rent at which it was first let, provided it was a bona fide tenancy controllable by the Rent Acts, e.g. not a furnished letting. If the house is let at a progressive rent the maximum rent payable under the tenancy is the standard rent. Where at the relevant date the rent was less than the rateable value, the rateable value at that date is treated as the standard rent (s. 12 (1) (a) / 1920 Act.

If it is not reasonably practicable by the above rules to obtain sufficient evidence for the purpose of ascertaining the standard rent of a house the sheriff court can fix the rent by reference to the standard rent of similar houses in the neighbourhood (s. 6 / 1933 Act: First Schedule / 1939 Act).

The court has power on the application of a landlord or a tenant to determine any questions as to the amount of rent, standard rent or net rent of a controlled dwelling-house (s. 11 / 1923 Act).

(2) *Reduction of recoverable rent on abolition of owners' rates*

Under the Valuation and Rating (Scotland) Act, 1956, an occupier became liable, as from the 16th May 1957, to pay all the rates leviable by a rating authority and owners' rates were abolished as from that date. If the local financial year commenced on a day other than the 16th May the change took place on that day.

To off-set the additional liability for rates so placed on an occupier the recoverable rent of a controlled tenancy has been reduced by the amount of the owner's liability for rates in the year 1956–57. This was done by the reduction of the standard rent by an amount equal to the "relevant fraction" of the net rent; and by the reduction of each permitted increase by an amount equal to the "relevant fraction" of that increase. The "relevant fraction" is a fraction of which the numerator is the number of pence per pound of rateable value payable by way of owners' rates in respect of the controlled dwelling in the year 1956–57 and the denominator is two hundred and forty, thus $\overline{240}$. Increases for cost of services and the repairs increase under the Act of 1954—not being rateable—were not reduced. This provision for reducing the net rent or standard rent does not apply to a standard rent settled by agreement or fixed by the court, or a rent tribunal, or a local authority, after the commencement of the financial year 1957–58.

Not later than the commencement of the year 1957–58 landlords were required to serve on their tenants a notice (prescribed by the Owners' Rates (Form of Notice) (Scotland) Regulations, 1957, S.I. No. 49 (s. 2)) showing the owners' share of rates for the year 1956–57 and the reduced rent payable (exclusive of rates) for rental periods beginning in the financial year 1957–58. Any dispute between a landlord and tenant as to the owner's share of rates can be referred to the rating authority for determination. Their decision is final.

(3) *Landlord's obligation to give statement of standard rent*

In addition to the above provision the landlord of a controlled dwelling in Scotland must supply at the written request of the tenant a statement in writing as to what is the standard rent of the house. If, without reasonable excuse, the landlord fails to do so within fourteen days, or supplies a statement which is false in any material particular, he is liable to a fine not exceeding £10 (s. 11 / 1920 Act).

2. Apportionment of standard rent and rateable value

Where a dwelling separately let is part of a controlled dwelling the standard rent of the part may be ascertained by the sheriff court by an apportionment of the standard rent of the whole house. The court may also apportion the rateable value of a house.

The power of apportionment may be exercised where the part dwelling was let before a "first letting" of the whole of the premises (s. 5 / 1938 Act). The tenant can recover any excess rent paid before the apportionment (s. 14 (1) / 1920 Act).

When the standard rent of a controlled property has been determined by a rent tribunal, then—

    (a) for the purpose of any apportionment for determining the standard rent of part of the property, the property (as a whole) is to be deemed to have been let at the rent deter-

mined by the tribunal or, if the tribunal determined an
excess (p. 119), that rent reduced by the amount of the
excess;

(b) any such apportionment made before the tribunal's determination may be varied accordingly.

When the standard rent of a dwelling-house, which is part of a
controlled dwelling, has been determined by a rent tribunal then,
in making any apportionment for the purpose of ascertaining the
standard rent of any other part of the property, no regard is to be
taken of the determination (s. 4 / 1949 Act).

If as the result of the operation of Section 28 of the Act of 1954
(p. 120), the standard rent of a controlled dwelling has been
increased by a rent tribunal, any apportionment of the rent of part
of the property made before the coming into operation of the increase
may be varied so as to accord with the tribunal's determination.
The apportionment so varied cannot take effect before the increase
comes into operation (s. 28 (3) *ibid.*).

3. Variation of standard rent by rent tribunal

For the purpose of controlling unduly high rents on "new control"
dwellings first let after the 1st September 1939, the Act of 1949
empowered rent tribunals—set up under the Rent of Furnished
Houses Control (Scotland) Act, 1943—to vary the standard rents
of new lettings. For this purpose the Secretary of State was authorised
(s. 6 / 1949 Act) to set up tribunals in any areas where they had not
been established for the purposes of the Act of 1943. The scope of
the provision is now limited to tenancies in existence before 6th July
1957, except in the case of a first letting after a landlord has obtained
possession on grounds of overcrowding (p. 92).

(1) *Lettings not subject to review*

In addition to there being no general right of reference in respect
of tenancies created on or after the 6th July 1957, no application
can be made to a tribunal in respect of any dwelling-house—

(a) for which a maximum rent has been fixed by a local authority
under Section 113 of the Housing (Scotland) Act, 1950, in
consequence of the payment of an improvement grant; or

(b) for which a maximum rent has been fixed by a local authority
under Section 3 of the Housing (Scotland) Act, 1952, under
a scheme for the provision of housing accommodation for
the agricultural population; or

(c) an interest in which ceased to belong to an exempted authority (p. 108), under the Act of 1954, and at the time there was no controlled tenancy or statutory tenancy subsisting in the whole of the premises (s. 28 (5) *ibid.*). The standard rent in that case could be fixed by the local authority under the now repealed Section 34 of that Act.

(2) *Variation of standard rents of "new control" lettings*

Where the standard rent of a dwelling-house is—

(a) the rent at which it was first let as a "new control" dwelling after the 1st September 1939, or

(b) an amount ascertainable by apportionment of such rent (whether or not the apportionment has been made),

the landlord or the tenant may apply to the rent tribunal to determine what rent is reasonable for the dwelling-house (s. 1 / 1949 Act). The tribunal must then make a determination and notify the parties of their decision.

The guidance given by the Act to the tribunal as to what is a reasonable rent is "the rent which is in all the circumstances reasonable on a letting of that dwelling-house on the terms and conditions, other than terms and conditions fixing the amount of rent, on which the dwelling-house is let at the time of the application". In fixing the rent of part of a house the tribunal must disregard the rent of the remainder or any other part of the house if no determination has been made in respect of those parts. No regard is to be had to the fact that any premium has been paid in respect of the grant, continuance or renewal of a tenancy. If the property is let at a progressive rent the rent fixed by the tribunal is to be the maximum rent under the letting.

No second application can be made for the review of a determination.

The rent so determined by the tribunal becomes the standard rent of the dwelling-house from the date of the determination.

If the recoverable rent (i.e. the standard rent plus the permitted increases) exceeds the standard rent, the tribunal must determine the amount of the excess; and if the rent as determined by the tribunal, reduced by the amount of the excess, differs from what the standard rent would otherwise be, the rent so determined and reduced becomes the standard rent of the dwelling-house as from the date of the tribunal's determination.

A tribunal has power to increase as well as to decrease a rent (s. 28 / 1954 Act).

(3) *Effect of previous determinations which increased rent*

Before the Act of 1954 came into force on the 30th August 1954 some tribunals had made increases in the rents of houses. Such determinations were unenforceable before that date. The Act, however, made such determinations valid (s. 28 (2)). But an increase in the standard rent effected by a determination before that date—

(a) did not operate until a date specified in a prescribed notice of increase served by the landlord on the tenant; and

(b) that date could not be earlier than four weeks after the service of the notice.

(4) *Procedure for obtaining a determination*

All applications to a tribunal must be made in writing and must specify the address of the dwelling-house to which the application relates, the name of the tenant, the name and address of the landlord or of his factor or agent, and the rent payable by the tenant.

Each party to the tenancy must be given an opportunity of a hearing before the tribunal or of making representations in writing. The time allowed within which the parties must give notice that they desire to be heard or to make representations is such period (not being less than seven days) as may be allowed by the tribunal. If any party desires to be heard the tribunal must give to each party not less than four clear days' notice in writing of the time and place of the hearing. Any interested party may appear in person or by counsel or a solicitor or by any other representative or may be accompanied by any person whom he may wish to assist him. The tribunal may determine their own procedure at a hearing and may postpone or adjourn the hearing from time to time. (The Landlord and Tenant (Rent Control) (Scotland) Regulations, 1949, S.I. No. 1257 (s. 90)). It is the duty of the tribunal to make the required entry in the register of determinations kept by them.

4. Permitted increases

(a) "*Old control*" houses

The permitted increases in the standard rents of "old control" houses are as follows (s. 2 (1) / 1920 Act):

(1) *Improvements and alterations (6 per cent. and 8 per cent.)*: Where between the 4th August 1914 and the 2nd July 1920 expenditure

had been incurred by the landlord on an improvement or structural alteration of a controlled dwelling-house the standard rent may be increased by not more than 6 per cent. per annum of the amount expended. If the improvement or alteration has been carried out since the 2nd July 1920, the rent may be increased by not more than 8 per cent. per annum of the amount expended (s. 2 (1) (a) / 1920 Act). Expenditure on the provision of additional or improved fixtures or fittings may be regarded as expenditure on the improvement of the house (s. 7 (1) / 1933 Act); but not on decoration or repairs.

(i) *Private street works qualify as improvements:* Where private street works are carried out at the expense of the landlord or a superior landlord under Sections 133 to 137, 141, 142, 150 and 151 of the Burgh Police (Scotland) Act, 1892; Section 39 of the Public Health (Scotland) Act, 1897; and Section 16 of the Burgh Police (Scotland) Act, 1903; or the corresponding provisions of any local Act, the works qualify as an improvement (s. 18 / 1957 Act).

The increase may be claimed only in respect of expenditure incurred by the landlord or a superior landlord on or after the 6th July 1957. Where the charges are payable by instalments the landlord is not entitled to include in his expenditure any interest payable on the charges.

If other premises belonging to the landlord or superior landlord benefit from the works the expenditure is to be apportioned between the controlled dwelling and the other premises by agreement in writing between the landlord and the tenant or determined by the sheriff.

(ii) *Expenditure and improvements which do not qualify:* The right to claim a permitted increase for improvements does not apply where in consequence of an improvement grant having been made under the Housing (Scotland) Act, 1950, the rent of the dwelling has been fixed under that Act (s. 125 *ibid.*).

Where the improvement includes the adaptation of fireplaces in dwellings in smokeless zones the amount of expenditure incurred on the work must be reduced by the amount of repayment made by the local authority under Section 12 of the Clean Air Act, 1956 (para. 31, Sixth Schedule / 1957 Act).

Where any statutory contribution is made which diminishes the liability for street works charges (e.g. under the Local Government (Street Works) (Scotland) Act, 1956) the expenditure on which the increase is claimed must be reduced by the amount of the contribution (s. 18 (3) / 1957 Act).

(iii) *Tenant's right of appeal against increase:* The tenant can apply to the sheriff court for an order suspending or reducing the permitted increase for improvements on the ground that the expenditure was wholly or partly unnecessary (s. 2 (1) (*a*) / 1920 Act). But the court cannot make an order unless the applicant proves either—

(*a*) that he was the tenant when the expenditure was incurred and did not give his written consent to the improvement or alteration and to the expenditure thereon; or

(*b*) that the landlord was in possession at the date when the expenditure was incurred and that the applicant was the first tenant subsequent to that date and became tenant without notice of—

(i) the nature of the improvement or alteration; and

(ii) the amount of expenditure thereon; and

(iii) the amount of the maximum increase of rent chargeable on account thereof (s. 7 (2) / 1933 Act).

The right of appeal does not apply in the case of an increase resulting from expenditure on private street works (s. 18 (4) / 1957 Act).

(2) *Increase for rates:* The Rent Acts have always provided that where the rent includes rates the landlord is entitled to claim from the tenant any increase above the amount paid at the time by reference to which the amount of the standard rent was fixed. In the application of this principle a limitation was set by the Act of 1920 in relation to owners' rates. Under Section 2 (1) (*b*), as read with Section 18 (1) (*b*), of the Act a landlord is entitled to claim any increase in the amount of occupiers' rates for the time being payable by the landlord in respect of the dwelling over the corresponding amount in the rating period for the year ending the 15th May 1915, or if no rates were payable for that period, the period when rates first became payable thereafter. But in the case of owners' rates there was a limit and the maximum permitted increase which the landlord could claim from the tenant was the increase in those rates in the year ending Whitsunday 1920, or for the time being payable, whichever is the less, over the corresponding amount paid in the rating period for the year ending the 15th May 1915, or if no rates were payable for that period, the period when rates first became payable thereafter.

Under the Valuation and Rating (Scotland) Act, 1956, the tenant (as occupier) has become responsible for all rates payable to the rating authority as from the beginning of the financial year 1957–58 and a corresponding reduction has been made in the recoverable rent to take account of the fact that the tenant has taken over the liability for the proportion of rates formerly borne by the owner (p. 116).

The net result of this change—as read with the Rent Acts—is that the full amount of any future increase in rates will be recoverable by the landlord from the tenant who pays an inclusive rent.

The transference of liability to the occupier does not affect the provisions of the House Letting and Rating (Scotland) Acts, 1911 and 1920, or of the Local Government (Scotland) Act, 1947, whereby an owner of a small dwelling-house is responsible in the first instance for payment of rates to the local authority or his rights of recovery against the occupier.

Where the landlord is allowed a commission for compounding with the rating authority for the payment of rates that discount is not taken into account in fixing the permitted increase; so that the landlord can charge the tenant more than he actually pays out as rates increase (s. 7 (2) / 1938 Act). If there is a subsequent reduction in the rates the permitted increase must be reduced accordingly.

(3) *40 per cent. increase:* In addition to the above increases the landlord is entitled to—

(a) an increase of an amount not exceeding 15 per cent. of the net rent (s. 2 (1) (c) / 1920 Act); and

(b) if he is responsible for the whole of the repairs, to a further increase of an amount not exceeding 25 per cent. of the net rent or, if he is responsible for part only of the repairs, such lesser amount as may be agreed with the tenant or as may be settled by the sheriff court on the application of either party (s. 2 (1) (d) *ibid.*).

The Acts do not attach any qualification for claiming the 15 per cent. increase but in both that case and in the case of the 25 per cent. increase the tenant had, until the commencement of the Act of 1957, the right to suspend payment of the increases if the property was not kept in repair.

By Section 9 (3) of the Act of 1957 the qualification that the property must be kept in good repair has been withdrawn, with the result that a tenant is no longer entitled to withhold the increases if the dwelling falls into disrepair. The subsection, however, provides safeguards where the dwelling was in disrepair on the 6th July 1957. The tenant—

(a) can obtain a court order suspending the amount of the increases for any rental period before that date, and court orders made before that date remain effective, or

(b) can withhold the increases if he had obtained a certificate of disrepair before that date and the defects have not been put right, or

(c) had applied for a certificate before that date and it is subsequently issued by the local authority.

(4) *Railway-owned houses:* Where houses are let by the railway authorities to their employees the standard rent may be increased by such amount, if any, as is required to give effect to the wages agreement of the 1st March 1920, or any agreement extending or modifying that agreement (s. 2 (1) (e) / 1920 Act).

(5) *Permitted increases in rent of sub-tenancies (10 per cent.):* When part of a controlled dwelling is lawfully sub-let and the part so sub-let is also a controlled dwelling, then in addition to the above increases the tenant may increase the sub-tenant's rent by 10 per cent. of the net rent of the dwelling let under the sub-tenancy. Five per cent. of the increase allowed in respect of the sub-tenancy is deemed to be a permitted increase in the rent of the head tenancy, and the landlord can increase the head tenant's rent by that amount. The effect is that the 10 per cent. allowed on sub-letting is shared equally between the landlord and the tenant. The landlord can claim his 5 per cent. if the tenant does not claim any increase from the sub-tenant (s. 7 (1) / 1923 Act).

If the tenant's interest is terminated and the sub-tenant becomes the tenant of the landlord, an increase of 5 per cent. only of the net rent of the sub-let part can be recovered from the tenant (i.e. the former sub-tenant).

No notice of increase (p. 126) is necessary in the case of a sub-tenancy.

(6) *Increased cost of services, repairs increase and 1957 Act increase:* The right of a landlord of "old control" houses to recover the increased cost of services is dealt with in paragraph 6 (p. 126) and his right to claim a repairs increase or the 1957 Act increase in Chapter XI.

(b) *"New control" houses*

The permitted increases in the standard rents of "new control" houses are (First Schedule / 1939 Act):

(1) *Improvements and alterations (8 per cent.):* For any improvement or structural alteration (including additional or improved fixtures or

fittings) carried out since the 2nd September 1939, or expenditure incurred after the 5th July 1957, on private street works (p. 121), the rent may be increased by 8 per cent. per annum of the amount expended. The increase cannot be claimed for expenditure on decorations or repairs and must be diminished in the case of grant-aided work (p. 121). The tenant has the same rights of appeal to the sheriff court against the increase on the ground that the expenditure was wholly or partly unnecessary as the tenant of an "old control" house (p. 122).

(2) *Increase for rates:* The landlord who pays the rates is permitted to recover from the tenant any future increases in rates, as in the case of "old control" property, and he has the same rights as to compounding allowances and obligations to make subsequent reductions in rates (p. 123).

(3) *Increased cost of services, repairs increase and 1957 Act increase:* The right of a landlord of "new control" property to recover the increased cost of services is dealt with in paragraph 6 (p. 126) and his right to claim a repairs increase or the 1957 Act increase in Chapter XI.

(c) Statutory sub-tenancies of property belonging to exempted authorities

Permitted increases in the standard rents of sub-tenancies of property belonging to exempted authorities (p. 111) may be claimed for improvements and alterations and for rates.

5. Notice of increase of rent

The Rent Acts do not enable a contractual tenancy to be broken during the currency of the contract and a permitted increase can be made only in respect of a period during which but for the Rent Acts the landlord would be entitled to possession (s. 3 (1) / 1920 Act).

It is provided, however, by Section 1 of the Rent Restrictions (Notices of Increase) Act, 1923, that a notice to increase rent has effect as if it were also a notice to terminate the existing tenancy—

(a) on the day preceding the day from which the increase is to take effect, or

(b) on the earliest day thereafter, on which, if the notice had been one to terminate the tenancy, it would have been effective for that purpose.

In any case at least four clear weeks' notice must be given of an intention to increase the rent (s. 3 (2) / 1920 Act), except where the increase is on account of an increase in rates where only one week's notice is necessary.

Where the rent has been increased after notice has been served on a former tenant, the increase may be continued without service of any fresh notice on a subsequent tenant (s. 3 (2) / 1920 Act), e.g. on a first letting after possession has been obtained on grounds of over-crowding.

No notice is necessary in respect of an increase permitted on sub-letting (s. 7 (1) / 1923 Act), but the tenant must give notice of the sub-letting to the landlord (p. 84); nor is a notice necessary in respect of increased cost of services (see below).

Any notice of intention to increase rent must be in the prescribed form or in a form to the like effect. The Rent Restrictions (Scotland) Regulations, 1939 (S.R.O. No. 1615 / s. 116), as amended by the Rent Restrictions (Scotland) Amendment Regulations, 1954 (S.I. No. 1081 (s. 104)) have prescribed the forms of notice to be served on a tenant in order to claim a permitted increase.

As to service of notice of increase in respect of a repairs increase or a 1957 Act increase, see Chapter XI.

The sheriff court can determine any question as to a permitted increase (s. 11 / 1923 Act) and may rectify any error or omission in a notice if satisfied that it was due to a bona fide mistake on the part of the landlord (s. 6 / 1923 Act). If a notice of increase contains any statement or representation which is false or misleading in any material respect the landlord is liable to a fine not exceeding £10 unless he can prove that the statement was made innocently and without intent to deceive (s. 3 (2) / 1920 Act).

6. Increased cost of services

Provision was made by Section 31 of the Act of 1954 for enabling a landlord to recover the increased cost of services provided under pre-1939 lettings.

The increase may be recovered in any case where a dwelling-house was let under a controlled tenancy, or is occupied by a statutory tenant, and—

    (a) the standard rent is the rent at which it was let on or before the 1st September 1939, or is an amount ascertainable by apportionment of a rent of such a letting, and

    (b) under the terms and conditions of the letting the landlord provides services for the tenant, or

    (c) services for the tenant are provided by the landlord.

"Services" include attendance, the provision of heating or lighting, the supply of hot water and any other privilege or facility connected with the occupancy of a dwelling-house (s. 39 (1) *ibid.*).

The increase may be claimed for both "old control" and "new control" tenancies, provided the standard rent was fixed by reference to a letting which began on or before the 1st September 1939. It need not be the same tenancy. But the provision does not apply to a tenancy the standard rent of which may be varied by a rent tribunal (p. 119).

Notwithstanding anything in the terms of the tenancy or statutory tenancy or any enactment (e.g. the limits imposed by the Rent Acts) the landlord is entitled to recover the amount of the increased cost of services as agreed with the tenant or a former tenant or determined by the rent tribunal on the application of the landlord.

The agreement must be in writing and must have been made after the 29th August 1954. It must show that it has been agreed that the landlord is entitled to an increase of rent of the amount specified in the agreement in respect of any rise, over the period between the 3rd September 1939 and the 30th August 1954, in the cost of the provision of the services.

The Act provides that at any time after the 29th August 1954 the landlord may apply to the rent tribunal for the area in which the house is situated for a determination that in all the circumstances it is just that he should be entitled to an increase of rent, as specified in the determination, in respect of any such rise as is mentioned above. Before making a determination the tribunal must make such enquiries as they think fit and must give the landlord and the tenant an opportunity of being heard or, at the option of the party, of submitting representations in writing. The procedure to be followed for obtaining a determination is laid down by the Housing Repairs and Rents (Rent Tribunal) (Scotland) Regulations, 1954 (S.I. 1156 (s. 110)), and is similar to the procedure for obtaining a determination of a standard rent (p. 120).

Any increase recoverable by virtue of an agreement runs from the date specified in the agreement; any increase recoverable by virtue of a tribunal's determination runs from the date of the determination.

7. Prohibition on premiums

Section 2 of the Landlord and Tenant (Rent Control) Act, 1949, makes it illegal to charge a premium on the grant, renewal, continuance or assignment of a controlled tenancy. See Chapter V.

8. Transfer of burdens and liabilities

Any transfer to a tenant of any burden or liability previously borne by the landlord which makes the terms of letting less favourable to the tenant is regarded as an increase in rent. The transfer from the landlord to the tenant of the liability for rates is not deemed to be an increase if a corresponding reduction is made in the rent. If the rent is increased by the landlord assuming responsibility for any burden or liability previously borne by the tenant, and the terms of letting on the whole are not less favourable to the tenant than the previous terms, the increase is not deemed to be an increase for the purposes of the Rent Acts (s. 2 (3) / 1920 Act).

Where any agreement or determination has been made in regard to increased cost of services (p. 126) and made in respect of services which the landlord is not liable to provide under the terms and conditions of the letting (sub-heading (c), para. 6, *ante*), any withholding or restoration of those services (whether in whole or in part) may be treated as a transfer from the landlord or the tenant, as the case may be, of a burden previously borne by him (s. 31 (3) / 1954 Act).

9. Increases in rents of subsidised private houses

Where private houses have been provided or improved with the aid of a grant from the State or local authorities and a condition is imposed as to the rent which may be charged in respect of the house, that limit may be exceeded by the amount of the repairs increase or the 1957 Act increase (s. 10 / 1957 Act). These conditions will continue to apply after any such house has become decontrolled.

The rule for increasing the rent as above applies in relation to houses in respect of which a subsidy is payable under conditions imposed, or by virtue of any undertaking or agreement entered into, under—

(a) Section 2 of the Housing (Financial Provisions) Act, 1924, where Government subsidy was provided towards the cost of houses built by a non-profit-making society, body of trustees or company established for the promotion of dwelling-houses for the working classes;

(b) Section 3 of the Housing (Rural Workers) Act, 1926, where grants were made by local authorities (with Government aid) for the reconditioning of private houses for agricultural workers and others engaged in rural industries;

(c) Section 101 of the Housing (Scotland) Act, 1950, where grants are made by local authorities (with Government aid) for the replacement of unsatisfactory houses occupied by agricultural workers and others;

(d) Section 114 (1) (c) (ii) of the Act of 1950 where grants are made by local authorities (with Government aid) towards the modernisation of older type houses by improvement and conversion schemes.

10. Application of the Rent Acts to grant-aided dwellings

Section 113 of the Housing (Scotland) Act, 1950, makes it the duty of a local authority, when they approve an application for an improvement grant, to fix the maximum rent which may be charged for any new dwelling provided, and for any improved dwelling which has not been let during the preceding five years. So long as the conditions which are laid down by that Act in relation to the dwelling are observed the provisions of the Rent Acts as to standard rent and permitted increases do not apply (s. 125 *ibid.*).

K

CHAPTER XI

Repairs and Increases in Rent for doing Repairs in Scotland

THE right of a landlord to claim the maximum rent of a controlled dwelling in Scotland continues to be based on the principles of the Housing (Repairs and Rents) (Scotland) Act, 1954, which allows increases in rent to be made for doing repairs. The scheme of the Act is that if a landlord can prove that a certain amount of money has been spent on work on a dwelling-house in the preceding twelve months and it is in good and tenantable repair and not in any other respect unfit for human habitation he can claim an increase in rent for keeping it in repair.

The amount of the increase, where the landlord is responsible for all repairs, was fixed by the Act of 1954 as an amount equal to two-fifths of the net rent payable immediately before the 30th August 1954. The Act of 1957 increases the fraction to one-half of that rent; it also enables a landlord who does not qualify for that increase to claim an increase—called "the 1957 Act increase"—equivalent to one-quarter of the 1954 rent without proof of expenditure on past repairs; and a tenant can no longer suspend payment of the 40 per cent. increase in rent on "old control" property on grounds of want of repair.

1. Responsibility for repairs

For the purpose of claiming the repairs increase under the Act of 1954 and the 1957 Act increase the landlord is deemed, as between himself and the tenant, to be wholly responsible for the repair of a dwelling-house in any case where the tenant is under no express liability to carry out repairs (s. 23 / 1954 Act: s. 8 (1) / 1957 Act).

In any case where the landlord is responsible for part only of the repairs the proportion on which he can claim the repairs increase and the 1957 Act increase is to be settled by comparing both the express and implied burden of responsibility of the landlord with the express responsibility of the tenant.

The implied responsibility placed on the landlord for any repairs for which neither he nor the tenant is expressly liable has the effect of avoiding any right of the tenant to challenge the landlord's claim to an increase in rent on the ground that he is not obliged to do the work.

The same division of responsibility is implied as between tenant and sub-tenant. In any such case the tenant (as landlord) may assume responsibility for any repairs for which the sub-tenant is under no express liability to carry out. The tenant can serve in his own right a notice of increase irrespective of being able to pass on, for example, a repairs increase claimed by the landlord.

Any question as to whether the landlord is responsible for repairs or as to the amount of any reduction of repairs increase or the 1957 Act increase where the tenant is expressly liable to carry out repairs must be settled by agreement in writing between the landlord and the tenant or by the sheriff on the application of either party (s. 16 (4) / 1954 Act: s. 7 (4) / 1957 Act).

Where the landlord claims the increased amount of the repairs increase under the Act of 1957 and the tenant is expressly liable for some repairs the proportion of the difference between two-fifths and one-half of the rent recoverable immediately before the 30th August 1954, must be agreed in writing between the landlord and the tenant or settled by the sheriff.

In considering the extent to which a landlord is liable for repairs regard should be had to the provisions of Sections 3 and 4 of the Housing (Scotland) Act, 1950. Section 3 provides that in any contract for letting for human habitation a house (which includes part of a house separately let and a flat) at a rent not exceeding £26 there shall, notwithstanding any stipulation to the contrary, be implied a condition that the house is at the commencement of the tenancy—and an undertaking that it will be kept by the landlord during the tenancy—in all respects reasonably fit for human habitation. This implied condition applies to houses let to workmen engaged in agriculture under a contract of employment (s. 4); but not to leases granted for a fixed term of three years or more where the tenant undertakes to put the property in a condition in all respects reasonably fit for human habitation; nor to tenancies of houses let before the 31st July 1923 at a rent of more than £16.

Section 13 (2) of the Act of 1954 excludes the implied condition in the case of a contract of letting by a local authority of any slum property purchased or retained by them under that Act for housing purposes.

2. "Good and tenantable repair" and "unfit for human habitation"

In determining whether a dwelling-house is in good and tenantable repair a landlord is entitled to disregard any defect due to any act, neglect or default by the tenant or any person claiming under him or to any breach by the tenant or such a person of an express agreement. None of these matters, however, may be disregarded by a local authority in deciding whether a certificate of disrepair, or a certificate of repair, or a certificate of service of a Housing Act notice, should be granted or revoked (p. 137). If the dwelling is part only of a building it will not be treated as in good and tenantable repair unless every part of the building which the tenant requires to use (e.g. a common entrance or staircase) in connection with his occupation of the dwelling-house is also in good and tenantable repair (s. 24 / 1954 Act: s. 8 (1) / 1957 Act).

The term "repair" includes maintenance, but does not include improvement or structural alteration or the provision of additional or improved fixtures or fittings (s. 39 (1): s. 8 (1) *ibid.*).

For the purpose of determining whether a house is fit for human habitation the provisions of Section 184 (2) of the Housing (Scotland) Act, 1950, are applied (s. 39 (2) / 1954 Act). The subsection provides that, for the purpose of such a determination, regard shall be had to the extent, if any, to which by reason of disrepair or sanitary defects the house falls short of the provisions of any building regulations in operation in the district. These will include such matters as lack of air space or of ventilation, darkness, dampness, absence of adequate and readily accessible water supply or of sanitary arrangements or of other conveniences and inadequate paving or drainage of courts, yards and passages. The remedying of some of these defects may constitute an improvement for which the landlord may claim a permitted increase (p. 120).

3. Repairs increase

If the landlord is responsible for the whole or part of the repairs of a dwelling which is let under a controlled tenancy or is occupied by a statutory tenant he can claim from the tenant an increase in rent—known as a "repairs increase"—for keeping the dwelling in good and tenantable repair. This increase is additional to the permitted increases of 15 per cent. and 25 per cent. (p. 123) and may be claimed notwithstanding anything in the terms of the tenancy or statutory tenancy or any enactment (s. 16 / 1954 Act).

(1) *The conditions justifying a repairs increase*

The increase can be claimed by the landlord—

(*a*) if and so long as the following conditions (known as "the conditions justifying an increase of rent") are fulfilled

   (i) that the dwelling-house is in good and tenantable repair (p. 132); and

   (ii) that it is not in any other respect unfit for human habitation (p. 132); and

(*b*) the landlord produces satisfactory evidence that work to a minimum value has been carried out on the dwelling-house.

Thus, in order to establish a claim a landlord must be able to satisfy three conditions—(1) that the property is in good and tenantable repair; (2) that it is not in any other respect unfit for human habitation; (3) that he has actually incurred the expenditure on work on the dwelling. Conditions (1) and (2) are continuing obligations; but to satisfy condition (3) it is necessary only to produce proof of costs of work done in the past when making the initial claim. After that it is assumed that condition (3) is fullfilled by the obligations imposed by conditions (1) and (2). In other words, the onus is on the landlord to prove his case in the first instance and after that the onus is on the tenant to prove that the increase is not justified.

The assumption to be made in regard to a landlord's responsibility for repairs are described in paragraph 1 (p. 130).

The tenancies which do not entitle a landlord to claim a repairs increase are referred to in sub-paragraph (14) (p. 142).

(2) *Amount of repairs increase*

Under the Act of 1954 the amount of the repairs increase is fixed at two-fifths of the rent recoverable immediately before the 30th August 1954 if the landlord is responsible for all repairs (s. 16 (2)). The amount of the increase must be reduced proportionately if the tenant is expressly liable for some repairs (para. 1 *ante*).

Section 9 of the Act of 1957 allows the amount of the increase to be raised to one-half of the rent recoverable immediately before the 30th August 1954; but a landlord who is in receipt of a repairs increase which is a proportion of two-fifths of the rent recoverable, on the ground that the tenant is responsible for some repairs, is only entitled to a proportion of the difference between two-fifths and one-half of the rent.

The amount of the increase cannot be more nor less than the fraction of two-fifths or one-half, as the case may be, subject to the proportionate reduction where the tenant is expressly liable for some repairs.

As to the meaning of "rent recoverable" for the purpose of fixing the repairs increase see page 146.

(3) *Claim for additional amount of repairs increase under the 1957 Act*

Where the landlord is in receipt of a repairs increase of two-fifths of the recoverable rent he cannot claim the additional amount to bring it up to one-half until he has given at least eight clear weeks' notice of the increase (s. 9 (2) / 1957 Act).

(4) *Proof of past repairs by landlord*

In order to establish a claim for a repairs increase a landlord must be prepared to produce satisfactory evidence that, during a period of twelve months immediately preceding the date of service of the notice of increase (p. 136) on the tenant, work specified in general terms in the notice, had been carried out on or for the benefit of the dwelling-house to a value of not less than three-fifths of the rent which was recoverable in respect of the dwelling-house immediately before the 30th August 1954. If the notice was served within six months from that date the landlord could show as an alternative test of proof of past expenditure that, during any continuous period of three years, falling within the four years ending with the date of service of the notice, he had carried out work to a value of not less than six-fifths of the recoverable rent (First Schedule / 1954 Act).

If the landlord is only partly responsible for repair (p. 130), the values of three-fifths and six-fifths, as the case may be, must be proportionately reduced.

The landlord may include in his claim items of expenditure for repairs not actually done on the site but which were done solely for the benefit of the dwelling-house. If the repairs were for the joint benefit of the tenant and others, e.g. repairs to the roof of a tenement building, a just proportion of the cost may be included in the claim.

In the case of a building containing two or more dwelling-houses (or other premises), e.g. a block of flats, the landlord is entitled to apportion the cost of work carried out during the appropriate period on all or any of the premises in the building, or on the building itself, on the basis of floor area or rateable value. The value of work regarded as having been carried out on a particular dwelling-house within the building can be ascertained as an amount bearing a like proportion to the total cost of the work as either—

(i) the floor area of the dwelling-house bears to the total floor areas, or

(ii) the rateable value of the dwelling-house bears to the total rateable values

of all the premises owned by the landlord in the building.

In computing floor areas for this purpose—

(a) the measurements must be made between the finished internal surface of the external or containing walls of the dwelling-house or other premises; and

(b) include any floor area formed by a bay or oriel window or occupied by a partition, chimney breast, fixed press or other fixture; and

(c) exclude

(i) any part of the floor where the ceiling is less than five feet;

(ii) the floor area of a water-closet, wash-house, store, passage or staircase which is used in common; and

(iii) any part of the floor which is occupied by a staircase in a dwelling-house consisting of more than one storey (Third Schedule / Housing (Repairs Increase) (Scotland) Regulations, 1954—S.I. No. 1082 (s. 105)).

The landlord, or any person authorised by him in writing, is entitled at reasonable times of the day, on giving twenty-four hours' notice in writing to the occupier, to enter any dwelling-house for the purpose of measuring the floor area.

In determining whether work to the required value (either as to the whole, or an apportioned, amount) has been carried out on a dwelling-house, the landlord is only entitled to take into account any work required for securing that premises used for human habitation are in good and tenantable repair and are not in any other respect unfit for human habitation.

A landlord cannot include in his expenditure the cost of any work carried out at the expense of the tenant, or a previous tenant, or a sub-tenant, or a previous sub-tenant; nor can he include the cost of any work which has been or will be reimbursed on a claim under the War Damage Act, 1943; or for the adaptation of fireplaces in dwellings in smokeless zones in so far as the cost is reimbursed by the local authority under Section 12 of the Clean Air Act, 1956 (para. 32 (3), Sixth Schedule / 1957 Act).

(5) *Notice of increase*

No sum is recoverable by way of repairs increase unless the landlord has served on the tenant, or a former tenant, a "notice of increase", containing the required declaration (s. 17 / 1954 Act). The forms of notice are prescribed in the Housing (Repairs Increase) (Scotland) Regulations, 1954, *supra.*).

The declaration to be made by the landlord is:

(1) that at the date of service of the notice

   (*a*) the dwelling-house was not the subject of statutory action by way of certificate, notice or intimation by the local authority because it was unsatisfactory in some respect (sub-para. (8) *post*); and

   (*b*) the conditions justifying an increase of rent were fulfilled, i.e.

      (i) that the dwelling-house was in good and tenantable repair; and

      (ii) that it was not in any other respect unfit for human habitation; and

(2) that during the specified period of twelve months or three years (see previous para.), work specified in the notice to the required value had been carried out.

The declaration as to work done must be accepted as the production of satisfactory evidence that the work has been carried out and the validity of a declaration cannot be questioned on the ground that the value of the work stated is less than that required (para. 5, First Schedule / 1954 Act). This provision seems to preclude any right of the tenant to call upon the landlord to produce accounts. The only way in which a declaration can be challenged is on an application to the sheriff court for a determination that the work has not been carried out (p. 139); or that the declaration is false.

The date when the repairs increase is to take effect must be specified in the notice; but no increase is recoverable before the expiration of eight clear weeks after service of the notice (s. 17 (2) *ibid.*).

(6) *Penalty for making a false declaration*

If a person makes a statement in a declaration which he knows to be false in a material particular or recklessly makes a statement which is false in a material particular he is liable to a fine not exceeding £30 (para. 6, First Schedule *ibid.*).

(7) *Tenant's rights to challenge notice*

There are two ways in which a tenant may challenge a notice of increase: (i) on the grounds that the conditions justifying the increase are not fulfilled, and (ii) that the work has not been carried out.

(i) *That the conditions are not fulfilled.* On the service of a notice of increase, or at any subsequent time, the tenant may apply to the local authority for a certificate that either or both the conditions justifying an increase in rent are not fulfilled (s. 18 *ibid.*). There is no time limit within which the tenant must make this application. If the local authority are satisfied that the dwelling-house fails to fulfil either or both of the conditions they must issue a certificate, in the prescribed form, to that effect. The local authority must serve a copy of the certificate on the landlord. The certificate is deemed to have been in force from the time when the tenant made his application. The effect of back-dating the certificate is to enable the tenant to recover any payments of repairs increase made since the date of his application; it also has the effect of precluding the tenant from claiming a refund before he has applied for the certificate. A fee of one shilling is payable on making the application and if a certificate is granted the tenant is entitled to deduct the fee from his rent (s. 18 (7) *ibid.*). Any certificate issued by a sanitary authority under the Rent Acts, that a dwelling-house is not in a reasonable state of repair, which was in force immediately before the 30th August 1954, continued to have effect as a certificate of disrepair; and a court order granted before that date, suspending the 40 per cent. permitted increase on grounds of disrepair, remained in force (s. 19 (2) *ibid.*).

In considering whether a dwelling-house is in good and tenantable repair for the purpose of an application for the granting or the revocation of a certificate of disrepair, or the revocation of a certificate as to service of a Housing Act notice (see below), a local authority cannot disregard any defect due to any act, neglect or default by the tenant or sub-tenant or to any breach by them of an express agreement. If the dwelling-house is part of a building it will not be regarded by the authority as being in good and tenantable repair unless every part of the building which the tenant requires to use (e.g. a common entrance or staircase) in connection with his occupation of the dwelling-house is also in good and tenantable repair (s. 24 *ibid.*). If the local authority refuse to grant a certificate of disrepair the tenant has no direct right of appeal but if he is of the opinion that it ought to have been issued he is not without remedy. If, in any proceedings for the recovery of a repairs increase, the tenant satisfies the court that during the period in respect of which the proceedings are brought either or both the conditions justifying an increase of rent were not fulfilled then, in respect of that period, no sum is recoverable by way of repairs increase (s. 18 (5) *ibid.*).

Where a local authority have served a notice under Section 7 of the Housing (Scotland) Act, 1950, requiring the execution of works on a dwelling-house in respect of which a notice of increase has been served they must serve on the landlord and the tenant a copy of a certificate that they have issued their notice under the said Section 7. That certificate—which operates as a certificate of disrepair—comes into force as from the date when the copy is served on the landlord (s. 18 (2) / 1954 Act).

When a copy of a certificate of disrepair which has been granted, or a copy certificate as to service of a notice under Section 7 of the Act of 1950, has been served on the landlord no sum is recoverable by way of repairs increase during the period in which either certificate is in force.

A landlord can apply to the local authority for the revocation of either type of certificate when he has carried out the necessary works required to fulfil both of the conditions justifying an increase of rent. A fee of one shilling is payable on making the application. Whether or not the local authority grant the application they must give the landlord notice of their decision (s. 18 (4) *ibid.*).

If a landlord is aggrieved—

(a) by the granting of a certificate of disrepair, or

(b) by the refusal of a local authority to revoke such a certificate or a certificate as to service of a notice under Section 7 of the Housing (Scotland) Act, 1950,

he may appeal to the sheriff within twenty-one days after the date of the service on him of the copy certificate of disrepair or of the notice of the decision refusing to revoke a certificate. If the sheriff is satisfied that, at the time the certificate was granted or, as the case may be, the local authority refused to revoke a certificate, the conditions justifying an increase of rent were fulfilled, he must revoke the certificate. In that case the certificate of disrepair is deemed never to have been in force or, as the case may be, such certificate or the certificate as to service of the Housing Act notice is deemed to have been revoked on the date on which the local authority refused to revoke it (s. 18 (6) *ibid.*).

(ii) *That the work of repair has not been carried out.* Within twenty-eight days after service of the notice of increase the tenant may apply to the sheriff court to determine whether work, to a value of not less than that required, has been carried out on the dwelling-house during the period specified in the landlord's declaration, and whether the value of the work done satisfies the provisions of the Act (para. 4, First Schedule / 1954 Act). If the sheriff is not satisfied that the work has been so carried out and that the value is at least the amount required he must issue a certificate to that effect, and thereupon the notice of increase is deemed always to have been of no effect. It is on an appeal of this nature that the landlord can be required to produce satisfactory evidence that the work has been carried out to the value stated (para. 5, *ibid.*). Any such application is conducted and disposed of under small debt procedure (s. 41 *ibid.*). In considering an application the sheriff may determine the extent of the landlord's responsibility for repairs and his determination is final.

(8) *Certificates of repair required for dwellings with structural defects*

Before serving a notice of increase in respect of certain classes of dwelling-houses which are defective a landlord must comply with the following additional requirements—

(i) he must obtain from the local authority a certificate of repair that the dwelling-house fulfils both the conditions justifying an increase in rent;

(ii) he must agree in writing with the tenant, or obtain a determination from the sheriff, that work to the proper value has been carried out during the specified period.

A certificate of repair has the effect of revoking any certificate of disrepair and any order of the court under the Rent Acts suspending the permitted increases on "old control" houses.

If the local authority refuse to grant a certificate of repair they must serve on the landlord and the tenant a copy of a certificate to that effect. That certificate has the effect of a certificate of disrepair. In that case the landlord has a right of appeal, within twenty-one days, to the sheriff. If the sheriff revokes the certificate issued by the local authority, they must forthwith issue a certificate of repair (Second Schedule *ibid.*).

The classes of dwelling-houses to which these special provisions apply are (s. 20 *ibid.*)—

(a) a dwelling-house in respect of which there was in force or operative at any time during the period between the 13th November 1953, and the 30th August 1954,

(i) a certificate of the sanitary authority under the Rent Acts that the dwelling-house was not in a reasonable state of repair, or

(ii) an order of the court under the Rent Acts suspending the 40 per cent. increase in respect of "old control" houses payable under the Act of 1920, or

(iii) a notice under Section 7 of the Housing (Scotland) Act, 1950, requiring the execution of works;

(b) a dwelling-house in respect of which an intimation under Section 19 or a notice under Section 20 of the Public Health (Scotland) Act, 1897, had been served on the owner between the 13th November 1953 and the 30th August 1954, concerning a nuisance arising from any want or defect of a structural character, or where the notice had been served, but not complied with, before the 13th November 1953. A nuisance which is not within the dwelling-house itself but which affects it, or the building which contains it, in such a way that an intimation or notice was served on the owner, is sufficient for the purpose of the restrictions.

(9) *1957 Act increase test of fitness applies to repairs increase*

Any certificate of a local authority (including a certificate of a sanitary authority having the same effect), or any notice served by them revoking such a certificate, and any finding or order of the sheriff, for the purpose of establishing whether either or both of the conditions justifying a 1957 Act increase have been fulfilled (p. 143), have effect for the purpose of establishing whether the landlord is entitled to claim a repairs increase (s. 8 (3) / 1957 Act).

(10) *Repairs increase not payable twice over*

Where a tenant is by virtue of any agreement (however expressed) affecting a controlled tenancy under an obligation to pay a repairs increase then, without prejudice to the recovery from him of any such increase under the procedure of the Act of 1954, he is relieved from the obligation under the agreement (s. 22 / 1954 Act).

(11) *Repairs increase payable by sub-tenants*

If a tenant, who is responsible for the payment of a repairs increase, has sub-let the whole or part of the dwelling-house he can pass on the increase, or part of it, to his sub-tenant, provided the sub-tenant is holding under a controlled tenancy or is a statutory tenant (s. 21 *ibid.*). This provision does not apply, for example, to a sub-tenant of a furnished letting.

Where the whole of the dwelling-house on which the repairs increase has been claimed has been sub-let, the tenant may increase the sub-tenant's rent by the total amount claimed. But if the tenant has sub-let part only of the dwelling-house on which the increase is claimed by the landlord, only a just proportion of the increase may be recovered from the sub-tenant. In any such case the proportion may be settled by written agreement between the tenant and the sub-tenant or by the sheriff court on the application of either party. The sheriff's decision is final.

The right to pass on a repairs increase to a sub-tenant does not prejudice a tenant's right, as immediate landlord of the sub-tenant, to claim a repairs increase for any repairs which he (the tenant) may be under an express liability to carry out. If the tenant is liable to do part of the repairs he is entitled to claim in his own right a repairs increase from the sub-tenant, provided the property has been put into good and tenantable repair and is not in any other respect unfit for human habitation; and that during the specified period work to the required value had been carried out.

The combined effect of being able to pass on a repairs increase to a sub-tenant and of being able to claim direct from him would result, in some cases, in the limits of the Act of 1954 being over-reached. The sub-tenant, however, is protected against any such result by a provision which limits the total amount which may be recoverable from him to not more than two-fifths of the recoverable rent payable in respect of the sub-tenant's premises immediately before the 30th August 1954 (p. 146) or, as amended by the Act of 1957, one-half of that rent.

A sub-tenant has the same right as a tenant to challenge a notice of increase by applying to the local authority for a certificate of disrepair. The tenant (as landlord of the sub-tenant), after executing the necessary work, can apply to the local authority for revocation of the certificate of disrepair; and appeal to the court that the certificate ought not to have been issued or that it or a certificate as to service of a Housing Act notice ought to be revoked (p. 138). A sub-tenant cannot challenge in the court the head landlord's declaration of expenditure made in connection with the repairs increase which has been passed on to him (sub-para. (7) (ii) *ante*); nor can he force the tenant to challenge it. But in addition to claiming that the tenant is charging more than a just proportion of the repairs increase the sub-tenant can refuse to pay the increase on the ground that it is not justified (p. 137).

A tenant, on whom a notice of increase has been served, cannot pass on to a sub-tenant all or any of the repairs increase demanded from him unless he has served on the sub-tenant or a former sub-tenant a notice in the prescribed form of an intention to increase the sub-tenant's rent. The tenant must give the sub-tenant at least four clear weeks' notice before passing on any repairs increase which, in any case, is not recoverable before the date on which the tenant's liability begins to run under the notice of increase served on him by his landlord.

(12) *Additional amount of repairs increase payable by sub-tenants*

Where the tenant has passed on to the sub-tenant the whole or part of a repairs increase claimed by the landlord under the Act of 1954, or has claimed the increase in his (the tenant's) own right from the sub-tenant, at least eight clear weeks' notice of the increased amount recoverable under the Act of 1957 (p. 134) must be given to the sub-tenant. If the tenant's notice passes on the whole or part of the additional increase claimed by the landlord the recovery of that amount from the sub-tenant cannot begin earlier than the date on which the increase begins to be recoverable from the tenant (s. 9 (2) / 1957 Act).

(13) *Sub-sub-tenancies*

The provisions in sub-paragraphs (11) and (12) above apply to sub-sub-tenants as they apply to sub-tenants.

(14) *Tenancies on which the repairs increase may not be imposed*

The repairs increase may not be claimed in any of the following cases (s. 16 (3) / 1954 Act):

    (*a*) if the standard rent of the dwelling-house is

        (i) the rent at which it was first let after the 1st September 1939; or

        (ii) an amount ascertainable by apportionment of such rent (whether or not the apportionment has been made); or

    (*b*) if the maximum rent of the dwelling-house has been fixed under Section 113 of the Housing (Scotland) Act, 1950, in consequence of the payment of an improvement grant; or

(c) if the standard rent of the dwelling-house has been fixed by a local authority in consequence of the premises ceasing to belong to an exempted authority (p. 111); or

(d) if a local authority have fixed the rent of a dwelling-house in respect of which assistance has been given under Section 3 of the Housing (Scotland) Act, 1952.

The effect of provision (a) above is that a repairs increase is not limited to "old control" houses; it can be claimed on a "new control" house provided it was let on or before the 1st September 1939.

4. 1957 Act increase

The landlord of a dwelling-house, which is subject to a controlled tenancy, who is not able to produce evidence of past expenditure on repairs in order to qualify for a repairs increase under the Act of 1954 may claim an increase at a lower rate than the repairs increase if the conditions—other than the expenditure test—which relate to that increase have been fulfilled.

(1) The conditions justifying the 1957 Act increase

Section 7 of the Act of 1957 provides that the increase—which is called the "1957 Act increase"—can be claimed by a landlord who is responsible for repairs (p. 130) if and so long as the following conditions in the Act of 1954 (known as "the conditions justifying an increase of rent") are fulfilled—

(i) that the dwelling-house is in good and tenantable repair (p. 132); and

(ii) that it is not in any other respect unfit for human habitation (p. 132).

Thus, the landlord does not have to prove that he has actually incurred expenditure on work on the dwelling before claiming the increase (cf. para. 3 (1) ante).

This increase is additional to the permitted increases of 15 per cent. and 25 per cent. (p. 123) but it cannot be claimed where a repairs increase is recoverable. On the other hand, it may be claimed notwithstanding anything in the terms of the tenancy or any enactment.

(2) Amount of 1957 Act increase

The amount of the 1957 Act increase is an amount equal to one-quarter of the rent recoverable in respect of the dwelling-house immediately before the 30th August 1954 (s. 7 (2) ibid.). The in-

crease cannot be more nor less than the fraction of one-quarter
where the landlord is responsible for all repairs but it must be
reduced proportionately where the tenant is under express liability
to carry out any repairs (see para. 1 *ante*).

As to the meaning of "rent recoverable" for the purpose of fixing
the 1957 Act increase see page 146.

(3) *Other repairs increase conditions applying to 1957 Act increase*

The following conditions which apply in making a claim for a
repairs increase are applied with certain modifications to the 1957
Act increase (s. 8 (1) *ibid.*).

(*a*) *Notice of increase and declarations:* Before a landlord can recover
a 1957 Act increase he must have served on the tenant, or a former
tenant, eight clear weeks' notice of increase containing a declaration
that at the date of service of the notice the dwelling-house was not
subject to statutory action by the local authority and that the
conditions justifying an increase of rent were fulfilled (p. 133).

(*b*) *Tenant's right to challenge notice:* At any time after service of
notice of increase the tenant can apply to the local authority for a
certificate of disrepair on the grounds that either or both of the
conditions justifying an increase of rent are not fulfilled (p. 137). If
the certificate is issued it operates from the time the tenant made his
application and he can recover any payments of the increase made
since that date. A fee of one shilling is payable to the local authority
when he applies for the certificate and if it is granted he can deduct
the amount of the fee from his rent. If the local authority refuse to
grant a certificate the tenant can challenge the landlord by refusing
to pay the increase. Where the local authority serve a Housing Act
notice to do repairs they must serve a copy of a certificate to that
effect on the landlord and the tenant. The certificate operates as a
certificate of disrepair (p. 138).

When the landlord has carried out the necessary works he can
apply to the local authority for the revocation of the certificate of
disrepair or of service of the Housing Act notice. A fee of one shilling
is payable on making the application. The same test of fitness applies
as in the case of a repairs increase.

Within twenty-one days after the granting of a certificate of
disrepair or the refusal to revoke such a certificate or a certificate in
regard to service of a Housing Act notice the landlord can appeal to
the sheriff. If the appeal is successful the certificate is deemed never
to have been in force or, as the case may be, revoked when application was made to the local authority.

(c) *Certificates of repair for sub-standard property:* Before a landlord can serve a notice of increase in respect of the classes of dwelling-houses set out in paragraph 3 (8) (p. 139) he must obtain a certificate of repair from the local authority as in the case of a claim being made for a repairs increase. In the case of the 1957 Act, however, the landlord does not have to agree with the tenant, or obtain a determination from the sheriff, that work to a specified value has been carried out.

(d) *Repairs increase test of fitness applies to 1957 Act increase:* Any certificate of a local authority (including a certificate of a sanitary authority having the same effect), or any notice served by them revoking such a certificate, and any finding or order of the sheriff in connection with a repairs increase or the Rent Acts, for the purpose of establishing whether either or both of the conditions justifying a repairs increase have been fulfilled, have effect for the purpose of establishing whether a landlord is entitled to claim a 1957 Act increase (s. 8 (3) / 1957 Act).

(e) *1957 Act increase not payable twice over:* Where a tenant is by virtue of any agreement (however expressed) affecting a controlled tenancy under an obligation to pay the 1957 Act increase then, without prejudice to the recovery from him of any such increase under the Act, he is relieved from the obligation under the agreement.

(f) *Passing on 1957 Act increase to sub-tenants:* A tenant can pass on to a sub-tenant the 1957 Act increase in the same way as a repairs increase. The sub-tenant has the same rights of appeal; he is protected against over-payment and can challenge the notice of increase on grounds of disrepair as in the case of the repairs increase.

(g) *Tenancies on which the 1957 Act increase may not be imposed:* The 1957 Act increase cannot be claimed in any of the cases where a repairs increase may not be imposed (p. 142) (s. 7 (3) (a) / 1957 Act).

5. Interchange between repairs increase and 1957 Act increase

A landlord cannot claim a repairs increase and a 1957 Act increase at the same time; but he can change from one to the other, provided he gives at least four months' notice. This provision enables a landlord to qualify for a repairs increase on proof of work done to the required value after he has been in receipt of the 1957 Act increase. A notice of intention to increase the rent by way of repairs increase cannot be served at any time within four months after a notice of

L

intention to increase rent by way of the 1957 Act increase (s. 9 (5) /
1957 Act); a notice of intention to increase rent by way of a 1957 Act
increase cannot be served at any time within four months after a
notice of intention to increase rent by way of a repairs increase
(Third Schedule, *ibid.*).

6. Meaning of "recoverable rent immediately before the 30th August 1954"

In calculating the recoverable rent immediately before the 30th
August 1954, for the purpose of fixing the repairs increase or the 1957
Act increase, in respect of a tenancy or sub-tenancy of a dwelling-
house—

(*a*) it is to be assumed that, even if any part of the rent was suspended at that time on the ground that the dwelling was
not in all respects reasonably fit for human habitation or
otherwise in a reasonable state of repair, the full rent of the
dwelling was recoverable;

(*b*) from that amount must be deducted:

(i) the amount of any occupiers' rates; and

(ii) any payment in respect of services or the use of
furniture

included in the rent (s. 39 (3) / 1954 Act).

Thus, the amount of rent obtained by these calculations may differ
from the actual amount of rent paid by the tenant or sub-tenant.

Any question arising as to the amount of recoverable rent must be
settled by agreement in writing between the parties concerned or, on
the application of either of them, by the sheriff.

7. Valuation and rating of houses subject to repairs increase

The Act of 1954 provides (s. 35) that no rates are payable on a
repairs increase. For this purpose the net annual value and the
rateable value of any dwelling-house in respect of which a repairs
increase is recoverable is the gross annual value thereof after
deducting such part of the rent as is equal to the amount of the
repairs increase.

For the purpose of identifying a dwelling-house in respect of
which a repairs increase is recoverable the letters "R.I." appear in
brackets in the column headed "Description" in the Valuation Roll
immediately after the description of the subject to which it relates
(The Valuation Roll (Scotland) Regulations, 1954—S.I. No. 1575

(s. 175)). Any question which cannot be settled by agreement as to whether a dwelling-house is one in respect of which a repairs increase is recoverable must be determined by the sheriff on the application of the owner, the tenant, the assessor under the Valuation Acts or the rating authority (s. 36 / 1954 Act).

These provisions are to be repealed on the 16th May 1961, when the new system of valuation for rating comes into effect (Seventh Schedule, Valuation and Rating (Scotland) Act, 1956).

CHAPTER XII
Mortgages

1. General

THE Rent Acts impose restrictions on the right to call in a mortgage and as to the amount of mortgage interest which may be charged in respect of mortgaged property which consists of or comprises one or more dwelling-houses which are controlled by the Acts (s. 1 / 1920 Act: First Schedule / 1939 Act). The restrictions apply to mortgages on residential property let on long tenancies when the tenancies become subject to the provisions of the Rent Acts by virtue of the Landlord and Tenant Act, 1954 (s. 6); and to mortgages on leasehold interests of residential property held under exempted authorities (Fourth Schedule / 1954 English Act: Third Schedule / 1954 Scottish Act).

In the application of the Acts to Scotland "mortgage" means a heritable security, including a security constituted by absolute disposition qualified by back bond or letter (s. 18 (1) / 1920 Act).

2. Mortgages excluded from the Acts

The following mortgages are excluded from the Acts (s. 12 (4) *ibid.*):

(*a*) any mortgage of premises comprising both controlled property and uncontrolled property if the rateable value of the controlled property is less than one-tenth of the rateable value of the whole of the property comprised in the mortgage;

(*b*) an equitable charge by deposit of title deeds or otherwise;

(*c*) any mortgage which was created after the 2nd July 1920 on "old control" property;

(*d*) mortgages on dwelling-houses let for a term of twenty-one years or less at a rent of less than two-thirds of the rateable value (s 12 (7) *ibid.*).

3. Decontrol under the 1957 Act

The provisions in the Act of 1957 which provide for the decontrol of dwelling-houses apply equally to release from control of mortgages on those houses. Thus a mortgage entered into on or after the

6th July 1957 in respect of a dwelling-house which on the 7th
November 1956 had a rateable value exceeding—

   (i) £40 in the Metropolitan Police District or the City of
        London;

  (ii) £30 elsewhere in England and Wales;

 (iii) £40 in Scotland

is not controlled.

As and when other dwelling-houses are released from control by
Ministerial order a mortgage entered into after the time of decontrol
in respect of such houses will not be controlled.

4. Protection for mortgagors of decontrolled mortgages

Where any mortgaged property becomes decontrolled the Rent
Acts continue to apply to the mortgage for fifteen months after the
time of decontrol (para. 12, Fourth Schedule / 1957 Act).

In any case of future decontrol by Ministerial order the period of
fifteen months may be shortened to a period of not less than six
months (para. 13 *ibid.*).

5. Splitting a mortgage on controlled and
uncontrolled property

If the mortgaged property consists of controlled property and
uncontrolled property and the rateable value of the controlled
property is more than one-tenth of the rateable value of the whole
of the mortgaged property, or a question arises as to whether the
Rent Acts continue to apply to a mortgage by reason of decontrol,
the mortgagee may apportion the principal money secured by
the mortgage between the controlled and uncontrolled property
(s. 12 (5) / 1920 Act: para. 12, Fourth Schedule / 1957 Act). To do
this the mortgagee must give one calendar month's notice in writing
to the mortgagor in which must be stated the particulars of the
apportionment. Before the notice expires the mortgagor is entitled
to dispute the amounts of the apportionment and, in default of
agreement, the matter must be determined by a single arbitrator
appointed by the President of the Royal Institution of Chartered
Surveyors. Except in the case of property decontrolled under the
Act of 1957, the Rent Acts cease to apply to the mortgage, at the
expiration of the calendar month's notice, in so far as it relates to
the uncontrolled property, and the mortgage then operates as two
mortgages.

6. Permitted rates of interest

(1) *Standard rates of interest*

The rate of interest on a mortgage of a controlled house must not exceed, by more than the amount permitted, the standard rate laid down by the Acts. The "standard rate" means:

(a) for a mortgage in force on the 3rd August 1914 on "old control" property, the rate of interest payable on that date or, if the mortgage has been created since that date, the original rate of interest (s. 12 (1) (b) / 1920 Act);

(b) for a mortgage in force on the 1st September 1939 on "new control" property, the rate of interest payable on that date or, if the mortgage has been created since that date, the original rate of interest (First Schedule / 1939 Act);

(c) for a mortgage in force on the 8th February 1952 of a leasehold interest held from the Crown, the rate of interest payable on that date or, if the mortgage has been created since that date, the original rate of interest (Crown Lessees (Protection of Sub-Tenants) Act, 1952);

(d) for a mortgage in force at the date of termination of a long tenancy of residential property, the rate of interest payable on that date or, if the mortgage has been created since that date, the original rate of interest (s. 6, Landlord and Tenant Act, 1954); and

(e) for a mortgage on a leasehold interest of residential property held under an exempted authority, where the mortgage was in force on the 11th November 1953, or between that date and the 30th August 1954, the rate of interest payable on the respective dates (Fourth Schedule / 1954 English Act: Third Schedule / 1954 Scottish Act).

Under these provisions the rate of interest on second and subsequent mortgages is not limited to the rate permitted for the first or other former mortgage.

(2) *Permitted increase in rate of mortgage interest*

In the case of a mortgage on "old control" property, the standard rate of interest may be exceeded by not more than 1 per cent. per annum, provided the rate does not exceed $6\frac{1}{2}$ per cent. per annum (s. 4 / 1920 Act).

No increase is permitted in the standard rate of interest on mortgages on "new control" property, or on a leasehold interest held from the Crown, or on residential property let on a long tenancy after the termination of the tenancy, or on a leasehold interest of residential property held under an exempted authority.

(3) *Recovery of overpayments*

If a mortgagor has been overcharged he can only recover the excess interest paid within two years from the date of payment (s. 14 (1) / 1920 Act: s. 7 (6) / 1938 Act).

7. Restriction on the calling in of mortgages

It is unlawful for any mortgagee under a mortgage of controlled property to call in his mortgage or to take any steps for exercising any right of foreclosure or sale, or for otherwise enforcing his security or for recovering the principal money thereby secured, so long as—

(a) interest at the permitted rate is paid and is not more than twenty-one days in arrear; and

(b) the covenants by the mortgagor (other than the covenant for the repayment of the principal money secured) are performed and observed; and

(c) the mortgagor keeps the property in a proper state of repair and pays all interest and instalments of principal recoverable under any prior incumbrance (s. 7 / 1920 Act).

This restriction does not apply—

(i) to a mortgage where the principal moneys secured are repayable by instalments extending over a period of not less than ten years from the creation of the mortgage; or

(ii) to affect any power of sale exerciseable by a mortgagee in possession on the 25th March 1920 in the case of "old control" property; or on the 1st September 1939 in the case of "new control" property; or on the 8th February 1952 in the case of a leasehold interest held from the Crown; or, in the case of residential property let on a long tenancy, at the date of termination of the long tenancy; in the case of a leasehold interest of residential property held under an exempted authority, on the 11th November 1953 (if the mortgage was then in force), or between that date and the 30th August 1954; or

(iii) to cases where the mortgagor consents to the exercise by the mortgagee of the powers conferred by the mortgage; or

(iv) if the property mortgaged is a leasehold interest, the mortgagee satisfies the county court or the sheriff court, as the case may be, that his security is seriously diminishing in value or is otherwise in jeopardy, and for that reason it is reasonable that the mortgage should be called in and enforced. In any such circumstances the court may by order authorise the mortgagee to call in and enforce the mortgage. Any such order may be made subject to a condition that it shall not take effect if, within a prescribed time, the mortgagor pays to the mortgagee such portion of the principal sum secured as corresponds to the diminution of the security.

CHAPTER XIII

Protection of Reserve and Auxiliary Forces

THE Reserve and Auxiliary Forces (Protection of Civil Interests) Act, 1951, provides for the protection of civil interests of persons (men and women) called up or volunteering for certain naval, military or air force service, or doing work or training under the National Service Act, 1948, by virtue of being conditionally registered under that Act as conscientious objectors. The Act includes provision for the protection against insecurity of tenure of the person's place of residence, whether furnished or unfurnished. Regular service men and women are outside the scope of the Act.

1. Service protected by the Act

The following forms of service are regarded as "relevant service" for the purposes of securing protection under the Act:

(1) (i) Service in pursuance of any notice or directions given under any enactment which provides for the calling out on permanent service, or the calling into actual service, or the embodiment, of any reserve or auxiliary force, or members thereof, or for the recall of service pensioners within the meaning of the Reinstatement in Civil Employment Act, 1950.

(ii) Service, other than for the purposes of training only, in pursuance of any obligation or undertaking, whether legally enforceable or not, to serve when called upon as a commissioned officer, not being an obligation or undertaking to accept a permanent or short-service commission.

(iii) Service in pursuance of any directions given under subsection (5) of Section 3, subsection (5) of Section 4, subsection (3) of Section 5, or subsection (3) of Section 6, of the Armed Forces (Conditions of Service) Act, 1939, or subsection (2) of Section 1 of the Naval and Marine Forces (Temporary Release from Service) Act, 1940 (as amended by the Naval Forces (Extension of Service) Act, 1944).

(iv) Service in pursuance of any enlistment for a period not exceeding eighteen months with a view to service in the Korean operations continuing at the passing of the Act or in other operations designated for the purposes of this sub-paragraph by Her Majesty by Order in Council.

(v) Service, other than for the purposes of training only, in response to any notice or request made or given by the competent naval, military or air force authority, to members of any reserve of the Women's Royal Naval Service, members of Queen Alexandra's Royal Naval Nursing Service Reserve or the Naval Voluntary Aid Detachment Reserve, persons who have served in the Auxiliary Territorial Service, members of the Princess Mary's Royal Air Force Nursing Service Reserve, or persons who have served in the Women's Auxiliary Air Force, whether or not there is any legal obligation to comply with the notice or request.

(vi) In the case of a person who, during his whole-time service under Part I of the National Service Act, 1948, has accepted a commission in any of the armed forces of the Crown under arrangements made by the competent naval, military or air force authority for treating commissioned service as equivalent to whole-time service under Part I of that Act, his service as a commissioned officer under those arrangements.

(vii) In the case of a person who, being liable under Part I of the National Service Act, 1948, to be called up for whole-time service, has accepted a commission in any of the armed forces of the Crown under any such arrangements as are mentioned in sub-paragraph (vi) of this paragraph and has served whole-time as a commissioned officer under those arrangements without having been called up under the said Part I, his service as a commissioned officer in the circumstances mentioned in this sub-paragraph.

(viii) In the case of a person serving whole-time as a commissioned officer under any such arrangements as aforesaid who has undertaken, with a view to service in such operations as are mentioned in sub-paragraph (iv) of this paragraph, to serve whole-time as a commissioned officer for a further period not exceeding twelve months immediately after the time when his service under the said arrangements would have ended, any further period of such service in pursuance of that undertaking.

(2) Service in consequence of being called up under Section 1 of the Reserve and Auxiliary Forces (Training) Act, 1951.

(3) Service of any of the descriptions specified in paragraphs 3, 4 and 5 of the table set out in subsection (1) of Section 1 of the Reserve and Auxiliary Forces (Training) Act, 1951, entered on by a person of any of the descriptions specified in those paragraphs as a volunteer.

(4) Service for a period of eighteen months for which an officer of any reserve force of the Royal Navy or of the Royal Marines, or an officer of reserve to, or on the retired or emergency list of, or holding a temporary commission in, the Royal Navy or the Royal Marines, volunteers.

(5) The following compulsory national service, that is to say—

(a) whole-time service undertaken by virtue of an enlistment notice served under Part I of the National Service Act, 1948; or

(b) work or training in pursuance of an order made or direction given under the said Part I as respects a conditional registered conscientious objector.

(6) The following compulsory national service, that is to say, service undertaken by virtue of a training notice served under Part I of the National Service Act, 1948.

(7) Service, for the purposes of training only, for a continuous period of seven days or longer performed, whether under an obligation or under voluntary arrangements, by—

(a) an officer or man of any reserve force of the Royal Navy or of the Royal Marines, or an officer of reserve to, or on the retired or emergency list of, or holding a temporary commission in, the Royal Navy or the Royal Marines;

(b) an officer of any army reserve of officers, a man of any army reserve force, an officer or man of the Territorial Army, or an officer of the Territorial Army Reserve of Officers;

(c) an officer of the Royal Air Force Volunteer Reserve or of any air force reserve of officers or on the retired list of the Royal Air Force, a man of any air force reserve force, or an officer

or man of the Royal Auxiliary Air Force or the Royal
Auxiliary Air Force Reserve;

(d) a member of any reserve of the Women's Royal Naval Service
or a member of the Naval Voluntary Aid Detachment
Reserve,

not being service of a description specified in any of the preceding
paragraphs of this Schedule.

2. Protection against insecurity of tenure of place of residence

The following provisions apply as to protection during service
(other than a short period of training), and for four months thereafter, for giving security of tenure of premises which at any time
during the period of protection are the rented family residence of a
service man. The protection does not apply to on-licensed premises
or to premises bona fide let at a rent which includes payments in
respect of board (s. 14 / 1951 Act).

(1) *Furnished lettings and shared accommodation*

If the rented family residence is a furnished letting or an unfurnished letting where the tenant has exclusive occupation of some
accommodation together with the use of other accommodation in
common with the landlord or with the landlord and other persons
and the landlord serves notice to quit, an application may be made
to the rent tribunal for security of tenure (p. 171) without any
application being made for a determination of rent (s. 15 *ibid*.).

This right to claim protection is not affected by the provisions
for the decontrol of furnished lettings in the Act of 1957 (s. 12 (3) /
1957 Act).

(2) *Extension of Rent Acts protection*

If the service man occupies any of the following premises—which
are not controlled premises—he is given the protection of the Rent
Acts during his period of service if his tenancy is terminated (s. 16 /
1951 Act):

(a) property with a rateable value which is outside the limits of
the Rent Acts;

(b) houses belonging to local authorities, development corpora-
tions, housing associations and trusts, and National Health
Service Executive Councils in Scotland (s. 33 (4) / 1954
English Act: s. 25 (4) / 1954 Scottish Act);

(c) houses decontrolled under the Act of 1957 where the tenant is not entitled to retain possession after the time of decontrol (paras. 25 and 33, Sixth Schedule / 1957 Act);

(d) houses erected or converted after the 29th August 1954 (s. 35 (3) / 1954 English Act: s. 27 (3) / 1954 Scottish Act);

(e) houses let with more than two acres of land;

(f) premises let at a rent which is less than two-thirds of the rateable value of the property; or

(g) premises under a tenancy which qualifies for protection as a long tenancy under the Landlord and Tenant Act, 1954 (para. 25, Sixth Schedule / 1957 Act).

If, in any of the above cases, the tenant shares accommodation with persons other than the landlord as well as occupying separate accommodation, the Rent Acts apply to the separate accommodation (s. 17 / 1951 Act). The Acts are applied also in the case where the service man is occupying premises under licence in consequence of his employment or under a rent-free letting (s. 18 *ibid.*).

The protection of the Rent Acts lasts only during the service man's period of service and for four months thereafter; and the property is protected—subject to appropriate modifications—to the same extent as premises which are subject to "new control" under the Act of 1939.

(3) *Rent limits*

Under the Act of 1957 the rent may be increased to the rent limits allowed by the Act (p. 20). But if the rent payable under the tenancy which was terminated or came to an end was greater than that rent limit the higher rent is the rent limit.

This higher rent is subject to adjustment for rates (p. 29), services and furniture (p. 32) and for improvements (p. 33) completed after the beginning of the statutory tenancy; and to a reduction in case of disrepair (p. 58). The landlord and tenant may agree to the payment of a lower rent than the rent limit and where this is done it cannot be increased except by agreement in writing between the parties (para. 6, Sixth Schedule / 1957 Act).

(4) *Unfurnished dwellings subject to decontrol*

The provisions for the decontrol of unfurnished lettings in the Act of 1957 do not affect any statutory tenancy created under the Act of 1951 which was existing on the 6th July 1957, or on the date specified in any subsequent Ministerial order for further decontrol (paras. 25 and 33 *ibid.*).

If the rented family residence becomes subject to decontrol the date in the landlord's notice to the tenant to give up possession of the premises cannot be earlier than fifteen months after the end of the period of residence protection (para. 2 (4), Fourth Schedule, *ibid.*). The period of fifteen months may be shortened in a subsequent Ministerial order for further decontrol to a period not less than six months (para. 13 *ibid.*).

(5) *Protection against ejectment for breach of obligation*

Where the civil employment of a service man constitutes an obligation of his tenancy, and the performance of his service (including any short period of training) prevents his carrying out those duties, he is not regarded as being in breach of his civil obligations because of his service commitments. The landlord cannot treat such acts of non-performance as a ground for recovery of possession of the premises under paragraph (*a*) of the First Schedule to the Act of 1933 (p. 80); nor can he apply for an order for possession, under paragraph (*g*) of the Schedule, on the ground that the property is required for another employee (s. 20 / 1951 Act).

(6) *Facilities for the representation of men serving abroad*

The court or rent tribunal may allow any fit and proper person to act on behalf of a service man who is serving abroad (s. 22 *ibid.*).

3. Protection during short period of training

Where a service man, who has been living with dependents in premises in right of a tenancy or licence (or, in Scotland, a right or permission otherwise than under a lease) granted in consequence of his employment, performs a short period of training, the leave of the court must be obtained during that period and for fourteen days thereafter to proceed—

(*a*) with the execution or other enforcement of any judgment or order made against any of them for the recovery of possession of any part of the premises in which they are living; or

(*b*) with any right to take possession or re-enter on any part of the premises (s. 25 *ibid.*).

CHAPTER XIV

Dwellings Controlled on De-requisitioning

THE Requisitioned Houses and Housing (Amendment) Act, 1955, which came into force on the 6th June 1955, provides for the winding-up of requisitioning land for housing purposes under Defence Regulation 51.

1. Termination of further requisitioning for housing

Section 14 of the Act ended the power of the Minister of Housing and Local Government and of the Secretary of State for Scotland to requisition premises for general housing purposes.

2. Transfer for limited period of existing requisitioned houses in England and Wales to local authorities

The possession of houses in England and Wales already requisitioned has been transferred from the Minister to local authorities, who have the right to use them for housing purposes up to the 31st March 1960, but no longer.

Any agreement made in respect of a requisitioned house on behalf of the Minister remains in force and continues as if made on behalf of the local authority. Such agreements may have provided for the payment of rental compensation on a different basis to that prescribed by the Compensation (Defence) Act, 1939; or for the use of a lift or hot water service for the benefit of a flat requisitioned in a block of flats; or for giving access to requisitioned premises. The local authority may continue to use the requisitioned premises for housing even if it is contrary to any covenant or easement affecting the house, such as sub-dividing into flats (s. 1 / 1955 Act).

The enactments relating to requisitioned houses continue to apply to such houses transferred to local authorities with the substitution of the local authority for the Minister. This provision applies in particular to the payment of compensation. It makes local authorities primarily responsible under the Compensation (Defence) Act, 1939, for the payment of rental compensation and terminal compensation to owners of requisitioned houses; although claims for terminal compensation are still settled by the district valuer. If

requisitioned houses, which are transferred to local authorities, are
compulsorily acquired the provisions in Part VIII of the Requisitioned Land and War Works Act, 1945, will continue to apply in
settling compensation payable on acquisition (s. 2 *ibid.*).

3. Requisitioned sites and camps

Other properties, such as camp sites and temporary huts, held
under requisitioning powers by the Minister are not covered by the
Act (s. 18 (1) *ibid.*).

4. Scotland

Requisitioned houses in Scotland held by the Secretary of State
were not transferred by the Act to local authorities and, apart from
the repeal of the power to requisition premises for general housing
purposes and amendments to Sections 94 and 150 of the Housing
(Scotland) Act, 1950, the Act does not apply to Scotland (s. 20 /
1955 Act).

5. Release of dwellings falling vacant

If no occupier's licence was in force on the 6th June 1955, or the
licence has since been terminated, in respect of a requisitioned
dwelling (whether constituting the whole or part of a house) the
local authority's right to retain possession expired or expires, as the
case may be, at the end of four weeks from the date of such termination (s. 3 (1) *ibid.*).

Within the four-week period the local authority have power to
apply to the Minister for permission to retain possession of the
dwelling. Where an application is made the right to retain possession
is not in any case terminated until the date on which the Minister's
decision is notified to the local authority (s. 3 (2) *ibid.*). The local
authority must not allow any person to enter into occupation of the
dwelling until the Minister's authorisation has been obtained
(s. 3 (5) *ibid.*). Before applying for an authorisation the local
authority must give notice of their intention to do so to the owner
of the dwelling. If within two weeks the owner commences proceedings for possession for his own or a relative's occupation (see
para. 14 *post*) no authorisation is to be given by the Minister until
the conclusion of the proceedings (s. 3 (6) *ibid.*).

(1) *Exceptions to release of vacant dwellings*

The right of a local authority to retain possession of a dwelling is
not terminated, and the Minister's authorisation is not required to

retain the premises, if within the four-week period a fresh licence is granted by the authority—

(a) to the former licensee, on different terms (e.g. with a change in rent);

(b) on the death of the licensee, to a statutory successor of his;

> A "statutory successor" is the widow of the licensee who was residing with him at the time of his death, or where the licensee leaves no such widow or is a woman, such member of the licensee's family who had been living with him for six months immediately before his death. This provision is based on the similar provision in the Rent Acts which provides for transmission of a statutory tenancy on the death of the tenant. It only operates once, so that when the claimant dies the tenancy does not pass to another member of the family (p. 15).

(c) to a new licensee under an exchange agreement with another licensee or tenant of any other dwelling in the possession of or belonging to the local authority (s. 3 (3) *ibid.*).

A local authority does not lose the right to retain possession of premises where the licence has been terminated in order to carry out repairs or because the licensee had not paid his rent if, within three months, they grant a fresh licence to the previous licensee (s. 3 (4) *ibid.*). A new licence cannot be granted to a statutory successor.

(2) *Minister's power to order vacant dwellings to be retained*

The Minister has power to direct a local authority to retain dwellings which fall vacant in order to provide accommodation for occupants who are displaced from houses released for occupation by an owner or his relatives (p. 164), or on the grounds of hardship (para. 14 (2) *post*) (s. 3 (7) *ibid.*).

In order to provide such a pool of accommodation the Minister has issued a general direction in Circular No. 39/55 to retain possession of all requisitioned dwellings which become vacant.

(3) *Release of parts of requisitioned dwellings*

A local authority cannot release a part of requisitioned premises without the owner's consent unless it was a separate dwelling before requisitioning (s. 8 *ibid.*).

M

6. Invitation to owner to accept licensee as statutory tenant

Any local authority may invite the owner of a requisitioned dwelling to accept the licensee as a statutory tenant under the Rent Acts on payment of special compensation. The Minister can direct a local authority to use this power (s. 4 (1) *ibid.*) and, in Circular No. 39/55, has issued directions to local authorities generally to issue invitations to the owners of houses which are not unfit or in the process of being acquired compulsorily.

7. Owner's acceptance of licensee as statutory tenant

If within the period specified in the invitation an owner agrees to accept a licensee as a statutory tenant—

(*a*) the dwelling is released to the owner at the expiration of one week from the day on which the next instalment of rent is payable by the licensee to the local authority;

(*b*) from the date of release the licensee becomes the statutory tenant of the owner.

The Act of 1957 does not disturb this procedure but some statutory tenants or their successors will not be entitled to retain possession after the 31st March 1965 (see para. 13 *post*).

If the owner is prohibited or restricted by covenant or otherwise in the grant of tenancies, such as a landlord's consent to sub-letting, he is not permitted to accept a licensee as tenant in contravention of the prohibition or restriction.

8. Special compensation for accepting tenant

If the licensee is accepted as a statutory tenant the local authority must pay to the landlord the special compensation specified in the invitation. The maximum rate of compensation is five times the annual rental compensation payable during the last year of requisitioning (The Requisitioned Houses (Compensation) Regulations, 1955—S.I. No. 1331). In the case of landlords who are leaseholders under leases with less than twenty-eight years still to run the compensation is scaled down from a maximum of four times the annual rental compensation to one year's rental compensation for the landlord holding under a lease with less than seven years to run.

9. Terms of statutory tenancy

Under the statutory tenancy the landlord is assumed to be responsible for the payment of rates and the provision of any services which were provided for the tenant during requisitioning; and any other terms and conditions of the licence are deemed to have been written into the terms of the tenancy (other than the term as to rent).

10. Original standard rent under the statutory tenancy

The Act (s. 4 (3)), as originally written, fixes the standard rent of the dwelling as the aggregate of—

(a) the annual rate of rental compensation payable immediately before the day on which the notice of invitation was given to the landlord;

(b) the statutory repairs deduction for the dwelling, i.e. the reduction in the gross value of controlled dwellings as shown in the Third Schedule (now repealed) to the Act of 1954 for the purpose of calculating the repairs increase under that Act;

(c) the rates payable for the financial year during which the invitation was given; and

(d) the annual cost of any services provided by the local authority during the time of requisitioning.

That standard rent is deemed to have been fixed by reference to a letting which began immediately before the 1st September 1939. The effect of this provision being that neither the landlord nor the tenant could apply to the rent tribunal for an adjustment of the rent. On the other hand the landlord was able to claim the repairs increase under the Act of 1954, but was expressly precluded from claiming the permitted increases of 15 per cent. and 25 per cent. under the Act of 1920 for accepting responsibility for repairs.

The Act provides that the tenant or his statutory successor should not until the 1st April 1965 pay more in rent than he paid as licensee, except in so far as the local authority may review the rent from time to time. The difference between this amount and the standard rent until that date being paid in arrear at intervals of three months by the local authority to the landlord. This subsidy is paid by the local authority only in respect of the first tenant or his statutory successor.

11. New rent limit under the 1957 Act

The Act of 1957 (s. 22) allows the landlord of a former requisitioned dwelling to claim the rent limits under that Act but until the 1st April 1965 the liability of the tenant is not changed and he will not be required to pay more in rent than he paid as licensee, except as the result of a local authority review of the rent. This rule applies whether or not the dwelling is above the rateable value limits for controlled dwellings. The difference being paid by the local authority until the 1st April 1965, so long as the dwelling is occupied by the first tenant or his statutory successor.

12. Procedure for obtaining new rent limit

Not later than three days after serving a notice of increase in respect of any rental period beginning before the 1st April 1965, the landlord must serve a copy of the notice on the local authority. If the landlord fails to serve the copy notice within that time the notice has no effect (s. 22 (1) (a) *ibid.*).

(1) *Local authority's powers of appeal*

The local authority have the same powers of application to the county court under the Act of 1957 as the tenant (s. 22 (1) (b) *ibid.*).

(2) *Local authority must be party to agreements and proceedings*

The local authority must be a party to any agreement (e.g. as to the provision of services or apportionment of gross value) and to any court proceedings affecting the amount of rent for any rental period beginning before the 1st April 1965 (s. 22 (1) (c) *ibid.*).

13. Decontrol of statutory tenancies of former requisitioned premises

The provisions in the Act of 1957 relating to decontrol are modified in the case of statutory tenancies created under the Act of 1955 (s. 11 (5) *ibid.*). Any licensee who has been accepted as statutory tenant before the 1st April 1965 is protected under the Rent Acts up to that date.

If either the tenant or his statutory successor is in occupation of a decontrolled dwelling he is entitled to remain in possession up to and including the 31st March 1965.

On the other hand, a tenant or his statutory successor of a dwelling which remains within the limits of control at that date can thereafter continue to claim the protection of the Rent Acts.

14. Earlier release of requisitioned premises

Provision is made for the release of requisitioned premises earlier than the 31st March 1960 in the following cases:

(1) *For owner's occupation*

An owner can apply to the county court for possession of a requisitioned dwelling if he requires it for occupation for—

    i) himself or his spouse; or

  (ii) any son or daughter of his over eighteen years of age; or

 (iii) his father or mother,

provided he was not a purchaser for value after the 30th November 1954. If the dwelling is occupied the court will not grant possession if greater hardship would be caused by making the order than by refusing to make it. The onus of proving "greater hardship" is on the licensee (s. 5 / 1955 Act).

(2) *In case of hardship*

The Minister can direct a local authority to release or, at their option, to make an offer to buy requisitioned property if he is satisfied that an owner will suffer severe hardship unless he can obtain vacant possession of his property or is able to dispose of it with vacant possession (s. 6 *ibid.*).

(3) *For improvement works*

An owner can secure release from requisitioning in order to carry out works which qualify for an improvement grant under Section 20 of the Housing Act, 1949, provided he is prepared afterwards to accept as tenant a nominee of the local authority (s. 7 *ibid.*). Any such tenant whose tenancy commences on or after the 6th July 1957 will not be protected by the Rent Acts.

CHAPTER XV

Furnished Lettings

THE main provisions of the Rent Acts have never applied to any dwelling-house bona fide let at a rent which includes payments in respect of board, attendance or use of furniture (s. 12 (2) / 1920 Act: s. 3 (2) / 1939 Act). A house is not regarded as being let furnished or with attendance unless the amount of rent representing the value of the attendance or the use of the furniture to the tenant forms a substantial portion of the whole rent (s. 10 (1) / 1923 Act). Sections 9 and 10 of the Act of 1920, which have been repealed by the Act of 1957, contained provisions for limiting the rent of houses let furnished. The sections proved difficult to enforce in the absence of security of tenure for the tenant and the absence of any power to call for the production of figures and had been largely superseded by the Rent of Furnished Houses Control (Scotland) Act, 1943, and the Furnished Houses (Rent Control) Act, 1946. These Acts (which are renewed annually—see the Expiring Laws Continuance Act, 1956) provide parallel schemes for the control of rents and for security of tenure for tenants holding under contracts for furnished lettings in Scotland and in England and Wales. The schemes are administered through tribunals appointed under the Acts and their proceedings are governed by the Rent of Furnished Houses Control (Scotland) Regulations, 1943 (S.R.O. No. 1774 (s. 62)) and the Furnished Houses (Rent Control) Regulations, 1946 (S.R.O. No. 781).

1. Rent tribunals

The Acts extend to any area in Scotland, consisting of the whole or part of any county or burgh and, in England and Wales, to any district, consisting of the whole or any part of the area of a local authority, in respect of which the Acts have been applied by order of the Secretary of State for Scotland or the Minister of Housing and Local Government. For each area or district a tribunal consisting of three members is appointed by the appropriate Minister. The members hold office during the Minister's pleasure. The same tribunal may act for more than one area or district (ss. 1 / 1943 and 1946 Acts).

The Act of 1949 gave security of tenure to the tenants of furnished lettings in Scotland (see page 7) and enabled tribunals in England,

Wales and Scotland to entertain further applications for security of tenure. The tribunals were given jurisdiction by the Act to fix rents of newly controlled unfurnished houses let for the first time since the 1st September 1939; to fix rents and grant security of tenure to tenants having exclusive possession of unfurnished premises and also sharing accommodation with the landlord (p. 12); and, by the Acts of 1954, to determine increases in controlled rents fixed before September 1939, to take account of the rise in the cost of services between the 3rd September 1939 and the 30th August 1954. In consequence of the Act of 1957 these duties in relation to unfurnished lettings will be confined to tribunals in Scotland, except where the tenant shares accommodation with the landlord. The work of a tribunal is likely to diminish having regard to the provisions for the decontrol of furnished houses (para. 3 *post*) and to the fact that rents of unfurnished tenancies created by contract on or after the 6th July 1957, are not subject to control, except on a re-let after the landlord has obtained possession on grounds of overcrowding. In England and Wales all questions as to recoverable rent of controlled unfurnished dwellings are now settled by the county court (s. 19 / 1957 Act), including adjustments as respects the provision of services (p. 32).

2. References to a tribunal

Under the Acts as originally written any contract which grants the right to occupy as a residence a house or part of a house in consideration of a rent which includes payment for the use of furniture or for services, may be referred by either party or the local authority to the tribunal (ss. 2 / 1943 and 1946 Acts). This right does not apply where the tribunal have already given security of tenure for a period shorter than three months (s. 11 (1) / 1949 Act). Furthermore, nothing in the Acts affect the provisions of the Rent Acts (s. 5 / 1943 Act: s. 7 / 1946 Act), and it is a matter for the courts to decide whether or not a furnished letting is controlled by the Acts (s. 19 / 1957 Act).

A local authority cannot refer a contract to a tribunal as a "test case", e.g., for settling the rents of furnished lettings in a district or in a block of flats, as the purpose of the Acts is "to deal with individual cases where hardship exists or may be reasonably supposed to exist" (*R.* v. *Paddington and St. Marylebone Rent Tribunal, ex parte Bell London and Provincial Properties Ltd.* [1949] 1 K.B. 666).

The Acts do not apply to a house or part of a house let at a rent which includes payment in respect of board if the value of such board to the tenant forms a substantial proportion of the whole rent

(s. 9 (3) / 1943 Act: s. 12 (3) / 1946 Act). In *R.* v. *Battersea, Wandsworth, Mitcham and Wimbledon Rent Tribunal, ex parte Parikh* (1957) it was held that the Act of 1946 applied to a "paying guest" who was given the exclusive occupation of one furnished room and the right to use other rooms.

In the case of a contract for part of a house it is immaterial whether the tenant shares other accommodation with any other person (ss. 2 *ibid.*).

Where the tenant pays separate sums for any two or more of the following:

(a) occupation of the premises;

(b) use of furniture; and

(c) services,

the expression "rent" means the aggregate of those sums, and where the sums are payable under separate contracts those contracts are treated as one contract (s. 9 (2) / 1943 Act: s. 12 (2) / 1946 Act). In the Act of 1943 "services" include attendance, the provision of heating or lighting, the supply of hot water and any other privilege or facility connected with the occupancy of a house or part of a house (s. 9 (1)); in the Act of 1946 they include attendance, the provision of heating or lighting, the supply of hot water and any other privilege or facility connected with the occupancy of a house or part of a house, not being a privilege or facility requisite for the purposes of access, cold water supply or sanitary accommodation (s. 12 (1)).

3. Decontrol of furnished lettings

The Act of 1957 restricts the application of the Acts of 1943 and 1946 to dwellings which if let unfurnished would remain within the rateable value limits of control under the Rent Acts (s. 12). The general effect of this provision is to decontrol from the 6th July 1957, a contract made on or after that date in respect of a furnished letting of any dwelling-house the rateable value of which on the 7th November 1956, exceeded—

(i) £40 in the Metropolitan Police District or the City of London;

(ii) £30 elsewhere in England and Wales;

(iii) £40 in Scotland.

This rule applies whether or not the contract of letting has been before the rent tribunal and registered under the Acts (p. 172). Furthermore, as and when a Ministerial order provides for the decontrol of other classes or descriptions of unfurnished dwellings any furnished lettings within those categories may be decontrolled. On the other hand, a landlord of a furnished letting within the rent limits does not secure decontrol on obtaining possession. The provision in Section 11 (2) of the Act which excludes from the Rent Acts any contractual tenancy of an unfurnished letting made on or after the 6th July 1957 (p. 91), does not apply to a contract made on or after that date in respect of a furnished letting within the controlled rent limits.

(1) *Short-term protection for tenants of decontrolled lettings*

If the furnished letting is terminable by notice and has become decontrolled then in most cases the tenant is entitled to at least three months' notice to quit—

(*a*) if the landlord has given notice before the time of decontrol (i.e. the 6th July 1957, or in the case of future decontrol the date or dates specified in the Ministerial order) it will not take effect earlier than three months after that time. Thus, if a landlord had given notice to quit on the 1st June 1957, in respect of a furnished dwelling in London with a rateable value of £60, the tenant is entitled to remain in possession up to and including the 5th October 1957.

The only exception to this rule is that if the rent tribunal have fixed a shorter period than three months the tenant is not entitled to possession after the expiration of the period fixed by the tribunal;

(*b*) if the landlord gives notice to quit within a year after the time of decontrol he must give at least three months' notice, e.g. a notice given on or after the 6th July 1957 and on or before the 5th July 1958, must not be shorter than three months.

So long as a contract of a furnished letting continues in force after the time of decontrol the rent payable thereunder remains the same as if the contract had not ceased to be subject to control (s. 12 (2) *ibid.*).

(2) *Forces reservists*

As to the special protection given to members of the Reserve Forces in possession of furnished lettings which become decontrolled see Chapter XIII, page 153.

(3) *Meaning of rateable value for decontrolled furnished lettings*

The rateable value on a particular date for the purposes of

decontrol of a furnished letting is ascertained in the same way as for an unfurnished letting (p. 97).

Where the valuation list is altered so as to vary the rateable value of a hereditament shown in the list on the 7th November 1956, or, as the case may be, on the date specified in a Ministerial order, and the alteration takes effect not later than such respective date (e.g., 7th November 1956), the rateable value or net annual value of a furnished dwelling for the purposes of decontrol is the amount of that value shown in the list as altered. This provision applies also for the purpose of making an apportionment of rateable value for part of a hereditament which is let furnished (para 4, Fifth Schedule / 1957 Act). In the application of this provision to Scotland, the term "valuation list" refers to the valuation roll; "hereditament" means lands and heritages; and the term "net annual value" does not apply.

4. Furnished premises not rated or with no separate rateable value

Before the Act of 1957 came into operation there was no limitation as to the size or type of furnished house which could be referred to a rent tribunal. The provisions relating to decontrol now make it necessary to determine whether or not a letting is controlled by the Acts of 1943 or 1946. The rules referred to in the previous sub-paragraph will apply in the case of premises which are rated at the particular date. These do not apply, however, to premises which were not rated at the time, e.g., a block of flats erected since that date. The Act makes provision for this type of case; and also places the onus on the landlord to prove that a rent tribunal has no jurisdiction to deal with a letting of a dwelling which is not separately rated.

(1) *Premises not rated*

Where a dwelling is or forms part of premises for which no rateable value was shown in the valuation list (or, in Scotland, the valuation roll) at the particular date (e.g. 7th November 1956), there is to be substituted for that date the first subsequent date on which a rateable value for the hereditament appears in the list (or roll) (s. 12 (4) *ibid.*).

(2) *Premises not separately rated*

Where a contract is referred to a rent tribunal in respect of a dwelling consisting of or comprising part only of premises which are not separately rated it is for the landlord to show that the case is outside the jurisdiction of the tribunal. In the course of the proceedings the landlord can ask for an adjournment to enable him to obtain an apportionment of the rateable value by the county court (or, in Scotland, by the sheriff). Unless the landlord commences proceedings in the court for an apportionment within two weeks of the adjournment the tribunal can assume jurisdiction, notwithstanding that no apportionment has been made, if it appears to them that they would have had jurisdiction if an apportionment had been made by the court (s. 12 (5) *ibid.*).

5. Proceedings before a tribunal

(1) *Application to Tribunal*

References to a tribunal must be made by written notice. The notice must specify the address of the house or part of the house to which the contract relates, if it is situated in England and Wales the names of the landlord and tenant, and the address of the landlord. If the notice relates to such property and is delivered to the office of the tribunal it is treated as having reached them on the day of delivery, if it is posted it is regarded as having reached the tribunal on the day when it would be delivered in the ordinary course of post. In the case of a reference for reconsideration of the rent entered in a register in respect of premises in Scotland the application must set forth the ground on which it is made (1943 and 1946 Regulations p. 166).

The tribunal may, by notice in writing, obtain from the landlord particulars of the letting. The landlord must be allowed at least seven days within which to supply the information (ss. 2 (1) / 1943 and 1946 Acts). If he fails to do so he is liable to a fine not exceeding £20 or to three months imprisonment or, under the Act of 1946, to both such fine and imprisonment (s. 7 (2) / 1943 Act; s. 9 (2) / 1946 Act).

The tribunal must consider every contract which is referred to them except where they are satisfied in the case of a reference not made by a local authority that, having regard to the length of time which has elapsed since a previous reference was made by the same party or to other circumstances, the reference is frivolous or vexatious.

(2) *Rules for the guidance of Tribunals*

In *R.* v. *Paddington and St. Marylebone Rent Tribunal, ex parte Bell London and Provincial Properties Ltd.* [1949] *supra*, the Court of Appeal laid down the following rules for the guidance of tribunals appointed under the Act of 1946:

"If premises are let furnished or if the landlord has contracted in the case of either furnished or unfurnished premises to supply or render services, the tribunal can only consider whether the rent is fair for that which the landlord has contracted to give. If he breaks his contract, that cannot be used as a ground for reducing the rent because the law does not allow a reduction of rent by way of damages. If, however, the landlord lets premises, but does not contract to give or render any services, the tribunal will have jurisdiction only if the premises are let furnished. If they are, the tribunal, in considering what is a fair rent, must take into account the services and amenities which the landlord, in fact, is supplying and the tenant enjoying and which there is every reason to suppose will be continued as, obviously, a tenant would be willing to pay a higher rent with the amenities and services than without them, and it is just that he should. So, too, if the premises are let furnished or unfurnished, but the landlord contracts to supply certain services and does, in fact, supply, though without obligation, to do so, other services and amenities. In either of these cases, if the landlord ceases for whatever reason to continue the supply of all or any of . . . the non-contractual services, the tribunal can reduce the rent to what would be fair with the contractual services plus such non-contractual services as he may continue to render. . . ."

(3) *The hearing*

Each party to the contract must be given an opportunity of a hearing before the tribunal or of making representations in writing. The time allowed within which the parties may give notice that they wish to be heard or to make representations is within the discretion of the tribunal, but it must not be less than seven days. If any party desires to be heard the tribunal must give to each party not less than seven clear days' (in Scotland not less than four clear days') notice in writing of the time and place at which they will be heard. If the contract relates to a council house the local authority must be given an opportunity of being heard or of submitting representations in writing. A party may appear in person or be represented or may be accompanied by any person to assist him. The tribunal may determine their own procedure at a hearing. A hearing may be postponed or adjourned as the tribunal think fit (1943 and 1946 Regulations p. 166).

(4) *The tribunal's decision*

After making any necessary inquiries and allowing the parties an opportunity of being heard or of submitting representations the tribunal must either—

(*a*) approve the rent payable under the contract; or

(*b*) reduce it to such sum as they think reasonable,

or dismiss the reference. If the tribunal dismiss a reference it does not mean that they approve the rent charged. The Act of 1946 provides that if the rent includes payment for services it may be increased to take account of any increase in the cost of services since the 3rd September 1939 (s. 2 (4)); but that is the only case where a rent tribunal can increase rent on a first reference. A majority decision of the tribunal is a sufficient determination; in England and Wales a notice of a decision must be sent to the local authority for registration.

6. Review of decisions

The tribunal may, on the application of the landlord or the tenant or the local authority, review any registered rent. The same rights of a hearing and of making representations are available to the parties and the local authority as in the case of an original reference to the tribunal.

On a review a tribunal have power to increase the rent (ss. 2 (3) / 1943 and 1946 Acts).

7. Limitation of decisions

An approval, reduction or increase may be limited to rent payable in respect of a particular period.

8. Register of rents

It is the duty of each local authority in England and Wales (p. 177) to keep a register of rents approved, reduced or increased by the tribunal in respect of premises situated in their area (s. 3 / 1946 Act). In Scotland the register is kept by the tribunal (s. 2 (4) / 1943 Act).

A certified copy of any entry in the register is acceptable as evidence in the courts (s. 8 / 1943 Act: s. 11 / 1946 Act).

9. Security of tenure

(1) *Automatic security on reference to tribunal*

A tenant who has referred his case to the tribunal, or where it has been referred by the local authority, is protected against eviction. If, after any such reference (whether an original or for review) the landlord serves notice to quit on the tenant at any time before the decision of the tribunal has been given or within three months thereafter, the notice does not take effect before the expiration of the said three months. The tribunal may, in their discretion, direct that a shorter period be substituted for the three months. If the reference is withdrawn the period during which the notice has been suspended ends at the expiration of seven days from the withdrawal of the reference. The effect of this provision is that in any case the tenant is entitled to three months security of tenure unless the period is cut down by the tribunal or by the withdrawal of the reference (s. 5 / 1946 Act: s. 17 (6) / 1949 Act).

(2) *Power of tribunal to extend the period of security of tenure*

Where a contract has been referred to a tribunal, and the reference has not been withdrawn, the tenant may, if subsequently he receives notice to quit, apply to the tribunal for an extension of the period of security of tenure. Subsequent applications may be made for further extensions of time. In any case the application must be made before the notice takes effect, whether by virtue of the contract or by the expiration of the period of automatic security or any further period granted by the tribunal. But if the hearing of the tribunal is adjourned and in the meantime the notice to quit has expired the tribunal has jurisdiction to hear the application (*R.* v. *Paddington (South) Rent Tribunal ex parte Millard* [1955] 1 W.L.R. 348). A further application may not be made if the tribunal have directed that the original period is to be less than three months (s. 11 / 1949 Act).

On an application being made for an extension of the period of security—

(*a*) the notice to quit does not take effect until after the application has been determined (unless it has been withdrawn);

(*b*) the tribunal may direct that the notice to quit is not to take effect for a further period not exceeding three months; before issuing a direction the tribunal must give the landlord and the tenant an opportunity of being heard or of submitting representations in writing;

(*c*) if the tribunal refuse to issue a direction the notice to quit does not take effect before the expiration of seven days from the determination of the application. It does not follow that seven days is the arbitrary period in every case. The period of the notice to quit may be longer or the period of a previous extension may not expire until a later date.

When the tribunal have refused to issue a direction no subsequent application may be made in respect of the same notice to quit.

The tribunal must notify the parties of their decision.

10. Minimum length of notice to quit

By virtue of Section 16 of the Act of 1957 no notice by a landlord or a tenant to quit any furnished premises—whether controlled or uncontrolled—is valid unless it is given not less than four weeks before the date on which it is to take effect.

11. Assignments of furnished houses not protected

In *R.* v. *Tottenham and District Rent Tribunal, ex parte Northfield (Highgate) Ltd.* [1956] 2 All E.R. 863, it was held that a rent tribunal has no jurisdiction to consider a reference by an assignee of a furnished letting. An assignee, although he may have a privity of estate, has no privity of contract and, therefore, is not a "party to the contract" as required by Section 2 of the Act of 1946.

12. The deserted wife

Where the tenant deserts his wife she is assumed to acquire a licence to remain in occupation of a furnished letting but she has no authority to apply to the tribunal in her own name or as agent for her husband unless she has his authority for that purpose (*R.* v. *Twickenham Rent Tribunal, ex parte Dunn* [1953] 2 Q.B. 425).

13. Limitations

A tenant cannot obtain protection under the Acts of 1943 or 1946—

(i) if his tenancy is one which will expire by effluxion of time;
(ii) except by a reference to a tribunal;
(iii) if the notice to quit has taken effect (s. 11 (1) / 1949 Act).

14. Furnished sub-lettings

A tenant of controlled premises does not lose the protection of the Rent Acts by reason only that he has sub-let part of the premises as a furnished letting (s. 9 *ibid.*).

15. Prohibition as to premiums

The payment of a premium as a condition of the grant, renewal, continuance or assignment of rights under a contract for a furnished letting which is controlled by the Acts of 1943 or 1946 is prohibited in the following cases (s. 12 *ibid.*):

(a) where the rent has been registered by a local authority or, in Scotland, by a tribunal;
(b) where the approval, reduction or increase made by a tribunal has been limited to rent payable in respect of a particular period, and that period has not expired.

For this purpose a "premium" includes any fine or other like sum and any other pecuniary consideration in addition to rent (s. 18 (2) *ibid.*).

(1) *Exemptions from prohibition*

The prohibition against premiums does not affect the validity of—

(*a*) a requirement to pay so much of any outgoings discharged by a grantor or assignor as is referable to any period after the grant or assignment takes effect;

(*b*) a requirement to pay a reasonable amount in respect of goodwill of a business, trade or profession, being goodwill transferred to a grantee or assignee in connection with the grant or assignment or accruing to him in consequence thereof;

(*c*) any premium payable by a sub-tenant under a Crown interest in respect of an agreement made before the 8th February 1952 (Crown Lessees (Protection of Sub-Tenants) Act, 1952).

(2) *Recovery of premiums paid*

Any premium paid under an agreement made after the 25th March 1949, is recoverable by the person by whom it was paid. An agreement made between that date and the 2nd June 1949, for the payment of a premium which was lawful under previous law, is voidable at the option of either party.

(3) *Penalty for demanding a premium*

Any person demanding a premium is liable to a fine not exceeding £100. The court may also order the refund of the premium (s. 12 (3) / 1949 Act).

(4) *Excessive prices for furniture, etc., to be treated as premiums*

Where the purchase of any furniture, fittings or other articles has been required as a condition of the grant, renewal, continuance or assignment of rights under a contract for a controlled furnished letting and the price exceeds the reasonable price of the articles, the excess is to be treated as if it were a premium. Any person required to purchase any such articles may request the seller to state in writing the price he is demanding. If, without reasonable excuse, the seller fails within fourteen days to give the written statement, or knowingly makes a false statement, he is liable to a fine not exceeding £10 (ss. 3, 12 (3) *ibid.*).

16. Rent books required for weekly tenancies

Where rent is payable weekly in respect of the tenancy of a controlled furnished letting the landlord is required by section 12 (6) of the Act of 1957 to provide a rent book or other similar document, containing particulars of the rent and of the other terms and conditions of the contract.

If at any time after the expiration of two months from the 6th July 1957, the landlord fails to comply with this requirement he, and any person who on his behalf demands or receives rent under the contract, is liable to a fine not exceeding £10 in respect of each week in which the failure occurs or continues.

17. Illegal payments and offences

It is illegal for any person to claim or receive any payment on account of rent which is in excess of the registered rent. The tenant may recover the amount of any payment so made (s. 3 / 1943 Act: s. 4 / 1946 Act).

The penalty for claiming or receiving excess rent may be a fine not exceeding £100 or six months' imprisonment or, in England and Wales, to both such fine and imprisonment. The court may also order the person found guilty of the offence to repay the amount of the excess rent (s. 7 (1) / 1943 Act: s. 9 (1) / 1946 Act).

No proceedings for any such offence in England and Wales may be instituted except by the local authority (s. 10 / 1946 Act).

18. Provisions as to local authorities

The local authorities for the purposes of the Acts of 1943 and 1946 are—

(a) in London, the Common Council of the City of London and the metropolitan borough councils;

(b) elsewhere in England and Wales, the borough, urban district and rural district councils (s. 6 (1) / 1946 Act); and

(c) in Scotland, county and town councils (s. 9 (1) / 1943 Act).

The powers of a local authority may be exercised by a duly authorised officer. Local authorities may publish information in regard to the provisions of the Acts (s. 4 / 1943 Act: s. 6 / 1946 Act).

N

CHAPTER XVI

Miscellaneous and Supplementary Matters

1. Recoverable rent under a controlled tenancy

THE rent limit, together with the permitted increases and adjustments, fixed by the Act of 1957 constitutes the recoverable rent of a controlled tenancy in England and Wales (Chapters III and IV); in Scotland it consists of the standard rent, permitted increases, the repairs increase or 1957 Act increase, and the increase for cost of services (Chapters X and XI). Any excess above these limits is irrecoverable from the tenant.

(1) *Recovery of overpaid rent*

If a tenant has been over-charged he can only recover the excess paid within two years from the date of payment. The amount over-paid can be recovered from the landlord or from his personal representatives by action, or it may be deducted from future rent (s. 14 (1) / 1920 Act: s. 8 (2) / 1923 Act: s. 7 (6) / 1938 Act: para. 1, Sixth Schedule / 1957 Act).

(2) *Recovery of arrears of rent on defective notice*

If a landlord's notice of increase is defective and is rectified by the court the amount of arrears recoverable in respect of the increase is limited to any rental period within six months before the date of the court order (s. 8 (1) / 1923 Act: para. 2, Sixth Schedule / 1957 Act).

2. No right to suspend payment of rent if house is unfit

A statutory tenant does not seem to be in any better position than a contractual tenant in regard to the suspension of payment of rent, and he remains liable for payment of the recoverable rent (subject to certain deductions) if the house becomes unfit for human habitation. In England and Wales he is entitled to an abatement of rent (p. 58) and, in Scotland, he can withhold the repairs increase or the 1957 Act increase, on grounds of disrepair; but the tenant cannot withhold payment of the whole rent (*Peach* v. *Lowe* [1947] 1 All E.R. 441). This principle appears to apply even in the case of a tenancy which attracts the implied condition of fitness in Section 2 of the Housing Act, 1936 (p. 46). In any such case the remedy of the tenant seems to be an action for damages (*Walker* v. *Hobbs* (1889) 23 Q.B.D. 458) in so far as the landlord's breach may render the house unfit for human habitation.

3. Levy of distress for recovery of rent

The tenant of controlled property is protected against the common law right of a landlord to seize and sell, without taking legal proceedings, the goods of his tenant in satisfaction of any arrears of rent that may be due and owing.

No distress for the rent of a controlled dwelling may be levied except with the leave of the county court; in Scotland diligence cannot be done without leave of the sheriff (s. 6 / 1920 Act). In regard to an application for such leave the court has the same powers with regard to adjournment, stay, suspension, postponement of proceedings as are conferred on it in relation to an application for recovery of possession (p. 84).

This provision does not apply to a distress levied under Section 134 of the County Courts Act, 1934, which enables a landlord to claim for rent in arrear where goods are seized in execution under process of a county court.

4. Effect of bankruptcy on the operation of the Rent Acts

Where the occupier, being a contractual tenant, goes bankrupt and the tenancy vests in the trustee, the occupier will not be protected by the Rent Acts (*Reeves* v. *Davies* [1921] 2 K.B. 486). This rule applies whether the trustee disclaims or not (*Stafford* v. *Levy* (1946) 62 T.L.R. 487). If the occupier is a statutory tenant and goes bankrupt he does not lose the protection of the Acts (*Sutton* v. *Dorf* [1932] 2 K.B. 304). Where the tenant remains in possession after his tenancy has been forfeited for non-payment of rent and pays the arrears he may become a statutory tenant entitled to retain possession even if he goes bankrupt (*Smith* v. *Odder* [1949] W.N. 249).

Where the occupier is a contractual sub-tenant, and his landlord goes bankrupt, his position seems to be uncertain. There is no difficulty if the trustee in bankruptcy does not disclaim. If the trustee does disclaim the sub-tenant may not be protected (following *Reeves* v. *Davies*). In any case there appears to be nothing to prevent the head landlord from calling on the sub-tenant to take a vesting order (s. 54 (6), Bankruptcy Act, 1914) which he may not be prepared to do if the bankrupt's tenancy contained repairing covenants (*In re Finley* (1888) 21 Q.B.D. 475). If the sub-tenant is a statutory tenant and his landlord goes bankrupt no problem will

arise if the trustee does not disclaim. If the trustee does disclaim the
sub-tenant may not lose his protection any more than the tenant
did in *Sutton* v. *Dorf*.

5. Rent books

It is the duty of the landlord of a dwelling-house which is controlled under the Rent Acts to provide a rent book or other similar
document where the rent is payable weekly. If he fails to do so and
either he or any person on his behalf demands or receives rent in
respect of the house they are liable to a fine not exceeding £10 for
each week during which the default continues (s. 6 / 1938 Act).

(1) *Information to be included in rent books*

Every rent book or similar document used by or on behalf of any
landlord in respect of a controlled house must contain the notice set
out in the Rent Restrictions Regulations, 1957 (S.I. 981), or a
notice to the like effect. The Rent Restrictions (Scotland) Amendment Regulations, 1954 (S.I. 1081 (s. 104)) perscribe a similar
notice for Scotland.

A landlord is liable to a fine not exceeding £50 if any rent book
or similar document which does not conform to the prescribed
requirements is used by him or on his behalf (s. 14 (3) / 1933 Act:
para. 20, Sixth Schedule / 1957 Act).

In the case of any house in England and Wales which is occupied,
or is of a type suitable for occupation, by persons of the working
classes, the name and address of the medical officer of health for the
district and of the landlord or other person who is directly responsible for keeping the house in all respects reasonably fit for human
habitation must be inscribed in the rent book. If a rent book is not
used this information must be delivered in writing to the tenant at
the beginning of the tenancy and before any rent is demanded or
collected. The penalty for failure to comply with these requirements
is a fine not exceeding forty shillings (s. 4, Housing Act, 1936).

In most areas every rent book or similar document must contain:

(*a*) a summary in prescribed form of the provisions of Sections 58,
59 and 61 of the Housing Act, 1936 (which relate to over-
crowding); and

(*b*) a statement of the permitted number of persons in relation
to the house (s. 62 *ibid.*). There is a similar provision in
Section 54 of the Housing (Scotland) Act, 1950. The
permitted number can be obtained from the local authority.

If so required an occupier must within seven days produce his rent book or similar document to an authorised officer of the local authority; failure to do so renders the occupier liable to a fine not exceeding forty shillings (s. 62 (1), Housing Act, 1936).

Every document containing a demand or receipt for rent which includes any sum for rates payable under any statutory enactment by the owner instead of the occupier must state the amount of the rates in accordance with the last rate demand (Statement of Rates Act, 1919). The House-Letting and Rating (Scotland) Act, 1920 (s. 2) contains a similar provision in regard to small dwelling-houses in Scotland.

(2) *Wrong entries in rent books*

If an entry is made in any rent book or similar document showing as arrears of rent any sum which is irrecoverable or if the landlord refuses or neglects for more than seven days to delete such entry on being requested to do so by the tenant, the person making the entry or the landlord may be liable to a fine not exceeding £50, unless he proves that at the time of the alleged offence the landlord had a bona fide claim that the sum was recoverable (s. 14 (2) / 1920 Act: s. 8 (2) / 1933 Act: paras. 1 and 17, Sixth Schedule / 1957 Act).

When the recoverable rent of any dwelling-house has been determined by the court the tenant can ask the court to call for the production of the rent book and direct the registrar or clerk of the court to correct any entries of arrears which have been determined as irrecoverable (s. 8 / 1933 Act: para. 4, Sixth Schedule / 1957 Act).

(3) *Furnished lettings*

The provision of rent books for furnished lettings is dealt with in Chapter XV.

6. Service of notices

As a general rule service is deemed to have been effected by properly addressing, prepaying and posting a letter containing the document to be served, and unless the contrary is proved to have been effected at the time at which the letter would be delivered in the ordinary course of post (s. 26, Interpretation Act, 1889).

In regard to the service of notices, certificates and documents required or authorised to be served under the Act of 1957:

(1) *In England and Wales*, they may be served either—

    (a) by delivering it to the person on whom it is to be served; or (*b*) by leaving it at the usual or last known place of abode of that person; or

(*c*) by sending it in a prepaid registered letter addressed to that person at his usual or last known place of abode; or

(*d*) in the case of an incorporated company or body, by delivering it to the secretary or clerk of the company or body at their registered or principal office or sending it in a prepaid registered letter addressed to the secretary or clerk of the company or body at that office; or

(*e*) if it is not practicable after reasonable inquiry to ascertain the name or address of an owner, lessee or occupier of land on whom it should be served, by addressing it to him by the description of "owner" or "lessee" or "occupier" of the premises (naming them) to which it relates, and by delivering it to some person on the premises or, if there is no person on the premises to whom it can be delivered, by affixing it, or a copy of it, to some conspicuous part of the premises (para. 23, Sixth Schedule / 1957 Act).

(2) *In Scotland* they may be served—

(*a*) by being sent by post in a prepaid letter or delivered to or at the residence or place of business of the person to whom it is addressed:

Provided that in the case of a person employed on any ship or vessel it shall be delivered to some person on board thereof and connected therewith; or

(*b*) in the case of an incorporated company or body, by being sent by post in a prepaid letter addressed to the secretary or clerk of the company or body at their registered or principal office or by delivering it to him at that office; or

(*c*) where the notice or other document relates to premises and the owner thereof resides beyond the area of the local authority, by being sent by post in a prepaid letter or delivered to or at the place of business of his known factor or agent or the person drawing the rents of the premises; or

(*d*) where the notice or other document relates to premises and the authority or other person requiring to effect the service are unable after reasonable inquiry to ascertain the address of the person upon whom it should be served, by addressing it to him

(i) by name, if his name is known; or

(ii) if his name is not known, by the description of "owner" or "occupier" of the premises (naming them) to which it relates;

and by delivering it to some person on the premises, or if there is no person on the premises to whom it can be delivered, by affixing it or a copy thereof to some conspicuous part of the premises.

Service of a copy of the notice, certificate or document is deemed to be service of the principal document; and service may be proved by a certificate under the hand of the person who posted or delivered or affixed the same attested by one witness who was present at such posting, delivery or affixing (para. 33 *ibid.*).

Any notice connected with a repairs increase or a 1957 Act increase and any copy of a certificate of disrepair or a certificate of service of a Housing Act notice of a local authority (p. 138) may be served by registered post (s. 37 / 1954 Act).

7. Agents

Any document authorised or required by the Rent Acts or by the Act of 1957 to be served by the tenant of a dwelling-house on the landlord may be served on any agent of the landlord named as such in the rent book or other similar document, or on the person who receives the rent of the house. If for the purpose of any proceedings under the Acts (including any prosecution for an offence) any person serves upon any such agent or person receiving the rent a notice in writing requiring him to disclose the full name and place of abode or place of business of the landlord, it is the duty of the agent or other person forthwith to comply with the notice. If he fails or refuses to do so he is liable to a fine not exceeding £5, unless he shows to the satisfaction of the court that he did not know, and could not with reasonable diligence have ascertained, such of the facts required by the notice as were not disclosed by him (s. 7 (5) / 1938 Act: paras. 23 and 24, Sixth Schedule / 1957 Act).

The Accommodation Agencies Act, 1953, prohibits the taking of certain commissions in dealings with persons seeking houses or flats to let, and unauthorised advertisements for lettings. The Act is due to expire on the 31st December 1957. So long as it is in operation any person who—

(a) demands or accepts payment of any sum of money in consideration of registering, or undertaking to register, the name or requirements of any person seeking the tenancy of a house; or in consideration of supplying, or undertaking to supply, to any person addresses or other particulars of houses to let; or

(b) issues any advertisement, list or other document describing any house as being to let without the authority of the owner of the house or his agent,

is guilty of an offence.

"House" includes any part of a building which is occupied or intended to be occupied as a dwelling; "owner" means the person having power to grant a lease of the house.

Any person found guilty is liable to a fine not exceeding £100 or to imprisonment for three months, or to both the fine and imprisonment. It is not an offence for a person to demand or accept payment from the owner of the house of any remuneration payable to him as agent of the owner; or for a solicitor to demand or accept payment of any remuneration in respect of business done by him as such; or for a person to demand or accept any payment in consideration of the display in a shop, or of the publication in a newspaper, periodical or magazine, of any advertisement or notice; or of the receiving of any such advertisement or notice for display or publication in the ordinary course of business.

8. Jurisdiction

The county court or, in Scotland, the sheriff has jurisdiction to deal with any claim or other proceedings arising out of the Rent Acts (s. 17 (2) / 1920 Act).

Under Section 19 of the Act of 1957 jurisdiction may be exercised either in the course of any proceedings relating to a dwelling or on an application made for the purpose by the landlord or the tenant,

(a) by the county court to determine any question as to the application of the Rent Acts, as to the rent limit, or the rent actually recoverable, under a controlled tenancy, as to the application of the Act of 1946 to any contract for a furnished letting or as to any matter which is or may become material for determining any of the foregoing questions;

(*b*) by the sheriff to determine any question as to the application of the Rent Acts or of the Act of 1943 or as to any matter which is or may become material for determining any such question.

Any apportionment by either court as to rates, gross value or rateable value, or expenditure for private street works is final and conclusive.

9. Local authorities and the Rent Acts

Local authorities for the purposes of the Rent Acts are

(*a*) *In London:* as respects the City of London, the Common Council of the City, and for the remainder of the administrative County of London, the metropolitan borough councils (s. 16 (4) / 1933 Act);

(*b*) *Elsewhere in England and Wales:* county borough councils; non-county borough councils; urban and rural district councils (s. 10 *ibid.*);

(*c*) *In Scotland:* burgh and county councils (s. 15 *ibid.*).

(1) *Power to give information*

Local authorities have power to publish information, for the assistance of landlords and tenants, as to their rights and duties under the Rent Acts and the Act of 1957, and as to the procedure for enforcement; and they may furnish particulars as to the availability, extent, and character of alternative accommodation (s. 10 / 1933 Act: para. 18, Sixth Schedule / 1957 Act).

(2) *Power to prosecute offences*

Local authorities have power to institute proceedings for any offence under the Rent Acts or the Act of 1957, including offences in regard to taking premiums contrary to the Act of 1949 (s. 11 / 1933 Act: paras. 18 and 33, Sixth Schedule / 1957 Act).

10. Metropolitan Police district

The areas comprising the Metropolitan Police District are (s. 16 and Fourth Schedule / Police Act, 1946):

The County of London, excluding the City of London;

The County of Middlesex;

The County Boroughs of Croydon, East Ham, West Ham;

and the following boroughs, urban districts and rural districts and parishes:

In the County of Essex: the boroughs of Barking, Chingford, Dagenham, Ilford, Leyton, Walthamstow, Wanstead and Woodford; and the urban districts of Chigwell, Waltham Holy Cross.

In the County of Herts: the urban districts of Barnet, Bushey, Cheshunt, East Barnet; the rural district of Elstree; and the parishes of Northaw in the rural district of Hatfield, and Aldenham in the rural district of Watford.

In the County of Kent: the boroughs of Beckenham, Bexley, Bromley, Erith; and the urban districts of Chislehurst and Sidcup, Crayford, Orpington, Penge.

In the County of Surrey: the boroughs of Barnes, Beddington and Wallington, Epsom and Ewell, Kingston, Malden and Coombe, Mitcham, Richmond, Surbiton, Sutton and Cheam, Wimbledon; and the urban districts of Banstead, Carshalton, Coulsdon and Purley, Esher, Merton and Morden.

11. Exclusion of statutory tenants from receipt of certain notices

Paragraph 3 (1) (*b*) of the First Schedule to the Acquisition of Land (Authorisation Procedure) Act, 1946, provides for the service of notice of the making of a compulsory purchase order "on every owner, lessee and occupier (except tenants for a month or any period less than a month)". In *Brown* v. *Minister of Housing and Local Government and Another* [1953] 1 W.L.R. 1370, it was held that a statutory tenant under the Rent Acts was an "occupier" entitled to be served with such a notice; and that failure to serve such a notice was a ground for quashing the order in so far as it affected premises occupied by the statutory tenant.

Section 50 of the Housing Repairs and Rents Act, 1954, provides for the avoidance of this rule by declaring that, for the purposes of the said paragraph 3 (1) (*b*) and any corresponding enactment (including a local Act) regulating the service of notices in connection with the compulsory acquisition of land, an occupier being a statutory tenant under the Rent Acts shall be deemed to be a tenant for a period less than a month. The effect of this provision is that as from the 30th August 1954 a statutory tenant has not been entitled to notice of the making (or confirmation) of a compulsory purchase order; nor does he appear to be entitled to make objections to the order or to be heard at any public local inquiry or hearing in connection therewith.

The section applies also to—

(*a*) the service of notices of the making of a redevelopment plan or a clearance order under the Housing Act, 1936;

(*b*) the service of notices of the making of an order designating a national park, or an order creating, diverting or extinguishing a public path, or an order giving public access to private land, under the National Parks and Access to the Countryside Act, 1949;

(*c*) any local enactment regulating the service of notices in respect of the proposed exercise of any powers in relation to land.

12. Minimum notice to quit

Section 16 of the Act of 1957 imposes a restriction on the operation of the common law by providing that no notice by a landlord or a tenant to quit any premises let (whether before, on or after the 6th July 1957) as a dwelling shall be valid unless it is given not less than four weeks before the date on which it is to take effect.

This is merely a provision for a minimum period and does not affect any tenancy agreement which requires longer notice to be given. The provision applies only where a notice to quit is required to determine the letting. The notice need not be in writing or in any particular form or served in any particular manner unless the agreement or any enactment so requires. The provision applies to any letting of premises as a dwelling whether in public or private ownership, controlled or uncontrolled, or furnished or unfurnished.

Although there is no definition of what is meant by a "dwelling" for the purpose of the section it would not seem to apply to premises let in lodgings unless the lodger has a sufficient occupation to give him an interest in the land (*Inman* v. *Stamp* (1815) 1 Stark. 12) or he has a right of separate occupation (*Wright* v. *Stavert* (1860) 2. E. & E. 721).

The provision applies also to Scotland (paras. 28 to 30, Sixth Schedule, *ibid.*).

13. Prescribed forms

The Rent Restrictions Regulations, 1957 (S.I. No. 981), prescribe the forms of notice and other documents for use for the purposes of the Act of 1957 in connection with dwelling-houses in England and Wales.

CHAPTER XVII

Long Tenancies and Business Tenancies

THE provisions of the Landlord and Tenant Act, 1954, which protect a tenant of residential premises holding on a lease granted for a term of more than twenty-one years at a low rent and tenants of business and professional premises are not affected by the provisions for decontrol in the Act of 1957. It does, however, extend the provisions of the Act of 1954 which relate to the protection of residential premises, to long tenancies not at a low rent.

1. Long tenancies

Section 12 (7) of the Act of 1920 provides that if the rent payable in respect of any tenancy of any dwelling-house is less than two-thirds of the rateable value of the house the Rent Acts do not apply to that rent or tenancy. The class of tenancy which is mostly affected by this provision is the building lease held at a ground rent; it applies, however, to any type of letting at a rent of less than two-thirds of the rateable value, e.g. to bounty tenancies and rent-free tenancies.

(1) *Tenancies protected*

The Leasehold Property (Temporary Provisions) Act, 1951, provided interim protection for families living in dwelling-houses under leases granted for more than twenty-one years certain which were due to expire by effluxion of time between the 24th June 1951 and the 24th December 1954, or who were holding over, or who had made short-term arrangements to remain in possession, after the long lease had expired, during that period. The Act did not impose any limitation as to the size of the property or as to the rent charged and it gave protection to dwellings which were outside the limits of the Rent Acts and in some cases provided an alternative to those Acts for claiming protection against the loss of possession.

Part I of the Landlord and Tenant Act, 1954, which provides the permanent legislation for the protection of tenants holding under long leases, restricts its application to property which was of Rent Acts size in 1954; it added the qualification that the tenancy must be let at a low rent; and, by virtue of Section 35 (1) of the Housing

Repairs and Rents Act, 1954, limits the right to claim protection to houses which were in being before the 30th August, 1954.

Section 11 (4) of the Act of 1957 provides that the provisions for immediate decontrol (p. 90) or future decontrol by Ministerial order (p. 90) or for decontrol by the landlord obtaining possession do not affect the operation of Part I of the Landlord and Tenant Act, 1954. Furthermore, Section 21 of the Act of 1957 provides that the Rent Acts shall not apply to any long tenancy and that Part I of the Act of 1954 shall apply to long tenancies not at a low rent as it applies to long tenancies at a low rent. On the other hand, the exclusion of the application of the Rent Acts to long tenancies does not prevent a sub-tenant protected by those Acts becoming the tenant of the landlord on the same terms if the long tenancy is determined (p. 74).

The general effect of Part I of the Act of 1954, as amended by the Act of 1957, is to protect a residential tenant holding under a tenancy granted for a term of more than twenty-one years, whether or not it has been subsequently extended by act of the parties or by any enactment, in respect of a dwelling with a rateable value not exceeding—

(a) £100 in the Metropolitan Police District or the City of London;

(b) £75 elsewhere in England and Wales (s. 2 (5) / 1954 Act: s. 25 (1) / 1957 Act).

Rateable value for this purpose is:

(a) if the dwelling had not been let at a low rent it would have been an "old control" house, the rateable value of the house on the 3rd August 1914;

(b) if the dwelling had not been let at a low rent it would have been a "new control" house,

(i) in the administrative County of London, the rateable value or net annual value, if it differs from the rateable value, on the 6th April 1939; and

(ii) elsewhere in England and Wales, on the 1st April 1939.

If the property was not assessed on the respective dates the rateable value is the first assessment after those dates (s. 12 (1) (e) / 1920 Act: First Schedule / 1939 Act).

The Act of 1957 also amends the provision on which a landlord of property subject to a long tenancy may claim possession for occupation by himself or a son or daughter over eighteen years of age or his father or mother on grounds of greater hardship, when the lease falls in if he purchased his interest, or a reversionary lease has been created in his favour, not later than the 7th November 1956 (para. 27, Sixth Schedule, *ibid.*).

(2) *Rents of statutory tenancies*

The scheme of the Act of 1954 enables a tenant to claim a statutory tenancy under the Act on a different footing to what is called a "statutory tenancy" under the Rent Acts. The rent, terms and conditions of a statutory tenancy under the Act of 1954 are settled by agreement between the landlord competent to negotiate the new tenancy and the tenant or, if they cannot agree, by the county court. By virtue of the Act of 1957 (para. 8, Sixth Schedule) the rent of any such existing statutory tenancies may be increased to the rent limit of the Act and it restricts to that limit the rent of such statutory tenancies created on or after the 6th July 1957 in respect of houses which at the time are within the rateable value limits of control under the Rent Acts.

(*a*) *Existing statutory tenancies:* In the case of any statutory tenancy created before the 6th July 1957, the rent under the tenancy may be increased to the rent limit under the Act of 1957, provided that—

(i) if the existing rent is higher than that limit it will remain at the higher figure;

(ii) if the existing rent has been fixed by agreement at a lower amount than the rent limit of the Act of 1957 it can be increased up to that limit only by agreement in writing made between the competent landlord for the time being and the tenant (para. 8 (2) *ibid.*).

The rent limit under the Act of 1957, or the existing higher rent, is subject to adjustment as respects rates (p. 29), or to increase on account of subsequent improvements (p. 33), and is subject to abatement on grounds of disrepair (p. 58) (para. 7 (2), First Schedule: para. 8 (1), Sixth Schedule / 1957 Act).

(*b*) *New statutory tenancies within range of control:* In the case of a statutory tenancy created on or after the 6th July 1957, where the dwelling would, apart from the long tenancy, remain controlled at the time of creating the statutory tenancy, the landlord can claim a rent not exceeding the rent limit under the Act of 1957, which will be subject to adjustment for rates, to increase for subsequent improvements, and to abatement for disrepair.

If the rent is fixed by agreement at a figure lower than the rent limit it can be increased up to that limit only by agreement in writing made between the competent landlord for the time being and the tenant.

(c) *New statutory tenancies outside the range of control:* If the dwelling-house is one which if it were not subject to a long tenancy it would, at the time of creating the statutory tenancy, have been decontrolled as from—

(i) the 6th July 1957, or

(ii) a date fixed by Ministerial order,

the competent landlord and the tenant may agree or the county court may fix the rent, terms and conditions of the tenancy under the provisions of the Act of 1954.

Any such rent agreed or determined is, however, subject to adjustment as respects rates, to increase for subsequent improvements and to abatement for disrepair (para. 8 (3) *ibid.*).

2. Business and professional premises

Part II of the Landlord and Tenant Act, 1954, provides security of tenure for tenants of premises used for business or professional purposes. A tenancy does not qualify for protection under that part of the Act if it is protected by the Rent Acts or would be if it were not let at a rent of less than two-thirds of the rateable value of the dwelling-house or if it is a long tenancy.

Where a tenancy of premises used for business or professional purposes is decontrolled under the Act of 1957 the tenant cannot claim protection under the Act against ejectment or increase of rent during the period of security of tenure (p. 93) even if he holds under a tenancy which would or might come to an end within that period by effluxion of time or notice to quit or he is a statutory tenant (paras. 2 (6), 11, Fourth Schedule). He must rely on the Act of 1954.

(1) *Protection for contractual tenants*

If the tenant is holding under a contractual tenancy at the time of decontrol the tenancy will continue until terminated by notice under the Act of 1954. Upon that notice being given the tenant is entitled to claim a new tenancy either by agreement with the competent landlord—as defined by the Act—or by application to the county court.

(2) *Protection for statutory tenants*

Where a tenant is a statutory tenant at the time of decontrol his tenancy is assumed to be continuing under the Act of 1954 as if it were an expired tenancy for a term of years certain.

In that case the tenancy continues on the same terms but the tenant can apply to the county court for a new tenancy or he can wait until the competent landlord gives notice to terminate the existing tenancy and then apply to the court for a new tenancy.

CHAPTER XVIII

Texts of the Acts

NOTE: *The words in italics show amendments made by subsequent legislation. Any part of an Act which has been repealed is omitted. Parts of Acts which have been repealed as respects England and Wales but still apply to Scotland are shown in square brackets.*

RENT ACT, 1957

5 & 6 ELIZ. 2

CHAPTER 25

An Act to amend the Rent and Mortgage Interest Restrictions Acts, 1920 to 1939, the Rent of Furnished Houses Control (Scotland) Act, 1943, the Furnished Houses (Rent Control) Act, 1946, the Housing (Repairs and Rents) (Scotland) Act, 1954, and certain other enactments relating to the control of rents and the right to retain possession of houses; to provide a minimum length for notice to terminate residential lettings; and for purposes connected with the matters aforesaid. [6th June, 1957]

Be it enacted by the Queen's most Excellent Majesty, by and with the advice and consent of the Lords Spiritual and Temporal, and Commons, in this present Parliament assembled, and by the authority of the same, as follows:—

REVISION OF RENT LIMITS OF CONTROLLED HOUSES IN
ENGLAND AND WALES

1. Rent limit of controlled houses

(1) Subject to the following provisions of this Act the rent recoverable for any rental period from the tenant under a controlled tenancy shall not exceed the following limit, that is to say a rent of which the annual rate is equal to the 1956 gross value of the dwelling multiplied by two (or, if the responsibility for repairs is such as is specified in Part I of the First Schedule to this Act, by the appropriate factor specified in the said Part I), together with—

    (*a*) the annual amount, ascertained in accordance with the Second Schedule to this Act, of any rates for the basic rental period, being rates borne by the landlord or a superior landlord; and

(b) such annual amount as may be agreed in writing between the landlord and the tenant or determined by the county court to be a reasonable charge for any services for the tenant provided by the landlord or a superior landlord during the basic rental period or any furniture which under the terms of the tenancy the tenant is entitled to use during that period.

(2) The limit on the rent recoverable under a controlled tenancy for any rental period (hereinafter referred to as "the rent limit") shall be subject to adjustment from time to time under sections three to five of this Act and to reduction as provided by Part II of the First Schedule to this Act in case of disrepair.

(3) Where under a controlled tenancy current at the commencement of this Act the rent recoverable for the basic rental period exceeds what would be the rent limit for that period if ascertained under subsection (1) of this section, the rent limit shall be the rent recoverable as aforesaid, subject however to the provisions of the foregoing subsection.

(4) The rent recoverable under a controlled tenancy for the rental period comprising the commencement of this Act shall, notwithstanding the repeals effected by this Act, remain the rent recoverable under that tenancy for any rental period for which it is neither increased nor reduced under this Act.

2. Procedure for increasing rents

(1) If the rent for the time being recoverable under a controlled tenancy is less than the rent limit it may be increased up to that limit subject to and in accordance with the following provisions of this section; and this subsection shall have effect notwithstanding anything in any enactment.

(2) Subject to the provisions of Part II of the First Schedule to this Act, the rent may be increased as aforesaid by the service by the landlord on the tenant of a notice of increase in the prescribed form specifying the amount of the increase; but—

(a) the increase shall not have effect as respects rental periods beginning before such date as may be specified in the notice, being a date not earlier (except in the cases authorised by the following provisions of this Act) than three months after the service of the notice;

(b) the total of the increases which may be specified in any notice or notices of increase as taking effect less than nine months after the service of the first notice (excluding any increases which under the following provisions of this Act are to be disregarded) shall not exceed seven shillings and sixpence per week, but a notice may specify more than one date and amount;

(c) except so far as may be necessary for giving effect to an adjustment under section three or five of this Act, a notice of increase shall be of no effect if given at a time when—

(i) the dwelling is within a clearance area under the Housing Act, 1936, or is or forms part of premises with respect to which a demolition order or closing order under that Act or a closing order under section ten or eleven of the Local Government (Miscellaneous Provisions) Act, 1953, has been made and has not ceased to be in force, or

(ii) works of repair remain unexecuted which were required to be executed by a notice or order given or made as respects the dwelling to or against the landlord, or any person receiving rent as agent for the landlord, under section nine of the Housing Act, 1936, section ninety-four of the Public Health Act, 1936, or paragraph 7 of the Fifth Schedule to the Public Health (London) Act, 1936, or

(iii) an order has been made under paragraph 9 of the Fifth Schedule to the Town and Country Planning Act, 1944, declaring the dwelling or a house of which it forms part unfit for human habitation and not capable at reasonable expense of being rendered so fit, and either the Minister has not yet decided whether to confirm the order or he has confirmed it and less than two years have elapsed since the confirmation,

and (except as aforesaid) if the date specified in a notice of increase in accordance with paragraph (a) of this sub-section falls at a time when the condition specified in sub-paragraph (i), (ii) or (iii) of this paragraph is fulfilled, no increase shall be recoverable by virtue of the notice for any rental period beginning at any such time.

(3) Where the landlord is a body corporate incorporated outside the United Kingdom, the foregoing provisions of this section shall have effect subject to the provisions of Part III of the First Schedule to this Act.

(4) If a notice of increase contains any statement or representation which is false or misleading in any material respect, the landlord shall be liable on summary conviction to a fine not exceeding fifty pounds unless he proves that the statement was made innocently and without intent to deceive.

3. Adjustment as respects rates borne by landlord

(1) Where any rates in respect of the dwelling are borne by the landlord or a superior landlord, then for any rental period for which the amount of the rates, ascertained in accordance with the Second Schedule to this Act, differs from the amount, so ascertained, of the rates for the basic rental period the rent limit shall be increased or decreased by the amount of the difference.

(2) In so far as a notice of increase relates to an increase of rent authorised by this section, the date specified by the notice may be any date not earlier than six weeks before the service of the notice, and where that date is earlier than the service of the notice any rent underpaid shall become due on the day after the service.

(3) Any increase of rent authorised by this section shall be disregarded for the purposes of paragraph (b) of subsection (2) of section two of this Act.

4. Adjustment as respects services and furniture

(1) Where, for any rental period, there is as respects—

(a) the provision of services for the tenant by the landlord or a superior landlord, or

(b) the use of furniture by the tenant under the terms of the tenancy,

or any circumstances relating thereto any difference, in comparison with the basic rental period, such as to affect the amount of the rent which it is reasonable to charge, the rent limit shall be increased or decreased by an appropriate amount; and where by virtue of this subsection the rent limit is increased for any rental period the rent for that period shall, notwithstanding anything in section two of this Act and without the service of any notice, be increased by the like amount.

(2) Any question whether, or by what amount, the rent limit is

increased or decreased by virtue of the foregoing subsection shall be determined by agreement in writing between the landlord and the tenant or by the county court; and any such determination—

(a) may be made so as to relate to past rental periods; and

(b) shall have effect as respects rental periods subsequent to the periods to which it relates until revoked or varied by such an agreement as aforesaid or by the county court.

5. Increase for improvements

(1) If an improvement has been effected in a dwelling and the improvement was completed after the commencement of this Act, the rent limit under any controlled tenancy of the dwelling for rental periods beginning after the completion of the improvement shall, subject to the following provisions of this section, be increased by eight per cent. per annum of the amount expended on the improvement by the landlord or any superior landlord or any person from whom the landlord or any superior landlord derives title.

(2) In so far as a notice of increase relates to an increase of rent authorised by this section, the date specified by the notice may be any date after the service of the notice, and any such increase shall be disregarded for the purposes of paragraph (b) of subsection (2) of section two of this Act.

(3) A tenant on whom a notice specifying an increase authorised by this section is served may, not later than one month after the service of the notice or such longer time as the court may allow, apply to the county court for an order cancelling or reducing the increase on the ground that the improvement was unnecessary or that a greater amount was expended on it than was reasonable, and the court may make an order accordingly, relating (if it is so provided by the order) not only to future but to past rental periods:

Provided that no application shall be made on the ground that an improvement was unnecessary if an improvement grant has been made in respect of the improvement under section twenty of the Housing Act, 1949, or if—

(a) a tenant under the controlled tenancy consented in writing to the improvement, and

(b) the consent contained an acknowledgement (however expressed) that the rent could be increased on account of the improvement.

(4) Where a grant has been made under the said section twenty or a repayment has been made under section twelve of the Clean

Air Act, 1956 in respect of an improvement, the reference in sub-section (1) of this section to the amount expended on the improvement shall be construed as a reference to that amount diminished by the amount of the grant or repayment.

6. Variation of rent under contractual tenancy

(1) In this section "contractual period" means a rental period beginning while a tenancy is current.

(2) Neither a notice of increase nor section four of this Act shall operate to increase the rent under a controlled tenancy for any contractual period except in so far as may be consistent with the terms of the tenancy.

(3) Where a notice of increase is served during the currency of a tenancy which could, by a notice to quit served by the landlord at the same time, be brought to an end before the date or earliest date specified in the notice of increase, the notice of increase shall operate to convert the tenancy into a statutory tenancy as from that date.

(4) Where the basic rental period of a controlled tenancy current at the commencement of this Act is a contractual period and the rent recoverable for that period includes an increase agreed or determined under section forty of the Housing Repairs and Rents Act, 1954, in respect of services which the landlord is not under the terms of the tenancy liable to provide, then, if those services are withheld in whole or in part during any contractual period, the rent recoverable for that period shall be decreased by an appropriate amount; and, without prejudice to the operation of section four of this Act in so far as it provides for a variation in the rent limit, subsection (2) of that section shall apply for the purpose of determining any question whether, or by what amount, the recoverable rent is decreased by virtue of this subsection.

(5) Subject to the last foregoing subsection, nothing in this Act shall affect the operation of any lease or agreement in so far as it provides for a reduction of rent during any contractual period.

INCREASE OF RENTS OF CONTROLLED HOUSES IN SCOTLAND

7. Increase of controlled rents

(1) Where a dwelling-house in Scotland is subject to a controlled tenancy, and the landlord is responsible, wholly or in part, for the repair of the dwelling-house, then, subject to the provisions of this and the next following section, if and so long as the conditions justifying an increase of rent, that is to say the conditions specified

in paragraph (a) of subsection (1) of section sixteen of the Housing (Repairs and Rents) (Scotland) Act, 1954 (in this and the three next following sections referred to as "the Act of 1954"), are fulfilled, the rent recoverable from the tenant shall, notwithstanding anything in the terms of the tenancy or any enactment, be increased by virtue of this subsection so as to exceed by the amount hereinafter mentioned the rent which apart from this subsection would be recoverable from the tenant under the terms of the tenancy and having regard to the provisions of any enactment.

(2) The amount of any increase payable by virtue of the foregoing subsection (which increase is hereinafter referred to as a "1957 Act increase") shall be an amount equal to one-quarter of the rent which was recoverable in respect of the dwelling-house immediately before the commencement of the Act of 1954:

Provided that where the landlord is responsible in part only for the repair of the dwelling-house, the amount of the 1957 Act increase shall be reduced proportionately.

(3) The foregoing provisions of this section shall not apply in relation to a dwelling-house—

(a) if it is one in relation to which, by virtue of subsection (3) of section sixteen of the Act of 1954, that section does not apply; or

(b) if it is one in respect of which a repairs increase is recoverable.

In this and the two next following sections the expression "repairs increase" has the same meaning as in the Act of 1954.

(4) Any question arising under the foregoing provisions of this section whether the landlord is responsible for repairs or as to the amount of any reduction under the proviso to subsection (2) of this section shall be determined by agreement in writing between the landlord and the tenant or, on the application of either of them, by the sheriff.

8. Supplementary provisions as to 1957 Act increases

(1) The provisions of sections seventeen to twenty-four and sections thirty-nine to forty-one of, and the Second Schedule to, the Act of 1954 shall apply in relation to a 1957 Act increase as they apply in relation to a repairs increase, and as so applied shall have effect subject to the modification that for any reference (except in section twenty) to Part II of the Act of 1954 and to a repairs increase or an increase under the said Part II there shall be substituted a

reference to section seven of this Act and to a 1957 Act increase and subject also to the further modifications set out in the Third Schedule to this Act.

(2) The rent recoverable from the tenant of a dwelling-house shall be subject to be increased by way of a repairs increase in accordance with the provisions of Part II of the Act of 1954 notwithstanding that that rent has already been increased by way of a 1957 Act increase, but no sum shall be recoverable by way of 1957 Act increase in respect of any period in respect of which any sum is recoverable by way of repairs increase.

(3) Any certificate of a local authority granted under Part II of the Act of 1954 (including the Second Schedule thereto), any notice served by a local authority revoking such a certificate, any certificate of a sanitary authority having effect as such a certificate of a local authority, and any finding or order of the sheriff made under the said Part II or under the Rent Acts, the effect of which is to establish whether either or both of the conditions justifying an increase of rent under that Act are fulfilled, shall have effect for the purpose of establishing whether the conditions justifying an increase of rent by way of a 1957 Act increase are fulfilled as if it were a certificate, notice, finding or order granted, served or made for the purposes of section seven of this Act; and any such certificate, notice, finding or order granted, served or made for the purposes of the said section seven shall have effect for the purpose of establishing whether either or both of the conditions justifying an increase of rent by way of a repairs increase are fulfilled as if it were granted, served or made for the purposes of the said Part II.

9. Amendments of Act of 1954 as to amount of repairs increase, etc.

(1) Subsection (2) of section sixteen of the Act of 1954 (which provides that the amount of the repairs increase shall be an amount equal to two-fifths of the rent recoverable immediately before the commencement of that Act) and subsection (3) of section twenty-one of that Act (which limits the amount recoverable from a sub-tenant by way of repairs increase) shall have effect with the substitution for the words "two-fifths" of the words "one-half".

(2) Where the rent recoverable from the tenant or sub-tenant of a dwelling-house has already been increased by way of a repairs increase of an amount ascertained in accordance with the Act of 1954 as originally enacted, no further increase shall be recoverable by virtue of the foregoing subsection unless the landlord or the

tenant has served on the tenant or sub-tenant or a former tenant or sub-tenant a notice in the prescribed form specifying a date, not earlier than eight clear weeks after the service of the notice and (in the case of a notice served on a sub-tenant) not earlier than the date on which the further increase begins to be recoverable from the tenant, as the date on which such further increase is to begin; and no sum shall be recoverable on account of such further increase before, or in respect of any period before, that date.

(3) Subsection (1) of section nineteen of the Act of 1954 (which subsection provides that the increases of rent permitted by paragraphs (c) and (d) of subsection (1) of section two of the Act of 1920 shall cease to be recoverable in respect of any period during which a certificate granted or having effect as if granted under subsection (1) or subsection (2) of section eighteen of the Act of 1954 is in force or a court is satisfied that either or both of the conditions justifying an increase of rent were not fulfilled) shall cease to have effect:

Provided that nothing in this subsection shall have effect as respects any period before the commencement of this Act or shall affect the operation of subsection (1) of the said section nineteen in relation to any such certificate as aforesaid granted before the commencement of this Act or granted after such commencement in pursuance of an application made before such commencement.

(4) In this section "prescribed" means prescribed by regulations made by the Minister by statutory instrument, and the provisions of subsection (3) of section seventeen of the Act of 1954 shall apply to a form prescribed for the purposes of this section as they apply to a form prescribed for the purposes of that section.

(5) A notice of intention to increase the rent by way of a repairs increase shall not be served under section seventeen of the Act of 1954 in respect of a dwelling-house at any time within a period of four months after a notice of intention to increase the rent thereof by way of a 1957 Act increase has been served in respect of the dwelling-house, and any notice served in contravention of this subsection shall be void.

10. Rents of subsidised private houses in Scotland

(1) The conditions which are mentioned in any of the enactments specified in the next following subsection or which have effect by virtue of any undertaking or agreement entered into in pursuance of any such enactment shall, in so far as they relate to the rent to be charged in respect of any dwelling-house in Scotland, limit that rent, and if imposed before the commencement of this Act shall have

effect as if they limited that rent, to an amount equal to the rent which might properly be charged in respect of that dwelling-house by virtue of those conditions together with any sum recoverable in respect thereof by way of repairs increase under the Act of 1954 or by way of 1957 Act increase.

(2) The enactments referred to in the foregoing subsection are—

    (*a*) section two of the Housing (Financial Provisions) Act, 1924;

    (*b*) section three of the Housing (Rural Workers) Act, 1926;

    (*c*) section one hundred and one of the Housing (Scotland) Act, 1950;

    (*d*) sub-paragraph (ii) of paragraph (*c*) of subsection (1) of section one hundred and fourteen of the Housing (Scotland) Act, 1950.

RELEASE FROM RENT ACTS AND FURNISHED HOUSES RENT CONTROL

11. Release from control under Rent Acts

(1) The Rent Acts shall not apply to any dwelling-house the rateable value of which on the seventh day of November, nineteen hundred and fifty-six, exceeded, in the Metropolitan Police District or the City of London forty pounds, elsewhere in England or Wales thirty pounds, and in Scotland forty pounds.

(2) The Rent Acts shall not apply to a tenancy created by a lease or agreement coming into operation at or after the commencement of this Act, and the tenant shall not by virtue of those Acts be entitled to retain possession as a statutory tenant on the coming to an end of such a tenancy:

Provided that this subsection shall not apply where the person to whom the tenancy is granted was immediately before the granting the tenant under a controlled tenancy and the premises comprised in one of the tenancies are the same as, or consist of or include part of, the premises comprised in the other.

(3) The Minister may by order provide that the Rent Acts shall not apply, as from such date as may be specified in the order, to dwelling-houses the rateable value of which, ascertained as on such date as may be specified in the order, exceeds such amount as may be so specified; and an order under this subsection may be made so as to relate to the whole of England and Wales, to the whole of Scotland, or to such area or areas in England and Wales or in Scotland as may be specified in the order, and so as to apply gener-

ally, or only to, or except to, such classes or descriptions of dwelling-houses as may be so specified.

The power conferred by this subsection to make orders shall be exercisable by statutory instrument, and no such order shall have effect until it is approved by a resolution of each House of Parliament.

(4) Nothing in the foregoing provisions of this section shall affect the operation of Part I of the Landlord and Tenant Act, 1954.

(5) Nothing in the foregoing provisions of this section shall affect the operation of section four of the Requisitioned Houses and Housing (Amendment) Act, 1955, but a person shall not be entitled to retain possession by virtue of this subsection after the thirty-first day of March, nineteen hundred and sixty-five.

(6) Where a controlled tenancy of a dwelling comes to an end by virtue of section sixty-five of the Housing Act, 1936, section fifty-five of the Housing (Scotland) Act, 1950, or section eleven of the Housing Repairs and Rents Act, 1954 (which relate to over-crowding), subsection (2) of this section shall not apply to the first tenancy created thereafter of the dwelling or any part thereof.

(7) The transitional provisions contained in the Fourth Schedule to this Act shall have effect in relation to dwelling-houses which cease to be subject to control by virtue of subsection (1) or (3) of this section; and those subsections shall have effect subject to the provisions of paragraph 3 of Part I of the Fifth Schedule to this Act.

12. Furnished houses

(1) Subject to the provisions of this section, the Furnished Houses (Rent Control) Act, 1946, shall not apply to a contract (whether registered under that Act or not) relating to a dwelling of any class or description in any area if the rateable value of the dwelling on any date as on which rateable value fell to be ascertained under subsection (1) of the foregoing section, or under an order which has come into force under subsection (3) thereof, was such that the Rent Acts do not apply to dwelling-houses of that class or description in that area and of that rateable value on that date.

(2) Where the said Act of 1946 ceases to apply to a contract (whether by virtue of the foregoing subsection or otherwise),—

   (a) a notice to quit given by the landlord before the time at which the said Act of 1946 ceases to apply to the contract shall not take effect earlier than the expiration of three months after that time unless the Tribunal constituted under section one of that Act have determined that the

notice shall take effect at the end of a period or extended
period expiring before the said three months;

(b) a notice to quit given by the landlord within a year after
the said time shall not take effect earlier than the
expiration of three months after the giving of the notice;

(c) so long as the contract continues in force, the rent payable
thereunder shall be the same as if the said Act of 1946
had not ceased to apply to the contract.

(3) As respects a notice to quit current during a service man's
period of residence protection (within the meaning of the Reserve
and Auxiliary Forces (Protection of Civil Interests) Act, 1951) and
relating to the rented family residence, the operation of section
eleven of the Landlord and Tenant (Rent Control) Act, 1949, and
of section fifteen of the said Act of 1951 (which relate to the suspension of notices to quit) shall not be affected by subsection (1) of this
section whether the notice was given before or after the beginning
of the period of residence protection:

Provided that nothing in this subsection shall apply where the
rented family residence is excluded by subsection (2) of section
fourteen of the said Act of 1951 from the operation of the said section
fifteen.

(4) Where a dwelling is or forms part of a hereditament for which
no rateable value was shown in the valuation list on a date referred
to in subsection (1) of this section, that subsection shall have effect,
in relation to that dwelling, as if for the first reference to that date
there were substituted a reference to the first subsequent date on
which a rateable value for that hereditament was shown in the
valuation list.

(5) Where a contract referred to a Tribunal under the said Act
of 1946 relates to a dwelling consisting of or comprising part only of
a hereditament, and no apportionment of the rateable or annual
value of the hereditament has been duly made, then unless the
landlord—

(a) in the course of the proceedings requires that an apportionment shall be made by the county court, and

(b) within two weeks of making the requirement brings proceedings in the county court for the making of the
apportionment,

the Tribunal shall have jurisdiction to deal with the reference,
notwithstanding that no apportionment has been made, if it appears

to them that if an apportionment had been made its result would have been such that they would have had jurisdiction.

(6) Where rent is payable weekly under any contract to which the Furnished Houses (Rent Control) Act, 1946, applies, it shall be the duty of the landlord to provide a rent book or other similar document for use in respect of the dwelling, containing particulars of the rent and of the other terms and conditions of the contract; and if at any time after the expiration of two months from the commencement of this Act the landlord fails to comply with the requirements of this subsection he, and any person who on his behalf demands or receives rent under the contract, shall in respect of each week in which the failure occurs or continues be guilty of an offence and liable on summary conviction to a fine not exceeding ten pounds.

(7) This section shall apply to Scotland subject to the following modifications, that is to say—

(a) for any reference to the Furnished Houses (Rent Control) Act, 1946, there shall be substituted a reference to the Rent of Furnished Houses Control (Scotland) Act, 1943;

(b) for references to a hereditament and to the valuation list there shall be substituted references to lands and heritages and to the valuation roll; and

(c) for references to the county court there shall be substituted references to the sheriff.

PROVISIONS AS TO PREMIUMS, ETC.

13. Premiums not to be charged for decontrolled tenancies

(1) As respects grant, renewal, continuance or assignment at any time during the period of three years beginning with the commencement of this Act, a tenancy excluded from the application of the Rent Acts by reason only of the provisions of subsection (1) or (2) of section eleven of this Act or of those provisions and of subsection (7) of section twelve of the Act of 1920 (which excludes from the Rent Acts tenancies where the rent is less than two-thirds of the rateable value) shall be treated as one to which section two of the Landlord and Tenant (Rent Control) Act, 1949, applies (which section prohibits the requiring of premiums on the grant, renewal, continuance or assignment of tenancies to which the Rent Acts apply):

Provided that this subsection shall not affect the assignment of a tenancy granted before the commencement of this Act and not renewed or continued thereafter, being a tenancy to which sub-section (7) of section twelve of the Act of 1920 applies.

(2) An order under subsection (3) of section eleven of this Act may provide that the foregoing subsection shall apply in relation to the order as it applies in relation to subsection (1) of the said section eleven, but with the substitution for the period mentioned in the foregoing subsection of such period, beginning with the date as from which the order excludes the application of the Rent Acts and ending not later than three years thereafter, as may be specified in the order.

14. Application to loans of provisions of Act of 1949 relating to premiums

(1) Subsections (1) and (2) of section two of the Landlord and Tenant (Rent Control) Act, 1949, and subsection (6) of that section so far as it provides for the trial and punishment of persons contravening that section, shall apply to requiring the making of any loan (whether secured or unsecured) as they apply to requiring the payment of a premium in addition to rent.

(2) The foregoing subsection shall not invalidate any agreement for the making of a loan or any security issued in pursuance of such an agreement, but any sum lent in circumstances involving a contravention of the said section two shall, notwithstanding anything in the agreement for the loan, be repayable to the lender on demand.

15. Restriction on requiring payment in advance of rent under decontrolled tenancies

(1) Where a tenancy is granted, continued or renewed in circumstances in which section thirteen of this Act applies, any requirement that rent shall be payable—

(a) before the beginning of the rental period in respect of which it is payable, or

(b) earlier than six months before the end of the rental period in respect of which it is payable, if that period is more than six months long,

shall be void, whether the requirement is imposed as a condition of the grant, renewal or continuance of the tenancy or under the terms thereof; and rent for any rental period to which a requirement avoided by this section relates shall be irrecoverable from the tenant.

(2) A person who purports to impose any requirement avoided by

the foregoing subsection shall be liable on summary conviction to a fine not exceeding one hundred pounds, and the court by which he is convicted may order any amount of rent paid in compliance with the requirement to be repaid to the person by whom it was paid.

16. Minimum length of notice to quit

No notice by a landlord or a tenant to quit any premises let (whether before or after the commencement of this Act) as a dwelling shall be valid unless it is given not less than four weeks before the date on which it is to take effect.

17. Provisions to facilitate exchange of controlled dwellings

(1) Where it is so agreed in writing between the tenant under a statutory tenancy of a dwelling and a person proposing to occupy that dwelling (hereinafter referred to as the "incoming tenant"), the incoming tenant shall subject as hereinafter provided be deemed as from such date as may be specified in the agreement (hereinafter referred to as the "date of exchange") to be the tenant of the dwelling under that statutory tenancy; and the question whether the provisions of the Rent Acts as to the succession by the widow of a deceased tenant or by a member of his family to the right to retain possession are capable of having effect in the event of the death of the incoming tenant shall be determined according as those provisions have or have not already had effect in relation to the statutory tenancy.

(2) An agreement under the foregoing subsection shall not have effect unless the landlord is a party thereto, and if the consent of any superior landlord would have been required to an assignment of the tenancy on the coming to an end of which the statutory tenancy arose the agreement shall not have effect unless the superior landlord is a party thereto.

(3) An agreement under subsection (1) of this section may provide that the provisions of the Rent Acts mentioned in that subsection shall be capable of having effect in the event of the death of the incoming tenant notwithstanding that they had effect in favour of the tenant to whom he succeeded.

(4) It shall be unlawful to require the payment of any pecuniary consideration for entering into an agreement under subsection (1) of this section; and—

(a) the amount of any payment made which under this sub-
     section could not lawfully be required shall be recover-
     able by the person by whom it was made either by
     proceedings for its recovery or, if it was made to the
     landlord, by deduction from any rent payable by the
     said person to the landlord;

(b) a person requiring the payment of any consideration in
     contravention of this subsection shall be liable on sum-
     mary conviction to a fine not exceeding one hundred
     pounds, and the court by which he is convicted may
     order the amount of the payment to be repaid by the
     person to whom it was paid:

Provided that subsection (4) of section two of the Landlord and
Tenant (Rent Control) Act, 1949 (which allows an assignor to
charge the assignee for apportioned outgoings, improvements, and
goodwill) shall apply with the substitution for the reference to
subsection (2) of that section of a reference to this subsection, and
for references to the assignor, the assignee and the taking effect of
the assignment of references to the tenant, the incoming tenant and
the date of exchange.

18. Private street works to count as improvements

(1) The following provisions of this section shall have effect for
the purposes of section five of this Act or, in Scotland, for the
purposes of paragraph (a) of subsection (1) of section two of the Act
of 1920.

(2) Where works have been carried out on a street under—

(a) section one hundred and fifty of the Public Health Act,
     1875, or

(b) the Private Street Works Act, 1892, or

(c) any of the enactments referred to in section one of the Local
     Government (Street Works) (Scotland) Act, 1956, or

(d) the corresponding provisions of any local Act,

and any dwelling having access to the street is the subject of a
controlled tenancy, the amount of any expenditure incurred after
the commencement of this Act by the landlord or a superior landlord
in the carrying out of the works, or of any liability so incurred by
the landlord or a superior landlord in respect of the works to the
authority by whom they were carried out (whether the liability is
dischargeable in a lump sum or by instalments, but in the case of

instalments exclusive of interest), shall (whether or not apart from this section it would be so treated) be treated as expenditure incurred by the landlord or superior landlord on improvement as mentioned in subsection (1) of section five of this Act or, as the case may be, in paragraph (a) of subsection (1) of section two of the Act of 1920:

Provided that if benefit accrues from the carrying out of the works not only to the dwelling but also to other premises of the landlord or superior landlord, the amount to be treated as aforesaid shall be so much only of the expenditure or liability as may be determined, by agreement in writing between the landlord and the tenant or by the county court, or in Scotland the sheriff, to be properly apportionable to the dwelling, having regard to the benefit accruing, from the carrying out of the works, to the dwelling and to the other premises.

(3) For the purposes of this section the amount of any expenditure shall be treated as diminished by the amount of any contribution made in respect thereof under any enactment.

(4) Subsection (3) of section five of this Act and the proviso to paragraph (a) of subsection (1) of section two of the Act of 1920 shall not apply to any increase authorised by virtue of this section.

19. Jurisdiction of county court or sheriff, and procedure

(1) The county court shall have jurisdiction, either in the course of any proceedings relating to a dwelling or on an application made for the purpose by the landlord or the tenant, to determine any question as to the application of the Rent Acts, as to the rent limit, or the rent actually recoverable, under a controlled tenancy, as to the application of the Furnished Houses (Rent Control) Act, 1946, to any contract, or as to any matter which is or may become material for determining any such question as aforesaid.

(2) In Scotland, the sheriff shall have jurisdiction, either in the course of any proceedings relating to a dwelling or on an application made for the purpose by the landlord or the tenant, to determine any question as to the application of the Rent Acts or of the Rent of Furnished Houses Control (Scotland) Act, 1943, or as to any matter which is or may become material for determining any such question.

(3) Section seventeen of the Act of 1920 (which relates to rules of procedure and the jurisdiction of the county court) shall apply in relation to this Act as it applies in relation to that Act.

(4) Any apportionment of rates, gross value or rateable value made by the county court or the sheriff for the purposes of this Act,

P

and any apportionment made by the court or sheriff under the proviso to subsection (2) of the foregoing section, shall be final and conclusive.

20. Rents of subsidised private houses

(1) In so far as the conditions mentioned in any of the following enactments, that is to say,—

    (a) section two of the Housing (Financial Provisions) Act, 1924;

    (b) section three of the Housing (Rural Workers) Act, 1926;

    (c) section three of the Housing (Financial Provisions) Act, 1938;

    (d) section twenty-three of the Housing Act, 1949;

    (e) section three of the Housing Act, 1952,

relate to the rent to be charged in respect of any dwelling they shall limit that rent, and if imposed before the commencement of this Act shall have effect as if they limited that rent, to the amount of the rent limit; but if the conditions were imposed before the commencement of this Act and then limited the rent to an amount exceeding what would be the rent limit if ascertained under subsection (1) of section one of this Act, the rent limit shall be that amount, subject however to the provisions of subsection (2) of that section.

(2) Where any such condition as aforesaid has been registered in the register of local land charges the proper officer of the local authority shall record in that register any change in that condition effected by this section.

(3) Where any such condition as aforesaid limits the rent under a tenancy which is not a controlled tenancy then, subject to the next following subsection,—

    (a) subsection (1) of this section shall have effect, in relation to that tenancy, as if for the reference to the amount of the rent limit there were substituted a reference to the amount which would be the rent limit if the tenancy were a controlled tenancy; and

    (b) in ascertaining that amount in a case where a dwelling was produced by the conversion of any premises and the conversion resulted in a change in the valuation list after the seventh day of November, nineteen hundred and fifty-six, any entry in that list before the change shall be disregarded; and

(c) the provisions of this Act enabling rents to be increased and conferring jurisdiction on the county court shall apply in relation to the tenancy as they apply in relation to a controlled tenancy.

(4) In relation to a tenancy falling within paragraph (c) or (d) of section thirty-three of the Housing Repairs and Rents Act, 1954 (which exclude from the operation of the Rent Acts certain tenancies where the interest of the landlord belongs to a housing association or a housing trust),—

(a) paragraphs (a) to (c) of the last foregoing subsection shall not apply; but

(b) the condition shall limit the rent, and if imposed before the commencement of this Act shall have effect as if it limited the rent, to such amount as may from time to time be agreed between the association or trust and the local authority (or the London County Council in the case of houses the construction of which was promoted by them or in respect of which improvement grants were made by them under the Housing Act, 1949) or as may, in default of agreement, be determined by the Minister; but if the condition was imposed before the commencement of this Act it shall, until the said amount has been agreed or determined under this paragraph, have effect as if this Act had not been passed.

21. Long tenancies

(1) The Rent Acts shall not apply to any long tenancy, without prejudice however to the operation of subsection (3) of section fifteen of the Act of 1920.

(2) Part I of the Landlord and Tenant Act, 1954, shall apply to long tenancies not at a low rent as it applies to long tenancies at a low rent.

22. Statutory tenancies of requisitioned houses

(1) The following provisions shall have effect in the case of a statutory tenancy subsisting under section four of the Requisitioned Houses and Housing (Amendment) Act, 1955 (which applies the Rent Acts to occupiers of certain dwellings formerly requisitioned and empowers the local authority to contribute to the rent):—

(a) a notice of increase applying to rent for any rental period beginning before the first day of April, nineteen hundred and sixty-five, shall not have effect unless not later than three days after the service of the notice the landlord serves a copy of the notice on the local authority;

(b) the local authority shall have such powers of applying to the county court as are conferred by this Act on the tenant;

(c) the local authority shall be a necessary party to any agreement, and to any proceedings in any court, affecting the amount of the rent for any such rental period as aforesaid.

In this subsection the expression "the local authority" means the local authority (within the meaning of the said Act of 1955) which gave the invitation by virtue of the acceptance of which the statutory tenancy arose.

(2) The said section four shall be amended as follows:—

(a) in paragraph (b) of subsection (2) the words from "at a rent" to "this section" shall be omitted, and after the words "terms and conditions" there shall be inserted the words "(other than terms as to rent)";

(b) in subsection (3) for the words "The standard rent" there shall be substituted the words "Subject to the provisions of subsection (4) of this section and of the Rent Act, 1957, the rent", and the words from "and for the purposes" to the end of the subsection shall be omitted.

23. Concurrence of superior landlords to agreements as to 1956 gross value and rateable value

Where the landlord is himself a tenant, then unless he is tenant under a tenancy having a term with more than seven years to run an agreement between him and his tenant relating to the amount of the 1956 gross value or of the rateable value of the dwelling-house shall not have effect, for the purposes of the provisions of this Act relating to controlled tenancies and to the application of the Rent Acts, except with the concurrence in writing of his immediate landlord.

24. Payments out of moneys provided by Parliament

There shall be paid out of moneys provided by Parliament any increase attributable to this Act in—

(a) the sums required by the Minister for making payments to local authorities under Part I of the Requisitioned Houses and Housing (Amendment) Act, 1955, and (*b*) the sums payable out of moneys provided by Parliament under Part I of the Local Government Act, 1948, or the Local Government (Financial Provisions) (Scotland) Act, 1954, as amended by the Valuation and Rating (Scotland) Act, 1956.

25. Interpretation

(1) In this Act, except so far as the context otherwise requires:—

"the Rent Acts", "the Act of 1920", "the Act of 1933", "landlord", "tenant", "tenancy", "statutory tenancy" and "local authority" have the meanings assigned to them by subsection (1) of section forty-nine of the Housing Repairs and Rents Act, 1954, or as respects Scotland by subsection (1) of section thirty-nine of the Housing (Repairs and Rents) (Scotland) Act, 1954;

"appropriate factor" means the number by which the 1956 gross value is to be multiplied in determining the rent limit;

"basic rental period" means the rental period comprising the commencement of this Act or, in the case of a controlled tenancy beginning thereafter, the first rental period of the tenancy;

"controlled tenancy" means a tenancy to which the Rent Acts apply or a statutory tenancy;

"dwelling", except in section sixteen of this Act, means in relation to a controlled tenancy the aggregate of the premises comprised in the tenancy, and in relation to a contract the aggregate of the premises to which the contract relates;

"improvement" includes structural alteration, extension or addition and the provision of additional fixtures or fittings, but does not include anything done by way of decoration or repair;

"long tenancy" and "tenancy at a low rent" have the meanings assigned to them by subsections (4) and (5) of section two of the Landlord and Tenant Act, 1954;

"1956 gross value", in relation to a dwelling, means, subject to the provisions of the Fifth Schedule to this Act, the gross value thereof as shown in the valuation list on the seventh day of November, nineteen hundred and fifty-six, or, where the dwelling forms part only of a hereditament shown in that list, such proportion of the gross value shown in that list for that hereditament as may be agreed in writing between the landlord and the tenant or determined by the county court;

"notice of increase" means a notice of increase under section two of this Act;

"prescribed" means prescribed by regulations under section fourteen of the Act of 1933, and references in this Act to a prescribed form include references to a form substantially to the same effect as the prescribed form;

"rateable value" shall be construed as provided in Part I of the Fifth Schedule to this Act;

"rates" includes water rents and charges but does not include an owner's drainage rate within the meaning of paragraph (a) of subsection (2) of section twenty-four of the Land Drainage Act, 1930; and any references in this Act to rates in respect of any dwelling include references to such proportion of any rates in respect of a hereditament of which the dwelling forms part as may be agreed in writing between the landlord and the tenant or determined by the county court;

"rental period" means a period in respect of which a payment for rent falls to be made;

"the Minister" means the Minister of Housing and Local Government, or as respects Scotland the Secretary of State;

"the valuation officer" has the same meaning as in Part III of the Local Government Act, 1948.

(2) Where a controlled tenancy is followed by a statutory tenancy of the same dwelling, the two shall be treated for the purposes of this Act, in its application to England and Wales, as together constituting one controlled tenancy.

(3) Any reference in this Act, in its application to England and Wales, to rent shall be construed as a reference to rent—

(a) exclusive of any sums recoverable as rent under section sixteen of the Landlord and Tenant Act, 1927 (which enables landlords to recover, as rent, sums in respect of increases in taxes, rates or fire premiums ascribable to improvements made by tenants) other than—

(i) sums so recoverable in respect of increases in rates, or

> (ii) sums referable to improvements executed by the tenant before the first day of April, nineteen hundred and fifty-six, or
>
> (iii) sums referable to improvements executed by him after that day but affecting the 1956 gross value by reason of a proposal made before the first day of April, nineteen hundred and fifty-seven;

(b) exclusive of any sums recoverable as rent under the First Schedule to the Landlord and Tenant Act, 1954;

(c) without taking into account any deduction falling to be made under the First Schedule to the Landlord and Tenant (Rent Control) Act, 1949 (which provides for the recovery of premiums by deduction from rent) or under paragraph 1 of the Second Schedule to the Landlord and Tenant Act, 1954 (which empowers the court to order a reduction of rent where the landlord fails to carry out initial repairs).

(4) References in this Act to any enactment are references to that enactment as amended by any other enactment, including, except where the context otherwise requires, this Act.

26. Application of enactments, minor amendments, transitional provisions and repeals

(1) The provisions of the Sixth Schedule to this Act shall have effect for applying certain enactments for the purposes of this Act and for making certain minor and consequential amendments of enactments.

(2) The transitional provisions contained in the Seventh Schedule to this Act shall have effect.

(3) The enactments specified in Part I of the Eighth Schedule to this Act are hereby repealed, in their application to England and Wales, to the extent specified in the third column of that Part of that Schedule; and the enactments specified in Part II of that Schedule are hereby repealed, in their application to Scotland, to the extent specified in the third column of the said Part II.

27. Short title, commencement and extent

(1) This Act may be cited as the Rent Act, 1957.

(2) This Act shall come into force on the expiration of the period of one month which begins with the date of the passing thereof.

(3) The following provisions of this Act, that is to say, sections seven to nineteen, sections twenty-three and twenty-five, subsections (1) and (3) of section twenty-six, this section, the Third and Fourth Schedules, Part I of the Fifth Schedule, the Sixth Schedule, and Part II of the Eighth Schedule shall, so far as applicable, and subject to any modification specified therein, extend to Scotland, but the other provisions of this Act shall not extend to Scotland.

(4) This Act shall not extend to Northern Ireland.

Section 1.

SCHEDULES

FIRST SCHEDULE

Adjustment of Rent in Respect of Repairs

Part I

Adjustment of Rent Limit

1.—(1) The following provisions shall have effect in ascertaining the rent limit by reference to the 1956 gross value.

(2) If under the terms of the tenancy the tenant is responsible for all repairs, the appropriate factor shall be four-thirds.

(3) If under the terms of the tenancy the tenant is responsible for some, but not all, repairs, the appropriate factor shall be such number less than two but greater than four-thirds as may be agreed in writing between the landlord and the tenant or determined by the county court.

2.—(1) In the foregoing paragraph the expression "repairs" does not include internal decorative repairs, but if the landlord is responsible for internal decorative repairs under the terms of the tenancy, or neither the landlord nor the tenant is responsible therefor under the terms of the tenancy but the landlord elects to be treated for the purposes of this Act as responsible therefor,—

(a) "seven-thirds" and "five-thirds" shall be substituted respectively for "two" and "four-thirds" in section one of this Act and the foregoing paragraph, and

(b) as respects any rental period beginning after the election, the question whether the rent limit is to be ascertained under subsection (1) or under subsection (3) of the said section one shall be determined as if the election had always had effect.

(2) An election under this paragraph shall be made by notice in the prescribed form served on the tenant and shall continue in force notwithstanding any change in the person of the landlord.

(3) An election under this paragraph shall not have effect if the tenant dissents from it in writing within one month of the service on the tenant of the notice under the foregoing sub-paragraph; but if the tenant duly dissents the First Schedule to the Act of 1933 shall thereafter have effect in relation to the dwelling as if the grounds for possession specified in paragraph (a) thereof included the ground that the tenant has failed to keep the dwelling in a reasonable state of internal decorative repair, having due regard to its age, character and locality.

PART II

ABATEMENT FOR DISREPAIR

Notification of disrepair to landlord

3. The provisions of this Part of this Schedule shall have effect where the tenant under a controlled tenancy serves on the landlord a notice in the prescribed form stating that the dwelling or any part thereof is in disrepair by reason of defects specified in the notice, and that those defects ought reasonably to be remedied, having due regard to the age, character and locality of the dwelling, and requesting the landlord to remedy them.

Landlord's undertaking to repair: and certificates of disrepair

4.—(1) If, on the expiration of six weeks from the service of a notice under the last foregoing paragraph, any of the defects specified in the notice remain unremedied, then unless the landlord has given an undertaking in the prescribed form to remedy those defects or such of them as the tenant may agree in writing to accept as sufficient, the tenant may in the prescribed form apply to the local authority for a certificate of disrepair.

Any such application shall be accompanied by a copy of the said notice.

(2) Where an application under this paragraph is made to a local authority and the local authority are satisfied that the dwelling or any part thereof is in disrepair by reason of defects specified in the said notice and that all or any of those defects ought reasonably to be remedied, having due regard to the age, character and locality of the dwelling, they shall issue to the tenant a certificate of disrepair accordingly and any such certificate shall be in the prescribed form and shall specify the defects as to which the local authority are satisfied as aforesaid, stating that the local authority are so satisfied.

(3) If on an application by the tenant the county court is satisfied, as respects any defects, that the local authority have failed to issue a certificate of disrepair which ought to have been issued, the court shall direct the authority to proceed on the footing that, in relation to those defects, they are satisfied as to the matters specified in the foregoing sub-paragraph; and if on an application by the tenant the county court is satisfied that any defect not specified in a certificate of disrepair ought to have been specified therein, the court shall order that the defect shall be deemed to have been specified in the certificate.

(4) The local authority shall not be concerned to inquire into any obligation as between a landlord and tenant or into the origin of any defect; but if on an application by the landlord the county court is satisfied, as respects any defect specified in a certificate of disrepair, that it is one for which the tenant is responsible, the court shall cancel the certificate as respects that defect.

(5) If on an application by the landlord the county court is satisfied as respects any defect specified in a certificate of disrepair that it ought not to

have been specified, the court shall cancel the certificate as respects that defect.

(6) Where a certificate of disrepair is cancelled under this paragraph as respects all the defects specified therein it shall be deemed never to have had effect, and where it is so cancelled as respects some only of the defects specified therein it shall be deemed never to have had those defects specified therein.

5. Notwithstanding anything in the last foregoing paragraph, a local authority shall not issue a certificate of disrepair until the expiration of three weeks from the service by them on the landlord of a notice in the prescribed form stating that the authority propose to issue the certificate of disrepair and specifying the defects to which it is to relate; and if within the said three weeks the landlord gives an undertaking in the prescribed form to remedy those defects and serves a copy of the undertaking on the local authority, the authority shall not issue the certificate:

Provided that where—

(a) a previous certificate of disrepair under this Schedule has been issued against the landlord in respect of the dwelling or any part thereof, or

(b) the landlord has previously become liable under subsection (3) of section ten of the Housing Act, 1936, as the person having control of the dwelling or of any premises comprising the dwelling, to repay to the local authority (within the meaning of that section) any expenses incurred by them under that section, or

(c) the landlord has previously given an undertaking under this Schedule in respect of the dwelling, or any other dwelling in the area of the local authority, and any of the defects to which that undertaking related remained unremedied on the expiration of six months from the giving thereof, or

(d) the landlord has previously been convicted of an offence under section ninety-five of the Public Health Act, 1936, of failing to comply with, or contravening, a nuisance order or an offence under paragraph 12 of the Fifth Schedule to the Public Health (London) Act, 1936, of failing to comply with an abatement order or contravening a prohibition order or a closing order,

the local authority may refuse to accept the undertaking and may issue a certificate of disrepair, and if they do so the undertaking shall be deemed never to have been given.

6.—(1) Where, after the issue of a certificate of disrepair, the landlord applies to the local authority for the cancellation of the certificate on the ground that the defects specified in the certificate have been remedied, the local authority shall serve on the tenant a notice to the effect that unless an objection from the tenant is received by them within three weeks from the

. service of the notice on the ground that the said defects or any of them have not been remedied, they propose to cancel the certificate.

(2) If no objection is received as aforesaid, or if in the opinion of the local authority the objection is not justified, they shall cancel the certificate as from the date of the application or such later date as appears to them to be the date on which the said defects were remedied.

(3) Where the landlord has applied to the local authority for the cancellation of a certificate of disrepair, and the authority have not cancelled the certificate, the landlord may apply to the county court, and if on the application the court is satisfied that the certificate ought to have been cancelled by the local authority the court shall order that the certificate shall cease to have effect as from the date of the order or such earlier date as may be specified in the order.

(4) Where the local authority have cancelled a certificate of disrepair, the tenant may apply to the county court, and if on the application the court is satisfied that the certificate ought not to have been cancelled the court may order that it shall be deemed not to have been cancelled.

Abatement of rent where certificate issued or undertaking not carried out

7.—(1) Where an application for a certificate of disrepair is granted, any notice of increase served during the period beginning six months before the date of the application and ending when the certificate ceases to be in force shall have no effect as respects any rental period beginning while the certificate is in force, except in so far as it specifies an increase authorised by section three or five of this Act.

(2) Where a certificate of disrepair is issued, then as respects any rental period beginning while the certificate is in force the appropriate factor shall be four-thirds, and the rent limit shall be ascertained under subsection (1) of section one of this Act notwithstanding anything in subsection (3) of that section or subsection (1) of section twenty of this Act or sub-paragraph (3) of paragraph 8 of the Sixth Schedule thereto.

(3) A notice of increase served while a certificate of disrepair is in force shall be void unless it contains a statement that it will not take effect while the certificate is in force except in so far as the increase specified in it is authorised by section three or five of this Act.

(4) Without prejudice to sub-paragraphs (1) to (3) of this paragraph, the tenant shall be entitled to withhold rent otherwise recoverable for rental periods beginning while the certificate of disrepair continues in force up to an aggregate amount equal to the aggregate amount of rent for rental periods which began—

(a) on or after the date of the application for the certificate of disrepair, and

(b) before the granting thereof,

being rent which would have been made irrecoverable by the foregoing provisions of this paragraph if the certificate had been in force throughout those rental periods, so however that for any rental period the amount of rent withheld by virtue of this sub-paragraph shall not exceed the amount of rent made irrecoverable by the foregoing provisions of this paragraph for the first rental period beginning while the certificate is in force.

(5) Where under paragraph 4 of this Schedule an application is made to the court for the cancellation of a certificate of disrepair as respects all the defects specified therein, and the application is made within three weeks after the issue of the certificate, the rent recoverable for any rental period beginning while proceedings on the application are pending shall, until those proceedings are concluded, be deemed to be the same as if the certificate had not been issued.

8.—(1) If on the expiration of six months from the giving of such an undertaking as is mentioned in paragraph 4 or 5 of this Schedule any defects to which the undertaking relates remain unremedied the same consequencies shall follow as if a certificate of disrepair had then been issued and had continued in force until the remedying of the defects, and (where the undertaking was given before any application for such a certificate had been made) as if such an application had been made when the undertaking was given.

(2) Where such an undertaking has been given the landlord or the tenant may apply to the local authority for a certificate under this sub-paragraph, and the local authority shall certify whether any, and if so which, of the defects to which the undertaking relates remain unremedied.

(3) A certificate under the foregoing sub-paragraph shall in any proceedings be evidence until the contrary is proved of the matters certified.

9.—(1) If a certificate of disrepair is issued to the tenant of a dwelling, and the dwelling, or any part thereof which is in disrepair by reason of defects specified in the certificate, is subject to a sub-tenancy, being a controlled tenancy, then unless a certificate of disrepair in respect of those defects has been issued to the sub-tenant the same consequences shall follow as between the tenant and the sub-tenant as if a certificate of disrepair had been issued to the sub-tenant when the certificate was issued to the tenant, had specified the same defects as the certificate issued to the tenant, had been issued on an application made by the sub-tenant when the tenant applied for the certificate issued to him, and had continued in force for the same period as that certificate.

(2) Where sub-paragraph (1) of the foregoing paragraph has effect as between the landlord and the tenant, the foregoing sub-paragraph shall have effect accordingly as between the tenant and the sub-tenant.

(3) Nothing in this paragraph shall prejudice the power of the sub-tenant to obtain a certificate of disrepair or the effect of any undertaking given to the sub-tenant.

General and supplemental

10. The provisions of this Part of this Schedule shall apply, while a controlled tenancy continues, notwithstanding any change in the person of the landlord or the tenant.

11.—(1) The defects which may be specified in a certificate of disrepair shall not include any defects in the state of internal decorative repair unless the landlord is responsible for internal decorative repairs under the terms of the tenancy or is to be treated as responsible therefor by virtue of an election under paragraph 2 of this Schedule.

(2) In considering whether or not to issue a certificate of disrepair or what defects to specify in such a certificate the local authority shall treat the landlord as responsible for internal decorative repairs if the application for the certificate alleges that he is responsible therefor or that he is to be treated as responsible therefor by virtue of such an election as aforesaid, but in any other case the local authority shall treat the landlord as not responsible for such repairs.

(3) Sub-paragraph (4) of paragraph 4 of this Schedule shall apply in relation to a defect in the state of internal decorative repair as if for the words "for which the tenant is responsible" there were substituted the words "for which the landlord is not responsible and is not to be treated as responsible by virtue of an election under paragraph 2 of this Schedule".

12.—(1) On any application to the local authority for a certificate of disrepair or a certificate under sub-paragraph (2) of paragraph 8 of this Schedule there shall be paid to the local authority a fee of two shillings and sixpence, but where a certificate of disrepair, or a certificate under the said sub-paragraph (2) certifying that any defects remain unremedied, is granted to the tenant he shall be entitled to deduct the fee from any subsequent payment of rent to the landlord.

(2) If a certificate of disrepair is cancelled by the court under paragraph 4 of this Schedule as respects all the defects specified in the certificate, any sum deducted under this paragraph may be recovered by the landlord.

(3) On any application to the local authority for the cancellation of a certificate of disrepair there shall be paid to the local authority a fee of two shillings and sixpence.

13. In the case of a controlled tenancy of a dwelling which forms part of any other premises owned by or under the control of the landlord or a superior landlord,—

(a) any disrepair of the roof or of any other part of those premises which results, or may result, in disrepair of the dwelling, and

(b) any disrepair of any staircase or other approach to the dwelling contained in those premises,

shall be treated for the purposes of this Part of this Schedule as if it were disrepair of the dwelling.

14. The local authority shall serve a copy of every certificate of disrepair issued by them on the landlord.

15. In this Part of this Schedule references to defects for which the tenant is responsible are references to defects for the remedying of which, as between the landlord and the tenant, the tenant is responsible, or defects which are due to any act, neglect or default of the tenant or any person claiming under him or any breach by the tenant or such a person of any express agreement.

16. Nothing in subsection (3) of section twenty of this Act shall be construed as applying the provisions of this Part of this Schedule to a tenancy which is not a controlled tenancy.

Part III

Overseas companies

17. In a case falling within subsection (3) of section two of this Act, except where the tenant is responsible for all repairs a notice of increase served in respect of the dwelling by the landlord referred to in the said subsection (3) shall not have effect unless either a certificate of repair has been issued to the landlord with respect to the dwelling not earlier than twelve months before the service of the notice of increase or a previous notice of increase served by that landlord in respect of the dwelling has had effect.

18.—(1) If, on an application for a certificate of repair made by the landlord in the prescribed form and stating the name of the tenant, the local authority are satisfied that the state of repair of the dwelling is such that (without regard to paragraph 11 of this Schedule) no certificate of disrepair could be issued in respect of the dwelling, the local authority shall issue the certificate of repair and shall serve a copy of the certificate on the tenant.

(2) On any application for a certificate of repair there shall be paid to the local authority a fee of two shillings and sixpence.

19. If on an application for a certificate of repair the local authority are not satisfied as aforesaid, the authority shall send to the landlord a statement of the defects in consequence of which they are unable to issue the certificate of repair; and if on an application to the county court the landlord proves that all the defects specified in the statement are either defects for which the tenant is responsible or defects amounting only to internal decorative disrepair and for which the landlord is not responsible, the court shall order the local authority to issue a certificate of repair.

20. If after the issue of a certificate of repair a certificate of disrepair is issued in respect of the same dwelling, the certificate of repair shall be deemed never to have been issued.

21. Paragraph 15 of this Schedule shall apply to this Part of this Schedule as it applies to Part II thereof.

Sections 1, 3.

SECOND SCHEDULE

Calculation of amount of rates

1. Subject to the following provisions of this Schedule, the amount of the rates for any rental period shall for the purposes of this Act be taken to be an amount which bears to the total rates payable during the rating period during which the rent for that rental period is payable the same proportion as the length of the rental period bears to the length of the rating period.

2. As respects rental periods which precede the making, by the authority levying the rates, of their first demand for, or for an instalment of, the rates for a rating period, the said amount shall be calculated on the basis that the rates for that rating period will be the same as the rates for the last preceding rating period.

3.—(1) On the making, by the authority levying the rates, of their first such demand, and on the making by them of any subsequent such demand, the said amount shall if necessary be recalculated on the basis that the rates for the rating period will be such as appears from the information given in the demand and any previous demands.

(2) Any such recalculation shall not affect the ascertainment of the rates for any rental period beginning more than six weeks before the date of the service of the demand giving rise to the recalculation.

4. If, as the result of the settlement of a proposal, the rates payable for any rating period are decreased, the said amount shall be recalculated so as to give effect to the decrease; but any such recalculation shall not affect the ascertainment of the rates for any rental period beginning more than six weeks before the date of the settlement of the proposal.

5. In computing the rates for any rating period for the purposes of this Schedule, any discount, and any allowance made under any of the enactments relating to allowances given where rates are paid by the owner instead of by the occupier, shall be left out of account, and accordingly the said rates shall be computed as if no such discount and no such allowance had fallen to be, or had been, allowed or made.

Section 8.

THIRD SCHEDULE

Modifications of provisions of Act of 1954 in

application to 1957 Act increases in Scotland

Section seventeen   ..   In subsection (1), paragraph (*b*) shall be omitted, and at the end of the section the following subsection shall be added—

"(4) A notice of intention to increase the rent by way of a 1957 Act increase shall not be served under this section in respect of a dwelling-house at any time within a period of four months after a notice of intention to increase the rent thereof by way of a repairs increase has been served in respect of the dwelling-house, and any notice served in contravention of this subsection shall be void".

Section twenty ..	In subsection (1) the words "and the First Schedule thereto" shall be omitted.
Section twenty-one ..	In subsection (3) for the word "two-fifths" there shall be substituted the word "one-quarter".
Section twenty-three ..	In subsection (1) the words "and the First Schedule thereto" shall be omitted.
Section thirty-nine ..	The definition of "controlled tenancy" and any reference to the First and Third Schedules to the Act of 1954 shall be omitted.
Section forty-one ..	Subsection (1) shall have effect as if among the enactments therein mentioned there were included subsection (4) of section seven of this Act.
Second Schedule ..	Any reference to section sixteen of the Act of 1954 shall include a reference to section seven of this Act.
	In paragraph 3, sub-paragraphs (b) and (c) shall be omitted.
	Paragraph 5 shall be omitted.

Section 11.

FOURTH SCHEDULE

TRANSITIONAL PROVISIONS ON DECONTROL

1. In this Schedule "the time of decontrol" means the time at which the Rent Acts cease to apply to a dwelling-house by virtue of subsection (1) or (3) of section eleven of this Act.

2.—(1) Where immediately before the time of decontrol the dwelling-house was the subject of a statutory tenancy or of a controlled tenancy which would or might come to an end within fifteen months of that time by effluxion of time or notice to quit, the tenant under that tenancy shall be entitled until the date hereinafter mentioned, and subject to the following provisions of this Schedule, to retain possession of the dwelling-house in the like circumstances, to the like extent and subject to the like provisions (including in particular provisions as to recovery of possession by the landlord) as if the Rent Acts had not ceased to apply to the dwelling-house.

(2) The said date is such date as may be specified in a notice served on

O

the tenant by the landlord at or after the time of decontrol, being a date not earlier than fifteen months after the time of decontrol nor than six months after the service of the notice, but nothing in this paragraph shall prevent the execution of an order for possession obtained by the landlord before the time of decontrol.

(3) Where for the purposes of section eleven of this Act the rateable value of the dwelling-house falls to be ascertained by apportionment, no notice shall be served under sub-paragraph (2) of this paragraph until the apportionment has been made in accordance with the provisions of this Act.

(4) Where sub-paragraph (1) of this paragraph applies and at any time between the time of decontrol and the time when the tenant ceases to be entitled to retain possession by virtue of this Schedule there is current, in relation to the tenant, a period of residence protection (within the meaning of the Reserve and Auxiliary Forces (Protection of Civil Interests) Act, 1951), the date which may be specified in a notice under sub-paragraph (2) of this paragraph shall not be earlier than the expiration of fifteen months after the end of the period of residence protection, and any such notice served before the beginning of that period which specifies an earlier date, being a notice which would have had effect apart from this sub-paragraph, shall have effect as if the date specified therein were the date on which the said fifteen months expires.

(5) Where the tenancy in respect of which a notice is served under sub-paragraph (2) of this paragraph is terminable by notice to quit but has not been terminated by the date specified in the notice, the notice shall operate to terminate the tenancy at that date.

(6) This paragraph shall not apply to a tenancy to which, immediately after the time of decontrol, Part II of the Landlord and Tenant Act, 1954, applies.

3. Where sub-paragraph (1) of the foregoing paragraph applies the rent recoverable from the tenant for any rental period beginning after the time of decontrol shall, whether the tenancy continues or he retains possession by virtue of this Schedule, be the same as would have been recoverable if section one of this Act had provided in all cases for a rent limit equal to the rent recoverable from the tenant for the last rental period beginning before the time of decontrol, that rent limit being subject to adjustment under section three of this Act but not to any other alteration.

4. If before the date specified under sub-paragraph (2) of paragraph 2 of this Schedule the landlord and tenant agree for the creation of a tenancy of the premises of which the tenant is entitled to retain possession by virtue of that paragraph, being a tenancy not expiring, or terminable by notice to quit given by the landlord, earlier than three years from the commencement thereof, the two last foregoing paragraphs shall cease to apply as from the commencement of that tenancy.

5.—(1) Where sub-paragraph (1) of paragraph 2 of this Schedule applies, then if the tenant gives up possession of the dwelling-house at the end of the tenancy therein mentioned, or on ceasing to retain possession by virtue of this Schedule, he shall be entitled, if he has made a claim for the purpose at any time before giving up possession, to be paid by his landlord compensation in respect of any improvement on the dwelling-house, not being a fixture which he is by law entitled to remove, which on his giving up possession adds to the value of the dwelling-house, being an improvement made by him, by any other person who retained possession of the dwelling-house by virtue of this Schedule, or by any other person being a tenant under the said statutory or controlled tenancy, and completed after the fifteenth day of August, nineteen hundred and forty-five.

(2) The sum to be paid as compensation for any improvement shall not exceed the net addition to the value of the dwelling-house as a whole which may be determined to be the direct result of the improvement, allowance being made for any benefits which may have been received from the landlord or his predecessors in title in consideration expressly or impliedly of the improvement; and in determining the amount of the said net addition regard shall be had to the purposes for which it is intended that the dwelling-house shall be used after possession has been given up, and, if it is shown that it is intended to demolish or to make structural alterations in the dwelling-house or any part thereof or to use it for a different purpose, regard shall be had to the effect of such demolition, alteration or change of use on the additional value attributable to the improvement, and to the length of time likely to elapse between the giving up of possession and the demolition, alteration or change of use.

(3) In determining the amount of compensation under this paragraph regard shall be had to any diminution in the value of any other property belonging to the same landlord, or to any superior landlord from whom the immediate landlord directly or indirectly holds, which is the direct result of the improvement.

(4) No compensation shall be payable under this paragraph if the improvement is one of a kind for which a claim for compensation may be made under section one of the Landlord and Tenant Act, 1927, or if the person by whom the improvement was made was under an obligation to make it in pursuance of a contract entered into for valuable consideration, or if the improvement was made in breach of the terms of the controlled tenancy, or if before the completion thereof the landlord notified the person by whom it was made, in writing, that the landlord objected to the improvement.

(5) Any question whether compensation is payable under this paragraph, or as to the amount of any such compensation, shall be determined by the county court; and if the court determines that, on account of the intention to demolish or alter, or to change the use of, the dwelling-house, no compensation or a reduced amount of compensation shall be paid, the court may authorise a further application for compensation to be made by the claimant if effect is not given to the intention within such time as may be fixed by the court.

(6) Where the landlord is himself a tenant of the dwelling-house, he may recover from his landlord such part (if any) of any compensation payable by him under this paragraph as may be agreed between the parties or determined by the county court to be just having regard to the terms of his tenancy, and in particular the length of the unexpired term thereof, and to all other relevant circumstances; and the foregoing provisions of this sub-paragraph shall apply in relation to sums recoverable thereunder as they apply to compensation under this paragraph.

(7) Section thirteen of the Landlord and Tenant Act, 1927 (which confers power to apply and raise capital money for the payment of compensation under that Act), shall apply to compensation or other sums (including costs, charges and expenses) payable by a landlord by virtue of this paragraph as it applies to such compensation and other sums as are mentioned in that section.

6. Where at the time of decontrol any proceedings are pending for the variation of the rent recoverable from the tenant no further steps shall be taken in the proceedings except in relation to costs.

7. Where a tenancy, not being one falling within sub-paragraph (1) of paragraph 2 of this Schedule, continues after the time of decontrol, and immediately before that time any part of the rent recoverable was so recoverable (by virtue of any enactment) in addition to the rent recoverable under the terms of the tenancy,—

> (a) neither the repeals effected by this Act nor anything in section eleven thereof shall affect the recovery of that part of the rent in respect of any rental period after the time of decontrol, but

> (b) if such a part of the rent consists of or includes an increase agreed or determined under section forty of the Housing Repairs and Rents Act, 1954, in respect of services which the landlord is not under the terms of the tenancy liable to provide, then if those services are withheld in whole or in part during any rental period after the time of decontrol the rent recoverable for that period shall be decreased by an appropriate amount, and sub-section (2) of section four of this Act shall apply for the purposes of determining any question whether, or by what amount, the recoverable rent is decreased by virtue of this paragraph.

8. Where at the time of decontrol any rent has been underpaid or any sum has been paid by way of rent which by virtue of the Rent Acts or this Act is irrecoverable from the tenant, nothing in this Act shall be taken to affect the right of any person to recover that sum from any other person from whom he could have recovered it if the Rent Acts had continued to apply to the dwelling-house; and where any sum could under the Rent Acts have been recovered from the landlord by a deduction from rent it shall continue to be so recoverable notwithstanding that the Rent Acts have ceased to apply to the dwelling-house.

9.—(1) Where a tenancy which immediately before the time of decontrol was a controlled tenancy not falling within sub-paragraph (1) of paragraph 2 of this Schedule contains a provision (however expressed) whereby the landlord is entitled, on or after the Rent Acts ceasing to apply to the dwelling-house, to increase the rent otherwise than in respect of rates, the provision of services or the use of furniture, and the amount by which the rent may be so increased is not specified by the terms of the tenancy, the tenant may by notice in writing served on the landlord not later than three months after the time of decontrol elect that as from the service of the notice the foregoing provisions of this Schedule shall apply as if the tenancy had been such a tenancy as is mentioned in sub-paragraph (1) of paragraph 2 of this Schedule.

(2) Where a notice is served under this paragraph the tenancy to which it relates, and any sub-tenancy thereof (whether or not an immediate sub-tenancy), shall come to an end on the service of the notice; and if any such sub-tenancy was one falling within the foregoing sub-paragraph, then as from the service of the notice the foregoing provisions of this Schedule shall apply as if the sub-tenancy had been such a tenancy as is mentioned in sub-paragraph (1) of paragraph 2 of this Schedule.

This sub-paragraph shall not prejudice the power of a sub-tenant to serve a notice under this paragraph where no such notice has been served by a superior tenant.

(3) In the case of a tenancy falling within sub-paragraph (1) of this paragraph, the rent shall not in any case be increased under the terms of the tenancy as respects a rental period beginning before the expiration of three months after the time of decontrol.

10. For the purposes of this Schedule the power of a tenant under a tenancy for a term of years to terminate the tenancy at a specified point during the term shall not be treated as a power to terminate the tenancy by notice to quit.

11. A statutory tenancy which, immediately before the time of decontrol, was one to which, but for paragraph (c) of subsection (1) of section forty-three of the Landlord and Tenant Act, 1954, Part II of that Act would have applied if it had been a tenancy within the meaning of that Act, shall after the time of decontrol be deemed for the purposes of that Act to be a tenancy to which Part II thereof applies, being a tenancy continuing by virtue of section twenty-four of that Act after the expiry of a term of years certain, and accordingly paragraph 2 of this Schedule shall not apply to it.

12. Where any mortgaged property consists of or comprises one or more dwelling-houses to which the Rent Acts applied immediately before the time of decontrol those Acts shall, until the expiration of fifteen months after the time of decontrol, have effect in relation to the mortgage as if they had not ceased to apply to the dwelling-house or dwelling-houses, and any question whether a mortgage is a mortgage to which those Acts apply, or whether or in what manner the principal moneys secured by a mortgage

can be apportioned under subsection (5) of section twelve of the Act of 1920, shall be determined accordingly.

13. An order under subsection (3) of section eleven of this Act may provide that, in the application of the foregoing provisions of this Schedule to dwelling-houses excluded from the Rent Acts by virtue of the order, for references to fifteen months there shall be substituted references to such shorter period, not being less than six months, as may be specified in the order.

14. As respects any time after the time of decontrol, references in this Schedule to the tenant include references to any other person who by virtue of paragraph (g) of subsection (1) of section twelve of the Act of 1920 would have been entitled on the death of the tenant to retain possession if the Rent Acts had not ceased to apply to the dwelling-house.

15. In the application of this Schedule to Scotland,—

(a) in paragraph 3 for the words from "be the same as" to the end of the paragraph there shall be substituted the words "be the same as was recoverable from him for the last rental period beginning before that time";

(b) in paragraph 5 for any reference to the county court there shall be substituted a reference to the sheriff, and in sub-paragraph (4) the words from "if the improvement is one" to "1927, or", and sub-paragraph (7) shall be omitted;

(c) in paragraph 7 for any reference to section forty of the Housing Repairs and Rents Act, 1954, there shall be substituted a reference to section thirty-one of the Housing (Repairs and Rents) (Scotland) Act, 1954, and for the words from "and subsection (2) of section four" to the end of the paragraph there shall be substituted the words "and any question whether, or by what amount, the recoverable rent is decreased by virtue of this paragraph shall be determined by agreement in writing between the landlord and the tenant or by the sheriff; and any such determination may be made so as to relate to past rental periods and shall have effect as respects rental periods subsequent to the periods to which it relates until revoked or varied by such an agreement as aforesaid or by the sheriff"; and

(d) "mortgage" means a heritable security, including a security constituted by absolute disposition qualified by back bond or letter, and "mortgaged" shall be construed accordingly.

Sections 11, 25.

FIFTH SCHEDULE

ASCERTAINMENT AND ADJUSTMENT OF RATEABLE VALUE
AND 1956 GROSS VALUE

PART I

ASCERTAINMENT OF RATEABLE VALUE AND ADJUSTMENTS
FOR PENDING PROPOSALS

1. In relation to any premises in England or Wales, any reference in this Act to the rateable value on a particular date (hereinafter referred to as the "date of ascertainment") shall subject to the following provisions of this Part of this Schedule be construed—

(a) if the premises are a hereditament for which a rateable value is then shown in the valuation list, as a reference to the rateable value of the hereditament, or where that value differs from the net annual value, the net annual value thereof, as shown in the valuation list on that date;

(b) if the premises form part only of such a hereditament, as a reference to such proportion of the said rateable value or net annual value as may be agreed in writing between the landlord and tenant or determined by the county court;

(c) if the premises consist of or form part of more than one such hereditament, to the aggregate of the rateable values (ascertained in accordance with the foregoing sub-paragraphs) of those hereditaments or parts.

2.—(1) The following provision shall have effect for the purposes of subsection (1) of section eleven of this Act or an order made under subsection (3) thereof, that is to say, where after the date of ascertainment the valuation list is altered so as to vary the rateable value of a hereditament, and the alteration has effect from a date not later than the date of ascertainment and is made in pursuance of a proposal to which this paragraph applies, the rateable value on the date of ascertainment of any dwelling-house consisting of or wholly or partly comprised in that hereditament shall be ascertained as if the amount of the rateable, or as the case may be net annual, value of that hereditament shown in the valuation list on the date of ascertainment had been the amount of that value shown in the list as altered.

(2) This paragraph applies to a proposal made—

(a) if the date of ascertainment is that specified in subsection (1) of section eleven of this Act, before the first day of April, nineteen hundred and fifty-seven;

(b) if the date of ascertainment is a date specified in an order under subsection (3) of the said section eleven, before such date as may be specified by the order for the purposes of this provision.

3.—(1) Where the application or non-application of the Rent Acts to a dwelling-house may be affected by an alteration in the valuation list made in pursuance of a proposal to which the foregoing paragraph applies, then—

(a) if the proposal is pending at the commencement of this Act, nothing in subsection (1) of section eleven thereof, and

(b) if it is pending at the date specified in an order under subsection (3) of that section as the date from which the Rent Acts are to cease to apply, nothing in the order,

shall exclude the application of the Rent Acts to the dwelling-house at any time before the proposal is settled.

(2) The foregoing sub-paragraph shall not have effect as respects the said subsection (1) in a case where the proposal is one for an alteration in the valuation list reducing the rateable value of the dwelling-house and that rateable value on the thirty-first day of March, nineteen hundred and fifty-six, was such that, if it had remained unaltered, the Rent Acts would apart from this and the last foregoing paragraph have ceased to apply to the dwelling-house by virtue of the said subsection (1); and in any such case the said subsection (1) (if it has effect in relation to the dwelling-house) shall have effect in relation thereto as from the commencement of this Act notwithstanding that at that date the proposal had not been settled.

4. The following provision shall have effect for the purposes of section twelve of this Act, that is to say, where after the date of ascertainment the valuation list is altered so as to vary the rateable value of a hereditament, and the alteration has effect from a date not later than the date of ascertainment, the rateable value on the date of ascertainment of any dwelling consisting of or comprised in that hereditament shall be ascertained as if the amount of the rateable, or as the case may be net annual, value of that hereditament shown in the valuation list on the date of ascertainment had been the amount of that value shown in the list as altered.

5. This Part of this Schedule shall apply to Scotland subject to the following modifications—

(a) for paragraph 1 there shall be substituted the following paragraph—

"1. In relation to any premises in Scotland, any reference in this Act to the rateable value on a particular date (hereinafter referred to as 'the date of ascertainment') shall, subject to the following provisions of this Part of this Schedule, be construed as a reference to the rateable value thereof as shown in the valuation roll on that date, or where the premises form part only of lands and heritages shown in that roll, to such proportion of the rateable value of those lands and heritages as may be agreed in writing between the landlord and the tenant or determined by the sheriff.";

(b) for references to the valuation list and to a hereditament there shall be substituted references to the valuation roll and to lands and heritages, and any reference to net annual value shall be omitted;

(c) for any reference to a proposal to which paragraph 2 of this Schedule applies there shall be substituted a reference to an appeal or complaint duly made in accordance with the provisions of the Lands Valuation (Scotland) Act, 1854, and the Acts amending that Act, against an entry in the valuation roll, and sub-paragraph (2) of paragraph 2 shall be omitted;

(d) in paragraph 3, for heads (a) and (b) of sub-paragraph (1) there shall be substituted the words "nothing in subsection (1) of section eleven of this Act or in an order under subsection (3) of that section", and in sub-paragraph (2) for the words "the thirty-first day of March" there shall be substituted the words "the fifteenth day of May";

(e) for the purposes of this Part of this Schedule an appeal or complaint shall be taken to be settled when an alteration is made in the valuation roll to give effect to it, or when the appeal or complaint (including any further appeal to the Lands Valuation Appeal Court) is finally determined, or when the appeal or complaint is withdrawn, whichever first occurs.

Part II
Modification, in special cases, of 1956 Gross Value

6. If, in pursuance of a proposal made before the first day of April, nineteen hundred and fifty-seven, or made on the ground of a change in the occupier or in the circumstances of occupation, the gross value shown for a hereditament in the valuation list is varied after the seventh day of November, nineteen hundred and fifty-six, then, as regards any rental periods (whether beginning before or after the variation) the 1956 gross value of a dwelling being or forming part of that hereditament shall be ascertained by reference to the gross value as so varied.

7. Where a dwelling is or forms part of a hereditament for which no gross value was shown in the valuation list on the said seventh day of November, the provisions of this Act defining the 1956 gross value shall have effect in relation to the dwelling as if for the references to that date there were substituted references to the first subsequent date on which a gross value for that hereditament was shown in the valuation list.

8. Where in pursuance of a proposal made on the ground of a change in the occupier or circumstances of occupation the gross value shown in the valuation list is varied so as to take account of the state of the dwelling at a date after the commencement of this Act, a reference to that date shall, in relation to that dwelling, be substituted for the reference in section five of this Act to the commencement thereof.

9. Where a dwelling is or forms part of a hereditament the gross value of which, as shown in the valuation list, was arrived at after such a reduction as is provided for in subsection (3) of section four of the Valuation for Rating Act, 1953 (which relates to certain hereditaments consisting partly of premises used wholly for the purposes of a private dwelling and partly of other premises) that gross value shall be deemed for the purposes of this Act to be further reduced by four-sevenths of so much thereof as is attributable to that part of the hereditament which is not used wholly for the purposes of a private dwelling or private dwellings; and a certificate of the valuation officer shall be conclusive evidence of the amount so attributable.

10. Where a dwelling consists of or forms part of more than one hereditament, the 1956 gross value of the dwelling shall be ascertained by determining the 1956 gross value of each hereditament or part as if it were a separate dwelling and aggregating the gross values so determined; but in determining for the purposes of this paragraph the 1956 gross value of any hereditament the gross value of which is ascertained in accordance with the definition of gross value in section sixty-eight of the Rating and Valuation Act, 1925, that gross value shall be taken to be reduced by four-sevenths.

PART III

REDUCTION OF 1956 GROSS VALUE AND RATEABLE VALUE IN CASE OF CERTAIN IMPROVEMENTS

11.—(1) Where the tenant, or any previous tenant, under a controlled tenancy current at the commencement of this Act has made or contributed to the cost of an improvement on the premises comprised in the tenancy and the improvement is one to which this Part of this Schedule applies, then, if the tenant, not later than six weeks after the commencement of this Act, serves on the landlord a notice in the prescribed form requiring him to agree to a reduction under this Part of this Schedule,—

(a) the 1956 gross value of the premises, and

(b) their rateable value as ascertained for the purposes of subsection (1) of section eleven of this Act,

shall be reduced by such amount, if any, as may be agreed or determined in accordance with the following provisions of this Part of this Schedule.

(2) This Part of this Schedule applies to any improvement made before the seventh day of November, nineteen hundred and fifty-six, by the execution of works amounting to structural alteration, extension or addition.

12.—(1) The amount of any such reduction may at any time be agreed in writing between the landlord and the tenant.

(2) Where, at the expiration of a period of six weeks from the service of a notice under paragraph 11 of this Schedule any of the following matters

has not been agreed in writing between the landlord and the tenant, that is to say,—

    (*a*) whether the improvement specified in the notice is an improvement to which this Part of this Schedule applies;

    (*b*) what works were involved in it;

    (*c*) whether the tenant or a previous tenant under the controlled tenancy has made it or contributed to its cost; and

    (*d*) what proportion his contribution, if any, bears to the whole cost;

the county court may on the application of the tenant determine that matter, and any such determination shall be final and conclusive.

(3) An application under the last foregoing sub-paragraph must be made within three weeks from the expiration of the period mentioned therein or such longer time as the court may allow.

13.—(1) Where, after the service of a notice under paragraph 11 of this Schedule, it is agreed in writing between the landlord and the tenant or determined by the county court—

    (*a*) that the improvement specified in the notice is one to which this Part of this Schedule applies, and what works were involved in it; and

    (*b*) that the tenant or a previous tenant under the controlled tenancy has made it or contributed to its cost, and, in the latter case, what proportion his contribution bears to the whole cost,

then if, at the expiration of a period of two weeks from the agreement or determination, it has not been agreed in writing between the landlord and the tenant whether any or what reduction is to be made under this Part of this Schedule, and the tenant, within two weeks from the expiration of that period, makes an application to the valuation officer for a certificate under the next following sub-paragraph, that question shall be determined in accordance with the certificate, unless the landlord and the tenant otherwise agree in writing.

(2) On any such application the valuation officer shall certify—

    (*a*) whether or not the improvement has affected the 1956 gross value and the rateable value on the seventh day of November, nineteen hundred and fifty-six (as ascertained for the purposes of sub-section (1) of section eleven of this Act), of the hereditament of which the premises consist or, as the case may be, in which they are wholly or partly comprised, and

    (*b*) if it has, the amount by which the said gross value and rateable value respectively would have been less if the improvement had not been made.

(3) An application for such a certificate shall be in the prescribed form and shall state the name and address of the landlord, and the valuation officer shall send a copy of the certificate to the landlord.

(4) Where the amount of the reduction under this Part of this Schedule falls to be determined in accordance with such a certificate, it shall be equal to the amount specified in pursuance of head (*b*) of sub-paragraph (2) of this paragraph, but proportionately reduced in any case where a proportion only of the cost was contributed by the tenant or a previous tenant under the controlled tenancy.

(5) Where at the time of an application for a certificate under this paragraph a proposal for an alteration in the valuation list relating to the hereditament is pending and the alteration would have effect from a date earlier than the eighth day of November, nineteen hundred and fifty-six, the valuation officer shall not issue the certificate until the proposal is settled.

14. Where the rateable value of a dwelling-house on the seventh day of November, nineteen hundred and fifty-six, as ascertained for the purposes of subsection (1) of section eleven of this Act, is reduced under this Part of this Schedule and, as reduced, is not such that the application of the Rent Acts to the dwelling-house is excluded by the said subsection (1), nothing in that subsection shall be taken to have excluded the application of those Acts to the dwelling-house between the commencement of this Act and the time at which the reduction is agreed or determined.

15. An order under subsection (3) of the said section eleven may make provision as to the reduction of the rateable value of dwelling-houses for the purposes of the order corresponding (with such modifications as may be provided in the order) to so much of the foregoing provisions of this Part of this Schedule as relates to rateable value.

PART IV

GENERAL PROVISIONS

16. Where, after a notice of increase has been served in respect of any dwelling, its 1956 gross value is reduced under paragraph 6 or under Part III of this Schedule, the notice shall not be invalidated but shall take effect so far as it can without causing the rent to exceed the rent limit.

17. For the purposes of this Schedule, a proposal shall be taken to be settled when an alteration is made in the valuation list so as to give effect to it, or to an agreement made in consequence of it, or when the proceedings on an appeal against, or a reference to arbitration relating to, an objection to the proposal (including any proceedings in consequence of such an appeal or reference to arbitration) are finally determined, or when the proposal is withdrawn, whichever first occurs.

Section 26.

SIXTH SCHEDULE

MINOR AND CONSEQUENTIAL AMENDMENTS AND APPLICATION OF ENACTMENTS

Amendments consequential on provisions as to rent

1. Section fourteen of the Act of 1920 (which relates to the recovery by the tenant of sums overpaid by way of rent and other related matters) shall have effect as if any sum in respect of rent which is irrecoverable by virtue of this Act (including any sum irrecoverable by virtue of section fifteen thereof) were irrecoverable by virtue of the Act of 1920.

2. Subsection (1) of section six and subsection (1) of section eight of the Rent and Mortgage Interest Restrictions Act, 1923 (which relate to the amendment of notices of increase of rent by the county court) shall apply to notices of increase under this Act.

3. In section sixteen of the Landlord and Tenant Act, 1927 (which enables landlords to recover, as rent, sums in respect of increases in taxes, rates or fire premiums ascribable to improvements made by tenants) for the words from "anything to the contrary" to the end of the section there shall be substituted the words "and shall be so recoverable notwithstanding anything in the Rent Act, 1957".

4. In section four and subsection (1) of section eight of the Act of 1933 (which relate to excessive charges for sublet parts of dwellings and to the rectification of rent books) the references to recoverable rent shall be construed as references to the rent which is or was for the time being recoverable having regard to the provisions of this Act, and references to rent which is irrecoverable shall be construed accordingly.

5. In paragraph 2 of the First Schedule to the Landlord and Tenant (Rent Control) Act, 1949 (which provides for the recovery of premiums by deduction from rent) for the words from "shall not" in sub-paragraph (1) to the end of sub-paragraph (2) there shall be substituted the words "shall not exceed the rent recoverable in accordance with the provisions of the Rent Act, 1957 (other than paragraph 5 of the Sixth Schedule thereto) less the rental equivalent of the premium".

6.—(1) As respects any statutory tenancy arising after the commencement of this Act under section sixteen, seventeen or eighteen of the Reserve and Auxiliary Forces (Protection of Civil Interests) Act, 1951, the provisions of the three following sub-paragraphs shall have effect in substitution for the provisions of those sections as to standard rents.

(2) Subject to the following provisions of this paragraph, the rent for any rental period for which it is neither increased nor reduced under the provisions of this Act other than this paragraph shall be of an amount equal to the rent limit ascertained under subsection (1) of section one of this Act.

(3) Where the rent payable for the last rental period of the tenancy qualifying for protection referred to in section sixteen or section seventeen of the said Act of 1951, (hereinafter referred to as "the contractual rent") was greater than the amount mentioned in the last foregoing sub-paragraph, the rent payable for any such rental period as is mentioned in that sub-paragraph shall be of an amount equal to the contractual rent; and where this sub-paragraph has effect the rent limit shall be an amount equal to the contractual rent, but subject to adjustment from time to time under sections three and four of this Act and under section five thereof except as respects improvements completed before the beginning of the statutory tenancy, and to reduction as provided by Part II of the First Schedule to this Act in case of disrepair.

(4) The foregoing provisions of this paragraph shall have effect subject to any agreement between the parties for the payment of a lower rent; and where a lower rent is agreed it shall not be increased under this Act, but may notwithstanding anything in this Act be increased up to the rent limit by agreement in writing between the parties.

7. In paragraph (b) of subsection (1) of section six of the Landlord and Tenant Act, 1954, for the words "so agreed or determined" there shall be substituted the words "agreed or determined in accordance with the next following section".

8.—(1) In relation to any statutory tenancy created under Part I of the Landlord and Tenant Act, 1954, after the commencement of this Act, any reference in sections seven and nine of that Act to the rent which is to be the standard rent of the dwelling-house during the period of the statutory tenancy shall be construed as a reference to the rent which during the period of the statutory tenancy is to be the rent for any rental period for which it is neither increased nor reduced under the provisions of this Act other than this paragraph.

(2) The last-mentioned rent shall, unless a lower rent is agreed, be an amount equal to the rent limit, ascertained under subsection (1) of section one of this Act; and where a lower rent is agreed it shall not be increased under this Act but notwithstanding anything therein may be increased up to that limit by agreement in writing between the landlord and the tenant.

(3) The foregoing sub-paragraph shall not apply to a dwelling-house such that at the beginning of the period of the statutory tenancy it would but for subsection (4) of section eleven of this Act be excluded from the Rent Acts by subsection (1) or subsection (3) of that section; but in the case of any such dwelling-house the rent limit during the period of the statutory tenancy shall, notwithstanding anything in subsection (1) of section one of this Act, be the rent agreed or determined under section seven of the Landlord and Tenant Act, 1954, subject however to the provisions of subsection (2) of section one of this Act.

9. At the end of paragraph 9 of the First Schedule to the Landlord and Tenant Act, 1954 (which provides, in certain cases, for the recovery of

instalments of a payment for accrued tenant's repairs as if it were rent) there shall be added the words "and shall be so recoverable notwithstanding anything in the Rent Act, 1957".

10. In the Second Schedule to the said Act of 1954, at the end of sub-paragraph (1) of paragraph 1 (which empowers the court to order a reduction of rent where the landlord fails to carry out initial repairs) there shall be added the words "and any such order shall have effect notwithstanding anything in the Rent Act, 1957".

Amendments consequential on section twenty

11. In paragraph (e) of subsection (2) of section three of the Housing (Financial Provisions) Act, 1924, for the words from "the appropriate normal rent" to "local authority themselves" there shall be substituted the words "the limit imposed by section twenty of the Rent Act, 1957".

12. In subsection (1) of section three of the Housing (Rural Workers) Act, 1926, the following paragraph shall be substituted for paragraph (b)—

"(b) the rent payable by the occupier in respect of the dwelling shall not exceed the limit imposed by section twenty of the Rent Act, 1957, and no fine, premium or other like sum shall be taken in addition to the rent".

13. In subsection (1) of section three of the Housing (Financial Provisions) Act, 1938, the following paragraph shall be substituted for paragraph (b)—

"(b) if let, is let at a rent not exceeding the limit imposed by section twenty of the Rent Act, 1957".

14. In subsection (1) of section twenty-three of the Housing Act, 1949, the following words shall be substituted for heads (i) and (ii) of paragraph (c)—

"the limit imposed by section twenty of the Rent Act, 1957".

Amendments consequential on section twenty-one

15.—(1) The Landlord and Tenant Act, 1954, shall be amended as follows.

(2) In subsection (1) of section two, the words "at a low rent" where they first occur shall be omitted, and for the words "if the tenancy had not been one at a low rent" there shall be substituted the words "if the tenancy had not been a long tenancy and (in the case of a tenancy at a low rent) had not been a tenancy at a low rent".

(3) In subsections (2) and (3) of section two and in sections eighteen and nineteen, the words "at a low rent" shall be omitted wherever those words occur.

(4) In subsection (3) of section three, for the words "if the tenancy in question were not one at a low rent" there shall be substituted the words 'if the tenancy in question were not a long tenancy and (in the case of a tenancy at a low rent) were not a tenancy at a low rent".

(5) In subsection (2) of section twelve, in paragraphs (a) and (b), for the words "if the tenancy were not one at a low rent" there shall be substituted the words "if the tenancy were not a long tenancy and (in the case of a tenancy at a low rent) were not a tenancy at a low rent".

(6) In subsection (1) of section nineteen, immediately before the words "the second tenancy" there shall be inserted the words "and the second tenancy is a tenancy at a low rent".

Miscellaneous amendments and application of enactments

16. Sections nine and ten of the Act of 1920 (which relate to furnished lettings) shall cease to have effect.

17. In subsection (2) of section fourteen of the Act of 1920 (which, as amended, imposes a penalty of twenty pounds for offences in connection with rent books), for the words "twenty pounds" there shall be substituted the words "fifty pounds".

18. In sections ten and eleven of the Act of 1933 (which confer on local authorities power to publish information and power to prosecute for offences) the references to the principal Acts shall be deemed to include references to the Landlord and Tenant (Rent Control) Act, 1949, and this Act.

19. The power conferred by section fourteen of the Act of 1933 to make regulations shall include power to make regulations prescribing forms for notices, certificates and other documents required or authorised under this Act and requiring such notices, certificates and documents to contain such information as may be specified in the regulations.

20. In subsection (3) of the said section fourteen (which imposes a penalty of ten pounds for the use of rent books not conforming to the prescribed requirements), for the words "ten pounds" there shall be substituted the words "fifty pounds".

21. For paragraph (h) of the First Schedule to the Act of 1933 (which relates to possession without proof of alternative accommodation), the following paragraph shall be substituted—

"(h) the dwelling-house is reasonably required by the landlord (not being a landlord who has become landlord by purchasing the dwelling-house or any interest therein after the seventh day of November, nineteen hundred and fifty-six) for occupation as a residence for—

(i) himself; or

(ii) any son or daughter of his over eighteen years of age; or

(iii) his father or mother."

22. Section two of the Housing Act, 1936 (which implies, in contracts for letting at rents below specified limits, a condition as to fitness for human habitation), shall have effect, in relation to contracts entered into after the commencement of this Act, as if for the words "forty pounds" and "twenty-

six pounds" there were substituted respectively the words "eighty pounds" and "fifty-two pounds".

23. Section one hundred and sixty-seven of the Housing Act, 1936 (which relates to the service of notices) shall apply to the service of notices, certificates and documents required or authorised to be served under this Act, and, without prejudice to the generality of the foregoing provision, shall apply to the service of such notices, certificates and documents by virtue of subsection (5) of section seven of the Increase of Rent and Mortgage Interest (Restrictions) Act, 1938, as applied by this Schedule on an agent of the landlord or a person receiving the rent.

24. Subsection (5) of section seven of the Increase of Rent and Mortgage Interest (Restrictions) Act, 1938 (which enables documents to be served on agents or persons receiving rent and compels such persons to disclose the name and address of the landlord) shall apply for the purposes of this Act as if references therein to the principal Act included references to this Act.

25.—(1) In subsection (2) of section sixteen of the Reserve and Auxiliary Forces (Protection of Civil Interests) Act, 1951, there shall be added at the end of paragraph (*bb*) the words "or by or under section eleven of the Rent Act, 1957", but the Rent Acts shall not apply by virtue of this sub-paragraph where on the coming to an end of the tenancy qualifying for protection the tenant is entitled to retain possession by virtue of the Fourth Schedule to this Act.

(2) Nothing in section eleven of this Act or any order thereunder shall affect any statutory tenancy which by virtue of the said Act of 1951 is subsisting at the commencement of this Act or the date specified in the order as the date on which the Rent Acts are to cease to apply.

(3) At the end of subsection (2) of section sixteen of the said Act of 1951 there shall be added the following paragraph:—

"(*f*) that the tenancy qualifying for protection was a long tenancy as defined in section two of the Landlord and Tenant Act, 1954".

(4) In subsection (4) of section nineteen of the said Act of 1951, for the words "as mentioned in subsection (2) of this section" there shall be substituted the words "as mentioned in subsection (1) of section sixteen or subsection (1) of section eighteen of this Act, or apply by virtue of section seventeen of this Act".

26.—(1) Section thirty-three of the Housing Repairs and Rents Act, 1954 (under which a tenancy where the interest of the landlord belongs to a housing association is not a controlled tenancy if the condition specified in subsection (2) of that section is fulfilled) shall have effect as if at the end of the said subsection (2) there were added the following:—

"or

(*c*) the premises comprised in the tenancy were provided by the housing association with the assistance of a local authority or county council under subsection (3) of section ninety-three of

R

the Housing Act, 1936, or were provided or improved by the housing association in accordance with arrangements made under section thirty-one of the Housing Act, 1949."

(2) Subsection (8) of the said section thirty-three (which provides for the variation of arrangements between housing associations and local authorities) shall apply in relation to agreements and arrangements entered into before the commencement of this Act in connection with the assistance mentioned in sub-paragraph (1) of this paragraph or under section thirty-one of the said Act of 1949 as it applies in relation to the arrangements mentioned in that subsection.

27.—(1) In section forty-three of the Landlord and Tenant Act, 1954, in paragraph (c) of subsection (1) after the words "1920" there shall be inserted the words "or subsection (1) of section twenty-one of the Rent Act, 1957".

(2) In paragraph 1 of the Third Schedule to the said Act of 1954, for the words "the twenty-first day of November, nineteen hundred and fifty" in paragraph (a) of the proviso there shall be substituted the words "the seventh day of November, nineteen hundred and fifty-six".

Provisions as to Scotland

28. Section five of the Removal Terms (Scotland) Act, 1886, shall have effect as if at the end thereof there were added the following:—

"Provided that in no case shall notice of removal be given less than twenty-eight days before the date on which it is to take effect."

29. Section thirty-eight of the Sheriff Courts (Scotland) Act, 1907, shall have effect as if at the end thereof there were added the following:—

"Provided that in no case shall notice of removal be given less than twenty-eight days before the date on which it is to take effect."

30.—(1) The House Letting and Rating (Scotland) Act, 1911, shall be amended as follows.

(2) In section four for the words "the next payment" in the first place where they occur there shall be substituted the words "a payment", and for those words in the second place where they occur there shall be substituted the words "that payment", and in paragraph (b) of the proviso for the words from "except" to the end of the section there shall be substituted the words "so, however, that in no case shall the notice be given less than twenty-eight days before the date on which it is to take effect."

(3) In section five for the words "forty-eight hours" there shall be substituted the words "twenty-eight days".

31. Where a repayment has been or will be made under section twelve of the Clean Air Act, 1956, in respect of an improvement the reference in paragraph (a) of subsection (1) of section two of the Act of 1920 to the amount expended on the improvement shall be construed as a reference to that amount diminished by the amount of the repayment.

32.—(1) Section twenty-five of the Housing (Repairs and Rents) (Scotland) Act, 1954 (under which a tenancy where the interest of the landlord belongs to a housing association is not a controlled tenancy if the condition specified in subsection (2) of that section is fulfilled) shall have effect as if at the end of the said subsection (2) there were added the following:—

"or

(c) the premises comprised in the tenancy were provided by the housing association with the assistance of a local authority under subsection (2) of section seventy-nine of the Housing (Scotland) Act, 1950, or were improved by the housing association in accordance with arrangements made under section one hundred and twenty-one of that Act".

(2) Subsection (7) of the said section twenty-five (which provides for the variation of arrangements between housing associations and local authorities) shall apply in relation to agreements and arrangements entered into before the commencement of this Act in connection with the assistance mentioned in sub-paragraph (1) of this paragraph or under section one hundred and twenty-one of the said Act of 1950 as it applies in relation to the arrangements mentioned in that subsection.

(3) Paragraph 9 of the First Schedule to the said Act of 1954 shall have effect as if at the end there were added the following sub-paragraph—

"(c) if or in so far as the cost thereof has been or will be repaid under section twelve of the Clean Air Act, 1956".

33.—(1) Paragraph 1, paragraphs 16 to 21, paragraphs 23 and 24, sub-paragraphs (1), (2) and (4) of paragraph 25, and paragraphs 28 to 32 of this schedule shall apply to Scotland subject to the modifications hereinafter mentioned, but save as aforesaid the foregoing provisions of this Schedule shall not apply to Scotland.

(2) Nothing in paragraph 19 shall apply to any notice served for the purposes of section seven or nine of this Act.

(3) In paragraph 23 for the reference to section one hundred and sixty-seven of the Housing Act, 1936, there shall be substituted a reference to section three hundred and forty-nine of the Local Government (Scotland) Act, 1947, subject however to the modification that any reference in that section to a local authority shall include a reference to any person other than a local authority.

Section 26.

SEVENTH SCHEDULE

GENERAL TRANSITIONAL PROVISIONS

1. If, at the commencement of this Act, any agreement or determination of a tribunal made or given for the purposes of paragraph (b) of subsection (3) of section twenty-four of the Housing Repairs and Rents Act, 1954, is in force in the case of a controlled tenancy, that agreement or determination shall, until an agreement or determination is made under paragraph (b) of subsection (1) of section one of this Act, be deemed to be an agreement or determination made under that paragraph.

2.—(1) The following provisions of this paragraph shall have effect with respect to improvements completed before the commencement of this Act.

(2) Where a notice of increase under section three of the Act of 1920 has been served in respect of the improvement but the service was effected less than four weeks before the commencement of this Act, sections one and two of this Act shall, subject to the following provisions of this paragraph, have effect, in relation to any rental period beginning more than four weeks after the service of the notice, as if the notice had taken effect as from the beginning of the basic rental period.

(3) Where the improvement was completed after the first day of April, nineteen hundred and fifty-six and has not affected the 1956 gross value of the dwelling, then, if the rent limit under a controlled tenancy of the dwelling falls to be ascertained under subsection (1) of section one of this Act, the rent limit shall, subject to the following provisions of this paragraph, be increased by eight per cent. per annum of the amount expended on the improvement by the landlord or any superior landlord or any person from whom the landlord or any superior landlord derives title.

(4) Subject to the following provisions of this paragraph, where the last foregoing sub-paragraph applies or a notice of increase was served in respect of the improvement under section three of the Act of 1920 less than four weeks before the commencement of this Act, subsections (3) and (4) of section five of this Act shall apply in relation to the increase authorised by the last foregoing sub-paragraph, or, as the case may be, specified in the said notice, as they apply in relation to an increase authorised by the said section five, but with the modification that, except where no notice of increase under the Act of 1920 was ever served in respect of the improvement, the period within which an application to the court may be made under the said subsection (3) shall be one month after the commencement of this Act or such longer time as the court may allow and that paragraph (b) of the proviso to the said subsection (3) shall not apply.

(5) Where before the commencement of this Act the tenant has applied to the court (under the proviso to paragraph (a) of subsection (1) of section two of the Act of 1920) for an order suspending or reducing an increase of

rent in respect of an improvement no application in respect thereof shall be made under the last foregoing sub-paragraph; but if the application under the said proviso has not been finally determined at the commencement of this Act, proceedings on the application may be continued notwithstanding the repeals effected by this Act and effect shall be given, in ascertaining the rent limit and the rent recoverable for any rental period, to any order made on the application.

(6) A certificate of the valuation officer that an improvement has or has not affected the 1956 gross value of a dwelling shall be conclusive for the purposes of sub-paragraph (3) of this paragraph.

3.—(1) Any certificate of a local authority under subsection (1) of section twenty-six of the Housing, Repairs and Rents Act, 1954, and any certificate of a sanitary authority having effect (under paragraph (a) of subsection (2) of section twenty-seven of that Act) as if it were a certificate under Part II thereof, being a certificate in force immediately before the commencement of this Act, shall, to the extent that it specifies any defects as regards the state of repair of any dwelling, have effect after the commencement of this Act as if it were a certificate of disrepair under this Act; but nothing in this paragraph or in the repeals effected by this Act shall affect the power of the county court in proceedings pending at the commencement of this Act to order that the certificate shall cease to be in force.

(2) Where any such certificate as aforesaid ceases to have effect (whether by virtue of an order of the court or in consequence of being cancelled by the local authority), sections one and two of this Act shall have effect, in relation to any rental period beginning after the date as from which it ceases to have effect, as if it had ceased to have effect immediately before the basic rental period.

4. Where any increase in the rent recoverable under a controlled tenancy current at the commencement of this Act took effect before the commencement of this Act but after the beginning of the basic rental period, section one of this Act shall have effect as if for references to the rent recoverable for the basic rental period there were substituted references to the rent that would have been recoverable for that period if the increase had taken effect before the beginning thereof.

Section 26.

EIGHTH SCHEDULE

Repeals

Part I

Enactments repealed as respects England and Wales

Session and Chapter	Short Title	Extent of Repeal
10 & 11 Geo. 5. c. 17.	The Increase of Rent and Mortgage Interest (Restrictions) Act, 1920.	In section one, the words "the rent of any dwelling-house to which this Act applies, or", the words "the increased rent or", the words "standard rent or", the words "the tenant or", the words "as the case may be", and the proviso. Section two. In section three, in subsection (1) the words "any increase of rent except in respect of a period during which but for this Act the landlord would be entitled to obtain possession, or" and the whole of subsections (2) and (3). Sections nine to eleven. In section twelve, in subsection (1), paragraphs (a), (c) and (d), in subsection (2) the words "either the annual amount of the standard rent or", in subsection (3), the words "standard rent or" and the words "the rent at the date in relation to which the standard rent is to be fixed, or", and in subsection (7) the words from "and this Act" to the end of the subsection.
13 & 14 Geo. 5. c. 13.	The Rent Restrictions (Notices of Increase) Act, 1923.	The whole Act.

Session and Chapter	Short Title	Extent of Repeal
13 & 14 Geo. 5. c. 32.	The Rent and Mortgage Interest Restrictions Act, 1923.	In section four, in subsection (7) of the section directed to be substituted for section five of the Increase of Rent and Mortgage Interest (Restrictions) Act, 1920, the words from "and in any such case" to the end of the subsection. Section seven. Subsection (3) of section eight. Subsection (2) of section ten. Section eleven. In section eighteen, subsections (2) and (3).
14 & 15 Geo. 5. c. 35.	The Housing (Financial Provisions) Act, 1924.	Subsection (3) of section three.
23 & 24 Geo. 5. c. 32.	The Rent and Mortgage Interest Restrictions (Amendment) Act, 1933.	In section four, in subsection (2) the words "neither an apportionment of standard rent as between the dwelling-house and the sublet part thereof" and the words "apportionment or", and in subsection (3) the words from the beginning to "apply, or" and the words "apportionment or". Sections six and seven. In the Second Schedule, the entry relating to section eighteen of the Rent and Mortgage Interest Restrictions Act, 1923.
26 Geo. 5 & 1 Edw. 8. c. 51.	The Housing Act, 1936.	Subsection (2) of section sixty-five.
1 & 2 Geo. 6. c. 26.	The Increase of Rent and Mortgage Interest (Restrictions) Act, 1938.	Section five. Subsections (2) and (4) of section seven. In the Second Schedule, the amendments of section fourteen of the Act of 1920, of section three of the Rent Res-

Session and Chapter	Short Title	Extent of Repeal
1 & 2 Geo. 6. c. 26—*cont.*	The Increase of Rent and Mortgage Interest (Restrictions) Act, 1938—*cont.*	trictions (Notices of Increase) Act, 1923, of section seven of the Rent and Mortgage Interest Restrictions Act, 1923, and of the First Schedule to the Act of 1933.
1 & 2 Geo. 6. c. 35.	The Housing (Rural Workers) Amendment Act, 1938.	Sections four and six.
2 & 3 Geo. 6. c. 71.	The Rent and Mortgage Interest Restrictions Act, 1939.	In the First Schedule— in the entry relating to section one of the Increase of Rent and Mortgage Interest (Restrictions) Act, 1920, the words "the increased rent or" the words "standard rent or" and the words "if the increased rent exceeds the standard rent by more than the amount permitted under this Act or, as the case may be", the whole of the entries relating to sections two, three, nine and ten of that Act and in the first paragraph of the entry relating to section twelve of that Act the words "(a) and"; the entry relating to section seven of the Rent and Mortgage Interest Restrictions Act, 1923; and the entry relating to section six of the Rent and Mortgage Interest Restrictions (Amendment) Act, 1933, and so much of the entry relating to the First Schedule to that Act as relates to paragraph (h) thereof.

Session and Chapter	Short Title	Extent of Repeal
9 & 10 Geo. 6. c. 34.	The Furnished Houses (Rent Control) Act, 1946.	In section seven, the words from the beginning to "save as aforesaid".
9 & 10 Geo. 6. c. 48.	The Housing (Financial and Miscellaneous Provisions) Act, 1946.	Subsection (2) of section thirteen.
12, 13 & 14 Geo. 6. c. 40.	The Landlord and Tenant (Rent Control) Act, 1949.	Sections one, four, five and six. In section eight, in subsection (2) the words "standard rent or", subsections (3) and (4), in subsection (8) the words "Without prejudice to the provisions of subsection (4) of this section" and subsection (9).
12, 13 & 14 Geo. 6. c. 47.	The Finance Act, 1949.	Subsection (10) of section forty.
12, 13 & 14 Geo. 6. c. 60.	The Housing Act, 1949.	Section twenty-two. In section twenty-seven, the proviso to subsection (2). In section twenty-eight, in subsection (2), the words "and six". Section twenty-nine.
14 & 15 Geo. 6. c. 65.	The Reserve and Auxiliary Forces (Protection of Civil Interests) Act, 1951.	In section sixteen, in subsection (1) the words from "but shall" to the end of the subsection and subsections (3) to (8). In section seventeen, in subsection (1) the words "then subject to the next succeeding subsection" and subsection (2). In section eighteen, subsection (2). In section nineteen, subsections (2) and (3).
15 & 16 Geo. 6. & 1 Eliz. 2. c. 40.	The Crown Lessees (Protection of Sub-Tenants) Act, 1952.	In section two, proviso (a) to subsection (1); and subsections (2) and (3). In the Schedule, paragraph (a)

Session and Chapter	Short Title	Extent of Repeal
15 & 16 Geo. 6. & 1 Eliz. 2. c. 40—*cont.*	The Crown Lessees (Protection of Sub-Tenants) Act, 1952—*cont.*	of the entry relating to section one of the Increase of Rent and Mortgage Interest (Restrictions) Act, 1920, and the whole of the entries relating to sections two, nine and ten of that Act and to section six of and the First Schedule to the Rent and Mortgage Interest Restrictions (Amendment) Act, 1933.
15 & 16 Geo. 6. & 1 Eliz. 2. c. 53.	The Housing Act, 1952.	In section three, in subsection (3) the words following paragraph (*b*). In section four, subsection (2).
2 & 3 Eliz. 2. c. 53.	The Housing Repairs and Rents Act, 1954.	In section sixteen, subsections (6) and (8). Sections twenty-three to thirty-two. Subsection (5) of section thirty-three. Sections thirty-four, thirty-six to thirty-eight, forty and forty-four. Subsection (1) of section forty-five. Sections forty-six to forty-eight. In section forty-nine, in subsection (1), the definitions of "Act of 1923", "Act of 1938", "good repair", "repair", "repairs" and "repairs increase"; and subsection (3). The Second and Third Schedules. In the Fourth Schedule, in the Table in paragraph 1 the words "section 2 (1) (*a*)", the words "section 2 (1) (*b*)", the words "section nine (1)", the words "section ten", and the words "Act of 1933 . . .

Session and Chapter	Short Title	Extent of Repeal
2 & 3 Eliz. 2. c. 53—*cont.*	The Housing Repairs and Rents Act, 1954—*cont.*	Schedule 1, paragraph (*h*)"; and paragraphs 2 and 4.
2 & 3 Eliz. 2. c. 56.	The Landlord and Tenant Act, 1954.	In section two, the words "at a low rent" in the first place where they occur in subsection (1) and where they occur in subsections (2) and (3). In section six, in subsection (1), the words "at a rent equal to the standard rent agreed or determined in accordance with the next following section"; in subsection (4) the words from "subject to the following adaptations" to "as aforesaid"; and subsection (5). In section seven, in subsection (1) the words "standard rent of the dwelling-house during the period of the statutory tenancy, and the other", and the words from "and for the avoidance of doubt" to the end of the subsection; and in subsection (2) the word "rent", in the first place where it occurs in paragraph (*b*) and the word "standard" in that paragraph. Section eleven. In sections eighteen and nineteen, the words "at a low rent" wherever they occur.
3 & 4 Eliz. 2. c. 24.	The Requisitioned Houses and Housing (Amendment) Act, 1955.	In section four, in paragraph (*b*) of subsection (2) the words from "at a rent" to "this section", and in subsection (3) the words from "and for the purposes" to the end of the subsection.

Session and Chapter	Short Title	Extent of Repeal
4 & 5 Eliz. 2. c. 9.	The Rating and Valuation (Miscellaneous Provisions) Act, 1955.	Section twelve.

PART II

ENACTMENTS REPEALED AS RESPECTS SCOTLAND

Session and Chapter	Short Title	Extent of Repeal
10 & 11 Geo. 5. c. 17.	The Increase of Rent and Mortgage Interest (Restrictions) Act, 1920.	Sections nine and ten.
13 & 14 Geo. 5. c. 32.	The Rent and Mortgage Interest Restrictions Act, 1923.	In section four, in subsection (7) of the section directed to be substituted for section five of the Increase of Rent and Mortgage Interest (Restrictions) Act, 1920, the words from "and in any such case" to the end of the subsection. Subsection (2) of section ten.
1 & 2 Geo. 6. c. 26.	The Increase of Rent and Mortgage Interest (Restrictions) Act, 1938.	Subsection (4) of section seven. In the Second Schedule, the amendments of section fourteen of the Act of 1920 and of the First Schedule to the Act of 1933.
2 & 3 Geo. 6. c. 71.	The Rent and Mortgage Interest Restrictions Act, 1939.	In the First Schedule the whole of the entries relating to sections nine and ten of the Increase of Rent and Mortgage Interest (Restrictions) Act, 1920; and so much of the entry relating to the First Schedule to the Rent and Mortgage Interest (Restrictions) (Amendment) Act, 1933, as relates to paragraph (h) thereof.

Session and Chapter	Short Title	Extent of Repeal
6 & 7 Geo. 6. c. 44.	The Rent of Furnished Houses Control (Scotland) Act, 1943.	In section five the words from the beginning to "save as aforesaid".
14 & 15 Geo. 6. c. 65.	The Reserve and Auxiliary Forces (Protection of Civil Interests) Act, 1951.	In section nineteen, subsection (2).
15 & 16 Geo. 6. & 1 Eliz. 2. c. 40.	The Crown Lessees (Protection of Sub-Tenants) Act, 1952.	In the Schedule the whole of the entries relating to sections nine and ten of the Increase of Rent and Mortgage Interest (Restrictions) Act, 1920, and the First Schedule to the Rent and Mortgage Interest Restrictions (Amendment) Act, 1933.
2 & 3 Eliz. 2. c. 50.	The Housing (Repairs and Rents) (Scotland) Act, 1954.	Sections twenty-six and thirty-four. In subsection (1) of section thirty-nine, in the definition of "dwelling-house", the words "or prospective controlled tenancy". In the Third Schedule, in the Table in paragraph 1, the words "Section 9 (1)", "section 10" and the words "Act of 1933 . . . Schedule 1, paragraph (h)".

INCREASE OF RENT AND MORTGAGE INTEREST (RESTRICTIONS) ACT, 1920

[10 & 11 GEO. 5]

CHAPTER 17

An Act to consolidate and amend the Law with respect to the increase of rent and recovery of possession of premises in certain cases, and the increase of the rate of interest on, and the calling in of securities on such premises, and for purposes in connection therewith.   [2nd July 1920]

Be it enacted by the King's most Excellent Majesty, by and with the advice and consent of the Lords Spiritual and Temporal, and Commons, in this present Parliament assembled, and by the authority of the same, as follows:—

RESTRICTIONS ON INCREASE OF RENT AND MORTGAGE INTEREST

1. Restriction on increasing rent and mortgage interest

Subject to the provisions of this Act, where [the rent of any dwelling-house to which this Act applies, or] the rate of interest on a mortgage to which this Act applies, has been, since the twenty-fifth day of March nineteen hundred and twenty, or is hereafter, increased, then, if [the increased rent or] the increased rate of interest exceeds by more than the amount permitted under this Act the [standard rent or] standard rate of interest, the amount of such excess shall, notwithstanding any agreement to the contrary, be irrecoverable from [the tenant or] the mortgagor, [as the case may be:

Provided that, where a landlord or mortgagee has increased the rent of any such dwelling-house or the rate of interest on any such mortgage since the said date, but before the passing of this Act, he may cancel such increase and repay any amount paid by virtue thereof, and in that case the rent or rate shall not be deemed to have been increased since that date.]

For "new control" houses the foregoing section reads as follows (see First Schedule / 1939 Act):

1. Subject to the provisions of this Act, where [the rent of any dwelling-house to which this Act applies, or] the rate of interest on a mortgage to which this Act applies, has been, since the first day of September nineteen hundred and thirty-nine, or is hereafter, increased, then, if [the increased rent exceeds the standard rent by more than the amount permitted under this Act or, as the case may be, if] the increased rate of interest exceeds the standard rate of interest, the amount of such excess shall, notwithstanding any agreement to the contrary, be irrecoverable from [the tenant or] the mortgagor, [as the case may be:

Provided that, where a landlord or mortgagee has increased the rent of any such dwelling-house or the rate of interest on the said mortgage since the said date, but before the commencement of the Rent and Mortgage Interest Restrictions Act, 1939, he may cancel such increase and repay any amount paid by virtue thereof, and in that case the rent or rate shall not be deemed to have been increased since that date.]

2. [Permitted increases in rent

(1) The amount by which the increased rent of a dwelling-house to which this Act applies may exceed the standard rent shall, subject to the provisions of this Act, be as follows,[1] that is to say:—

(a) Where the landlord has since the fourth day of August nineteen hundred and fourteen[2] incurred, or hereafter incurs, expenditure on the improvement or structural alteration of the dwelling-house (not including expenditure on decoration or repairs), an amount calculated at a rate per annum not exceeding six, or, in the case of such expenditure incurred after the passing of this Act,[3] eight per cent. of the amount so expended:[4]

Provided that the tenant may apply to the county court for an order suspending or reducing such increase on the ground that such expenditure is or was unnecessary in whole or in part, and the court may make an order accordingly:[5]

(b) An amount not exceeding any increase in the amount for the time being payable by the landlord in respect of rates over the corresponding amount paid in respect of the yearly, half-yearly or other period which included the third day of August nineteen hundred and fourteen,[6] or in

---

[1] See also s. 7 / 1923 Act as to increases for sub-letting.
[2] For "new control" houses substitute the 2nd September 1939 (1st Sch. / 1939 Act).
[3] The words underlined do not apply to "new control" houses (*ibid.*).
[4] See also s. 7 (1) / 1933 Act.
[5] See also s. 7 (2) / 1933 Act.
[6] For "new control" houses substitute the 1st September 1939 (1st Sch. / 1939 Act).

the case of a dwelling-house for which no rates were payable in respect of any period which included the said date, the period which included the date on which the rates first became payable thereafter:[1]

(c)[2] In addition to any such amounts as aforesaid, an amount not exceeding fifteen per centum of the net rent:

Provided that, except in the case of a dwelling-house to which this Act applies but the enactments repealed by this Act did not apply, the amount of such addition shall not, during a period of one year after the passing of this Act, exceed five per cent.:

(d)[2] In further addition to any such amounts as aforesaid—

(i) where the landlord is responsible for the whole of the repairs, an amount not exceeding twenty-five per cent. of the net rent; or

(ii) where the landlord is responsible for part and not the whole of the repairs, such lesser amount as may be agreed, or as may, on the application of the landlord or the tenant, be determined by the county court to be fair and reasonable having regard to such liability:

(e)[2] In the case of dwelling-houses let by a railway company to persons in the employment of the company, such additional amount, if any, as is required in order to give effect to the agreement dated the first day of March nineteen hundred and twenty, relating to the rates of pay and conditions of employment of certain persons in the employment of railway companies, or any agreement, whether made before or after the passing of this Act, extending or modifying that agreement.]

(2) (Repealed by 1954 Acts.)

[(3) Any transfer to a tenant of any burden or liability previously borne by the landlord shall, for the purposes of this Act, be treated as an alteration of rent, and where, as the result of such a transfer, the terms on which a dwelling-house is held are on the whole less favourable to the tenant than the previous terms, the rent shall be deemed to be increased, whether or not the sum periodically payable

[1] See s. 7 (2) / 1938 Act as to compounding allowances and discounts.
[2] This paragraph does not apply to "new control" houses (1st Sch. / 1939 Act).

by way of rent is increased, and any increase of rent in respect of any transfer to a landlord of any burden or liability previously borne by the tenant where, as the result of such transfer, the terms on which any dwelling-house is held are on the whole not less favourable to the tenant than the previous terms, shall be deemed not to be an increase of rent for the purposes of this Act: Provided that, for the purposes of this section, the rent shall not be deemed to be increased where the liability for rates is transferred from the landlord to the tenant, if a corresponding reduction is made in the rent.]

$\left.\begin{matrix}(4)\\(5)\end{matrix}\right\}$ (Repealed by 1954 Acts.)

[(6) Any question arising under subsection (1), (2) or (3) of this section shall be determined on the application either of the landlord or the tenant by the county court, and the decision of the court shall be final and conclusive.][1]

3. Limitation as to permitted increases in rent

(1) Nothing in this Act shall be taken to authorise [any increase of rent except in respect of a period during which but for this Act the landlord would be entitled to obtain possession, or] any increase in the rate of interest on a mortgage except in respect of a period during which, but for this Act, the security could be enforced.

[(2) Notwithstanding any agreement to the contrary, where the rent of any dwelling-house to which this Act applies is increased, no such increase shall be due or recoverable until or in respect of any period prior to the expiry of four clear weeks, or, where such increase is on account of an increase in rates, one clear week, after the landlord has served upon the tenant a valid notice in writing of his intention to increase the rent, which notice shall be in the form contained in the First Schedule to this Act, or in a form substantially to the same effect. If a notice served as aforesaid contains any statement or representation which is false or misleading in any material respect, the landlord shall be liable on summary conviction to a fine not exceeding ten pounds unless he proves that the statement was made innocently and without intent to deceive. Where a notice of an increase of rent which at the time was valid has been served on any tenant, the increase may be continued without service of any fresh notice on any subsequent tenant.[2]

---

[1] See also s. 7 (3) 1923 Act.
[2] See s. 1 / 1923 Notices Act and s. 7 (1) / 1923 Act.

S

(3) A notice served before the passing of this Act[1] of an intention
to make any increase of rent which is permissible only by virtue of
this Act shall not be deemed to be a valid notice for the purpose of
this section.]

4.[2] Permitted increase in rate of mortgage interest

The amount by which the increased rate of interest payable in
respect of a mortgage to which this Act applies may exceed the
standard rate, shall be an amount not exceeding one per cent. per
annum:

Provided that—

  (a) the rate shall not be increased so as to exceed six and a half
      per cent. per annum; and

  (b) except in the case of a dwelling-house to which this Act
      applies but the enactments repealed by this Act did not
      apply, the increase during a period of one year after the
      passing of this Act shall not exceed one-half per cent. per
      annum.

FURTHER RESTRICTIONS AND OBLIGATIONS ON LANDLORDS AND
MORTGAGEES

5. (See substituted section in S. 4 / 1923 Act—Subsection (1) of
that substituted section replaced by SS. 3, 4 (1) of and First
Schedule to 1933 Act.)

6. Restriction on levy of distress for rent

No distress for the rent of any dwelling-house to which this Act
applies shall be levied except with the leave of the county court, and
the court shall, with respect to any application for such leave, have
the same or similar powers with respect to adjournment, stay,
suspension, postponement and otherwise as are conferred by the
last preceding section of this Act in relation to applications for the
recovery of possession:

Provided that this section shall not apply to distress levied under
section one hundred and sixty of the County Courts Act, 1888.

The provisions of this section shall be in addition to and not in
derogation of any of the provisions of the Courts (Emergency
Powers) Act, 1914, or any Act amending or extending the same,
except so far as those provisions are repealed by this Act.

---

[1] For "new control" houses read "before the 2nd September 1939" (1st Sch. /
1939 Act).
[2] This section does not apply to "new control" houses (*ibid.*).

7. Restriction on calling in of mortgages

It shall not be lawful for any mortgagee under a mortgage to which this Act applies, so long as—

(*a*) interest at the rate permitted under this Act is paid and is not more than twenty-one days in arrear; and

(*b*) the covenants by the mortgagor (other than the covenant for the repayment of the principal money secured) are performed and observed; and

(*c*) the mortgagor keeps the property in a proper state of repair and pays all interest and instalments of principal recoverable under any prior encumbrance,

to call in his mortgage or to take any steps for exercising any right of foreclosure or sale, or for otherwise enforcing his security or for recovering the principal money thereby secured:

Provided that—

(i) this provision shall not apply to a mortgage where the principal moneys secured thereby is repayable by means of periodical instalments extending over a term of not less than ten years from the creation of the mortgage, nor shall this provision affect any power of sale exercisable by a mortgagee who was on the twenty-fifth day of March nineteen hundred and twenty[1] a mortgagee in possession, or in cases where the mortgagor consents to the exercise by the mortgagee of the powers conferred by the mortgage; and

(ii) if, in the case of a mortgage of a leasehold interest the mortgagee satisfies the county court that his security is seriously diminishing in value or is otherwise in jeopardy, and that for that reason it is reasonable that the mortgage should be called in and enforced, the court may by order authorise him to call in and enforce the same, and thereupon this section shall not apply to such mortgage; but any such order may be made subject to a condition that it shall not take effect if the mortgagor within such time as the court directs pays to the mortgagee such portion of the principal sum secured as appears to the court to correspond to the diminution of the security.

8. (Repealed by 1949 Act.)

---

[1] For "new control" houses substitute the 1st September 1939 (1st Sch. / 1939 Act).

9.
10. } (Repealed by 1957 Act.)

11. [Statement to be supplied as to standard rent

A landlord of any dwelling-house to which this Act applies shall, on being so requested in writing by the tenant of the dwelling-house, supply him with a statement in writing as to what is the standard rent of the dwelling-house, and if, without reasonable excuse, he fails within fourteen days to do so, or supplies a statement which is false in any material particular, he shall be liable on summary conviction to a fine not exceeding ten pounds.]

APPLICATION AND INTERPRETATION OF ACT

12. Application and interpretation

(1) For the purpose of this Act, except where the context otherwise requires:—

[(a) The expression "standard rent" means the rent at which the dwelling-house was let on the third day of August nineteen hundred and fourteen,[1] or, where the dwelling-house was not let on that date, the rent at which it was last let before that date, or, in the case of a dwelling-house which was first let after the said third day of August, the rent at which it was first let:[2]

Provided that, in the case of any dwelling-house let at a progressive rent payable under a tenancy agreement or lease, the maximum rent payable under such tenancy agreement or lease shall be the standard rent; and, where at the date by reference to which the standard rent is calculated, the rent was less than the rateable value the rateable value at that date shall be the standard rent;]

(b) The expression "standard rate of interest" means, in the case of a mortgage in force on the third day of August nineteen hundred and fourteen,[1] the rate of interest payable at that date, or, in the case of a mortgage created since that date, the original rate of interest;

[(c) The expression "net rent" means, where the landlord at the time by reference to which the standard rent is

---

[1] For "new control" houses substitute the 1st September 1939 (1st Sch. / 1939 Act).
[2] See s. 2 (1) / 1952 Act as to Crown sub-tenants.

calculated paid the rates chargeable on, or which but for
the provisions of any Act would be chargeable on the
occupier, the standard rent less the amount of such
rates, and in any other case the standard rent;]

(d) (Repealed by 1957 Act.)

(e) The expression "rateable value" means the rateable value
on the third day of August nineteen hundred and fourteen, or, in the case of a dwelling-house or a part of
dwelling-house first assessed after that date, the rateable
value at which it was first assessed;

For "new control" houses paragraph (e) was revised by the 1939
Act as follows—

(e) The expression "rateable value", in relation to any
dwelling-house, means the value shown, with respect to
that dwelling-house, on the appropriate day in the valuation list then in force, as the rateable value or, where the
net annual value differs from the rateable value, as the
net annual value; and the expression "the appropriate
day" means, in relation to a dwelling-house within the
administrative county of London, the sixth day of April
nineteen hundred and thirty-nine or, in relation to a
dwelling-house in any other part of England, the first
day of April nineteen hundred and thirty-nine; and in
relation to a dwelling-house first assessed after the said
sixth day of April or the said first day of April, as the
case may be, any reference in the preceding provisions
of this paragraph to the appropriate day shall be construed as a reference to the day on which the dwelling-
house was first assessed (First Schedule / 1939 Act);

(f) The expressions "landlord," "tenant," "mortgagee," and
"mortgagor" include any person from time to time
deriving title under the original landlord, tenant, mortgagee, or mortgagor;

(g) The expression "landlord" also includes in relation to any
dwelling-house any person, other than the tenant, who
is or would but for this Act be entitled to possession of the
dwelling-house, and the expressions "tenant and
tenancy" include sub-tenant and sub-tenancy, and the
expression "let" includes sub-let; and the expression
"tenant" includes the widow of a tenant ****[1] who was

---

[1] The words "dying intestate" were omitted by the 1935 Act (see p. 5).

residing with him at the time of his death, or, where a tenant ****[1] leaves no *such*[2] widow or is a women, such member of the tenant's family so residing as aforesaid as may be decided in default of agreement by the county court;[3]

(h) The expression "mortgage" includes a land charge under the Land Transfer Acts, 1875 and 1897;

(i) The expressions "statutory undertaking" and "statutory duties or powers" include any undertaking, duties or powers, established, imposed or exercised under any order having the force of an Act of Parliament.

(2)[4] This Act shall apply to a house or a part of a house let as a separate dwelling, where [either the annual amount of the standard rent or] the rateable value does not exceed—

(a) in the metropolitan police district, including therein the City of London, one hundred and five pounds;

(b) in Scotland, ninety pounds; and

(c) elsewhere, seventy-eight pounds;

and every such house or part of a house shall be deemed to be a dwelling-house to which this Act applies:

Provided that—

(i) this Act shall not, save as otherwise expressly provided, apply to a dwelling-house bona fide let at a rent which includes payments in respect of board, attendance, or use of furniture;[5] and

(ii) the application of this Act to any house or part of a house shall not be excluded by reason only that part of the premises is used as a shop or office or for business, trade, or professional purposes; and

(iii) for the purposes of this Act, any land or premises let together with a house shall, if the rateable value of the land or premises let separately would be less than one-quarter of the rateable value of the house, be treated as part of the house, but, subject to this provision, this Act shall not apply to a house let together with land other than the site of the house.

---

[1] The words "dying intestate" were omitted by the 1935 Act (see p. 5).
[2] Inserted by 1954 Acts.
[3] See s. 13 / 1933 Act.
[4] This subsection does not apply to "new control" houses (1st Sch. / 1939 Act).
[5] See s. 10 (1) / 1923 Act.

(3) Where, for the purpose of determining the [standard rent or] rateable value of any dwelling-house to which this Act applies, it is necessary to apportion [the rent at the date in relation to which the standard rent is to be fixed, or] the rateable value of the property in which that dwelling-house is comprised, the county court may, on application by either party, make such apportionment as seems just, and the decision of the court as to the amount to be apportioned to the dwelling-house shall be final and conclusive.[1]

(4) Subject to the provisions of this Act, this Act shall apply to every mortgage where the mortgaged property consists of or comprises one or more dwelling-houses to which this Act applies, or any interest therein, except that it shall not apply—

(a) to any mortgage comprising one or more dwelling-houses to which this Act applies and other land if the rateable value of such dwelling-houses is less than one-tenth of the rateable value of the whole of the land comprised in the mortgage; or

(b) to an equitable charge by deposit of title deeds or otherwise; or

(c)[2] to any mortgage which is created after the passing of this Act.

(5) When a mortgage comprises one or more dwelling-houses to which this Act applies and other land, and the rateable value of such dwelling-houses is more than one-tenth of the rateable value of the whole of the land comprised in the mortgage, the mortgagee may apportion the principal money secured by the mortgage between such dwelling-houses and such other land by giving one calendar month's notice in writing to the mortgagor, such notice to state the particulars of such apportionment, and at the expiration of the said calendar month's notice this Act shall not apply to the mortgage so far as it relates to such other land, and for all purposes, including the mortgagor's right of redemption, the said mortgage shall operate as if it were a separate mortgage for the respective portions of the said principal money secured by the said dwelling-houses and such other land, respectively, to which such portions were apportioned:

Provided that the mortgagor shall, before the expiration of the said calendar month's notice, be entitled to dispute the amounts so apportioned as aforesaid, and in default of agreement the matter

---

[1] See also s. 17 (2) / 1933 Act and s. 5 / 1938 Act.
[2] This paragraph does not apply to "new control" houses (1st Sch. / 1939 Act).

shall be determined by a single arbitrator appointed by the President of the Surveyors' Institution.

(6) Where this Act has become applicable to any dwelling-house or any mortgage thereon, it shall continue to apply thereto whether or not the dwelling-house continues to be one to which this Act applies.

(7) Where the rent payable in respect of any tenancy of any dwelling-house is less than two-thirds of the rateable value thereof, this Act shall not apply to that rent or tenancy nor to any mortgage by the landlord from whom the tenancy is held of his interest in the dwelling-house, [and this Act shall apply in respect of such dwelling-house as if no such tenancy existed or ever had existed.]

(8) Any rooms in a dwelling-house subject to a separate letting wholly or partly as a dwelling shall, for the purposes of this Act, be treated as a part of a dwelling-house let as a separate dwelling.

(9)[1] This Act shall not apply to a dwelling-house erected after or in course of erection on the second day of April nineteen hundred and nineteen, or to any dwelling-house which has been since that date or was at that date being bonâ fide reconstructed by way of conversion into two or more separate and self-contained flats or tenements; [but, for the purpose of any enactment relating to rating, the gross estimated rental or gross value of any such house to which this Act would have applied if it had been erected or so reconstructed before the third day of August nineteen hundred and fourteen, and let at that date, shall not exceed—

    (a) if the house forms part of a housing scheme to which section seven of the Housing, Town Planning, &c. Act, 1919, applies, the rent (exclusive of rates) charged by the local authority in respect of that house; and

    (b) in any other case the rent (exclusive of rates) which would have been charged by the local authority in respect of a similar house forming part of such a scheme as aforesaid.]

(10)[1] Where possession has been taken of any dwelling-houses by a Government department during the war, under the Defence of the Realm regulations, for the purpose of housing workmen, this Act shall apply to such houses as if the workmen in occupation thereof at the passing of this Act were in occupation as tenants of the landlords of such houses.

---

[1] This subsection does not apply to "new control" houses (1st Sch. / 1939 Act).

13. (Repealed by the Statute Law Revision Act, 1927.)

14. Recovery of sums made irrecoverable, &c.

(1) Where any sum has, whether before or after the passing of this Act,[1] been paid on account of any rent or mortgage interest, being a sum which is by virtue of this Act, or any Act repealed by this Act,[1] irrecoverable by the landlord or mortgagee, the sum so paid shall be recoverable from the landlord or mortgagee who received the payment or his legal personal representative by the tenant or mortgagor by whom it was paid, and any such sum, and any other sum which under this Act is recoverable by a tenant from a landlord or payable or repayable by a landlord to a tenant, may, without prejudice to any other method of recovery, be deducted by the tenant or mortgagor from any rent or interest payable by him to the landlord or mortgagee.[2]

(2) If—

    (a) any person in any rent book or similar document makes an entry showing or purporting to show any tenant as being in arrear in respect of any sum which by virtue of any such Act is irrecoverable; or

    (b) where any such entry has, ****,[3] been made by or on behalf of any landlord, the landlord on being requested by or on behalf of the tenants so to do, refuses or neglects to cause the entry to be deleted within seven days,

that person or landlord shall, on summary conviction, be liable to a fine not exceeding *fifty*[4] pounds, *unless he proves that at the time of the making of the entry or of the neglect or refusal to cause it to be deleted, as the case may be, the landlord had a bona fide claim that the sum was recoverable.*[5]

15. Conditions of statutory tenancy

(1) A tenant who by virtue of the provisions of this Act retains possession of any dwelling-house to which this Act applies shall, so long as he retains possession, observe and be entitled to the benefit of all the terms and conditions of the original contract of tenancy, so far as the same are consistent with the provisions of this Act, and

---

[1] See First Schedule / 1939 Act as to "new control" houses.
[2] See s. 8 (2) / 1923 Act as to limitations.
[3] Words omitted by the 1933 Act.
[4] Substituted by the 1957 Act.
[5] Substituted by the 1933 Act.

shall be entitled to give up possession of the dwelling-house only on giving such notice as would have been required under the original contract of tenancy, or, if no notice would have been so required, on giving not less than three months' notice:

Provided that, notwithstanding anything in the contract of tenancy, a landlord who obtains an order or judgment for the recovery of possession of the dwelling-house or for the ejectment of a tenant retaining possession as aforesaid shall not be required to give any notice to quit to the tenant.

(2) Any tenant retaining possession as aforesaid shall not as a condition of giving up possession ask or receive the payment of any sum, or the giving of any other consideration, by any person other than the landlord, and any person acting in contravention of this provision shall be liable on summary conviction to a fine not exceeding one hundred pounds, and the court by which he was convicted may order any such payment or the value of any such consideration to be paid to the person by whom the same was made or given, but any such order shall be in lieu of any other method of recovery prescribed by this Act.[1]

(3) Where the interest of a tenant of a dwelling-house to which this Act applies is determined, either as the result of an order or judgment for possession or ejectment, or for any other reason, any sub-tenant to whom the premises or any part thereof have been lawfully sublet shall, subject to the provisions of this Act, be deemed to become the tenant of the landlord on the same terms as he would have held from the tenant if the tenancy had continued.

16. Minor amendments of law

[(1) Section three of the Poor Rate Assessment and Collection Act, 1869, shall, except so far as it relates to the metropolis, have effect as though for the limits of value specified in that section there were substituted limits twenty-five per cent. in excess of the limits so specified, and that section and section four of the same Act shall have effect accordingly.]

(2) It shall be deemed to be a condition of the tenancy of any dwelling-house to which this Act applies that the tenant shall afford to the landlord access thereto and all reasonable facilities for executing therein any repairs which the landlord is entitled to execute.

(3) Where the landlord of any dwelling-house to which this Act applies has served a notice to quit on a tenant, the acceptance of

[1] See s. 9 (2) / 1923 Act.

rent by the landlord for a period not exceeding three months from the expiration of the notice to quit shall not be deemed to prejudice any right to possession of such premises, and, if any order for possession is made, any payment of rent so accepted shall be treated as mesne profits.

17. Rules as to procedure

(1) The Lord Chancellor may make such rules and give such directions as he thinks fit for the purpose of giving effect to this Act, and may, by those rules or directions, provide for any proceedings for the purposes of this Act being conducted so far as desirable in private and for the remission of any fees.

(2) A county court shall have jurisdiction to deal with any claim or other proceedings arising out of this Act or any of the provisions thereof, notwithstanding that by reason of the amount of claim or otherwise the case would not but for this provision be within the jurisdiction of a county court, and, if a person takes proceedings under this Act in the High Court which he could have taken in the county court, he shall not be entitled to recover any costs.

18. Application to Scotland and Ireland

(1) This Act shall apply to Scotland, subject to the following modifications:—

(a) "Mortgage" and "encumbrance" mean a heritable security including a security constituted by absolute disposition qualified by back bond or letter; "mortgagor" and "mortgagee" mean respectively the debtor and the creditor in a heritable security; "covenant" means obligation; "mortgaged property" means the heritable subject or subjects included in a heritable security; "rateable value"[1] means yearly value according to the valuation roll; "rateable value on the third day of August nineteen hundred and fourteen"[1] means yearly value according to the valuation roll for the year ending fifteenth day of May nineteen hundred and fifteen; "assessed" means entered in the valuation roll; "land" means lands and heritages; "rates" means assessments as defined in the House Letting and Rating (Scotland) Act, 1911; "Lord Chancellor" and "High Court" mean the

---

[1] Does not apply to "new control" houses (1st Sch. / 1939 Act).

Court of Session; "rules" means act of sederunt; "county court" means the sheriff court; "sanitary authority" means the local authority under the Public Health (Scotland) Act, 1897; "mesne profits" means profits; the Board of Agriculture for Scotland shall be substituted for the Minister of Agriculture and Fisheries; the twenty-eighth day of May shall be substituted for the twenty-fourth day of June; the reference to the county agricultural committee shall be construed as a reference to the body of persons constituted with respect to any area by the Board of Agriculture for Scotland under subsection (2) of section eleven of the Corn Production Act, 1917; references to levying distress shall be construed as references to doing diligence; the reference to the President of the Surveyors' Institution shall be construed as a reference to the Chairman of the Scottish Committee of the Surveyors' Institution; a reference to section five of the Housing, Town Planning, &c. (Scotland) Act, 1919, shall be substituted for a reference to section seven of the Housing, Town Planning, &c. Act, 1919; and a reference to section one of the House Letting and Rating (Scotland) Act, 1911, shall be substituted for a reference to section three of the Poor Rate Assessment and Collection Act, 1869:

(b) Nothing in paragraph (b) of subsection (1) of the section of this Act relating to permitted increases in rent shall permit any increase in rent in respect of any increase after the year ending Whitsunday nineteen hundred and twenty in the amount of the rates payable by the landlord other than rates for which he is responsible under the House Letting and Rating (Scotland) Act, 1911:

(c) Paragraph (d) of subsection (1) of the section of this Act relating to application and interpretation shall not apply:

(d) Where any dwelling-house, to which the Acts repealed by this Act applied, is subject to a right of tenancy arising from a yearly contract or from tacit relocation, and ending at Whitsunday nineteen hundred and twenty-one, the year ending at the said term of Whitsunday shall be deemed to be a period during which, but for this Act, the landlord would be entitled to obtain possession of such dwelling-house.

(2) (This subsection applied the Act to Ireland subject to modifications.)

19. Short title, duration and repeal

(1) This Act may be cited as the Increase of Rent and Mortgage Interest (Restrictions) Act, 1920.

(2) Except as otherwise provided, this Act shall continue in force until the twenty-fourth day of June nineteen hundred and twenty-three:

Provided that the expiration of this Act or any part thereof shall not render recoverable by a landlord any rent, interest or other sum which during the continuance thereof was irrecoverable, or affect the right of a tenant to recover any sum which during the continuance thereof was under this Act recoverable by him.

(3) The enactments mentioned in the Second Schedule to this Act are hereby repealed to the extent specified in the third column of that schedule:

Provided that, without prejudice to the operation of section thirty-eight of the Interpretation Act, 1889, nothing in this repeal shall render recoverable any sums which at the time of the passing of this Act were irrecoverable, or affect the validity of any order of a court, or any rules or directions made or given under any enactment repealed by this Act, all of which orders, rules, and directions if in force at the date of the passing of this Act shall have effect as if they were made or given under this Act, and any proceedings pending in any court at the date of the passing of this Act, under any enactment repealed by this Act, shall be deemed to have been commenced under this Act.

SCHEDULES

Sections 3 and 18.

FIRST SCHEDULE.

Form of Notice by Landlord.

(Section 14 (1) / 1933 Act enables the Minister of Housing and Local Government and, as read with Section 15, the Secretary of State for Scotland to make regulations prescribing a form to be substituted for the form in this Schedule to be used by landlords for increasing rent. This power has been exercised and the present regulations are:

> For England and Wales—The Rent Restrictions Regulations, 1957 (S.I. 981).

> For Scotland—The Rent Restrictions (Scotland) Regulations, 1939 (S.R.O. 1615).

In consequence of the exercise of these powers the form in the Schedule has ceased to have effect (s. 14 (2) / 1933 Act).)

Section 19.

SECOND SCHEDULE.

Enactments Repealed.

Session and Chapter	Short Title	Extent of Repeal
5 & 6 Geo. 5. c. 97.	The Increase of Rent and Mortgage Interest (War Restrictions) Act, 1915.	The whole Act.
7 & 8 Geo. 5. c. 25.	The Courts (Emergency Powers) Act, 1917.	Ss. 4, 5 and 7.
9 & 10 Geo. 5. c. 7.	The Increase of Rent and Mortgage Interest (Restrictions) Act, 1919.	The whole Act.
9 & 10 Geo. 5. c. 90.	The Increase of Rent, &c. (Amendment) Act, 1919.	The whole Act.

INCREASE OF RENT AND MORTGAGE INTEREST RESTRICTIONS (CONTINUANCE) ACT, 1923.

(This Act provided for the continuance of the Act of 1920 until the 31st July 1923. It was repealed by the Statute Law Revision Act, 1950.)

RENT RESTRICTIONS
(NOTICES OF INCREASE) ACT, 1923*
[13 & 14 Geo. 5]

CHAPTER 13

[AN Act to amend the Increase of Rent and Mortgage Interest
(Restrictions) Act, 1920, with respect to the effect of notices to
increase rent given thereunder; and for purposes consequential
thereon.   [7th June 1923.]

Be it enacted by the King's most Excellent Majesty, by and with
the advice and consent of the Lords Spiritual and Temporal, and
Commons, in this present Parliament assembled, and by the authority of the same, as follows:—

1. Effect of notices to increase rent under principal Act

(1) Where notice of intention to increase rent has, whether before
or after the passing of this Act, been served on a tenant in con-
formity with subsection (2) of section three of the Increase of Rent
and Mortgage Interest (Restrictions) Act, 1920 (hereinafter referred
to as the principal Act), and a notice to terminate the tenancy was
necessary in order to make such increase effective, the notice of
intention to increase the rent shall have effect and shall be deemed
always to have had effect as if it were or had been also a notice to
terminate the existing tenancy on the day immediately preceding the
day as from which the increase is or was first to take effect, or on the
earliest day thereafter on which if it had been a notice to terminate
the tenancy, it would have been effective for that purpose, and in the
latter case a notice of increase served before the passing of this Act
shall be deemed to have had effect as if such earliest date had been
specified in the notice as the date as from which the increase was to
take effect:

Provided that—

(a) nothing in this Act shall entitle a landlord after the passing
of this Act to recover from a tenant, in respect of any
period before the first day of December, nineteen hundred
and twenty-two, the increase of rent made valid by this
Act, or any sums which have been recovered from the

---

*This Act has been repealed as to England and Wales by the 1957 Act.

landlord before that date by means of deductions from rent or otherwise, or any rent due before that date which has not been paid by reason of such deductions having been made therefrom; but section fourteen, subsection (1), of the principal Act shall not apply to an increase of rent made valid by this Act which was paid by, or recovered from, a tenant prior to the first day of December, nineteen hundred and twenty-two;

(b) nothing in this Act shall affect the right to enforce any judgment of a court of competent jurisdiction given before the fifteenth day of February, nineteen hundred and twenty-three, or render recoverable any sum paid under such a judgment.

(2) Any increase of rent made valid by this Act is hereinafter referred to as a validated increase of rent.

2. Payment of arrears by instalments

(1) The amount due under this Act on account of any arrears of rent, that is to say,—

(a) any validated increase of rent in respect of the period from the first day of December, nineteen hundred and twenty-two to the date of the passing of this Act, both inclusive; and

(b) any sum which during the said period has been recovered by the tenant from the landlord by deductions from rent or otherwise, and which would not have been so recoverable had this Act been then in force;

shall be payable by instalments with and as part of the periodical payments of rent, each instalment being fifteen per cent. of the standard rent for the week, month, or other period for which the rent is payable, fractions of a penny being disregarded; and such instalments shall continue payable until the whole of the amount of such arrears is paid off:

Provided that—

(i) the tenant may at any time pay to the landlord the full amount of such arrears subject to the deduction of the aggregate amount of the instalments (if any) already paid; and

(ii) if a tenant by whom any such instalments are payable gives up possession of the premises either voluntarily or on any order or judgment of a court, the balance of the sum payable by instalments shall immediately become due and recoverable.

(2) A landlord claiming that a sum on account of arrears of rent is due to him under this Act shall serve on the tenant a notice to that effect, and the notice shall specify the amount so claimed and the amount of the instalments claimed to be payable, and the first instalment shall not be payable until after the expiration of one clear week from the date of the notice. If such notice contains any statement or representation which is false or misleading in any material respect, the landlord shall be liable on summary conviction to a fine not exceeding ten pounds unless he proves that the statement was made innocently and without intent to deceive.

(3) The notice shall be in the form contained in the Schedule to this Act, or in a form substantially to the same effect, and the landlord shall furnish the tenant with details in writing showing how the amount claimed is arrived at, and how the amount of the instalments has been calculated.

(4) Any question as to the amount of arrears due from a tenant, or the amount of any instalment, shall be determined on the application either of the landlord or the tenant by the county court, and the decision of the court shall be final and conclusive.

3. Power to suspend liability if premises unfit for human habitation or in state of disrepair

(1) A tenant, who becomes by virtue of this Act liable to pay any sum by way of rent or on account of arrears, or the sanitary authority, may apply to the county court for an order suspending such liability on the ground that the house is not in all respects reasonably fit for human habitation or that it is otherwise not in a reasonable state of repair, and section two of the principal Act shall apply as if the application had been made under subsection (2) of that section.

(2) Where the liability in respect of the payment of instalments is so suspended, the instalments which would have become payable during the period of suspension, shall, for the purpose of calculating the aggregate amount of instalments paid, be deemed to have been paid.

(3) Where a tenant has obtained from the sanitary authority a certificate that the house is not in a reasonable state of repair, and has served a copy of the certificate upon the landlord, it shall be a good defence to any claim against the tenant for the payment of any

T

sum which the tenant is by virtue of this Act liable to pay by way of rent or on account of arrears in respect of any subsequent rental period that the house was not in a reasonable state of repair during that period, and in any proceedings against the tenant for the enforcement of such claim (including proceedings for recovery of possession or ejectment on the ground of non-payment of rent so far as the rent unpaid includes any such sum), the production of the said certificate shall be sufficient evidence that the house was and continues to be in the condition therein mentioned unless the contrary is proved:

Provided that the foregoing provision shall not apply in any case where and so far as the condition of the house is due to the tenant's neglect or default or breach of express agreement.

(4) (Repealed by the 1938 Act.)

(5) An instrument purporting to be a certificate of a sanitary authority and to be signed by an officer of the authority shall, without further proof, be taken to be a certificate of the authority unless the contrary is proved.

(6) (Repealed by the Local Government (Scotland) Act, 1947.)

4. Short title and construction

This Act may be cited as the Rent Restrictions (Notices of Increase) Act, 1923, and shall be construed as one with the principal Act, except that this Act shall not extend to Ireland.]

TEXTS OF THE ACTS

SCHEDULE

FORM OF NOTICE BY LANDLORD

RENT RESTRICTIONS (NOTICES OF INCREASE) ACT, 1923

Date

To

Address of premises to which⎱
this notice refers   .   .⎰

TAKE NOTICE that I claim that the sum of
is due to me from you as tenant of the above premises on account of arrears
of rent under the above-mentioned Act.

The amount due on account of such arrears is payable by instalments
with, and as part of, your weekly [*monthly, or other periodical*] rent until the
amount of such arrears is paid off. The first instalment will be payable on
the   day of   *

The amount of the instalments claimed by me is
a week [*month, or other period, as the case may be*].

If you wish to dispute the amount of the sum claimed or of the instalments,
you are entitled to apply to the county court of

You are entitled to apply to the county court for an order suspending any
sum due from you by way of rent, or on account of arrears, under the above-
mentioned Act, if you consider that the premises are not in all respects
reasonably fit for human habitation or otherwise not in a reasonable state
of repair. You will be required to satisfy the county court, by a report of the
sanitary authority or otherwise, that your application is well founded, and
for this purpose you are entitled to apply to the sanitary authority for a
certificate. A fee of one shilling is chargeable, but, if the certificate is
granted, you can deduct this sum from the sum due from you as aforesaid.
The address of the sanitary authority is

If at any time you give up possession of the above premises, either
voluntarily or on an order or judgment of the court, the balance of the sum
payable by instalments will immediately become due.

A statement is sent herewith showing how the amount of the above claim
is arrived at, and how the amount of the instalments has been calculated.

Signed

Address

* The date to be inserted will be the first rent day after the expiration of one
clear week from the date of the notice.
(This footnote is part of the Act.)

RENT AND MORTGAGE INTEREST RESTRICTIONS ACT, 1923
[13 & 14 Geo. 5]
CHAPTER 32

An Act to amend and prolong the duration of the Increase of Rent and Mortgage Interest (Restrictions) Act, 1920, and any enactment amending that Act, and to make provision as to the rent and recovery of possession of premises in certain cases after the expiry of that Act, and for purposes in connection therewith.

[31st July 1923.]

Be it enacted by the King's most Excellent Majesty, by and with the advice and consent of the Lords Spiritual and Temporal, and Commons, in this present Parliament assembled, and by the authority of the same, as follows:—

Part I
AMENDMENT AND PROLONGATION OF DURATION OF PRINCIPAL ACT

1. (Repealed by the Statute Law Revision Act, 1950.)

2.[1] Exclusion of dwelling-houses from application of principal Act in certain cases

(1) Where the landlord of a dwelling-house to which the principal Act applies is in possession of the whole of the dwelling-house at the passing of this Act, or comes into possession of the whole of the dwelling-house at any time after the passing of this Act, then from and after the passing of this Act, or from and after the date when the landlord subsequently comes into possession, as the case may be, the principal Act shall cease to apply to the dwelling-house:

Provided that, where part of a dwelling-house to which the principal Act applies is lawfully sub-let, and the part so sub-let is also a dwelling-house to which the principal Act applies, the principal Act shall not cease to apply to the part so sub-let by reason of the tenant being in or coming into possession of that part, and, if the landlord is in, or comes into possession of, any part not so sub-let, the principal Act shall cease to apply to that part, notwithstanding

---

[1] The operation of this section was restricted by s. 2 / 1933 Act; further by s. 3 / 1938 Act and by virtue of s. 2 / 1939 Act it ceased to provide for further decontrol on possession as from the 2nd September 1939.

that a sub-tenant continues in, or retains, possession of any other part by virtue of the principal Act:

Provided also that, where a landlord comes into possession under an order or judgment made or given after the passing of this Act, on the ground of non-payment of rent, the principal Act shall, notwithstanding anything in the foregoing provisions of this subsection, continue to apply to the dwelling-house.

(2) Where, at any time after the passing of this Act, the landlord of a dwelling-house to which the principal Act applies grants to the tenant a valid lease of the dwelling-house for a term ending at some date *not earlier than one year after the date fixed at the time at which the lease is granted for the expiration of the principal Act,*[1] being a term of not less than two years, or enters into a valid agreement with the tenant for a tenancy for such a term, the principal Act shall, as from the commencement of the term, cease to apply to the dwelling-house, and nothing in the principal Act shall be taken as preventing or invalidating the payment of any agreed sum as part of the consideration for such lease or agreement:

Provided that, where part of the dwelling-house is lawfully sub-let at the commencement of the term, and is a dwelling-house to which the principal Act applies, that part shall, notwithstanding anything in the foregoing provisions of this subsection, continue to be a dwelling-house to which the principal Act applies.

(3) For the purposes of this section, the expression "possession" shall be construed as meaning "actual possession", and a landlord shall not be deemed to have come into possession by reason only of a change of tenancy made with his consent.

3.[2] Determination of certain leases and tenancies

Where before the passing of this Act the landlord of a dwelling-house to which the principal Act applies has granted to the tenant a valid lease of the dwelling-house for a term ending at some date after the twenty-fourth day of June, nineteen hundred and twenty-three, or has entered into a valid agreement with the tenant for a tenancy for such a term, and the rent thereby reserved is reserved at a rate which after but not before such last mentioned date exceeds the standard rent and the increases permitted under the principal Act or this Act, the landlord may, by three months notice in writing expiring not earlier than the twenty-first day of December, nineteen

---

[1] Substituted by s. 1 / 1925 Act.
[2] This section does not apply to "new control" houses (1st Sch. / 1939 Act).

hundred and twenty-three, and not later than the thirty-first day of March, nineteen hundred and twenty-four, determine the said lease or tenancy, provided that, if within one month of the receipt of such notice the lessee or tenant shall give to the landlord notice in writing that he elects to abide by the said lease or agreement and the terms thereof, then the said lease or agreement shall remain in full force and effect in every respect including the amount of the rent thereby expressed to be reserved unaffected by the principal Act or this Act.

4. Restriction on right to possession

The following section shall be substituted for section five of the principal Act, namely:—

"**5.**—(1) (Repealed by 1933 Act.)

"(2) At the time of the application for or the making or giving any order or judgment for the recovery of possession of any such dwelling-house, or for the ejectment of a tenant therefrom, or in the case of any such order or judgment which has been made or given, whether before or after the passing of this Act, and not executed at any subsequent time, the court may adjourn the application, or stay or suspend execution on any such order or judgment, or postpone the date of possession for such period or periods as it thinks fit, and subject to such conditions (if any) in regard to payment by the tenant of arrears of rent, rent, or mesne profits and otherwise as the court thinks fit, and, if such conditions are complied with, the court may, if it thinks fit, discharge or rescind any such order or judgment.

"(3)[1] Where any order or judgment has been made or given before the passing of this Act but not executed, and, in the opinion of the court, the order or judgment would not have been made or given if this Act had been in force at the time when such order or judgment was made or given, the court may, on application by the tenant, rescind or vary such order or judgment in such manner as the court may think fit for the purpose of giving effect to this Act.

"(4)[2] *Notwithstanding anything in section one of the Small Tenements Recovery Act, 1838, every warrant to enter and give possession of any dwelling-house to which this Act applies shall remain in force for three months from the date of the issue of the warrant and for such further period or periods, if any, as the court shall from time to time, whether before or after the expiration of such three months, direct.*

---

[1] This subsection does not apply to "new control" houses (1st Sch. / 1939 Act).
[2] This subsection is printed as revised by the Second Schedule to the Administration of Justice Act, 1956.

"(5) An order or judgment against a tenant for the recovery of possession of any dwelling-house or ejectment therefrom under this section shall not affect the right of any sub-tenant to whom the premises or any part thereof have been lawfully sub-let before proceedings for recovery of possession or ejectment were commenced, to retain possession under this section, or be in any way operative against any such sub-tenants.

"(6) Where a landlord has obtained an order or judgment for possession or ejectment under this section on the ground that he requires a dwelling-house for his own occupation, and it is subsequently made to appear to the court that the order or judgment was obtained by misrepresentation or the concealment of material facts, the court may order the landlord to pay to the former tenant such sum as appears sufficient as compensation for damage or loss sustained by that tenant as the result of the order or judgment.

"(7) The provisions of the last preceding subsection shall apply in any case where the landlord has, after the thirty-first day of July, nineteen hundred and twenty-three,[1] obtained an order or judgment for possession or ejectment on any of the grounds specified in *paragraphs (g) and (h) of the First Schedule to the Act of 1933*,[2] and it is subsequently made to appear to the court that the order or judgment was obtained by misrepresentation or concealment of material facts, ****.[3]

5.—(Repealed by the 1954 Acts.)

6. Notice of increase of rent

(1) The county court, if satisfied that any error or omission in a notice of intention to increase rent, whether served before or after the passing of this Act, is due to a bonâ fide mistake on the part of the landlord, shall have power to amend such notice, by correcting any errors and supplying any omissions therein, which, if not corrected or supplied, would render the notice invalid, on such terms and conditions as respects arrears of rent or otherwise as appear to the court to be just and reasonable, and, if the court so directs, the notice as so amended shall have effect and be deemed to have had effect as a valid notice.

(2) (Repealed by the Statute Law Revision Act, 1950.)

[1] For "new control" houses substitute the 2nd September 1939 (1st. Sch./ 1939 Act).
[2] Substituted by the Second Schedule / 1933 Act.
[3] Words omitted by the 1957 Act.

7.[1] Permitted increases of sub-tenancies

[(1) Where part of a dwelling-house to which the principal Act applies is lawfully sub-let, and the part so sub-let is also a dwelling-house to which the principal Act applies, then, in addition to any increases permitted by paragraphs (*a*) to (*e*) of subsection (1) of section two of the principal Act, an amount not exceeding ten per cent. of the net rent of the dwelling-house comprised in the sub-tenancy shall be deemed to be a permitted increase in the case of that dwelling-house, and an amount equivalent to five per cent. of the net rent of the dwelling-house comprised in the sub-tenancy shall be deemed to be a permitted increase in the case of the dwelling-house comprised in the tenancy. Subsection (2) of section three of the principal Act shall not apply as respects any increase permitted under this subsection:

Provided that, if the interest of the tenant in the dwelling-house comprised in the tenancy is determined and the sub-tenant becomes the tenant of the landlord, then, notwithstanding anything in subsection (3) of section fifteen of the principal Act (which provides that in such circumstances a sub-tenant becomes the tenant of the landlord on the same terms as he would have held from the tenant if the tenancy had continued) the maximum additional amount of rent which is allowed by this subsection to be charged in respect of the dwelling-house comprised in the sub-tenancy shall be reduced to five per cent. of the net rent thereof.[2]]

[(2) Where part of any such dwelling-house is so sub-let, the tenant shall, on being so requested in writing by the landlord, supply him, within fourteen days thereafter, with a statement in writing of any sub-letting, giving particulars of occupancy, including the rent charged, and should the tenant without reasonable excuse fail to do so or supply a statement which is false in any material particulars he shall be liable on summary conviction to a fine not exceeding two pounds.]

[(3) In subsection (6) of section two of the principal Act the expression "landlord" shall, in relation to a sub-tenancy, be taken to include not only the person who is immediate landlord of the sub-tenant but also the landlord of that person.]

8. Limitation on recovery of overpayments or arrears

(1) No increase of rent which becomes payable by reason of an amendment of a notice of increase made by order of the county

---

[1] This section does not apply to "new control" houses (1st Sch. / 1939 Act).
[2] This proviso was added by the Second Schedule / 1938 Act.

court under this Act shall be recoverable in respect of any rental period which ended more than six months before the date of the order.

(2) Any sum paid by a tenant or mortgagor which, under sub-section (1) of section fourteen of the principal Act is recoverable by the tenant or mortgagor shall be recoverable at any time within *two years*[1] from the date of payment but not afterwards, or in the case of a payment made *not earlier than six months before the passing of the Increase of Rent and Mortgage Interest (Restrictions) Act, 1938*,[1] at any time within *two years from the date of payment*[1] but not afterwards.[2]

[(3) Nothing in this section shall affect the operation of the Rent Restriction (Notices of Increase) Act, 1923.]

9. Excessive charges for furniture, &c., taken over in connexion with tenancies

(1) (Repealed by the 1949 Act.)

(2) Where a tenant who by virtue of the principal Act retains possession of a dwelling-house to which that Act applies requires that furniture or other articles shall be purchased as a condition of giving up possession, the price demanded shall, at the request of the person on whom the demand is made, be stated in writing, and, if the price exceeds the reasonable price of the articles, the excess shall be treated as a sum asked to be paid as a condition of giving up possession, and the provisions of subsection (2) of section fifteen of the principal Act (including penal provisions) shall apply accordingly.

10. Amendment of provisions of the principal Act as to houses let with furniture, &c.

(1) For the purposes of proviso (i) to subsection (2) of section twelve of the principal Act (which relates to the exclusion of dwelling-houses from the principal Act in certain circumstances),[3] a dwelling-house shall not be deemed to be bonâ fide let at a rent which includes payments in respect of attendance or the use of furniture unless the amount of rent which is fairly attributable to the attendance or the use of the furniture, regard being had to the value of the same to the tenant, forms a substantial portion of the whole rent.

---

[1] Substituted by s. 7 (6) / 1938 Act.
[2] In the case of "new control" houses substitute the 2nd September 1939 for the date of passing of the Act of 1938 (1st Sch. / 1939 Act).
[3] For "new control" houses a reference to s. 3 (2) (b) of the Act of 1939 is substituted for the reference to s. 12 (2) (i) of the Act of 1920 (1st Sch. / 1939 Act).

(2) (Repealed by the 1957 Act.)

11. Power of county court to determine questions as to standard rent, &c.

[(1) The county court shall have the power on the applicatio n o a landlord or a tenant to determine summarily any questions as to the amount of the rent, standard rent or net rent of any dwelling-house to which the principal Act applies, or as to the increase of rent permitted under that Act or this Part of this Act.

(2) The Lord Chancellor may, by rules and directions made and given under section seventeen of the principal Act, provide for any questions arising under or in connection with the principal Act or this Part of this Act being referred by consent of the parties interested for final determination by the judge or registrar of a county court sitting[1] as an arbitrator or by an arbitrator appointed by such judge.]

Part II

RESTRICTIONS AFTER EXPIRY OF PRINCIPAL ACT

12–17. (Repealed by the 1933 Act.)

Part III

GENERAL

18. (1) (Repealed by the 1954 Acts.)

[(2) On any application to a county agricultural committee for a certificate for the purpose of *sub-paragraph (ii) of paragraph (g) of the First Schedule to the Rent and Mortgage Interest Restrictions (Amendment) Act, 1933*, a fee shall be payable by the applicant to the county agricultural committee of such amount as the Minister of Agriculture and Fisheries shall by regulation determine.

(3) An instrument purporting to be a certificate or report ****[2] of a county agricultural committee and to be signed by an officer of the authority or committee shall, without further proof, be taken to be a certificate or report of the ****[2] committee unless the contrary is proved.]

(4)
(5) } (Repealed by the 1954 Acts.)

---

[1] See s. 19.
[2] Words omitted by the 1954 Acts.

19. Application to Scotland

This Act shall apply to Scotland subject to the following modifications:—

(a) The twenty-eighth day of May shall be substituted for the twenty-fourth day of June; the Scottish Board of Health shall be substituted for the Minister of Health; references to the registrar of a county court shall not apply; and "exciseable liquor" shall be substituted for "intoxicating liquor";

(b) For removing doubts, it is hereby declared that nothing in the principal Act affects the operation of the House Letting and Rating (Scotland) Act, 1920, and the reference in subsection (2) of section one of the last mentioned Act to the provisions of Acts repealed by the principal Act shall be construed as a reference to the provisions of section three of the principal Act.

20. Short title, construction and extent

This Act may be cited as the Rent and Mortgage Interest Restrictions Act, 1923, and shall be construed as one with the principal Act, save that this Act shall not apply to Ireland, and the principal Act, the Increase of Rent and Mortgage Interest Restrictions (Continuance) Act, 1923, the Rent Restrictions (Notices of Increase) Act, 1923, and this Act may be cited together as the Rent and Mortgage Interest Restrictions Acts, 1920 and 1923.

PREVENTION OF EVICTION ACT, 1924

[14 & 15 Geo. 5]

CHAPTER 18

An Act to prevent unreasonable eviction of tenants.

[14th July 1924.]

Be it enacted by the King's most Excellent Majesty, by and with the advice and consent of the Lords Spiritual and Temporal, and Commons, in this present Parliament assembled, and by the authority of the same, as follows:—

1. (Repealed by the 1933 Act.)

2. Application of Act to pending proceedings

(1) Where any order or judgment has been made or given before the passing of this Act but not executed, and in the opinion of the court the order or judgment would not have been made or given if this Act had been in force at the time when such order or judgment was made or given, the court, on application by the tenant, may rescind or vary the order or judgment in such manner and subject to such conditions as the court shall think fit for the purpose of giving effect to this Act.

(2) Where a landlord has, on or after the fifteenth day of April, nineteen hundred and twenty-four, taken possession of a dwelling-house under a judgment or order so rescinded as aforesaid, such possession shall not in any case exclude the dwelling-house from the operation of the Rent and Mortgage Interest (Restrictions) Acts, 1920 and 1923.

3. Short title

This Act may be cited as the Prevention of Eviction Act, 1924, and shall be construed as one with the Rent and Mortgage Interest (Restrictions) Acts, 1920 and 1923, and those Acts and this Act may be cited together as the Rent and Mortgage Interest (Restrictions) Acts, 1920 to 1924.

RENT AND MORTGAGE INTEREST (RESTRICTIONS CONTINUATION) ACT, 1925

[15 & 16 Geo. 5]

CHAPTER 32

An Act to prolong the duration of the Increase of Rent and Mortgage Interest (Restrictions) Act, 1920, as amended by any subsequent enactment, and to postpone the date of expiry of Part II of the Rent and Mortgage Interest Restrictions Act, 1923, and for purposes consequential thereon.   [28th May 1925.]

Be it enacted by the King's most Excellent Majesty, by and with the advice and consent of the Lords Spiritual and Temporal, and Commons, in this present Parliament assembled, and by the authority of the same, as follows:—

1.—(1) (2) (Repealed by the 1933 Act.)

(3) Accordingly the Rent and Mortgage Interest Restrictions Act, 1923, shall have effect as if—

(a) (Repealed by the 1933 Act.)

(b) in section two thereof for the words "after the twenty-fourth day of June, nineteen hundred and twenty-six" there were substituted the words "not earlier than one year after the date fixed at the time at which the lease is granted for the expiration of the principal Act";

(c)
(d) }(Repealed by the 1933 Act.)
(e)

2. Short title

This Act may be cited as the Rent and Mortgage Interest (Restrictions Continuation) Act, 1925; and the Rent and Mortgage Interest (Restrictions) Acts, 1920 to 1924, and this Act may be cited together as the Rent and Mortgage Interest (Restrictions) Acts, 1920 to 1925.

RENT AND MORTGAGE INTEREST RESTRICTIONS (AMENDMENT) ACT, 1933

[23 & 24 Geo. 5]

CHAPTER 32

An Act to amend and continue the Rent and Mortgage Interest (Restrictions) Acts, 1920 to 1925.   [18th July 1933.]

Be it enacted by the King's most Excellent Majesty, by and with the advice and consent of the Lords Spiritual and Temporal, and Commons, in this present Parliament assembled, and by the authority of the same, as follows:—

1.—(1)
       (2) } (Repealed by the 1939 Act.)

(3)[1] Where any dwelling-house to which the principal Acts apply consists of or comprises premises licensed for the sale of intoxicating liquor for consumption on the premises, the principal Acts shall, as from the said twenty-ninth day of September or as from the date on which the premises are first so licensed, whichever is the later date, cease to apply to that dwelling-house.

(4)
(5) } (Repealed by the 1939 Act.)
(6)

(7) Part II of the Act of 1923 (which contains provisions as to restrictions after the expiry of the principal Acts) is hereby repealed.

2. (Repealed by the 1938 and 1939 Acts.)

3. Amendments as to restriction on right to possession

(1) No order or judgment for the recovery of possession of any dwelling-house to which the principal Acts apply or for the ejectment of a tenant therefrom shall be made or given unless the court considers it reasonable to make such an order or give such a judgment, and either—

    (a) the court has power so to do under the provisions set out in the First Schedule to this Act; or

---

[1] This subsection does not apply to "new control" houses (1st Sch. / 1939 Act)—see parallel provision for such houses in s. 3 (2) (a) of 1939 Act.

(*b*) the court is satisfied that suitable alternative accommodation is available for the tenant or will be available for him when the order or judgment takes effect.

(2) A certificate of the housing authority for the area in which the said dwelling-house is situated, certifying that the authority will provide suitable alternative accommodation for the tenant by a date specified in the certificate, shall be conclusive evidence that suitable alternative accommodation will be available for him by that date.

(3) Where no such certificate as aforesaid is produced to the court, accommodation shall be deemed to be suitable[1] if it consists either—

(*a*) of a dwelling-house to which the principal Acts apply; or

(*b*) of premises to be let as a separate dwelling on terms which will, in the opinion of the court, afford to the tenant security of tenure reasonably equivalent to the security afforded by the principal Acts in the case of a dwelling-house to which those Acts apply,

and is, in the opinion of the court, reasonably suitable to the needs of the tenant and his family as regards proximity to place of work, and either—

(i) similar as regards rental and extent to the accommodation afforded by dwelling-houses provided in the neighbourhood by any housing authority for persons whose needs as regards extent are, in the opinion of the court, similar to those of the tenant and his family; or

(ii) otherwise reasonably suitable to the means of the tenant and to the needs of the tenant and his family as regards extent and character.

(4) For the purposes of the last foregoing subsection any certificate of a housing authority stating—

(*a*) the extent of the accommodation afforded by dwelling-houses provided by it to meet the needs of tenants with families of such number as may be specified in the certificate; and

(*b*) the amount of the rent charged by it for dwelling-houses affording accommodation of that extent,

shall be conclusive evidence of the facts so stated.

(5) Any document purporting to be a certificate of a housing authority named therein issued for the purposes of this section and to be signed by the clerk to that authority shall be received in evi-

---

[1] See s. 7 (3) / 1938 Act as to overcrowding.

dence and be deemed to be such a certificate without further proof unless the contrary is shown.

4. Prevention of excessive charges for sublet parts of dwelling-houses

(1) Notwithstanding anything in the last foregoing section, an order or judgment for the recovery of possession of a dwelling-house to which the principal Acts apply or for the ejectment of a tenant therefrom may be made or given where the court considers it reasonable so to do, if the court is satisfied that the rent charged after the passing of this Act by the tenant for any sublet part of the dwelling-house which is also a dwelling-house to which the principal Acts apply was in excess of the recoverable rent of that part.

(2) Where, in any proceedings under the last foregoing subsection for the recovery of possession of a dwelling-house or for the ejectment of a tenant therefrom, it appears to the court that [neither an apportionment of standard rent as between the dwelling-house and the sublet part thereof] nor a determination of the recoverable rent of the sublet part has previously been made by the county court, the court shall make such an [apportionment or] determination, whether or not an order or judgment is made or given for the recovery of possession or the ejectment of the tenant.

(3) [Where an apportionment of standard rent has been made by the county court as between a dwelling-house to which the principal Acts apply and any sublet part thereof which is also a dwelling-house to which the principal Acts apply, or] where the county court has determined the recoverable rent of any such sublet part, then, if, after the [apportionment or] determination, the rent charged after the passing of this Act by the tenant for that sublet part is in excess of the recoverable rent of that part, the tenant shall, unless he proves that he did not know and could not by reasonable enquiry have ascertained that the rent charged by him was so in excess as aforesaid or that the excess was solely due to an accidental miscalculation, be guilty of an offence and liable on summary conviction thereof to a fine not exceeding one hundred pounds.

(4) Where the tenant of a dwelling-house to which the principal Acts apply has sublet any part thereof which is also a dwelling-house to which the principal Acts apply, the tenant shall within fourteen days after the subletting, or, in the case of a subletting effected before the date of the passing of this Act,[1] within three months after that

---

[1] For "new control" houses substitute "before the 2nd September 1939" (1st Sch. / 1939 Act).

date, supply the landlord with a statement in writing of the sub-
letting giving particulars of occupancy, including the rent charged,
and if without reasonable excuse he fails to do so or supplies a
statement which is false in any material particular, he shall be liable
on summary conviction to a fine not exceeding ten pounds:

Provided that it shall not be necessary to supply a statement of
the subletting of any such part as aforesaid where the particulars to
be given therein as to the rent and other conditions of the sub-
tenancy would be the same as in the last statement supplied in
accordance with the requirements of this subsection with respect to
a previous subletting of that part.

5. (Repealed by the 1939 Act.)

6. Amendment as to ascertainment of standard rent

[If, in any proceedings in which the standard rent of any dwelling-
house to which the principal Acts apply is required to be determined,
the court is satisfied that it is not reasonably practicable to obtain
sufficient evidence to enable the court to ascertain the rent at which
the dwelling-house was let on the third day of August, nineteen
hundred and fourteen,[1] or, where the dwelling-house was not let on
that date, the rent at which it was last let before that date, or, in the
case of a dwelling-house which was first let after the said third day of
August, the rent at which it was first let, the court shall have power
to determine the standard rent as being, for the purposes of those
proceedings, of such amount as the court thinks proper having
regard to the standard rents of similar dwelling-houses in the
neighbourhood, and as from the date on which any such determination is made under this section the standard rent of the dwelling-
house shall, unless the court making the determination otherwise
orders, be deemed for all purposes to be of that amount.]

7. Amendments as to permitted increase of rent in respect of improvements and structural alterations

[(1) For the purposes of paragraph (a) of subsection (1) of section
two of the Act of 1920, expenditure after the passing of this Act on
the provision of additional or improved fixtures or fittings in a
dwelling-house (not being expenditure on decoration or repairs)
shall be deemed to be expenditure on the improvement of the
dwelling-house.

---

[1] For "new control" houses substitute the 1st September 1939.
U

(2) The county court shall not make an order under the proviso to the said paragraph (*a*) upon the application of any person unless he proves either—

    (*a*) that he was the tenant when the expenditure was incurred and had not given his written consent to the improvement or alteration and the expenditure thereon; or

    (*b*) that, the landlord having been in possession of the premises at the date when the expenditure was incurred, the applicant is the first tenant subsequent to that date and became tenant without notice of the following particulars, that is to say—

        (i) the nature of the improvement or alteration; and

        (ii) the amount of the expenditure thereon; and

        (iii) the amount of the maximum increase of rent chargeable on account thereof.]

8. Ratification of rent books

(1) Where the recoverable rent of any dwelling-house to which the principal Acts apply is determined by any court, that court shall have power, on the application of the tenant, whether in those proceedings or in any subsequent proceedings, to call for the production of the rent book or any similar document relating to the dwelling-house and may direct the registrar or clerk of the court to correct any entries therein showing, or purporting to show, the tenant as being in arrear in respect of any sum which the court has determined to be irrecoverable.

(2) Paragraph (*b*) of subsection (2) of section fourteen of the Act of 1920 (which relates to the refusal or neglect of landlords to delete from rent-books and similar documents entries purporting to show as arrears sums which are irrecoverable) shall have effect in relation to entries made after the passing of the Act of 1920 as well as in relation to entries made before that date, and in the said subsection (2) there shall be substituted for the words "unless he proves that he acted innocently and without intent to deceive" the words "unless he proves that at the time of the making of the entry or of "the neglect or refusal to cause it to be deleted, as the case may be, "the landlord had a bona fide claim that the sum was recoverable."

9. Temporary continuance of provisions as to mortgages where property decontrolled by this Act

[1]Where any mortgaged property consists of or comprises one or

---

[1] This section does not apply to "new control" houses (1st Sch. / 1939 Act).

more dwelling-houses to which the principal Acts ceased to apply as from the twenty-ninth day of September, nineteen hundred and thirty-three, by virtue of the provisions of section one of this Act, the principal Acts shall, until the expiration of the period of six months next after the passing of this Act, nevertheless have effect in relation to the mortgage as if those Acts had not ceased to apply to that dwelling-house or those dwelling-houses, and any question whether a mortgage is a mortgage to which those Acts apply, or whether or in what manner the principal moneys secured by a mortgage can be apportioned under subsection (5) of section twelve of the Act of 1920, shall be determined accordingly.

10. Powers of local authorities for the purposes of giving information

(1) The council of every county borough and of every county district shall have power to publish information, for the assistance of landlords and tenants, as to their rights and duties under the principal Acts, and as to the procedure for enforcing such rights or securing performance of such duties, and to furnish particulars as to the availability, extent, and character of alternative accommodation.

(2) The functions of a council under this section may in accordance with directions given by the council be exercised by a committee of the council appointed under this section or under any other enactment; and the council may appoint as additional members of any such committee for the purpose of exercising the said functions such persons as they think fit, whether members of the council or not.

(3) Any expenses incurred under this section by the council, or by any such committee as aforesaid with the permission or approval of the council by whom the committee was appointed, shall be defrayed out of the general rate.

11. Power of local authorities to prosecute offences

The council of a county borough or county district in England shall have power to institute proceedings for any offence under the principal Acts or this Act.

12. (Repealed by the Acts of 1954.)

13. Amendment as to application of Acts in relation to family of deceased tenant

So much of paragraph (g) of subsection (1) of section twelve of the

Act of 1920 as enacts that the expression "tenant" shall, in the case of a tenant ****[1] leaving no widow or being a woman, include such member of the tenant's family residing with him at the time of his death as may be decided in default of agreement by the county court shall not, as respects tenants dying after the passing of this Act, apply to any such member unless he was residing with the tenant for not less than six months immediately before the death.

14. Regulations

(1) The Minister of Health may make regulations prescribing—

(a) forms to be substituted for the form contained in the First Schedule to the Act of 1920;

(b) the matters as to which notice is to be given to tenants of dwelling-houses to which the principal Acts apply by means of notices inserted in rent books and similar documents, and the forms of such notices;

(c) the form of application for registration under section two of this Act.

(2) Upon the coming into force of regulations prescribing a form to be substituted for the form contained in the First Schedule to the Act of 1920, the form contained in the said Schedule shall cease to have effect.

(3) If any rent book or similar document which does not conform to the prescribed requirements is used by or on behalf of any landlord, the landlord shall be guilty of an offence and liable on summary conviction thereof to a fine not exceeding *fifty*[2] pounds.

(4) All regulations made under this section shall, as soon as may be after they are made, be laid before each House of Parliament, and if either House, within the next subsequent twenty-eight days on which that House has sat after any such regulations are laid before it, resolves that the regulations be annulled, the regulations shall thenceforth be void, but without prejudice to anything previously done thereunder or to the making of new regulations.

15. Application to Scotland

This Act shall, in its application to Scotland, be subject to the following modifications, that is to say:—

---

[1] The words "dying intestate" were omitted by the 1935 Act (p. 5).
[2] Substituted by the 1957 Act.

(a) for any reference to the Minister of Health there shall be substituted a reference to a Secretary of State, for any reference to the Minister of Agriculture and Fisheries there shall be substituted a reference to the Department of Agriculture for Scotland, for any reference to the Housing Act, 1925, there shall be substituted a reference to the Housing (Scotland) Act, 1925, ...[1]

(b) for any reference to the twenty-fourth day of June, nineteen hundred and thirty-eight, there shall be substituted a reference to the twenty-eighth day of May, nineteen hundred and thirty-eight, and for references to the twenty-eighth and twenty-ninth days of September there shall be substituted, respectively, references to the twenty-seventh and twenty-eighth days of November:

(c) ****;[2] "assessed" means entered in the valuation roll; "intoxicating liquor" means exciseable liquor; "county court" means sheriff court; "sanitary authority" means a county or a town council; "mortgage" means a heritable security, including a security constituted by absolute disposition qualified by back bond or letter, and any reference to mortgaged property shall be construed accordingly; "licensing justices" means licensing court; and "licence" means a certificate as defined in Part VII of the Licensing (Scotland) Act, 1903:

(d) for references to a county borough and a county district there shall be substituted respectively references to a burgh and a county:

(e) any expenses incurred by a county or town council under this Act or by any committee under section ten of this Act shall be defrayed out of such rate payable by owners and occupiers in equal proportions as the council may determine:

(f)[3]

(g) in determining for the purposes of the First Schedule to this Act whether any rent lawfully due from a tenant has or has not been paid in any case where the rent is payable in advance, any sums paid by the tenant in satisfaction of

---

[1] Words omitted by the 1954 Scottish Act.
[2] Words omitted by the 1939 Act.
[3] Repealed by the 1939 Act.

a decree or decrees for rent and expenses shall, if the action in which any such decree was obtained was raised before the expiry of the period in respect of which the rent sued for was due, be imputed wholly to rent and not to expenses:

(*h*) where the landlord of a dwelling-house to which the principal Acts apply and of which the rent is payable in advance raises any proceedings for recovery of rent or for removing or ejection before the expiry of the period for which the rent sued for or in respect of the non-payment of which removing or ejection is craved is payable, the court shall not award any expenses to the landlord unless it considers it reasonable to do so after consideration of the whole circumstances of the case, including any offer made by the tenant prior to the bringing of the proceedings to pay the rent by instalments.

16. Interpretation

(1) In this Act, unless the context otherwise requires, the following expressions have the meanings hereby respectively assigned to them, that is to say:—

****1

"Dwelling-house" has the same meaning as in the principal Acts, that is to say, a house let as a separate dwelling or a part of a house being a part so let;

"Housing authority" means a local authority for the purposes of Part III of the Housing Act, 1925; and "area", in relation to such an authority, means the area for supplying the needs of which the authority has powers under the said Part of that Act;

"Prescribed" means prescribed by regulations under this Act;

*****1

"Recoverable rent" means, in relation to any dwelling-house, the maximum rent which, under the provisions of the principal Acts, is or was recoverable from the tenant;

"Rent Restrictions Acts" means the principal Acts and the Acts repealed by the Increase of Rent and Mortgage Interest (Restrictions) Act, 1920;

---

[1] Repealed by the 1939 Act.

"The Act of 1920" means the Increase of Rent and Mortgage Interest (Restrictions) Act, 1920;

"The Act of 1923" means the Rent and Mortgage Interest Restrictions Act, 1923.

(2) (Repealed by the 1939 Act.)

(3) References in this Act to the principal Acts or to any of them or to any provision of those Acts or of any of them shall, unless the context otherwise requires, be construed as references to those Acts, that Act or that provision, as the case may be, as amended by any subsequent enactment, including this Act.

(4) References in this Act to county boroughs and county districts and to the councils thereof shall be construed, for the purposes of the application of this Act to the City of London, as references to the City of London and the common council, and for the purposes of the application of this Act to the remainder of the administrative County of London, as references to metropolitan boroughs and the councils thereof.

17. Consequential and minor amendments to principal Acts

(1) The amendments in the second column of the Second Schedule to this Act (which relate to consequential matters and to matters of minor detail) shall be made in the enactments specified in the first column of that Schedule.

(2) In subsection (3) of section twelve of the Act of 1920 (which relates to the apportionment of rateable value) the references to rateable value shall be construed as including references to "rateable value on the appointed day" as defined by this Act.

18. Short title, citation, extent and repeal

(1) This Act may be cited as the Rent and Mortgage Interest Restrictions (Amendment) Act, 1933, and this Act and the principal Acts may be cited together as the Rent and Mortgage Interest Restrictions Acts, 1920 to 1933.

(2) This Act shall not extend to Northern Ireland.

(3) (Repealed by the Statute Law Revision Act, 1950.)

SCHEDULES

Sections 3 and 15.

FIRST SCHEDULE

POSSESSION OR EJECTMENT WITHOUT PROOF OF
ALTERNATIVE ACCOMMODATION

A court shall, for the purposes of section three of this Act, have power to make or give an order or judgment for the recovery of possession of any dwelling-house to which the principal Acts apply or for the ejectment of a tenant therefrom without proof of suitable alternative accommodation (where the court considers it reasonable so to do) if—

(a) any rent lawfully due from the tenant has not been paid, or any other obligation of the tenancy (whether under the contract of tenancy or under the principal Acts), so far as the obligation is consistent with the provisions of the principal Acts, has been broken or not performed;

(b) the tenant or any person residing or lodging with him or being his sub-tenant has been guilty of conduct which is a nuisance or annoyance to adjoining occupiers, or has been convicted of using the premises or allowing the premises to be used for an immoral or illegal purpose, or the condition of the dwelling-house has, in the opinion of the court, deteriorated owing to acts of waste by, or the neglect or default of, the tenant or any such person, and, where such person is a lodger or sub-tenant, the court is satisfied that the tenant has not, before the making or giving of the order or judgment, taken such steps as he ought reasonably to have taken for the removal of the lodger or sub-tenant;

(c) the tenant has given notice to quit, and, in consequence of that notice, the landlord has contracted to sell or let the dwelling-house or has taken any other steps as a result of which he would, in the opinion of the court, be seriously prejudiced if he could not obtain possession;

(d) the tenant without the consent of the landlord has at any time after the thirty-first day of July, nineteen hundred and twenty-three,[1] assigned or sublet the whole of the dwelling-house or sublet part of the dwelling-house, the remainder being already sublet;

(e) the dwelling-house consists of or includes premises licensed for the sale of intoxicating liquor not to be consumed on the premises, and the tenant has committed an offence as holder of the licence

---

[1] For "new control" houses substitute the 1st September 1939.

or has not conducted the business to the satisfaction of the licensing justices or the police authority, or has carried it on in a manner detrimental to the public interest, or the renewal of the licence has for any reason been refused:

(*f*) [the dwelling-house is so overcrowded as to be dangerous or injurious to the health of the inmates, and the court is satisfied that the overcrowding could have been abated by the removal of any lodger or sub-tenant (not being a parent or child of the tenant) whom it would, having regard to all the circumstances of the case, including the question whether other accommodation is available for him, have been reasonable to remove, and that the tenant has not taken such steps as he ought reasonably to have taken for his removal;]

(*g*) the dwelling-house is reasonably required by the landlord for occupation as a residence for some person engaged in his whole-time employment or in the whole-time employment of some tenant from him or with whom, conditional on housing accommodation being provided, a contract for such employment has been entered into, and [either—

(i) the tenant was in the employment of the landlord or a former landlord, and the dwelling-house was let to him in consequence of that employment and he has ceased to be in that employment; or

(ii) the court is satisfied by a certificate of the county agricultural committee, or where there is no such committee, of the Minister of Agriculture and Fisheries, that the person for whose occupation the dwelling-house is required by the landlord is, or is to be, employed on work necessary for the proper working of an agricultural holding or as an estate workman on the maintenance and repair of the buildings, plant, or equipment, of agricultural holdings comprised in the estate;]

(*h*)[1] *the dwelling-house is reasonably required by the landlord (not being a landlord who has become landlord by purchasing the dwelling-house or any interest therein after the seventh day of November, nineteen hundred and fifty-six) for occupation as a residence for—*

(i) *himself; or*

(ii) *any son or daughter of his over eighteen years of age; or*

(iii) *his father or mother*

Provided that an order or judgment shall not be made or given on any ground specified in paragraph (*h*) of the foregoing provisions of this Schedule if the court is satisfied that having regard to all the circumstances

---

[1] Substituted by the 1957 Act.

of the case, including the question whether other accommodation is available for the landlord or the tenant, greater hardship would be caused by granting the order or judgment than by refusing to grant it.

Section 17.

SECOND SCHEDULE

CONSEQUENTIAL AND MINOR AMENDMENTS

Provision to be amended	Amendment
Section 5 of the Act of 1920	For subsection (1) there shall be substituted the provisions of section three and subsection (1) of section four of this Act and of the First Schedule thereto; and in subsection (7) for the reference to the grounds specified in paragraph (d) of subsection (1) of that section there shall be substituted a reference to the grounds specified in paragraphs (g) and (h) of the First Schedule to this Act.
Section 12 of the Act of 1920	In subsection (9), the words from "but for the purpose of any enactment relating to rating" to the end of the subsection shall cease to have effect except in the application of the Act to Scotland.
[Section 18 of the Act of 1923	In subsection (2) there shall be substituted for the reference to paragraph (ii) of subsection (1) of section five of the principal Act, a reference to subparagraph (ii) of paragraph (g) of the First Schedule to this Act.]

Section 18.

THIRD SCHEDULE

ENACTMENTS REPEALED

(Repealed by the Statute Law Revision Act, 1950.)

INCREASE OF RENT AND MORTGAGE INTEREST (RESTRICTIONS) ACT, 1935

[25 Geo. 5]

CHAPTER 13

An Act to amend the interpretation of "tenant" in paragraph (g) of subsection (1) of section twelve of the Increase of Rent and Mortgage Interest (Restrictions) Act, 1920, and the provisions of section thirteen of the Rent and Mortgage Interest Restrictions (Amendment) Act, 1933.   [28th March 1935.]

Be it enacted by the King's most Excellent Majesty, by and with the advice and consent of the Lords Spiritual and Temporal, and Commons, in this present Parliament assembled, and by the authority of the same, as follows:—

1. Amendment of interpretation of "tenant"

Paragraph (g) of subsection (1) of section twelve of the Increase of Rent and Mortgage Interest (Restrictions) Act, 1920, and section thirteen of the Rent and Mortgage Interest Restrictions (Amendment) Act, 1933, shall have effect as if the words "dying intestate" in all places where they occur were omitted.

2. Short title and citation

This Act may be cited as the Increase of Rent and Mortgage Interest (Restrictions) Act, 1935, and this Act and the Rent and Mortgage Interest Restrictions Acts, 1920 to 1933, may be cited together as the Rent and Mortgage Interest Restrictions Acts, 1920 to 1935.

INCREASE OF RENT AND MORTGAGE INTEREST (RESTRICTIONS) ACT, 1938

[1 & 2 Geo. 6]

CHAPTER 26

An Act to amend and continue the Rent and Mortgage Interest Restrictions Acts, 1920 to 1935.   [26th May 1938.]

Be it enacted by the King's most Excellent Majesty, by and with the advice and consent of the Lords Spiritual and Temporal, and Commons, in this present Parliament assembled, and by the authority of the same, as follows:—

1. (Repealed by the 1939 Act.)

2. Decontrol of certain houses

(1) Subject to the provisions of this Act relating to registration, the principal Acts, as from the twenty-ninth day of September nineteen hundred and thirty-eight, shall not apply to any dwelling-house unless it is a dwelling-house to which they applied immediately before the passing of this Act or then formed part of such a dwelling-house, and it is also a dwelling-house of which the rateable value on the appointed day did not exceed—

(a) in the metropolitan police district or the city of London, thirty-five pounds;

(b) in Scotland, thirty-five pounds;

(c) elsewhere, twenty pounds.

(2) Where part of a dwelling-house to which the principal Acts applied immediately before the commencement of this Act was on the sixth day of December nineteen hundred and thirty-seven lawfully sublet and occupied as, or vacant and to let as, a separate dwelling, the rateable value of the whole dwelling-house on the appointed day shall be treated for the purposes of subsection (1) of this section (but not for the purposes of any other provision of this Act) as not having exceeded the respective amount mentioned therein, if, after subtracting the rateable value on the appointed day of the said part, it would not exceed that amount.

Where the rateable value on the appointed day of the whole of a dwelling-house is by virtue of this subsection treated as not having exceeded a particular amount, then, so long as the principal Acts continue to apply to that dwelling-house, the rateable value on the appointed day of any dwelling-house which forms part thereof shall, irrespective of the actual facts, also be treated as not having exceeded that amount.

(3) The transitional provisions set out in the First Schedule to this Act (being certain transitional provisions of the Act of 1933 adapted for the purposes of this Act) shall have effect in relation to dwelling-houses to which the principal Acts cease to apply by virtue of this section.

3. Discontinuance, except in certain cases, of system of decontrol on landlord recovering possession

(1) Save as provided in this and the next succeeding section, section two of the Act of 1923 (which provides for the exclusion of dwelling-houses from the application of the principal Acts on the landlord recovering possession and in certain other cases) shall cease to have effect.

(2) (Repealed by the 1939 Act.)

4. (Repealed by the 1939 Act.)

5. Amendment as to standard rent

[Where a dwelling-house to which the principal Acts apply is part of another dwelling-house to which those Acts apply, the standard rent of the first-mentioned dwelling-house as from the twenty-ninth day of September nineteen hundred and thirty-eight shall be a standard rent ascertained by apportioning the standard rent of the second-mentioned dwelling-house, and subsection (3) of section twelve of the Act of 1920 shall apply accordingly notwithstanding that the first-mentioned dwelling-house was let as a separate dwelling on or before the first day of August nineteen hundred and fourteen or on or before the date on which the second-mentioned dwelling-house was first let.]

6. Provision of rent books

(1) Where the rent of a dwelling-house to which the principal Acts apply is payable weekly, it shall be the duty of the landlord to provide a rent book or other similar document for use in respect of the dwelling-house.

(2) If the landlord of a dwelling-house fails to comply with the requirements of this section, he, and any person who on his behalf demands or receives rent in respect of the dwelling-house, shall in

respect of each week in which the failure occurs or continues be guilty of an offence and liable on summary conviction to a fine not exceeding ten pounds.

(3) This section shall come into force on the expiration of three months from the passing of this Act.

7. Miscellaneous amendments

(1) If any question arises in any proceedings whether the principal Acts apply to a dwelling-house, it shall be deemed to be a dwelling-house to which those Acts apply unless the contrary is shown.

[(2) In computing whether any and, if so, what increase in the rent of a dwelling-house to which the principal Acts apply is permissible under paragraph (*b*) of subsection (1) of section two of the Act of 1920 (which paragraph relates to increases of rent corresponding to increases in rates) the amount of any allowance made to the landlord under any of the enactments relating to allowances given where rates are paid by the owner instead of by the occupier shall be treated as part of the amount payable by the landlord in respect of rates:

Provided that this subsection shall not come into operation with respect to any dwelling-house in England until the date on which a demand for the general rate in respect thereof is first made on or after the first day of October nineteen hundred and thirty-eight, not being a demand for a sum which had already been demanded before that date.]

(3) Accommodation shall not be deemed for the purposes of section three of the Act of 1933 (which relates to alternative accommodation for tenants of dwelling-houses to which the principal Acts apply) to be suitable to the needs of a tenant and his family, if the result of their occupation thereof would be that it would be an overcrowded dwelling-house for the purposes of the Housing Act, 1936.

(4) (Repealed by the 1957 Act.)

(5) Any document authorised or required by the principal Acts to be served by the tenant of a dwelling-house on the landlord thereof shall be deemed to be duly so served if it is served on any agent of the landlord named as such in the rent book or other similar document, or on the person who receives the rent of the dwelling-house; and if for the purpose of any proceedings brought or intended to be brought under the principal Acts or the Act of 1933 (including any prosecution for an offence under any of those Acts)

any person serves upon any such agent or person receiving the rent as aforesaid a notice in writing requiring him to disclose to him the full name and place of abode or place of business of the landlord, it shall be the duty of the agent or person receiving the rent forthwith to comply with the notice, and if he fails or refuses so to do, he shall be liable on summary conviction to a fine not exceeding five pounds, unless he shows to the satisfaction of the court that he did not know, and could not with reasonable diligence have ascertained, such of the facts required by the notice to be disclosed as were not disclosed by him.

(6) The period fixed by subsection (2) of section eight of the Act of 1923 for the recovery by a tenant or mortgagor of certain over-payments is hereby extended, in relation to payments made not earlier than six months before the passing of this Act, to two years from the date of payment.

(7) The minor and consequential amendments specified in the second column of the Second Schedule to this Act shall be made in the enactments mentioned in the first column of that Schedule.

8. Interpretation and application to Scotland

(1) In this Act the expression "the Act of 1933" means the Rent and Mortgage Interest Restrictions (Amendment) Act, 1933.

(2) Other expressions have the same meanings as in the Act of 1933, ****.[1]

(3) This Act shall apply to Scotland subject to the following modifications:—

    (a) for any reference to the twenty-fourth day of June nineteen hundred and forty-two, there shall be substituted a reference to the twenty-eighth day of May nineteen hundred and forty-two, and for references to the twenty-eighth and twenty-ninth days of September nineteen hundred and thirty-eight, there shall be substituted respectively references to the twenty-seventh and twenty-eighth days of November nineteen hundred and thirty-eight;

    (b) for references to a county borough and a county district there shall be substituted respectively references to a burgh and a county;

---

[1] Words omitted by the 1939 Act.

(c) for any reference to the Housing Act, 1936, there shall be substituted a reference to the Housing (Scotland) Act, 1935;

(d) the second column of the Second Schedule shall have effect as if—

      (i) (Repealed by the 1954 Scottish Act.)

      (ii) in the amendment to the First Schedule to the Act of 1933 the words "Paragraph (f) shall cease to have effect and" were omitted.

9. Short title, citation and extent

(1) This Act may be cited as the Increase of Rent and Mortgage Interest (Restrictions) Act, 1938, and this Act and the Rent and Mortgage Interest Restrictions Acts, 1920 to 1935, may be cited together as the Rent and Mortgage Interest Restrictions Acts, 1920 to 1938.

(2) This Act shall not extend to Northern Ireland.

SCHEDULES

Section 2.

FIRST SCHEDULE

TRANSITIONAL PROVISIONS

1. A person who, on the twenty-eighth day of September nineteen hundred and thirty-eight is, by virtue only of the principal Acts, tenant of a dwelling-house to which those Acts cease to apply as from the following day by virtue of the provisions of section two of this Act shall be entitled to retain possession of the dwelling-house until the date specified in a notice served upon the tenant under this paragraph by or on behalf of the landlord after the passing of this Act, and shall be so entitled in the like manner and subject to the like terms and conditions as if the principal Acts had not ceased to apply to the dwelling-house.

2. Any notice served under the last preceding paragraph shall be in writing and shall inform the tenant, either that he is required to give up possession of the dwelling-house on the date specified in the notice, or that he will be so required unless before that date an agreement for a new tenancy has been made between the tenant and the landlord, so, however, that the date specified in any such notice shall be not earlier than the twenty-ninth day of September nineteen hundred and thirty-eight, and not earlier than one month after the service of the notice.

3. The acceptance of rent or mesne profits by the landlord after the date specified in a notice served in respect of any dwelling-house under the said paragraph shall not affect the validity of the notice, and if any such notice contains or is accompanied by an offer in writing of the terms on which the landlord is willing to grant a new tenancy of the dwelling-house, and a written statement that, if the tenant retains possession of the dwelling-house after the date aforesaid without having made an agreement with the landlord on any other terms, he will by virtue of this Act be deemed to do so upon the terms so offered as aforesaid, then, if the tenant so retains possession, he shall be deemed to do so on those terms.

4. Where upon the expiration of such a notice as aforesaid a tenant ceases to be entitled by virtue of this Act to retain possession of a dwelling-house, the provisions of the Landlord and Tenant Act, 1927, shall apply in respect of the premises as if they had been held under a lease (as defined by that Act) terminated by that notice, and if, before the expiration of the notice, either—

    (a) the tenant has, under section five of that Act, served on the landlord a notice requiring a new lease of the premises; or

    (b) the landlord has under section two or section four of that Act, served on the tenant notice that he is willing and able to grant

v

to the tenant or obtain the grant to him of a renewal of the tenancy,

so much of the last foregoing paragraph as provides that in the circumstances therein mentioned the tenant of a dwelling-house will, if he retains possession thereof after the expiration of a notice requiring him to give up possession, be deemed to do so upon terms offered by the landlord, shall not apply.

5. Where any mortgaged property consists of or comprises one or more dwelling-houses to which the principal Acts cease to apply as from the twenty-ninth day of September nineteen hundred and thirty-eight by virtue of the provisions of section two of this Act, the principal Acts shall, until the expiration of the period of six months next after the passing of this Act, nevertheless have effect in relation to the mortgage as if those Acts had not ceased to apply to that dwelling-house or those dwelling-houses, and any question whether a mortgage is a mortgage to which those Acts apply, or whether or in what manner the principal moneys secured by a mortgage can be apportioned under subsection (5) of section twelve of the Act of 1920, shall be determined accordingly.

SECOND SCHEDULE

Sections 7, 8.

MINOR AND CONSEQUENTIAL AMENDMENTS.

Provision to be amended	Amendment
****	
[Section 3 of the Rent Restrictions (Notices of Increase) Act, 1923.	Subsection (4) shall cease to have effect.]
[Section 7 of the Rent and Mortgage Interest Restrictions Act, 1923.	In subsection (1) at the end of the first paragraph there shall be inserted the following proviso:— "Provided that, if the interest of the tenant in the dwelling-house comprised in the tenancy is determined and the sub-tenant becomes the tenant of the landlord, then, notwithstanding anything in subsection (3) of section fifteen of the principal Act (which provides that in such circumstances a sub-tenant becomes the tenant of the landlord on the same terms as he would have held from the tenant if the tenancy had continued) the maximum additional amount of rent which is allowed by this subsection to be charged in respect of the dwelling-

Provision to be amended	Amendment
	house comprised in the sub-tenancy shall be reduced to five per cent. of the net rent thereof."]
Section 18 of the Rent and Mortgage Interest Restrictions Act, 1923.	In subsection (1) the words down to "a reasonable state of repair, and" shall cease to have effect, and for the words "the purposes aforesaid" there shall be substituted the words "the purposes of the principal Act and this Act."
Section 2 of the Act of 1933.	Subsection (1) shall cease to have effect; in subsection (2), for the words "it is proved," there shall be substituted the words "it appears"; in subsection (5), after the word "proceedings," there shall be inserted the words "or on any application for that purpose "made by the tenant or by the landlord"; and in subsection (6) for the words "the respective amount "mentioned in subsection (1) of this section" there shall be substituted the words ", or is by virtue of "subsection (2) of section two of the Increase of "Rent and Mortgage Interest (Restrictions) Act, "1938, to be treated for the purposes of that section "as not having exceeded, in the metropolitan police "district, the city of London or Scotland thirty-five "pounds, or elsewhere twenty pounds."

RENT AND MORTGAGE
INTEREST RESTRICTIONS ACT, 1939
[2 & 3 Geo. 6]

CHAPTER 71

AN Act to continue and amend the Rent and Mortgage Interest Restrictions Acts, 1920 to 1938. [1st September 1939.]

Be it enacted by the King's most Excellent Majesty, by and with the advice and consent of the Lords Spiritual and Temporal, and Commons, in this present Parliament assembled, and by the authority of the same, as follows:—

1. Continuance of Acts

Subject to the provisions of this Act, the principal Acts shall continue in force until six months after such date as His Majesty may by Order in Council declare to be the date on which the emergency that was the occasion of the passing of this Act came to an end.

2. (Repealed by the Statute Law Revision Act, 1950.)

3. Application of Acts

(1) Without prejudice to the operation of the two preceding sections in relation to any dwelling-house to which the principal Acts applied immediately before the commencement of this Act, the principal Acts, as amended by the last preceding section, shall, subject to the provisions of this section, apply to every other dwelling-house of which the rateable value on the appropriate day did not exceed—

  (a) in the metropolitan police district or the city of London, one hundred pounds;

  (b) in Scotland, ninety pounds; or

  (c) elsewhere, seventy-five pounds;

and in relation to any such dwelling-house as aforesaid, not being a dwelling-house to which the principal Acts applied immediately before the commencement of this Act, the provisions of the Rent and Mortgage Interest Restrictions Acts, 1920 to 1933, set out in the first column of the First Schedule to this Act shall have effect as if there were made in those provisions the modifications respectively prescribed by that Schedule.

(2) The principal Acts shall not, by virtue of this section, apply—

    (*a*) to any dwelling-house consisting of, or comprising, premises licensed for the sale of intoxicating liquor for consumption on the premises; or

    (*b*) save as is expressly provided in the said Acts, as amended by virtue of this section, to any dwelling-house bona fide let at a rent which includes payments in respect of board, attendance or use of furniture; or

    (*c*) (Repealed by the 1954 Acts.)

(3) Subject to the provisions of paragraph (*a*) of the last preceding subsection, the application of the principal Acts, by virtue of this section, to any dwelling-house shall not be excluded by reason only that part of the premises is used as a shop or office or for business, trade or professional purposes; and for the purposes of the Rent and Mortgage Interest Restrictions Acts, 1920 to 1938, as amended by virtue of this section, any land or premises let together with a dwelling-house shall, unless the land or premises so let consists or consist of agricultural land exceeding two acres in extent, be treated as part of the dwelling-house; but, save as aforesaid, the principal Acts shall not, by virtue of this section, apply to any dwelling-house let together with land other than the site of the dwelling-house.

4. Application of Act to pending proceedings

Where, in relation to any dwelling-house to which the principal Acts apply by virtue only of the last preceding section, any order or judgment has been made or given by a court before the commencement of this Act, but has not been executed, and, in the opinion of the court, the order or judgment would not have been made or given if this Act had been in operation at the time when the order or judgment was made or given, the court may, on application by the tenant, rescind or vary the order or judgment in such manner as the court thinks fit for the purpose of giving effect to this Act.

5. (Repealed by the Statute Law Revision Act, 1950.)

6. Exercise of power to make rules when Great Seal in Commission

Any power vested in the Lord Chancellor to make rules or give directions for the purpose of giving effect to the principal Acts may, when the Great Seal is in commission, be exercised by any Lord Commissioner.

7. Interpretation

(1) In this Act the following expressions have the meanings hereby respectively assigned to them, that is to say:

"agricultural land" has the meaning assigned to that expression by section two of the Rating and Valuation (Apportionment) Act, 1928;

"rateable value on the appropriate day," in relation to any dwelling-house, means (subject to the following provisions of this section) the value shown, with respect to that dwelling-house, on that day in the valuation list then in force, as the rateable value or, where the net annual value differs from the rateable value, as the net annual value; and

"the appropriate day" means, as respects the administrative county of London, the sixth day of April, nineteen hundred and thirty-nine, or, as respects the remainder of England, the first day of April, nineteen hundred and thirty-nine;

and other expressions have the same meanings as in the Rent and Mortgage Interest Restrictions (Amendment) Act, 1933.

(2) In relation to any dwelling-house of which the rateable value on the appropriate day was not on that day separately assessed, any reference in the preceding provisions of this Act to the rateable value on the appropriate day shall be construed as a reference to such proportion of the rateable value on that day of the property in which the dwelling-house is comprised as may be apportioned to the dwelling-house by the county court in accordance with the provisions of subsection (3) of section twelve of the Increase of Rent and Mortgage Interest (Restrictions) Act, 1920.

(3) In relation to any dwelling-house first assessed after the appropriate day, any reference in the preceding provisions of this Act to the rateable value on the appropriate day shall be construed as a reference to the rateable value on the day on which the dwelling-house was first assessed.

(4) References in this Act or in the Rent and Mortgage Interest (Restrictions) Act, 1938, to the principal Acts or to any of them or to any provision of the principal Acts or of any of them shall, unless the context otherwise requires, be construed as references to the principal Acts, to that one of them or to that provision, as the case may be, as amended by any subsequent enactment, including this Act.

8. Application to Scotland

In the application of this Act to Scotland—

(a) "the appropriate day" means the sixteenth day of May, nineteen hundred and thirty-nine;

(b) "valuation list" means valuation roll;

(c) "agricultural land" means land used for agricultural or pastoral purposes only or as woodlands, market gardens, orchards, allotments or allotment gardens and any lands exceeding one-quarter of an acre used for the purpose of poultry farming, but does not include any lands occupied together with a house as a park, garden or pleasure ground or any land kept or preserved mainly or exclusively for sporting purposes;

(d) (Repealed by the 1954 Scottish Act.)

9. Short title, citation, extent, repeal and commencement

(1) This Act may be cited as the Rent and Mortgage Interest Restrictions Act, 1939; and the Rent and Mortgage Interest Restrictions Acts, 1920 to 1938, and this Act may be cited together as the Rent and Mortgage Interest Restrictions Acts, 1920 to 1939.

(2) This Act shall not extend to Northern Ireland.

(3) (Repealed by the Statute Law Revision Act, 1950.)

(4) This Act shall come into operation on such date as His Majesty may by Order in Council appoint.

(NOTE—This subsection (4) was repealed by the Statute Law Revision Act, 1950, but that does not affect the binding force, operation or construction of the 1939 Act.)

SCHEDULES

Section 3 (1).

FIRST SCHEDULE

MODIFICATION OF THE RENT AND MORTGAGE INTEREST RESTRICTIONS
ACTS, 1920 TO 1933, FOR THE PURPOSES OF SECTION THREE
OF THIS ACT.

THE INCREASE OF RENT AND MORTGAGE INTEREST (RESTRICTIONS)
ACT, 1920.

Section 1 . For the reference to the twenty-fifth day of March, nineteen hundred and twenty, there shall be substituted a reference to the date of the passing of this Act, and for the reference to the passing of the Act there shall be substituted a reference to the commencement of this Act; and for the words "if [the increased rent or] the increased "rate of interest exceeds by more than the amount "permitted under this Act the [standard rent or] "standard rate of interest" there shall be substituted the words " [if the increased rent exceeds the standard rent "by more than the amount permitted under this Act or, "as the case may be,] if the increased rate of interest "exceeds the standard rate of interest."

[Section 2 . In paragraph (a) of subsection (1) for the reference to the fourth day of August, nineteen hundred and fourteen, there shall be substituted a reference to the date of the commencement of this Act, and the words "six, or in the "case of such expenditure incurred after the passing of "this Act" shall be omitted.

In paragraph (b) of subsection (1) for the reference to the third day of August, nineteen hundred and fourteen, there shall be substituted a reference to the day before the date of the commencement of this Act.

Paragraphs (c) and (d) and (e) of subsection (1) shall not apply.

Subsections (2) and (4) shall not apply.]

[Section 3 . In subsection (3) for the reference to the passing of the Act there shall be substituted a reference to the commencement of this Act.]

Section 4 . This section shall not apply.

Section 5   .   Subsection (3) shall not apply.
In subsection (7) for the reference to the thirty-first day of
July, nineteen hundred and twenty-three, there shall be
substituted a reference to the commencement of this Act.

Section 6   .   For the reference to the Courts (Emergency Powers) Act,
1914, there shall be substituted a reference to the Courts
(Emergency Powers) Act, 1939.

Section 7   .   In proviso (i) for the reference to the twenty-fifth day of
March, nineteen hundred and twenty, there shall be
substituted a reference to the date of the passing of this
Act.

Section 8   .   In subsection (1) for the reference to the twenty-fifth day
of March, nineteen hundred and twenty, there shall be
substituted a reference to the date of the passing of this
Act; for the reference to the passing of the Act there
shall be substituted a reference to the commencement of
this Act; and the words "but the enactments repealed
"by this Act did not apply" shall be omitted.
****[1]
****[1]

Section 12   .   In paragraphs [(a) and] (b) of subsection (1), for the
references to the third day of August, nineteen hundred
and fourteen, there shall be substituted references to the
day before the date of the commencement of this Act.

For paragraph (e) of subsection (1) there shall be substituted the following paragraph:—

"(e) The expression 'rateable value,' in relation to
any dwelling-house, means the value shown, with
respect to that dwelling-house, on the appropriate day
in the valuation list then in force, as the rateable value
or, where the net annual value differs from the rateable
value, as the net annual value; and the expression 'the
appropriate day' means, in relation to a dwelling-
house within the administrative county of London, the
sixth day of April, nineteen hundred and thirty-nine,
or, in relation to a dwelling-house in any other part
of England, the first day of April, nineteen hundred
and thirty-nine; and in relation to a dwelling-house
first assessed after the said sixth day of April or the
said first day of April, as the case may be, any reference
in the preceding provisions of this paragraph to the
appropriate day shall be construed as a reference to

[1] Words omitted by the 1957 Act.

Section 12—*cont.*   the day on which the dwelling-house was first assessed;"

Subsection (2) shall not apply.

Paragraph (c) of subsection (4) shall not apply.

Subsections (9) and (10) shall not apply.

Section 14 . In subsection (1) for the words "whether before or after "the passing of this Act" there shall be substituted the words "since the beginning of the date of the passing of "the Rent and Mortgage Interest Restrictions Act, "1939"; and the words "or any Act repealed by this Act" shall be omitted.

Section 18 . In paragraph (a) of subsection (1) the definition of "rateable value" and of "rateable value on the third day of "August, nineteen hundred and fourteen" shall be omitted.

The Rent and Mortgage Interest Restrictions Act, 1923.

Section 3 . This section shall not apply.

[Section 7 . This section shall not apply.]

Section 8 . In subsection (2) for the references to the passing of the Act there shall be substituted references to the commencement of this Act.

Section 10 . In subsection (1) for the reference to proviso (i) to subsection (2) of section twelve of the Increase of Rent and Mortgage Interest (Restrictions) Act, 1920, there shall be substituted a reference to paragraph (b) of subsection (2) of section three of this Act.

The Rent and Mortgage Interest Restrictions (Amendment) Act, 1933.

Section 1 . Subsection (3) shall not apply.

Section 4 . In subsection (4) for the reference to the passing of the Act there shall be substituted a reference to the commencement of this Act.

Section 5 . This section shall not apply.

[Section 6 . For the references to the third day of August, nineteen hundred and fourteen, there shall be substituted references to the day before the date of the commencement of this Act.]

Section 9 . This section shall not apply.

The First   . In paragraph (*d*) for the reference to the thirty-first day of
Schedule   July, nineteen hundred and twenty-three, there shall be
               substituted a reference to the date of the passing of this
               Act.
****1

<h1 style="text-align:center">SECOND SCHEDULE</h1>

Section 9 (3).

ENACTMENTS REPEALED.

(Repealed by the Statute Law Revision Act, 1950).

---

¹ Words omitted by the 1957 Act.

LANDLORD AND TENANT (RENT CONTROL) ACT, 1949

[12 & 13 Geo. 6]

CHAPTER 40

An Act to provide in certain cases for the determination by a Tribunal of standard rents for the purposes of the Rent and Mortgage Interest Restrictions Acts, 1920 to 1939; further to restrict the requiring of premiums in connection with tenancies to which those Acts apply; to make further provision for the purposes of those Acts where the tenant shares part of his accommodation with his landlord or other persons or sublets part of his dwelling-house furnished; to amend the Rent of Furnished Houses Control (Scotland) Act, 1943, and the Furnished Houses (Rent Control) Act, 1946, as respects security of tenure and the requiring of premiums and as respects the districts for which Tribunals are constituted; to make certain minor amendments of the said Acts in so far as they apply to Scotland; and for purposes connected with the matters aforesaid.   [2nd June 1949]

Be it enacted by the King's most Excellent Majesty, by and with the advice and consent of the Lords Spiritual and Temporal, and Commons, in this present Parliament assembled, and by the authority of the same, as follows:—

1. Variation of standard rents fixed by reference to new lettings

[(1) Where apart from this section the standard rent of a dwelling-house would be—

(a) the rent at which it was let on a letting beginning after the first day of September, nineteen hundred and thirty-nine, or

(b) an amount ascertainable by apportionment of the rent at which a property of which it formed part was let on such a letting as aforesaid (whether such an apportionment has been made or not),

then, subject to the provisions of this section, the landlord or the tenant may make application to the Tribunal to determine what rent is reasonable for that dwelling-house, and on any such application the Tribunal shall determine that rent and shall notify the parties of their determination:[1]

Provided that an application shall not be made in respect of a dwelling-house if a previous application in respect thereof has been made under this subsection.

(2) Subject to the provisions of the next following subsection, if the rent so determined by the Tribunal as aforesaid *differs from*[2] what would be the standard rent apart from this section, it shall, as from the date of the determination thereof, be the standard rent of the dwelling-house.

(3) If on the hearing of the application it appears to the Tribunal that the limit imposed by the principal Acts on the rent recoverable in respect of the dwelling-house exceeds what would be the standard rent apart from this section, the Tribunal shall determine the amount of the excess; and if the rent determined in accordance with subsection (1) of this section, reduced by the amount of the excess, *differs from*[2] what would be the standard rent apart from this section, the rent so determined and reduced shall as from the date of the Tribunal's determination be the standard rent of the dwelling-house.

(4) Subject to the provisions of this section, the rent which is reasonable for a dwelling-house shall, for the purposes of this section, be the rent which is in all the circumstances reasonable on a letting of that dwelling-house on the terms and conditions, other than terms and conditions fixing the amount of rent, on which the dwelling-house is let at the time of the application.

(5) In determining under this section what rent is reasonable for a dwelling-house, no regard shall be had to the fact that any premium has been paid in respect of the grant, continuance or renewal of a tenancy; but the provisions of Part I of the First Schedule to this Act shall have effect in relation to such premiums paid before the commencement of this Act.

(6) In determining under this section what rent is reasonable for a dwelling-house forming part of another dwelling-house to which the principal Acts apply, regard shall not be had to the rent of the said other dwelling-house or any part thereof if no determination in

---

[1] See s. 2 (2) / 1952 Act as to Crown sub-tenants.
[2] Substituted by the 1954 Acts.

respect of the dwelling-house or part has been made under this section.

(7) No application shall be made under this section in respect of any house—

   (a) (Repealed by the 1954 Acts.)
   (b) while any limitation of the rent is in force, being a limitation imposed by or under any enactment not contained in the principal Acts or this Act.

(8) In relation to a dwelling-house or property let at a progressive rent, subsection (1) of this section shall have effect with the substitution, for references to the rent at which the dwelling-house or property was let, of references to the maximum rent under the letting.]

2. Prohibition of premiums on grant or assignment of tenancy

(1) A person shall not, as a condition of the grant, renewal or continuance of a tenancy to which this section applies, require the payment of any premium in addition to the rent.

(2) Subject to the provisions of Part II of the First Schedule to this Act, a person shall not, as a condition of the assignment of a tenancy to which this section applies, require the payment of any premium.[1]

(3) This section applies to any tenancy of a dwelling-house, being a tenancy to which the principal Acts apply, such that when the dwelling-house is let under the tenancy it is a dwelling-house to which the principal Acts apply.

(4) Notwithstanding anything in subsection (2) of this section, an assignor may, if apart from this section he would be entitled so to do, require the payment by the assignee—

   (a) of so much of any outgoings discharged by the assignor as is referable to any period after the assignment takes effect;
   (b) of a sum not exceeding the amount of any expenditure reasonably incurred by the assignor in carrying out any structural alteration of the dwelling-house or in providing or improving fixtures therein, being fixtures which as against the landlord he is not entitled to remove;

---

[1] See s. 38 / 1954 English Act and s. 29 / 1954 Scottish Act as to the modification of this provision.

(c) where the assignor became a tenant of the dwelling-house by virtue of an assignment of the tenancy thereof, of a sum not exceeding any reasonable amount paid by him to his assignor in respect of expenditure incurred by that assignor, or by any previous assignor of the tenancy, in carrying out any such alteration or in providing or improving any such fixtures as are mentioned in the last foregoing paragraph; or

(d) where part of the dwelling-house is used as a shop or office, or for business, trade or professional purposes, of a reasonable amount in respect of any goodwill of the business, trade or profession, being goodwill transferred to the assignee in connection with the assignment or accruing to him in consequence thereof.

(5) Where, under an agreement made after the twenty-fifth day of March, nineteen hundred and forty-nine, any premium has been paid which, or the whole of which, could not lawfully be required under the foregoing provisions of this section (or, if the premium was required before the commencement of this Act, which could not lawfully have been required if this Act had then been in force), the amount of the premium, or so much thereof as could not lawfully be required or have been required, as the case may be, shall be recoverable by the person by whom it was paid:

Provided that where an agreement has been made since the said twenty-fifth day of March and before the commencement of this Act, and the agreement includes provision for the payment of a premium which could lawfully be required under the enactments hereby repealed but which, if paid in pursuance of the agreement, would be recoverable, wholly or in part, by virtue of the foregoing provisions of this subsection, the agreement shall, without prejudice to the operation of this section, be voidable at the option of either party thereto.

(6) A person requiring any premium in contravention of this section shall be liable on summary conviction to a fine not exceeding one hundred pounds, and the court by which he is convicted may order the amount of the premium, or so much thereof as cannot lawfully be required under this section, to be repaid to the person by whom it was paid.

(7) Section eight of the Increase of Rent and Mortgage Interest (Restrictions) Act, 1920, is hereby repealed; but, without prejudice

to the operation of section thirty-eight of the Interpretation Act, 1889, nothing in this section shall be construed as affecting the operation of the said section eight as respects anything done before the commencement of this Act.

(8) For the avoidance of doubt it is hereby declared that nothing in this section shall render any amount recoverable more than once.

3. Excessive prices for furniture, &c. to be treated as premiums

(1) Where—

    (a) whether before or after the commencement of this Act the purchase of any furniture, fittings or other articles has been required as a condition of the grant, renewal, continuance or assignment of a tenancy to which the last foregoing section applies, and

    (b) the price exceeds the reasonable price of the articles,

the excess shall be treated, for the purposes of the foregoing provisions of this Act and, so far as they continue to have effect, of the provisions of section eight of the Increase of Rent and Mortgage Interest (Restrictions) Act, 1920, as if it were a premium required to be paid as a condition of the grant, renewal, continuance or assignment of the tenancy.

(2) Where after the commencement of this Act any such purchase as is mentioned in paragraph (a) of the last foregoing subsection is required as therein mentioned, the price demanded shall, at the request of the person on whom the demand is made, be stated in writing; and if, without reasonable excuse, a person required to give such a statement in writing fails within fourteen days to do so, or knowingly gives a statement which is false in any material particular, he shall be liable on summary conviction to a fine not exceeding ten pounds.

(3) Subsection (1) of section nine of the Rent and Mortgage Interest Restrictions Act, 1923, is hereby repealed, but without prejudice to the effect of any statement of the price of articles given under that subsection before the commencement of this Act.

4. Provisions as to apportionment where s. 1 applies

[(1) Where, in the case of a property being a dwelling-house to which the principal Acts apply, the standard rent of the property is a rent determined under section one of this Act, then—

(a) for the purpose of any apportionment under the principal Acts which is necessary for determining the standard rent of a dwelling-house comprised in that property, the property shall be deemed, at the date in relation to which the standard rent of the dwelling-house is to be fixed, to have been let at the rent determined under subsection (1) of section one of this Act or, where the Tribunal determine the excess mentioned in subsection (3) of that section, the said rent reduced by the amount of the excess;

(b) any such apportionment made before the determination under section one of this Act, whether it was made before or after the commencement of this Act, may be varied accordingly:

Provided that nothing in this subsection shall affect rent in respect of any period before the determination under section one of this Act.

(2) Where the standard rent of a dwelling-house, being part of a property which is a dwelling-house to which the principal Acts apply, has been determined under section one of this Act, then, in making any apportionment under the principal Acts for the purpose of ascertaining the standard rent of any other part of the property, no regard shall be had to the determination under section one of this Act.]

5. Register of determinations of Tribunal

[(1) The local authority[1] shall prepare and keep up to date a register for the purposes of section one of this Act, and shall make the register available for inspection in such place or places and in such manner as the Minister may direct.

(2) The register shall be so prepared and kept up to date as to contain, with regard to any dwelling-house in respect of which a determination has been made under section one of this Act, being a dwelling-house in the area of the local authority,—[1]

(a) a specification of the dwelling-house to which the determination relates;

(b) the prescribed particulars with regard to the terms and conditions of the tenancy;

(c) the reasonable rent determined under subsection (1) of the said section one and any determination of the Tribunal under subsection (3) of that section; and

---

[1] In Scotland, the tribunal.

AA

(*d*) the matters required to be contained in the register by the provisions in that behalf of the First Schedule to this Act.

(3) Section eight of the Rent of Furnished Houses Control (Scotland) Act, 1943 (which relates to certificates as to premises entered in the register kept under subsection (4) of section two of that Act), shall have effect as if the reference to that register included a reference to the register kept under this section.

(4) ⎫
(5) ⎬ (Repealed by the 1957 Act.)
(6) ⎭

(7) In this section the expression "prescribed" means prescribed by regulations made by the Minister.]

6. Tribunal for purposes of s. 1

[(1) For the purposes of section one of this Act, the Tribunal shall, for any district in which the Act of 1946 is in force, be the Tribunal constituted under section one of that Act.

(2) Where the Act of 1946 is not in force, the Minister shall by order constitute such districts, of which each shall be the whole or part of the area of a local authority for the purposes of the last foregoing section, as after consultation with such authorities appear to him expedient, and for each such district the Tribunal for the purposes of section one of this Act shall be a Tribunal constituted in accordance with the Schedule to the Act of 1946 and the provisions of that Schedule shall apply thereto:

Provided that if the Minister so directs the same Tribunal may act for more than one district constituted under this subsection.

(3) Where the whole or any part of a district constituted under the last foregoing subsection becomes comprised in a district in which the Act of 1946 is in force, that subsection and any order made thereunder shall cease to apply thereto.

(4) Any order under subsection (2) of this section may be varied by a subsequent order thereunder made in the like manner and subject to the like provisions.

(5) Paragraphs (*a*) and (*b*) of section eight of the Act of 1946 (which empower the Minister to make regulations with regard to the tenure of office of members of Tribunals under that Act and with regard to proceedings before such Tribunals) shall apply for the purposes of this section.]

7. Provisions where tenant shares accommodation with landlord

Where under any contract—

(a) a tenant has the exclusive occupation of any accommodation,

(b) the terms on which he holds the accommodation include the use of other accommodation in common with his landlord or with his landlord and other persons, and

(c) by reason only of the circumstances mentioned in paragraph (b) of this section, the accommodation referred to in paragraph (a) thereof is not a dwelling-house to which the principal Acts apply,

the Act of 1946 shall apply to the contract notwithstanding that the rent does not include payment for the use of furniture or for services.

8. Provisions where tenant shares accommodation with other persons but not with landlord

(1) Where—

(a) a tenant has the exclusive occupation of any accommodation (in this section referred to as "the separate accommodation"),

(b) the terms as between the tenant and his landlord on which he holds the separate accommodation include the use of other accommodation (in this section referred to as "the shared accommodation") in common with another person or other persons, not being or including the landlord, and

(c) by reason only of the circumstances mentioned in paragraph (b) of this subsection, the separate accommodation would not apart from this section be a dwelling-house to which the principal Acts apply,

the separate accommodation shall be deemed to be a dwelling-house to which those Acts apply, and the following provisions of this section shall have effect.

(2) For the avoidance of doubt it is hereby declared that where for the purpose of determining the [standard rent or] rateable value of the separate accommodation it is necessary to make an apportionment under the principal Acts, regard is to be had to the circumstances mentioned in paragraph (b) of the last foregoing subsection.

[(3) For the purpose of ascertaining the standard rent, a previous letting of the separate accommodation shall not be deemed not to be a letting of the same dwelling-house by reason only of any such change of circumstances as the following, that is to say, any increase or diminution of the rights of the tenant to use accommodation in common with others, or any improvement or worsening of accommodation so used by the tenant.]

[(4) For the purposes of any provisions of the principal Acts relating to increases of rent, or to the transfer to tenants of burdens or liabilities previously borne by landlords,—

(a) any such change of circumstances as is mentioned in the last foregoing subsection, being a change affecting so much of the shared accommodation as is living accommodation, shall be deemed to be an alteration of rent;

(b) where, as the result of any such change as is mentioned in the last foregoing paragraph the terms on which the separate accommodation is held are on the whole less favourable to the tenant than the previous terms, the rent shall be deemed to be increased, whether or not the sum periodically payable by way of rent is increased;

(c) any increase of rent in respect of any such change as is mentioned in paragraph (a) of this subsection where, as a result of the change and of the increase of rent, the terms on which the separate accommodation is held are on the whole not less favourable to the tenant than the previous terms, shall be deemed not to be an increase of rent.]

(5) In this section the expression "living accommodation" means accommodation of such a nature that the fact that it constitutes or is included in the share accommodation is sufficient to bring the tenancy within paragraph (c) of subsection (1) of this section.

(6) While the tenant is in possession of the separate accommodation by virtue either of the contract of tenancy or of the provisions of the principal Acts, any term or condition of the contract of tenancy terminating or modifying, or providing for the termination or modification of, his right to the use of any of the shared accommodation which is living accommodation shall be of no effect:

Provided that where the terms and conditions of the contract of tenancy are such that at any time during the tenancy the persons in common with whom the tenant is entitled to the use of the shared accommodation could be varied, or their number could be increased, nothing in this subsection shall prevent those terms and conditions from having effect so far as they relate to such variation or increase as aforesaid.

(7) Subject to the provisions of the next following subsection and without prejudice to the enforcement of any order made thereunder, while the tenant is in possession as aforesaid of the separate accommodation no order or judgment for the recovery of any of the shared accommodation or for the ejectment of the tenant therefrom shall be made or given, whether on the application of the immediate landlord of the tenant or on the application of any person under whom the said landlord derives title, unless a like order or judgment has been made or given, or is made or given at the same time, in respect of the separate accommodation; and section three of the Rent and Mortgage Interest Restrictions (Amendment) Act, 1933 (which restricts the landlord's right to possession of a dwelling-house to which the principal Acts apply) shall apply accordingly.

(8) [Without prejudice to the provisions of subsection (4) of this section,] the county court upon the application of the landlord may make such order, either terminating the right of the tenant to use the whole or any part of the shared accommodation other than living accommodation, or modifying his right to use the whole or any part of the shared accommodation, whether by varying the persons or increasing the number of persons entitled to the use of that accommodation, or otherwise, as to the court seems just:

Provided that no order shall be made under this subsection so as to effect any termination or modification of rights of the tenant which, apart from subsection (6) of this section, could not be effected by or under the terms of the contract of tenancy.

(9) Any question arising under subsection (4) of this section shall be determined on the application either of the landlord or of the tenant by the county court, and the decision of the court shall be final and conclusive.

9. Certain sublettings not to exclude operation of principal Acts.

Where the tenant of any premises, being a house or part of a house, has sublet a part, but not the whole, of the premises, then as against his landlord or any superior landlord (but without prejudice to the rights against and liabilities to each other of the tenant and any person claiming under him, or of any two such persons) no part of the premises shall be treated as not being a dwelling-house to which the principal Acts apply by reason only—

    (*a*) that the terms on which any person claiming under the
tenant holds any part of the premises include the use of
accommodation in common with other persons, or

    (*b*) that part of the premises is let to any such person at such a
rent as is mentioned in proviso (i) to subsection (2) of
section twelve of the Increase of Rent and Mortgage
Interest (Restrictions) Act, 1920 (which relates to furnished lettings).

10. Application of three last foregoing sections

The three last foregoing sections shall apply whether the letting
in question began before or after the commencement of this Act, but
not so as to affect rent in respect of any period before the commencement thereof or anything done or omitted during any such period.

11. Power of Tribunal under Act of 1946 to extend security of tenure

(1) Where a contract to which the Act of 1946 applies has been
referred to a Tribunal under that Act, and the reference has not been
withdrawn, the lessee may, at any time when a notice to quit has
been served and the period at the end of which the notice takes
effect (whether by virtue of the contract, of the Act of 1946 or of this
section) has not expired, apply to the Tribunal for the extension of
that period:

Provided that an application shall not be made under this section
where the Tribunal have directed, under paragraph (*a*) of the
proviso to section five of the Act of 1946,[1] that a shorter period shall
be substituted for the period of three months specified in that section
as the period before the end of which a notice to quit shall not have
effect.

(2) On an application being made under this section—

    (*a*) the notice to quit to which the application relates shall not,
unless the application is withdrawn, have effect before
the determination of the application;

    (*b*) the Tribunal, after making such inquiry as they think fit,
and giving to each party an opportunity of being heard,
or, at his option, of submitting representations in writing,
may direct that the notice to quit shall not have effect
until the end of such period, not exceeding three months
from the date at which the notice to quit would have

---

[1] For Scotland, substitute s. 17 (6) (*c*) of this Act.

effect apart from the direction, as may be specified in the direction;

(c) if the Tribunal refuse a direction under this section, the notice to quit shall not have effect before the expiration of seven says from the determination of the application.

(3) On coming to a determination on an application under this section the Tribunal shall notify the parties of their determination.

(4) Where on an application under this section the Tribunal have refused a direction under subsection (2) thereof, no subsequent application under this section shall be made in relation to the same notice to quit.

(5) This section shall be construed as one with the Act of 1946, [and references in this section to that Act shall be construed as references to that Act as extended by section seven of this Act.]

12. Prohibition of premiums on grant or assignment of furnished lettings

(1) Where the rent payable for any premises is entered in the register under the provisions of the Act of 1946, and, in a case in which the approval, reduction or increase made by the Tribunal is limited to rent payable in respect of a particular period, that period has not expired, the following provisions of this section shall apply in relation to the premises.

(2) Save as hereinafter provided, a person shall not, as a condition of the grant, renewal, continuance or assignment of rights under a contract to which the Act of 1946 applies, require the payment of any premium:

Provided that this subsection shall not prevent—

(a) a requirement that there shall be paid so much of any outgoings discharged by a grantor or assignor as is referable to any period after the grant or assignment takes effect;

(b) a requirement that there shall be paid a reasonable amount in respect of goodwill of a business, trade or profession, being goodwill transferred to a grantee or assignee in connection with the grant or assignment or accruing to him in consequence thereof.

(3) Subsections (5), (6) and (8) of section two, and section three, of this Act shall with the necessary modifications apply for the

purposes of this section as they apply for the purposes of the said section two.

(4) The following provisions of the Act of 1946, that is to say—

> (a) paragraph (b) of subsection (1) of section four (which prohibits the requiring of premiums on a grant, continuance or renewal of a letting where the rent payable is registered under the Act of 1946);
>
> (b) in subsection (2) of that section, the words "or consideration", "or value" and "or given";
>
> (c) in subsection (1) of section nine of the Act of 1946, the words "or any consideration", "or the value of the consideration given", and "or the consideration given",

are hereby repealed:

Provided that, without prejudice to the operation of section thirty-eight of the Interpretation Act, 1889, nothing in this section shall be construed as affecting the operation of the said provisions of the Act of 1946 as respects anything done before the commencement of this Act.

13. Jurisdiction of county court

Subsection (2) of section seventeen of the Increase of Rent and Mortgage Interest (Restrictions) Act, 1920 (which extends the jurisdiction of county courts in respect of proceedings under that Act) shall have effect in relation to any claim or proceedings for the recovery of any sum which is recoverable by virtue of this Act as it applies to the claims and proceedings mentioned in that subsection.

14. Division of areas constituted under Act of 1946

Where the Minister has made an order directing that the provisions of the Act of 1946 shall have effect in any district, he may by subsequent order direct that such part of the district as may be specified in the order shall be excepted therefrom and be a separate district in which that Act has effect.

15. Expenses

Any increase attributable to the provisions of this Act in the sums payable out of moneys provided by Parliament under paragraph 5 of the Schedule to the Act of 1946 (which provides for the remuneration and expenses of Tribunals) shall be defrayed out of moneys so provided.

16. Orders and regulations

Any power to make regulations or an order conferred on the Minister by this Act shall be exercisable by statutory instrument.

17. Application to Scotland

(1) The provisions of this section shall have effect for the purpose of the application of this Act to Scotland.

(2) For any reference to the Minister of Health there shall be substituted a reference to the Secretary of State; for references to the Furnished Houses (Rent Control) Act, 1946, to sections four, eight and nine thereof and to paragraph 5 of the Schedule thereto there shall be respectively substituted references to the Rent of Furnished Houses Control (Scotland) Act, 1943, to sections three, six and seven and to subsection (3) of section one thereof; for any reference to the Housing Act, 1936, there shall be substituted a reference to the Housing (Scotland) Act, 1935; for any reference to the county court, there shall be substituted a reference to the sheriff; for any reference to the grant, continuance or renewal of a term there shall be substituted a reference to the grant, continuance or renewal of a tenancy, and for any reference to a term in relation to a tenancy there shall be substituted a reference to the period for which a tenancy is granted, continued or renewed; and for any reference to a district in relation to a Tribunal there shall be substituted a reference to an area.

(3) Section five of this Act shall have effect as if
  (i) for any reference to a local authority there were substituted a reference to a Tribunal;
  (ii) subsections (3), (4), (5) and (6) were omitted; and
  (iii) there were inserted after subsection (2) the following subsection—

   "(3) Section eight of the Rent of Furnished Houses Control (Scotland) Act, 1943 (which relates to certificates as to premises entered in the register kept under subsection (4) of section two of that Act), shall have effect as if the reference to that register included a reference to the register kept under this section".

(4) Section six of this Act shall have effect as if for the reference to the local authorities therein mentioned there were substituted a reference to county and town councils.

(5) The First Schedule to this Act shall have effect as if in paragraph 8 thereof for the definition of the expression "reversion"

there were substituted the following definition:—

"reversion", in relation to the grant, continuance or renewal of a tenancy of a dwelling-house, means the estate or interest in the dwelling-house which immediately after the grant, continuance or renewal of the tenancy belonged to the immediate landlord of the tenant under the tenancy.

(6) If, after a contract to which the Rent of Furnished Houses Control (Scotland) Act, 1943, applies has been referred to a Tribunal by the lessee or by the local authority (either originally or for reconsideration), a notice to quit the premises to which the contract relates is served by the lessor on the lessee at any time before the decision of the Tribunal is given or within three months thereafter, the notice shall not take effect before the expiration of the said three months:

Provided that—

(a) the Tribunal may, if they think fit, direct that a shorter period shall be substituted for the said three months in the application of this subsection to the contract that is the subject of the reference; and

(b) if the reference is withdrawn the period during which the notice is not to take effect shall end on the expiry of seven days from the withdrawal of the reference.

(7) Section eleven of this Act shall have effect as if—

(i) the last foregoing subsection were contained in the Rent of Furnished Houses Control (Scotland) Act, 1943; and

(ii) for the reference to paragraph (a) of the proviso to section five of the Furnished Houses (Rent Control) Act, 1946, there were substituted a reference to paragraph (a) of the proviso to the last foregoing subsection.

(8) The amendments specified in the second column of the Second Schedule to this Act, being amendments relating to minor matters, shall be made in the enactments specified in the first column of that Schedule.

18. Short title, interpretation and extent

(1) This Act may be cited as the Landlord and Tenant (Rent Control) Act, 1949.

(2) In this Act—

the expression "the Minister" means the Minister of Health,

the expression "premium" includes any fine or other like sum
and any other pecuniary consideration in addition to rent,

the expression "the principal Acts" means the Rent and Mortgage Interest Restrictions Acts, 1920 to 1939,

the expression "the Act of 1946" means the Furnished Houses
(Rent Control) Act, 1946,

and other expressions have the same meanings as in the principal
Acts.

(3) This Act shall not extend to Northern Ireland.

SCHEDULES

Sections 1, 2, 5, 17.

FIRST SCHEDULE

Transitional Provisions as to Premiums

Part I

Adjustments, where s. 1 applies, for premiums paid before commencement of Act

1. Where on an application under section one of this Act made within twelve months from the date of the commencement of this Act it appears to the Tribunal that before the commencement of this Act any premium has been paid (whether lawfully required or not) in respect of the grant, continuance or renewal of a tenancy of the dwelling-house to which the application relates, whether by the tenant or by a previous tenant of the dwelling-house, and has not been fully repaid or recovered, the Tribunal shall, if the tenant so requires, certify that this Part of this Schedule applies, and thereupon—

 (a) except in a case falling within the next following sub-paragraph, the rent payable shall be limited in accordance with paragraph 2 of this Schedule;

 (b) where the Tribunal are satisfied that since the premium was paid and before the twenty-fifth day of March, nineteen hundred and forty-nine, the reversion had been conveyed or assigned for a consideration in money or money's worth, and so certify, the tenant of the dwelling-house at the time of the Tribunal's determination shall be entitled to recover from the person to whom the premium was paid such amount, if any, as is provided by paragraph 3 of this Schedule:

Provided that this paragraph shall not have effect where the Tribunal are satisfied that since the said grant, continuance or renewal the landlord has granted a tenancy of the dwelling-house under which, as against the landlord, a person became entitled to possession other than the person who was so entitled to possession of the dwelling-house immediately before that tenancy began.

2.—(1) Subject to the provisions of this paragraph, where sub-paragraph (a) of the last foregoing paragraph has effect, the rent payable by the tenant, or by any subsequent tenant, for any rent-period beginning after the Tribunal have issued their certificate and before the relevant date *shall not exceed the rent recoverable in accordance with the provisions of the Rent Act, 1957 (other than paragraph 5 of the Sixth Schedule thereto) less the rent equivalent of the premium.*[1]

---

[1] Substituted by the 1957 Act—sub-paragraph (2) of the paragraph was repealed by the amendment.

(3) Nothing in the foregoing provisions of this paragraph shall affect the rent payable for any rent-period after the landlord has granted a tenancy of the dwelling-house under which, as against the landlord, a person became entitled to possession other than the person who was so entitled to possession of the dwelling-house immediately before that tenancy began.

3.—(1) Where, in a case in which the Tribunal issue a certificate under sub-paragraph (b) of paragraph 1 of this Schedule, the existing rent is equal to or greater than the reasonable rent, the tenant shall be entitled to recover as mentioned in the said sub-paragraph (b) an amount equal to the product of—

(a) the rental equivalent of the premium, and

(b) the number of complete rent-periods in the period beginning with the date of the Tribunal's determination under section one of this Act and ending with the relevant date.

(2) Where, in any such case as aforesaid, the existing rent is less than the reasonable rent, but the difference between them is less than the rental equivalent of the premium, the tenant shall be entitled to recover as mentioned in the said sub-paragraph (b) an amount equal to the product of—

(a) the amount by which the rental equivalent of the premium exceeds the difference between the reasonable rent and the existing rent, and

(b) the number of complete rent-periods mentioned in head (b) of the last foregoing sub-paragraph.

(3) Where the rent payable under the tenancy is a progressive rent, the foregoing provisions of this paragraph shall have effect as if for the references therein to the existing rent there were substituted references to the average rent payable under the tenancy over the period beginning with the commencement of the term, or of the continuance or renewal of a term, in respect of which the premium was paid and ending with the relevant date.

(4) In this paragraph the expression "existing rent" means the rent which would be payable by the tenant, apart from the provisions of section one of this Act and of this Schedule, for the rent-period comprising the date of the Tribunal's determination of the reasonable rent.

4.—(1) Notwithstanding anything contained in the principal Acts, where the Tribunal issue a certificate under paragraph 1 of this Schedule with respect to any premium, so much of that premium as at the time when the certificate is issued has not been repaid or recovered shall not thereafter be recoverable otherwise than under the foregoing provisions of this Schedule.

(2) Save as provided in the last foregoing sub-paragraph, nothing in this Part of this Schedule shall prejudice any criminal proceedings against a person for having required any payment or the giving of any consideration in contravention of section eight of the Increase of Rent and Mortgage Interest (Restrictions) Act, 1920.

PART II

*Premiums allowed on assignment where before commencement of Act
premium paid on grant of tenancy*

5.—(1) Where—

(a) before the commencement of this Act a premium has been lawfully required, and paid, in respect of the grant, continuance or renewal of a tenancy to which section two of this Act applies, and

(b) since the said grant, continuance or renewal the landlord has not granted a tenancy of the dwelling-house under which, as against the landlord, a person became entitled to possession other than the person who was so entitled to possession of the dwelling-house immediately before that tenancy began,

then, subject to the provisions of this paragraph, subsection (2) of the said section two shall not prevent the requiring, on any assignment of the first-mentioned tenancy or of any subsequent tenancy of the same dwelling-house, of a premium not exceeding the amount hereinafter specified.

(2) Subject to the provisions of the next following sub-paragraph, the said amount is the amount which bears to the premium paid on the said grant, continuance or renewal the same proportion as the period beginning with the date at which the assignment takes effect and ending with the relevant date bears to the period beginning with the said grant, continuance or renewal and ending with the relevant date.

(3) Where before the assignment in question the Tribunal have issued a certificate under sub-paragraph (b) of paragraph 1 of this Schedule, then if the case falls within the following provisions of this sub-paragraph the foregoing provisions of this paragraph shall have effect subject to the following provisions, that is to say:—

(a) if the existing rent is equal to or greater than the reasonable rent, the foregoing provisions of this paragraph shall not apply;

(b) if the existing rent is less than the reasonable rent, but the difference between them is less than the rental equivalent of the premium therein mentioned, the last foregoing sub-paragraph shall apply as if the said premium were reduced by the product of—

(i) the amount by which the rental equivalent of that premium exceeds the difference between the reasonable rent and the existing rent, and

(ii) the number of complete rent-periods in the period beginning with the grant, continuance or renewal in respect of which the premium was paid and ending with the relevant date.

In this sub-paragraph the expression "existing rent" means the rent which would be payable by the tenant, apart from the provisions of section one of this Act and of this Schedule, for the rent-period comprising the date of the Tribunal's determination of the reasonable rent.

PART III
Supplementary

6.—(1) For the purposes of paragraphs 2, 3 and 5 of this Schedule the relevant date, in the case of an application to the Tribunal on which they issue a certificate under paragraph 1 of this Schedule as respects a premium paid in respect of the grant, continuance or renewal of any term, shall be ascertained as follows.

(2) Where the term is a term of years certain current when the application to the Tribunal is made, being a term exceeding seven years, or the continuance or renewal was for such a term of years certain, the relevant date shall be the date of the expiration of that term of years certain.

(3) In any case not falling within the last foregoing sub-paragraph, the relevant date shall be the date of the expiration of seven years from the commencement of the term, or of the continuance or renewal of a term, in respect of which the premium was paid.

(4) For the purposes of the two last foregoing sub-paragraphs, a term of years shall be deemed to be certain notwithstanding that it is liable to determination by re-entry or on the happening of any event other than the giving of notice by the landlord to determine the term; and a term of years determinable by the giving of such a notice as aforesaid by the landlord shall be deemed to be a term of years certain expiring on the earliest date on which such a notice given after the issuing of the certificate of the Tribunal would be capable of taking effect.

7. For the purposes of sub-paragraph (2) of paragraph 5 of this Schedule, the relevant date, in relation to an assignment taking effect where no such application has been made to the Tribunal as is mentioned in the last foregoing paragraph, shall be the date which would be the relevant date under the last foregoing paragraph in the case of such an application made at the date when the assignment takes effect.

8. In this Schedule the following expressions have the meanings hereby assigned to them respectively, that is to say:—

"reasonable rent" means the reasonable rent determined by the Tribunal under subsection (1) of section one of this Act;

"rent-period" means the period (whether weekly, monthly, annual or other) for which payments of rent are made;

"rental equivalent" means, in relation to any premium, the amount of the premium, or so much thereof as at the time of the issue of a certificate of the Tribunal under paragraph 1 of this Schedule has not been repaid or recovered, divided by the number of rent-periods between the commencement of the term, or of the continuance or renewal of a term, in respect of which the premium was paid and the relevant date;

"reversion", in relation to the grant, continuance or renewal of a tenancy of a dwelling-house, means the estate or interest in the dwelling- house which, immediately after the grant, continuance or renewal of the tenancy, was expectant upon the determination of the term granted, continued or renewed.

9. Where, on an application to the Tribunal on which they issue a certificate under paragraph 1 of this Schedule, the rental equivalent of the premium exceeds the reasonable rent,—

    (*a*) there shall be determined the date, being a date coinciding with the end of a rent-period, such that if that date were the relevant date the rental equivalent of the premium would be reduced so as to be as nearly as may be equal to, but not greater than, the reasonable rent; and

    (*b*) paragraphs 2 to 7 of this Schedule shall have effect, in relation to that application, as if the date determined under the last foregoing sub-paragraph were the relevant date and the rental equivalent of the premium were reduced accordingly.

10.—(1) It shall be the duty of the Tribunal, on any application to them on which they issue a certificate under paragraph 1 of this Schedule, to determine such of the following matters as are required to be determined for the purposes of the application, that is to say—

    (*a*) the rental equivalent of a premium;

    (*b*) the relevant date; and

    (*c*) the date referred to in sub-paragraph (*a*) of the last foregoing paragraph, and the amount which would be the amount of the rental equivalent of a premium if that date were the relevant date;

and the determination by the Tribunal of any of the said matters shall be conclusive for all purposes.

(2) The matters required to be contained in the register kept under section five of this Act shall include, in relation to any dwelling-house as respects which a certificate has been issued under paragraph 1 of this Schedule,—

    (*a*) that certificate and any other certificate issued under this Schedule as respects that dwelling-house;

    (*b*) any determination of the Tribunal made as respects that dwelling-house under any of the provisions of this Schedule.

Section 17.

SECOND SCHEDULE

Minor Amendments

Section	Amendment
Rent of Furnished Houses Control (Scotland) Act, 1943	
Section two	In subsection (1) for the words from "it shall be the duty" to the end of the subsection there shall be

Section   *Amendment*

Section two—*cont.*

substituted the words "they may by a notice in writing served on the lessor require him to give to them within such period (which shall not be less than seven days from the date of the service of the notice) as may be specified in the notice such information as they may reasonably require regarding such of the prescribed particulars relating to the contract as are specified in the notice"; in subsection (2) after the word "Tribunal" where it first occurs there shall be inserted the words "then, unless at any time before the Tribunal have entered upon consideration of the reference it is withdrawn by the party or authority by whom it was made", and after the word "reasonable" there shall be inserted the words "or may if they think fit in all the circumstances dismiss the reference"; after subsection (3) there shall be inserted the following subsections:—

"(3A) Notwithstanding anything in the foregoing provisions of this section, a Tribunal shall not be required to entertain a reference made otherwise than by the local authority if they are satisfied having regard to the length of time elapsing since a previous reference made by the same party or to other circumstances that the reference is frivolous or vexatious."

"(3B) An approval, reduction or increase under this section may be limited to rent payable in respect of a particular period";

and for subsection (4) there shall be substituted the following subsection:—

"(4) The Tribunal shall keep a register and shall cause to be entered therein with regard to any contract under which a rent is payable that has been approved, reduced or increased under this section,—

(*a*) the prescribed particulars with regard to the contract, including a specification of the premises to which the contract relates, and the rent, as approved, reduced or increased under this section, and

BB

Section	*Amendment*

Section two—*cont.*

    (*b*) in a case in which the approval, reduction or increase is limited to rent payable in respect of a particular period, a specification of that period.

    The Tribunal shall make the register available for inspection in such place or places and in such manner as the Secretary of State may direct."

Section three   ..   In subsection (1), after the words "such entry" there shall be inserted the words "(or in a case in which a particular period is specified, in respect of that period)".

Section seven   ..   In subsection (2) for the words from "to comply with" to "under this Act" there shall be substituted the words "within the time limited in that behalf to comply with the provisions of any notice served under subsection (1) of section two of this Act".

CROWN LESSEES
(PROTECTION OF SUB-TENANTS) ACT, 1952
[15 & 16 Geo. 6 & 1 Eliz. 2]

CHAPTER 40

An Act to abolish exemptions from the Rent and Mortgage Interest Restrictions Acts, 1920 to 1939, the Rent of Furnished Houses Control (Scotland) Act, 1943, the Furnished Houses (Rent Control) Act, 1946, and the Landlord and Tenant (Rent Control) Act, 1949, which arise by reason of the subsistence of a superior interest belonging to the Crown, the Duchy of Lancaster or the Duchy of Cornwall.   [1st August, 1952.]

Be it enacted by the Queen's most Excellent Majesty, by and with the advice and consent of the Lords Spiritual and Temporal, and Commons, in this present Parliament assembled, and by the authority of the same, as follows:—

1. Crown exemption from Rent Control Acts not to extend to mesne tenants or assignees from Crown

(1) Notwithstanding any rule of law excluding the operation of any of the Rent Control Acts where there subsists, or at any material time subsisted, an interest belonging to Her Majesty in right of the Crown or of the Duchy of Lancaster, or to the Duchy of Cornwall, or belonging to a Government department or held in trust for Her Majesty for the purposes of a Government department, the Rent Control Acts shall, subject to the provisions of this Act, apply in relation to premises in which there subsists, or at any material time subsisted, an interest belonging or held as aforesaid as they apply in relation to premises in which no such interest subsists or ever subsisted.

(2) A tenant, lessee or mortgagor shall not be protected by virtue of this section at any time when the interest of the landlord, lessor or mortgagee belongs or is held as aforesaid.

(3) Subsection (1) of this section shall not affect the requiring of a premium, or of any sum which in accordance with any provision of the Landlord and Tenant (Rent Control) Act, 1949, is to be treated as if it were a premium—

(a) as a condition of the grant, continuance or renewal of a tenancy or of rights under a contract by a landlord or lessor whose interest belongs or is held as aforesaid; or

(b) as a condition of the assignment of a tenancy or of rights under a contract by a tenant or lessee where the interest of the landlord or lessor is an interest so belonging or held.

Nothing in paragraph (a) of this subsection shall be construed as limiting the generality of the last foregoing subsection.

(4) In this Act the expression "the Rent Control Acts" means the Rent and Mortgage Interest Restrictions Acts, 1920 to 1939, the Rent of Furnished Houses Control (Scotland) Act, 1943, the Furnished Houses (Rent Control) Act, 1946, and the Landlord and Tenant (Rent Control) Act, 1949.

2. Consequential provisions

(1) In so far as the Rent and Mortgage Interest Restrictions Acts, 1920 to 1938 have effect by virtue of the foregoing section, they shall subject as hereinafter provided have effect as they have effect in relation to a dwelling-house to which they were applied by the Rent and Mortgage Interest Restrictions Act, 1939:

Provided that—

[(a) paragraph (a) of subsection (1) of section twelve of the Increase of Rent and Mortgage Interest (Restrictions) Act, 1920, which defines standard rent, shall have effect as if for the words from "the rent at which the dwelling-house was let" to "at which it was first let" there were substituted the words "the rent at which the dwelling-house was let on the critical date as defined in the Crown Lessees (Protection of Sub-Tenants) Act, 1952";]

(b) the enactments specified in the Schedule to this Act shall have effect subject to the adaptations specified in that Schedule.

[(2) Where under the foregoing provisions of this Act the standard rent for any premises would be a rent or amount such as is mentioned in paragraph (a) or (b) of subsection (1) of section one of the Landlord and Tenant (Rent Control) Act, 1949—

(a) the said provisions shall have effect subject to the said section one, and

(b) those provisions shall not be treated as such a limitation of rent as is mentioned in paragraph (b) of subsection (7) of the said section one (which paragraph excludes the operation of that section while a limitation of rent is in force which is imposed by or under certain enactments).]

[(3) In this section, and in the Schedule to this Act, the expression "the critical date" in relation to a dwelling-house means—

(a) if a tenant of the dwelling-house was protected by virtue of the foregoing section immediately after the commencement of this Act, the eighth day of February, nineteen hundred and fifty-two, or, if the dwelling-house was not then let, the date on which it was first let thereafter;

(b) in any other case, the first date after the commencement of this Act on which a tenant of the dwelling-house is protected by virtue of the foregoing section.]

(4) Where any order or judgment has been made or given by a court before the commencement of this Act, but has not been executed, and in the opinion of the court the order or judgment would not have been made or given if this Act had been in operation at the time when the order or judgment was made or given, the court may, on application by the tenant, rescind or vary the order or judgment in such manner as the court thinks fit for the purpose of giving effect to this Act.

(5) In subsection (3) of section fifteen of the Reserve and Auxiliary Forces (Protection of Civil Interests) Act, 1951, for the words from the beginning to the second "quit" there shall be substituted the words "The subsistence of a Crown interest in premises shall not affect the operation of this section", and paragraph (c) of subsection (2) of section sixteen of that Act shall cease to have effect; but nothing in the foregoing provisions of this subsection shall be construed as excluding the operation of Part II of that Act, as amended by those provisions, in cases where there subsists a Crown interest (as defined in the said Part II) not being the reversion immediately expectant on the tenancy in question.

(6) In the application of the last foregoing subsection to Scotland any reference to the reversion immediately expectant on a tenancy shall be construed as a reference to the interest of the immediate landlord of the tenant under the tenancy.

3. Short title, interpretation, extent and commencement

(1) This Act may be cited as the Crown Lessees (Protection of Sub-Tenants) Act, 1952.

(2) In this Act the expressions "lessee" and "lessor", in relation to premises in England or Wales, have the same meanings as in the Furnished Houses (Rent Control) Act, 1946, and, in relation to premises in Scotland, have the same meanings as in the Rent of Furnished Houses Control (Scotland) Act, 1943; and other expressions used in this Act and in the Rent and Mortgage Interest Restrictions Acts, 1920 to 1939, or the Landlord and Tenant (Rent Control) Act, 1949, have the same meanings in this Act as in those Acts.

(3) This Act shall not extend to Northern Ireland.

(4) This Act shall come into operation on the first day of September, nineteen hundred and fifty-two.

SCHEDULE

Section 2.

CONSEQUENTIAL ADAPTATION OF ENACTMENTS

Adaptations of Acts of 1920 to 1938 as modified by Act of 1939

Section one of the Increase of Rent and Mortgage Interest (Restrictions) Act, 1920 (which restricts increases of rent and mortgage interest) shall have effect—

[(a) so far as it related to rent, as if for the reference to the passing of the Rent and Mortgage Interest Restrictions Act, 1939, there were substituted a reference to the critical date, and in relation to a tenant protected by virtue of section one of this Act immediately after the commencement thereof, as if for the reference to the commencement of the said Act of 1939 there were substituted a reference to the commencement of this Act, and]

(b) so far as it relates to the rate of interest on a mortgage, as if for the reference to the passing of the said Act of 1939 there were substituted a reference to the eighth day of February, nineteen hundred and fifty-two and for the reference to the commencement of that Act there were substituted a reference to the commencement of this Act.

[In paragraphs (a) and (b) of subsection (1) of section two of the said Act of 1920 (which specify permitted increases of rent for improvements, structural alterations and increases in rates) for the references to the commencement of the said Act of 1939 there shall be substituted references to the critical date.]

In paragraph (i) of the proviso to section seven of the said Act of 1920 (which provides certain exceptions from the restriction imposed by that section on the calling in of mortgages) for the reference to the date of the passing of the said Act of 1939 there shall be substituted a reference to the eighth day of February, nineteen hundred and fifty-two.

****1

Paragraph (b) of subsection (1) of section twelve of the said Act of 1920 (which defines "standard rate of interest") shall have effect as if the reference to a mortgage in force on the day therein mentioned were a reference to a mortgage in force on the eighth day of February, nineteen hundred and fifty-two.

In subsection (4) of section four of the Rent and Mortgage Interest

---

1 Words omitted by the 1957 Act.

Restrictions (Amendment) Act, 1933 (which requires a tenant to supply the landlord with particulars of any subletting) for the reference to the commencement of the said Act of 1939 there shall be substituted a reference to the commencement of this Act.

[In section six of the said Act of 1933 (which enables the court to determine the standard rent where it is not reasonably practicable to obtain sufficient evidence) for the words from "at which the dwelling-house was let" to "the rent at which it was first let" there shall be substituted the words "at which the dwelling-house was let on the critical date (as defined in the Crown Lessees (Protection of Sub-Tenants) Act, 1952)".]

****1

Adaptation of 12, 13 & 14 Geo. 6. c. 40

Sections two and twelve of the Landlord and Tenant (Rent Control) Act, 1949 (which prohibit the requiring of premiums on the grant, continuance, renewal or assignment of unfurnished and furnished lettings respectively) shall not affect the payment of any premium or other sum required under an agreement made before the eighth day of February, nineteen hundred and fifty-two.

In head (a) of sub-paragraph (1) of paragraph 5 of the First Schedule to the said Act of 1949, for the words from "before" to "paid" there shall be substituted the words "a premium has been lawfully required and paid under an agreement made before the commencement of the Crown Lessees (Protection of Sub-Tenants) Act, 1952."

---

1 Words omitted by the 1957 Act.

RENT OF FURNISHED HOUSES CONTROL (SCOTLAND) ACT, 1943

[6 & 7 Geo. 6.]

CHAPTER 44

An Act to make provision with regard to the rent of houses or parts thereof in Scotland let at a rent which includes payment for the use of furniture or for services. [11th November 1943.]

Be it enacted by the King's most Excellent Majesty, by and with the advice and consent of the Lords Spiritual and Temporal, and Commons, in this present Parliament assembled, and by the authority of the same, as follows:—

1. Application of Act by Order of the Secretary of State, and appointment of Tribunal

(1) Where the Secretary of State is satisfied on representation by, or after consultation with, the council of any county or burgh that it is expedient that the provisions of this Act should have effect in any area consisting of the whole or part of that county or burgh, he may, by Order, direct that this Act shall have effect in that area as from such day as may be specified in the Order, and this Act shall thereupon come into force in that area.

(2) For each area in which this Act is in force there shall be a Tribunal constituted in accordance with the Schedule to this Act, and the provisions of that Schedule shall apply to each Tribunal:

Provided that, if the Secretary of State so directs, the same Tribunal may act for more than one such area.

(3) The sums required for the payment of remuneration and salaries and allowances to the members, acting members, clerks and officers and servants of a Tribunal shall be paid out of moneys provided by Parliament.

2. Reference to Tribunal of contracts for furnished letting

(1) Where a contract has, whether before or after the passing of this Act, been entered into whereby one person (hereinafter referred to as the "lessor") grants to another person (hereinafter referred to as the "lessee") the right to occupy as a residence a house or part of a house situated in an area in which this Act is in force in consideration of a rent which includes payment for the use of furniture or for

services, whether or not, in the case of such a contract with regard
to part of a house, the lessee is entitled, in addition to exclusive
occupation thereof, to the use in common with any other person of
other rooms or accommodation in the house, it shall be lawful for
either party to the contract or for the local authority for the area to
refer the contract to the Tribunal for the area, and where any such
contract (hereinafter referred to as a contract to which this Act
applies) is so referred to the Tribunal, *they may by a notice in writing
served on the lessor require him to give to them within such period (which
shall not be less than seven days from the date of the service of the notice) as may
be specified in the notice such information as they may reasonably require
regarding such of the prescribed particulars relating to the contract as are
specified in the notice.*[1]

(2) Where any contract to which this Act applies is referred to a
Tribunal, *then, unless at any time before the Tribunal have entered upon
consideration of the reference it is withdrawn by the party or authority by
whom it was made,*[2] the Tribunal shall consider the case and, after
making such enquiry as they think fit, and giving to each party (and
to the local authority if the house is or forms part of a house or
dwelling to which section thirty-nine of the Housing (Scotland) Act,
1935 applies) an opportunity of being heard or, in his option of
submitting representations in writing, shall approve the rent payable
under the contract or reduce it to such sum as they may, in all the
circumstances, think reasonable, *or may if they think fit in all the
circumstances dismiss the reference,*[2] and shall notify the parties and the
local authority of their decision in each case.

(3) Where the rent payable for any premises has been entered in
the register in accordance with the provisions hereinafter contained,
it shall be lawful for the lessor or the lessee or the local authority to
refer the case to the Tribunal for reconsideration of the rent so
entered on the ground of change of circumstances, and the provisions
of subsection (2) of this section shall apply on any such reference in
like manner as they apply on a reference under subsection (1) of this
section subject to the modification that the Tribunal shall have
power to increase the rent payable.

(3A) *Notwithstanding anything in the foregoing provisions of this section,
a Tribunal shall not be required to entertain a reference made otherwise than
by the local authority if they are satisfied having regard to the length of time*

---

[1] Substituted by the 1949 Act.
[2] Added by the 1949 Act.

elapsing since a previous reference made by the same party or to other circum-stances that the reference is frivolous or vexatious.[1]

(3B) *An approval, reduction or increase under this section may be limited to rent payable in respect of a particular period.*[1]

(4) *The Tribunal shall keep a register and shall cause to be entered therein with regard to any contract under which a rent is payable that has been approved, reduced or increased under this section,—*

  (a) *the prescribed particulars with regard to the contract, including a specification of the premises to which the contract relates, and the rent, as approved, reduced or increased under this section, and*

  (b) *in a case in which the approval, reduction or increase is limited to rent payable in respect of a particular period, a specification of that period.*

The Tribunal shall make the register available for inspection in such place or places and in such manner as the Secretary of State may direct.[2]

3. Rents in excess of registered rents and premiums illegal

(1) Where the rent payable for any premises is entered in the register under the provisions of this Act, it shall not be lawful to require or receive,

  (a) on account of rent for those premises in respect of any period subsequent to the date of such entry (*or in a case in which a particular period is specified, in respect of that period*),[1] payment of any sum in excess of the rent so entered; or,

  (b) (Repealed by the 1949 Act.)

(2) Where any payment ****[3] has been made or received in contravention of the last foregoing subsection, the amount ****[3] thereof shall be recoverable by the person by whom it was made ****[3]

4. Provisions as to powers and expenses of local authorities

(1) The powers of a local authority under this Act may, if the local authority so resolve, be exercised by one of their officers appointed by the authority for the purpose.

(2) A local authority shall have power to publish information regarding the provisions of this Act.

---

[1] Added by the 1949 Act.
[2] Substituted by the 1949 Act.
[3] Omitted by the 1949 Act.

(3) (Repealed by the Local Government (Scotland) Act, 1947.)

5. ****¹ nothing in this Act shall affect any provisions of the Rent and Mortgage Interest Restrictions Acts, 1920 to 1939.

6. Regulations

The Secretary of State may make regulations—
    (a) with regard to the tenure of office of Chairmen and other members of Tribunals;
    (b) with regard to proceedings before Tribunals under this Act;
    (c) for prescribing anything which is required by this Act to be prescribed; and
    (d) generally for carrying into effect the provisions of this Act.

7. Offences

(1) A person who requires or receives any payment ****² in contravention of section three of this Act shall be guilty of an offence and liable on summary conviction to a fine not exceeding one hundred pounds or to imprisonment for any period not exceeding six months, and without prejudice to any other method of recovery, the court by which he is convicted may order the amount paid ****² to be repaid to the person by whom the payment was made ****²

(2) If the lessor under a contract to which this Act applies refuses or fails without reasonable cause *within the time limited in that behalf to comply with the provisions of any notice served under subsection (1) of section two of this Act,*³ he shall be guilty of an offence and liable on summary conviction to a fine not exceeding twenty pounds or to imprisonment for any period not exceeding three months.

8. Certificates to be evidence

A document purporting to be a certificate signed by the clerk or other authorised officer of a Tribunal relating to any premises entered in the register shall, until the contrary is shown, be deemed to have been signed by such clerk or other officer, and shall be sufficient evidence of the matters therein contained.

9. Interpretation and saving

(1) In this Act—
    the expression "Tribunal" means a Tribunal appointed in pursuance of section one of this Act;

---

¹ Omitted by the 1957 Act.
² Omitted by the 1949 Act.
³ Substituted by the 1949 Act.

the expression "local authority" means a county or a town council;

the expression "register" means the register kept by a Tribunal in pursuance of subsection (4) of section two of this Act;

the expression "services" includes attendance, the provision of heating or lighting, the supply of hot water and any other privilege or facility connected with the occupancy of a house or part of a house.

(2) Where separate sums are payable by the lessee of any premises to the lessor for any two or more of the following, namely:—

(a) occupation of the premises;

(b) use of furniture; and

(c) services;

the expression "rent" shall, in relation to those premises, mean the aggregate of those sums, and where such sums are payable under separate contracts, those contracts shall be deemed to be one contract.

(3) Nothing in this Act shall apply to a house or part of a house let at a rent which includes payment in respect of board:

Provided that a house or part of a house shall not be deemed to be let at such a rent unless the value of such board to the lessee forms a substantial proportion of the whole rent.

10. Short title, extent and duration

(1) This Act may be cited as the Rent of Furnished Houses Control (Scotland) Act, 1943, and shall extend to Scotland only.

(2) This Act shall continue in force until the expiry of six months from the date when the Emergency Powers (Defence) Act, 1939, ceases to be in force.

SCHEDULE

Section 1.

PROVISIONS REGARDING CONSTITUTION OF TRIBUNALS.

1. The Tribunal shall consist of a Chairman and two other members.

2. The Chairman and the other members of the Tribunal shall be appointed by the Secretary of State. During the absence or incapacity of any member a person appointed by the Secretary of State shall act in his place.

3. The members and acting members of the Tribunal shall receive such remuneration and such travelling and other allowances as the Secretary of State may, with the consent of the Treasury, determine.

4. The Secretary of State shall assign to the Tribunal a clerk and such other officers and servants, and there shall be paid to them such salaries and allowances, as the Secretary of State, with the consent of the Treasury, may determine.

FURNISHED HOUSES (RENT CONTROL) ACT, 1946

[9 & 10 GEO. 6.]

CHAPTER 34

An Act to make provision with respect to the rent of houses or parts thereof let at a rent which includes payment for the use of furniture or for services. [26th March 1946.]

Be it enacted by the King's most Excellent Majesty, by and with the advice and consent of the Lords Spiritual and Temporal, and Commons, in this present Parliament assembled, and by the authority of the same, as follows:—

1. Application of Act by order of Minister of Health, and appointment of tribunal

(1) Where, as respects a district consisting of the whole or part of the area of a local authority, the Minister of Health (hereinafter referred to as "the Minister") is satisfied on representation by, or after consultation with, the local authority that it is expedient that the provisions of this Act should have effect in that district, he may, by order, direct that this Act shall have effect in that district as from such day as may be specified in the order, and this Act shall thereupon come into force in that district.

(2) For each district in which this Act is in force there shall be a tribunal constituted in accordance with the Schedule to this Act, and the provisions of that Schedule shall apply to each tribunal:

Provided that, if the Minister so directs, the same tribunal may act for more than one such district.

2. Reference to tribunal of contracts for furnished letting

(1) Where a contract has, whether before or after the passing of this Act, been entered into whereby one person (hereinafter referred to as the "lessor") grants to another person (hereinafter referred to as the "lessee") the right to occupy as a residence a house or part of a house situated in a district in which this Act is in force in consideration of a rent which includes payment for the use of furniture or for services, whether or not, in the case of such a contract with regard to part of a house, the lessee is entitled, in addition to exclusive occupation thereof, to the use in common with

any other person of other rooms or accommodation in the house, it shall be lawful for either party to the contract or for the local authority to refer the contract to the tribunal for the district, and where any such contract (hereinafter referred to as "a contract to which this Act applies") is so referred to the tribunal, they may by a notice in writing served on the lessor require him to give to them, within such period (which shall not be less than seven days from the date of the service of the notice) as may be specified in the notice, such information as they may reasonably require regarding such of the prescribed particulars relating to the contract as are specified in the notice.

(2) Where any contract to which this Act applies is referred to a tribunal, then, unless at any time before the tribunal have entered upon consideration of the reference it is withdrawn by the person or authority by whom it was made, the tribunal shall consider it and, after making such inquiry as they think fit, and giving to each party (and, if the house is one the general management whereof is vested in and exercisable by a housing authority, to that authority) an opportunity of being heard, or, in his option, of submitting representations in writing, shall approve the rent payable under the contract or reduce it to such sum as they may, in all the circumstances, think reasonable, or may, if they think fit in all the circumstances, dismiss the reference, and shall notify the parties and the local authority of their decision in each case.

(3) Where the rent payable for any premises has been entered in the register in accordance with the provisions hereinafter contained, it shall be lawful for the lessor or the lessee or the local authority to refer the case to the tribunal for reconsideration of the rent so entered on the ground of change of circumstances, and the provisions of subsection (2) of this section shall apply on any such reference in like manner as they apply on a reference under subsection (1) of this section subject to the modification that the tribunal shall have power to increase the rent payable.

(4) Where on any reference of a contract, the rent whereunder includes payment for services, the tribunal are of opinion that it would be proper that the rent payable for the premises should include an amount in respect of increase since the third day of September, nineteen hundred and thirty-nine, in the cost of providing such services, and are also of opinion that in all the circumstances a rent higher than the rent payable under the contract might properly be chargeable for the premises in order to include an

amount in respect of such increase, they may approve a rent higher by not more than such amount as they think reasonable in that respect.

(5) An approval, reduction or increase under this section may be limited to rent payable in respect of a particular period.

(6) Notwithstanding anything in the foregoing provisions of this section, a tribunal shall not be required to entertain a reference made otherwise than by the local authority if they are satisfied, having regard to the length of time elapsing since a previous reference made by the same party or to other circumstances, that the reference is frivolous or vexatious.

3. Register of rents

(1) The local authority shall prepare and keep up to date a register for the purposes of this Act, and shall make the register available for inspection in such place or places and in such manner as the Minister may direct.

(2) The register shall be so prepared and kept up to date as to contain, with regard to any contract under which a rent is payable that has been approved, reduced or increased under the last foregoing section (being a contract relating to premises situated in the area of the local authority), entries of—

    (a) the prescribed particulars with regard to the contract;

    (b) a specification of the premises to which the contract relates; and

    (c) the rent as approved, reduced or increased by the tribunal, and, in a case in which the approval, reduction or increase is limited to rent payable in respect of a particular period, a specification of that period.

(3) It shall be the duty of the tribunal, when they notify, under subsection (2) of the last foregoing section, the local authority of their decision in a case, to furnish to the local authority such particulars as are requisite for enabling them to discharge their functions under the foregoing provisions of this section.

4. Rents in excess of registered rents and premiums illegal

(1) Where the rent payable for any premises is entered in the register under the provisions of this Act, it shall not be lawful to require or receive—

CC

   (*a*) on account of rent for those premises in respect of any period subsequent to the date of such entry, (or, in a case in which a particular period is specified, in respect of that period) payment of any sum in excess of the rent so entered; or

   (*b*) (Repealed by the 1949 Act.)

(2) Where any payment ****¹ has been made or received in contravention of the foregoing subsection, the amount ****¹ thereof shall be recoverable by the person by whom it was made ****¹

5. Provision as to notice to quit served after reference to tribunal

If, after a contract to which this Act applies has been referred to a tribunal by the lessee or by the local authority (either originally or for reconsideration), a notice to quit the premises to which the contract relates is served by the lessor on the lessee at any time before the decision of the tribunal is given or within three months thereafter, the notice shall not take effect before the expiration of the said three months:

Provided that—

   (*a*) the tribunal may, if they think fit, direct that a shorter period shall be substituted for the said three months in the application of this section to the contract that is the subject of the reference; and

   (*b*) if the reference is withdrawn, the period during which the notice is not to take effect shall end on the expiration of seven days from the withdrawal of the reference.

6. Provisions as to local authorities

(1) For the purposes of this Act, the local authority shall be—

   (*a*) elsewhere than in the administrative county of London, the council of the borough, urban district or rural district;

   (*b*) in the administrative county of London other than the City of London, the council of the metropolitan borough;

   (*c*) in the City of London, the common council.

(2) The powers of the local authority under this Act may, if the local authority so resolve, be exercised by one of their officers appointed by them for the purpose.

---

¹ Omitted by the 1949 Act.

(3) The local authority shall have power to publish information regarding the provisions of this Act.

(4) Any expenses incurred under this Act by the common council of the City of London shall be defrayed out of the general rate.

7. ****[1] nothing in this Act shall affect any provisions of the Rent and Mortgage Interest Restrictions Acts, 1920 to 1939.

8. Regulations

The Minister may make regulations—

(a) with regard to the tenure of office of chairmen and other members of tribunals;

(b) with regard to proceedings before tribunals under this Act;

(c) for prescribing anything which is required by this Act to be prescribed; and

(d) generally for carrying into effect the provisions of this Act.

9. Offences

(1) A person who requires or receives any payment ****[2] in contravention of section four of this Act shall be guilty of an offence and be liable on summary conviction to a fine not exceeding one hundred pounds or to imprisonment for a period not exceeding six months or to both such fine and such imprisonment, and, without prejudice to any other method of recovery, the court by which he is found guilty may order the amount paid ****[2] to be repaid to the person by whom the payment was made ****[2]

(2) If the lessor under a contract to which this Act applies fails without reasonable cause, within the time limited in that behalf, to comply with the provisions of any notice served under subsection (1) of section two of this Act, he shall be guilty of an offence and liable on summary conviction to a fine not exceeding twenty pounds or to imprisonment for a period not exceeding three months or to both such fine and such imprisonment.

10. Institution of proceedings

The local authority shall have power to institute proceedings for an offence under this Act, and no such proceedings shall be instituted otherwise than by them.

---

[1] Omitted by the 1957 Act.
[2] Omitted by the 1949 Act.

11. Evidence

(1) A copy of an entry in the register certified under the hand of an officer duly authorised in that behalf by the local authority shall be receivable in evidence of that entry in all courts and in any proceedings.

(2) Any person requiring such a certified copy as aforesaid shall be entitled to obtain it on payment of the prescribed fee.

12. Interpretation and saving

(1) In this Act, unless the context otherwise requires, the following expressions have the meanings hereby respectively assigned to them, that is to say:—

"housing authority" means a council which is a local authority for the purposes of Part V of the Housing Act, 1936;

"local authority" has the meaning assigned to that expression by section six of this Act;

"register" means the register kept by the local authority in pursuance of section three of this Act;

"services" includes attendance, the provision of heating or lighting, the supply of hot water and any other privilege or facility connected with the occupancy of a house or part of a house, not being a privilege or facility requisite for the purposes of access, cold water supply or sanitary accommodation;

"tribunal" means a tribunal appointed in pursuance of section one of this Act.

(2) Where separate sums are payable by the lessee of any premises to the lessor for any two or more of the following, namely:—

(*a*) occupation of the premises;

(*b*) use of furniture; and

(*c*) services;

the expression "rent" shall, in relation to those premises, mean the aggregate of those sums, and where such sums are payable under separate contracts, those contracts shall be deemed to be one contract.

(3) Nothing in this Act shall apply to a house or part of a house let at a rent which includes payment in respect of board:

Provided that a house or part of a house shall not be deemed to be let at such a rent unless the value of such board to the lessee forms a substantial proportion of the whole rent.

(4) Nothing in this Act shall apply to accommodation registered for the purposes of Regulation sixty-eight CB of the Defence (General) Regulations, 1939, which is let in accordance with the terms and conditions so registered.

13. Short title, extent and duration

(1) This Act may be cited as the Furnished Houses (Rent Control) Act, 1946.

(2) This Act shall not extend to Scotland or to Northern Ireland.

(3) This Act shall continue in force until the thirty-first day of December nineteen hundred and forty-seven.

SCHEDULE

Section 1.

PROVISIONS REGARDING CONSTITUTION OF TRIBUNALS

1. A tribunal shall consist of a chairman and two other members.

2. The chairman and the other members of a tribunal shall be appointed by the Minister. During the absence or incapacity of any member a person appointed by the Minister shall act in his place.

3. The members and acting members of a tribunal shall receive such remuneration and such travelling and other allowances as the Minister may, with the consent of the Treasury, determine.

4. A tribunal may appoint a clerk and, with the approval of the Minister as to numbers, such other officers and servants as they think fit, and there shall be paid to the clerk and other officers and servants such salaries and allowances as the Minister, with the consent of the Treasury, may determine.

5. The remuneration and allowances of members and acting members of a tribunal, the salaries and allowances of the clerk and other officers and servants appointed as aforesaid, and such other expenses of a tribunal as the Treasury may determine, shall be defrayed out of moneys provided by Parliament.

Index

Possession orders—*cont.*
over-charging sub-tenants, 84, 288
overcrowding, 82, 85, 203, 297
statutory powers, exercise of, 86
sub-divided houses, 85
sub-letting, 82, 296
suspension of, 84, 278
tenant ceasing to occupy, 86
tenant's breach of obligation, 80, 296
tenant's change of status, 86
tenant's notice to quit, 82, 296
Premises let for mixed purposes, 13, 262
used for professional purposes (*see* Business premises)
Premiums
Crown property, 65, 339
excessive price of furniture treated as, 68, 320, 327
general prohibition on, 7, 65, 318, 327
decontrolled houses, 69, 205
exchange of statutory tenancies, 18, 207
furnished lettings, 175, 327
loans count as, 9, 70, 206
long leases, 66, 69
meaning of, 65, 331
payable before 2nd June, 1949, 66, 318, 332
payments not treated as, 18, 66, 176, 208, 318, 327
penalty for demanding, 67, 176, 208, 319, 327
recovery of, 67, 176, 319, 332
Prescribed forms, 187
Private street works qualify as improvements, 34, 35, 121, 125, 208
Procedure for increasing rents (*see* Rents)
Property unfit, rent restrictions on, 28, 49, 195

Railway-owned houses, 124, 256
Rateable value
aggregation of, 98, 231
apportionment of, 98, 117, 231
ascertainment where proposals pending, 99, 231
concurrence of landlords on, 106, 212
control limits, 11, 90, 202
furnished lettings not rated, 170, 204
not separately rated, 170, 204

meaning of, 97, 214, 231
furnished lettings, 169, 232
reduction for tenant's improvements, 100, 102, 234
Rates
adjustments as respects, 29, 196
calculation of, 28, 224
discount on, 29, 123, 224, 302
included in rent, 21, 28, 193
meaning of, 28, 214
permitted increases in Scotland, 122, 125, 255
sub-tenants, 30
Recoverable rent, meaning of, 178
Recovery of overpayments, 151, 178, 265, 303
Rectification of notices, 26, 126, 279
Registers of rents, 173, 321, 347, 353
Registration of houses as decontrolled, 5
Relatives right to claim statutory tenancy, 5, 15, 261
Rent
abatement for disrepair, 58, 220
acceptance after notice to quit, 85, 266
adjustments
furniture, 32, 196
premiums, 67, 332
services, 25, 32, 196
in Scotland, 127
advance payments restrictions, 9, 70, 206
arrears, recovery of, 178, 237, 280
calculation of, 23, 214
distress for, 179, 258
houses formerly requisitioned, 163, 211
increases in
improvements, 33, 36, 197, 244
limitation on, 27, 195
exceptions to, 27, 39, 196, 197
notice of (q.v.)
procedure for, 26, 194
repairs increase (Scotland) (q.v.)
the 1957 Act increase (Scotland) (q.v)
limits in England and Wales, 20, 193
higher rent permitted, 23, 194
in Scotland, 115
no right to suspend, 178
overpayments, recovery of, 178, 237, 265, 281, 303

Rent—*cont.*
  payable after decontrol, 95, 96, 226
  permitted increases (Scotland) 3, 6,
    120, 255, 312
  rates included in (q.v.)
  recoverable, 178
    before 30th August, 1954, in
      Scotland, 146
  registers, 120, 173, 321, 347, 353
  restrictions on disrepair, 45, 220
    certificates of disrepair, 53, 54, 220
      in Scotland, 137, 144
      local authority's action, 52, 195
      tenant's notice of disrepair, 53, 220
  standard (Scotland), 3, 115, 260
    variation of, 7, 118, 316
  subsidised private houses, 37, 128,
    201, 210
  variation under contract, 24, 198
Rent Acts
  application of, 11
    after decontrol, 93, 225
  furnished lettings excluded from, 30,
    166, 262
  history of, 1
  long tenancies excluded from, 112,
    211
  responsibility for repairs under, 45,
    130, 220, 222
Rent books
  furnished lettings, 177, 205
  unfurnished lettings, 180, 237, 240,
    243, 265, 290, 292, 301
Rent tribunals
  appointment of, 166, 345, 351
  lettings not subject to review by, 118,
    167
  proceedings before, 171
  references to, 119, 167, 316, 345, 351
  review of decisions by, 173, 346, 352
  rules for guidance of, 171
  security of tenure by, 174, 330, 354
  services, increased cost of, 127
  standard rent, power to vary, 7, 118,
    316
  unfurnished houses rents, 167, 316
Repair, certificates of (*see* Certificates of
  repair)
Repairs
  adjustment of factor for, 20, 21, 217
  assumptions as to responsibility for,
    55, 218, 222, 223

furnished lettings, 45
internal decorations, 22, 217
landlord's liability, 45
  right to execute, 15, 266
  undertaking to do, 54, 218
meaning of, 47
  Scotland, 132
notices, 50, 195
proof of (Scotland), 134
provisions run with property, 62, 222
reduction of factor for, 20, 58, 220
rent increases for (Scotland), 130,
  198, 200
responsibility for, 45, 222, 223, 240
  Scotland, 130
tenant's liability, 47, 223
unfurnished lettings, 45
Repairs increase (Scotland)
  additional amount of, 134, 142, 200
  amount of, 133, 200
  conditions justifying, 133
  notice of, 136
  interchange with 1957 Act increase,
    145, 201
  not payable twice, 140
  proof of past repairs, 134
  tenancies which do not qualify, 142
  test of fitness for, 140
  valuation of, 146
Reports
  Guthrie Committee, 7
  Hunter Committee, 2
  Leasehold Committee, 7
  Marley Committee, 4
  Onslow Committee, 3
  Ridley Committee (1937), 5
  Ridley Committee (1945), 6
  Salisbury Committee, 3
Requisitioned dwellings
  decontrol, 92, 164, 203
  release of, 8, 159, 160, 161, 164, 165
  retention of, 159, 161
  statutory successors, 161
  statutory tenants, 8, 162
Requisitioned sites and camps, 160
Reserve forces
  decontrol of dwellings held by, 157,
    226
  possession orders against, 81, 83
  protection of, 8, 158
  Rent Acts, extension for, 156
  rent limits, 157, 237